Economic Capital

Economic Capital
How It Works and What Every Manager Needs to Know

Pieter Klaassen and Idzard van Eeghen

AMSTERDAM • BOSTON • HEIDELBERG • LONDON
NEW YORK • OXFORD • PARIS • SAN DIEGO
SAN FRANCISCO • SINGAPORE • SYDNEY • TOKYO

Elsevier
30 Corporate Drive, Suite 400, Burlington, MA 01803, USA
525 B Street, Suite 1900, San Diego, California 92101-4495, USA
84 Theobald's Road, London WC1X 8RR, UK

This book is printed on acid-free paper. ∞

Library of Congress Cataloging-in-Publication Data
Klaassen, Pieter.
    Economic capital : how it works and what every manager needs to know / Pieter
Klaassen, Idzard van Eeghen.
       p. cm.
       ISBN 978-0-12-374901-7 (hbk. : alk. paper) 1. Bank capital. 2. Bank
management. 3. Banks and banking--Risk management. I. Eeghen, Idzard van. II. Title.
    HG1616.C34K49 2009
    332.1068'1--dc22   2009011193

British Library Cataloguing in Publication Data
A catalogue record for this book is available from the British Library

ISBN 13: 978-0-12-374901-7

For information on all Elsevier publications
visit our Web site at www.elsevierdirect.com

Printed in the United States of America
09 10 9 8 7 6 5 4 3 2 1

Working together to grow
libraries in developing countries

www.elsevier.com | www.bookaid.org | www.sabre.org

ELSEVIER   BOOK AID
             International   Sabre Foundation

Contents

Acknowledgments

This book might never have been written without the takeover of our employer, ABN AMRO Bank in The Netherlands. In the unavoidable uncertainty and changes that followed, the idea developed to put on paper some of our experiences with and ideas about the implementation and use of economic capital. Brainstorming resulted in the outline of a hypothetical book. We decided to float the idea to see whether it would sink or sail. The enthusiasm with which the book proposal was received provided the extra stimulus to really embark on this project. Before we knew it, we had passed the point of no return. In the midst of the storm that the sub-prime crisis caused in the financial industry, we were able to stay on course to complete our journey. We hope that you as reader, conclude that it has been a worthwhile one.

Writing this book is also a way to express our gratitude to our (former) employer, who allowed us to explore the developing world of economic capital and initiate new and exciting projects. This would not have been possible without the vision and support of two successive Chief Risk Officers, Jan Sijbrand and David Cole. Furthermore, we thoroughly enjoyed the lively debates and exchanges of views with our many colleagues in different parts of the world, whether part of LaSalle Bank in the United States, Banco Real in Brazil, Hoare Govett in the United Kingdom, or ABN AMRO in Asia and The Netherlands. Our experience has been enriched by the views and experiences they shared with us over many years. Still, this book is not about how economic capital was measured and used in ABN AMRO. Rather, it reflects the insights obtained from continuous learning, asking questions, and appreciating different points of view that we want to share in this book; not what we did or failed to do.

We are indebted to various colleagues who were willing to review parts of this book. They often helped us fill the gaps in our knowledge. Specifically, we want to thank Erwin Charlier, who not only reviewed part of the manuscript but also performed various calculations that are included in the book; and Ton Vorst, Elisabeth Minkner, Bas de Mik, and Boudewijn Posthumus Meyjes.

One former colleague, Carol Oliver, has helped us in more ways than one reasonably could have asked. She acted as co-reader and provided us with valuable comments, ideas, and suggestions. This book would have been different without her.

Now that we have come to the end of this journey, we want to thank our families, and in particular Margot and Marian, for their patience and unwavering support. In a year that was not short of changes and emotions, they have made it possible for us to find the time and peace of mind to write this book. The influence of family is also indirectly visible in this book through the imprint that our parents left on us. It is the influence of our respective fathers, both deceased, that is probably most visible for those who have known them. It is to them that we dedicate this book.

Pieter Klaassen   Idzard van Eeghen
Meilen, Switzerland   Hilversum, The Netherlands
pklaassen@alum.mit.edu   idzard.v.eeghen@planet.nl

Introduction

In the summer of 2006, bankers and financial engineers lived in a rose garden. Financial markets were booming, risk premiums were low, financial engineers and their models were in high demand, and regulators had adopted Basel II regulations, which many bankers expected would allow them to reduce their capital requirements and grow their business further. Two years later, the garden had changed into a wasteland with credit losses mounting on the products developed by the same financial engineers, and spreading like wildfire to other areas of the financial markets. As a result, a number of banks (nearly) failed, the two largest mortgage providers in the United States and the largest insurer in the world were de facto nationalized, investment banks became an endangered species, and a USD 700 billion bail-out operation was launched by the US government, later supplemented by additional measures, to regain the market's trust in the financial system.

Across the ocean, the crisis had taken its toll in the form of bank rescues in several European countries, notably Germany, the United Kingdom, and the Benelux countries. Several European governments injected unprecedented amounts of capital into banks, increased the size of their deposit-guarantee schemes, and provided guarantees on bank debt. Other countries around the world followed with similar actions to protect their banks.

The unanticipated nature and magnitude of the crisis were illustrated by the October 2007 issue of *The Banker*, which had Merrill Lynch's CEO on the cover with the text, "Unmoved by the Crisis, Merrill Lynch's Stan O'Neal sticks to his strategy." Only shortly after that, on October 30, 2007, Stan O'Neal was forced to resign as a result of the investment bank's worst quarterly loss in its 93-year history. Even a year later, the nature and depth of the crisis were not fully understood. Among others, the CEOs of Bear Stearns and Lehman Brothers found that they had done too little too late to replenish their capital levels leading to the demise of their institutions in the summer of 2008. On the other hand, there were also CEOs whose banks had been relatively unscathed by the crisis, and who boasted about the risk management capabilities of their institutions. No wonder that with these conflicting signals, many observers wondered whether risk models and risk management practices were at the root of the failure of many institutions, or whether risk models and practices had saved the institutions that suffered limited losses.

In the decades before the sub-prime crisis, financial techniques and models had taken an enormous flight, supporting the development of many innovative financial products. With the ups and downs common to innovations, they had helped the financial industry to significantly outpace the growth of the economy in general. During the same period, economic capital models were developed that helped to determine how much capital an institution should hold in relation to the risks to which it is exposed. These models gave managers comfort that their institutions held sufficient capital against the risks and that the returns were commensurate with these risks. Over time, risk models and risk management grew in complexity to encompass these innovative products, and senior management increasingly relied on specialists to understand and manage the risks. Regulators observed that their regulations became outdated in the face of all these new products and started to work on a more advanced and risk-sensitive approach to determine the minimum capital that an institution should have. They took their inspiration from the economic capital models that banks had developed. Though stopping short of allowing banks to apply their own risk models to determine the required level of capital, with the introduction of the Basel II regulations[1] this economic capital technology had become increasingly mainstream.

During the sub-prime crisis, doubts about the performance of some risk models started to surface when a number of structured credit products that had been developed and rated on the basis of complex credit risk models proved to contain more risks than the models and the rating agencies previously had indicated. Seemingly secure, highly rated investments were downgraded rapidly, in a short period of time, across scores of securities and issuers. Losses mounted to levels that seemed to contradict the economic capital models. Rating agencies and bank CEOs all of a sudden were questioned about the quality of their risk models. Did these models capture the risks adequately? Worse, could they be a source of risks themselves? The events during the sub-prime crisis also made the banking regulators concerned about the robustness of the Basel II capital adequacy framework that they had just designed and approved. The credibility of the Basel II framework was undermined further when the UK building society Northern Rock was the subject of a classic bank run, only a few months after it had received the approval for the Basel II advanced approaches.

In response to the events in the sub-prime crisis, banking regulators focused on the areas that had been shown to be vulnerable during the crisis. This included liquidity risk, credit risk for traded products, and credit and market risk for securitizations. Some regulators proposed to complement risk-based capital measures with a simple leverage ratio to avoid being exposed to uncertainties with respect to the way risks are measured.[2] Nevertheless, all regulators agreed that the advancement of risk models and risk management practices should be stimulated, that banks should apply internally developed methodologies to assess the adequacy of their capital levels, and that banking supervisors should review these assessments. Furthermore, economic capital models continued to be considered as "best practice" for these assessments. However, regulators stipulated that, more than in the past, senior management of banks should be actively involved and "recognize the importance of using economic capital measures in conducting the bank's business and capital planning, and should take measures to ensure the meaningfulness and integrity of the economic capital measures.... At the same time, management should fully understand the limitations of economic capital measures."[3]

The question of how much capital a financial institution should hold is more relevant than ever. Moreover, institutions increasingly have to justify that they allocate capital to activities that provide an acceptable return in relation to the risks they take. As such, economic capital will remain an important risk measure for managers of financial institutions, regulators, and investors. However, the events of the sub-prime crisis have uncovered a number of shortcomings in the measurement, implementation, and use of economic capital. A number of assumptions that were made in the models clearly did not hold up in reality. The risk that this happens exists with any model, since every model is a simplification of the real world and therefore subject to model risk. The events during the sub-prime crisis have underlined the importance of model risk. Rather than reject economic capital models because they are subject to model risk, we believe that modelers and managers should be aware of these model risks, improve the models based on the experience gained from their use, and take remaining model risk explicitly into account.

In this book, we aim to clarify the main concepts, assumptions, and dilemmas that underlie many of the modeling practices of economic capital, and how these are—or should be—linked to the intended use of economic capital for managing risk in financial institutions and creating value for shareholders and other stakeholders. We make use of the experiences of many financial institutions with economic capital and illustrate important issues related to measuring and using economic capital with historic and recent events in financial markets.

This book is aimed at senior managers who want to effectively measure and manage risk while remaining in control of the risk models that help them with this task and, hence, feel the need to understand the key choices and assumptions without going into the technical detail of formulas and mathematics. This knowledge is becoming increasingly relevant as market participants and supervisors require that senior managers inform them about the working of their risk models and how the outcomes are used in risk identification and decision making within the organization. The book is also relevant for senior managers who use, or plan to use, economic capital and related performance measures to optimize the profitability of the institution. They should be aware of the strengths and limitations of their performance measures, the trade-offs between using economic capital for risk management or for a performance measurement, and finally, the incentives created by applying economic capital-related performance measures.

The book is also valuable to regulators and supervisors of the financial industry. They have embraced the economic capital concept because it provides a comprehensive and analytical means of quantifying how much capital an institution should have as a buffer against the combined risks assumed. To ensure that economic capital provides an adequate reflection of the risks, they should understand the choices that managers have to make when setting up an economic capital framework.

Another potential audience for this book consists of analysts of, and investors in, financial institutions, because these constituents must interpret risk data in relation to the capital maintained by an institution and assess whether an institution uses its capital efficiently. Economic capital can be an aid in this analysis, provided that the scope, key modeling assumptions, and sensitivities of the methodologies that are used to quantify economic capital are transparent and well understood.

This book starts by introducing economic capital and associated concepts in Chapter 1. In Chapter 2, we describe why the economic capital concept was developed and how it relates to the objectives of the main stakeholders in a financial institution. Chapters 1 and 2 define the context and set the stage for the more in-depth discussion of economic capital in the subsequent chapters.

In Chapter 3 we explore what choices have to be made when making the general definition of economic capital that was presented in Chapter 1 operational. How to measure economic capital is discussed in detail in Chapter 4. We describe the main ideas behind various approaches that can be used to quantify economic capital for a large number of risk types, their potential strengths and limitations, what choices need to be made, and how to make these consistently between risk types. As the focus is on the main concepts, strengths and limitations of various modeling approaches, we abstain from the use of mathematics. Many examples are given to illustrate that measuring economic capital is a challenging and sometimes daunting task. Nevertheless, important insights can be gained by modeling risks, provided one is also aware of the underlying choices and assumptions, and the model risks involved.

After economic capital has been quantified, it has to be implemented in the organization. A successful implementation requires that many practical issues are dealt with in a comprehensive and transparent manner, ranging from governance and dealing with complex products to the setting of hurdle rates and the impact on incentives for managers and staff. These issues, among various others, are discussed in Chapter 5. As with any risk measure, economic capital should not be used or managed in isolation. In Chapter 6, the relationships between economic capital and stress testing, enterprise risk management, and regulatory capital are discussed.

Finally, in Chapter 7, we assess how the measurement and use of economic capital is likely to evolve in the future and how capital adequacy regulations may benefit from further progress in this area.

For the efficient reader, each chapter begins by introducing the main topics of that chapter and ends with a brief summary and conclusion.

Notes

[1]Basel Committee on Banking Supervision (2006). "International Convergence of Capital Measurement and Capital Standards—A Revised Framework." Bank for International Settlements, June.

[2]For an early advocate see "Statement of Sheila C. Bair, Chairman Federal Deposit Insurance Corporation on the Interagency Proposal Regarding the Basel Capital Accord, before the Committee on Banking, Housing and Urban Affairs;" U.S. Senate; September 26, 2006 (www.banking.senate.gov/public/_files/ACF4A61.pdf). For a European advocate see Hildebrand, Philipp M., "Is Basel II enough? The benefits of a leverage ratio," speech at the Financial Markets Group Lecture, London School of Economics, London, 15 December 2008.

[3]Basel Committee on Banking Supervision (2009). "Range of practices and issues in economic capital frameworks," March.

1 Measuring the Unexpected: Understanding Economic Capital

In this chapter we introduce economic capital: what it is and what the key underlying concepts are. The origin of economic capital usually is traced back to the late 1970s, when Bankers Trust introduced the RAROC (risk-adjusted return on capital) concept for the evaluation of the profitability of its transactions, using economic capital as uniform measure of risk.[1] Since then, an increasing number of banks have adopted economic capital and RAROC in their decision making. Subsequently, other financial institutions such as insurance companies have caught on to the concept.

When tracing back to the roots of economic capital, an important development was the growth of the trading activities, and in particular the trading of derivative instruments, by financial institutions. This increased the sensitivity of a bank's profit to market variables such as interest rates, exchange rates, and equity prices. To manage these risks, value-at-risk (VaR) models were developed to measure the worst loss that can be incurred from holding a portfolio of securities over a given time and with a specified probability. As the experience of banks with these models grew, regulators became comfortable to allow their use to determine how much capital a bank should hold as buffer against these risks.[2]

Up to that moment, credit risk management did not make much use of quantitative methods. However, the growth of the credit derivative market introduced market risk elements into the credit arena. Modelers started to apply VaR-like models to credit risk, which was still the single most important risk type for most banks. The innovation of Bankers Trust was to use economic capital in performance management by adjusting returns for the economic risks associated with an activity or transaction. Although the fate of Bankers Trust, which was taken over in 1998 by Deutsche Bank after suffering heavy losses, indicates that economic capital and RAROC are no guarantee for success, the underlying ideas proved to be conceptually so appealing that many others continued with its further development and use.

The appeal of economic capital was enhanced by the growth in scale and complexity of many financial institutions, because as a comprehensive risk measure it can be used to monitor and manage the risks efficiently and consistently across the organization. The scope gradually has been extended from market and credit risk to cover all material risks to which an institution is exposed.

The actual use of economic capital was made possible because of the tremendous increase in the power of computers and associated possibilities of information technology. This has enabled the efficient handling of large data sets and performance of complex financial calculations in a fast manner, both of which are crucial for economic capital calculations.

In Section 1.1, we will explain what economic capital intends to measure, and how it relates to the available capital of an institution. Section 1.2 introduces the concepts of expected and unexpected loss, and we indicate their relationship with economic capital. In Section 1.3 we review two conceptual issues related to economic capital as risk measure. The first one concerns the distinction between risk and uncertainty, and we discuss how and to what extent economic capital can reflect both. The second issue concerns a property that one would like any risk measure to possess, but that economic capital (and, in fact, any type of value-at-risk measure) could violate. As we will discuss, this violation does not tend to cause problems in realistic settings, however. Although we believe that economic capital is a valuable and important risk measure for financial institutions, no single risk measure can capture the full spectrum of risks that an institution faces. In Section 1.4 we review reasons for, and examples of, other risk measures that financial institutions use in addition to economic capital.

1.1   What Is Economic Capital?

The *capital* of a firm protects the firm against insolvency in case the difference in value between its assets and its liabilities decreases. Such a decrease can occur if the value of the liabilities increases more than the value of the assets, or if the value of the assets decreases more than the value of the liabilities. Insolvency occurs if the value of the assets falls below the value of the liabilities and the amount of capital becomes negative. Assuming a given level of capital, the more volatile the difference in value between assets and liabilities is, the more likely it is that insolvency will occur. Increasing the amount of capital will decrease the likelihood of insolvency, but it will not be possible to prevent insolvency with 100 percent certainty. This would also not be an attractive proposition for the providers of capital, because they want to earn an attractive return on their investment. Hence, capital will protect a firm only against insolvency with a certain probability. This probability typically is referred to as the *confidence level.*

Economic capital represents an estimate of the worst possible decline in the institution's amount of capital at a specified confidence level, within a chosen time horizon. As such, it is a direct function of the risks to which an institution is exposed. If the confidence level at which economic capital is calculated equals the probability with which an institution wants to remain solvent over the chosen time horizon, then economic capital can be viewed as the amount of capital that an institution should possess. The confidence level and time horizon have to be specified by the institution in order to make the definition operational. We will discuss this in Chapter 3.

Financial institutions will not be able to operate normally long before they become insolvent. Once doubts arise whether the amount of capital of an institution is sufficient in relation to the institution's risks, investors, depositors, clients, and other financial institutions will sell the stock, withdraw money, and stop doing business with the institution. This will cause immediate continuity problems. Hence, financial institutions typically do not fail because their capital is depleted, but because the *probability* of potential capital depletion is deemed too high. It is thus crucial for a financial institution to ensure that its capital is large enough that the probability of insolvency is sufficiently low. This is where economic capital can help to prevent an institution's failure, on which we will elaborate in Chapter 2.

The adjective *economic* in economic capital reflects that the aim of economic capital is to measure potential changes in the economic value of assets and liabilities, as opposed to changes in value that are determined by accounting rules. The choice for economic values relates to the fact that most firms use economic capital as a measure of risk in risk-return evaluations of their activities. Such risk-return evaluations typically aim to maximize value for the firm's shareholders, and shareholders will focus on the economic value of a firm as opposed to its value according to accounting rules. This obviously presupposes that shareholders are able to determine the economic value of a firm, and the extent to which it differs from the accounting value, something that may not in all cases be straightforward. We will see in Chapter 3 that there will be some tension in the precise definition of economic capital depending on whether economic capital is used in the context of solvency assessment or shareholder value maximization. Differences between accounting values and economic values for assets and liabilities contribute to this tension.

1.2 Expected and Unexpected Losses

When defining economic capital for financial institutions, we need to distinguish between expected and unexpected losses. In the course of doing business, a financial institution expects to incur a certain amount of losses. From experience, a bank knows that there will be a number of customers who will not be able to repay in full the money that was lent by the bank, giving rise to credit losses. Similarly, insurance companies expect to face payouts on a certain number of insurance policies in the normal course of business. In addition, both banks and insurers will account for a certain amount of operational losses to occur. The amount that an institution expects to lose is called the *expected loss*.

Expected loss can be viewed as a cost of doing business. Consequently, the pricing of products will incorporate a margin to compensate for expected losses. Otherwise, a firm would structurally lose money. We can thus reasonably assume that the pricing of products covers expected losses, and there is therefore no need to hold capital for expected losses. In fact, expected loss does not represent risk, as it constitutes the amount of loss that a financial institution should anticipate to incur.

In any period, however, actual losses will either be higher or lower than the expected amount of losses. Statistically speaking, the probability of ending up exactly with the expected amount of losses is almost zero. To the extent that actual losses are higher than the expected losses, we call them *unexpected losses*. The size of the unexpected losses is what constitutes risk for a financial institution. If unexpected losses are not too large, they may be compensated by the profit margin in the product pricing if this profit margin is larger than strictly necessary to compensate for expected losses. In that case, the realized profit will be lower than the expected profit, but the capital of the institution is not impaired. If unexpected losses are large, however, then they may exceed the profit margin and eat into the capital of the institution. The potential decline of a financial institution's capital is thus directly related to the potential for (large) unexpected losses.

The sub-prime crisis of 2007–2008 has presented many illustrations of the impact of unexpected losses on capital. During this crisis, many banks had to report large net losses that reduced the amount of available capital. As a result, several banks have sought new capital injections from outside investors to maintain their desired capital levels.

Graph 1.1 illustrates the concepts of expected loss, unexpected loss, and economic capital. The curved line depicts a loss distribution. On this loss distribution, we have indicated the amount of expected loss, as well as the amount of economic capital corresponding to a 99.95% confidence level. Unexpected losses are the losses that exceed the expected loss. For future reference, we also have indicated below the graph what constitutes the "body" of the distribution (i.e., the range of losses around the expected loss that have the highest probability of occurring) and the "tail" of the distribution (i.e., the area corresponding to large but unlikely losses).

We note that the distinction between expected and unexpected losses is not directly applicable to all types of risk. For example, for trading activities we focus on potential changes in market values, and there is no natural interpretation of expected loss in this case. Market values are such that the expected return is sufficiently positive for market participants to invest in the assets. If the actual return falls short of the expected return, then the difference can be viewed as unexpected loss.

1.3 Conceptual Issues with Economic Capital

Economic capital has intuitive appeal, as it can be used as a direct estimate of the amount of capital that a financial institution should possess. There are, however, also drawbacks attached to its use as a risk measure. The first one

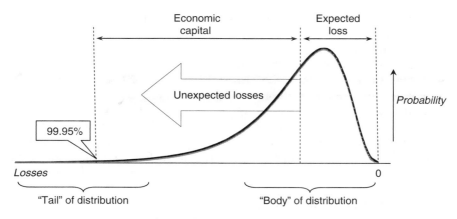

Graph 1.1   Graphic depiction of expected loss, unexpected loss, and economic capital.

relates to the fact that economic capital is an estimate of a very improbable event. As the confidence level that is used in the definition of economic capital is typically around 99.95%, we are trying to estimate a loss that will be exceeded in only 0.05% of all possible situations (or once every 2000 years if we measure economic capital over a one-year horizon and assume a constant universe). Being an estimate of such an improbable event, economic capital is unavoidably surrounded by uncertainty. In Section 1.3.1 we discuss the difference between risk and uncertainty, and how they impact the measurement of economic capital.

A second drawback relates to the mathematical properties of economic capital as a risk measure. Like the value-at-risk (VaR) measure, it violates one of the properties that have been postulated in the academic literature for coherent risk measures. In Section 1.3.2 we elaborate on this issue.

1.3.1   Risk Versus Uncertainty

Models that are used to calculate economic capital typically yield an estimate of the full probability distribution of potential gains and losses of a firm's assets and liabilities. We will often refer to this probability distribution as loss distribution, but it may also reflect potential gains. Estimating a loss distribution may not always be possible, however. Frank Knight already pointed out in 1921 that in many cases in economics and business it is very difficult if not impossible to know the loss distribution. He refers to risk when the probability distribution of events is known (measurable), and to uncertainty when this probability distribution is not known (immeasurable).[3]

An example of a situation in which we face risk is the throw of a fair die. All possible outcomes are known as well as their likelihood of occurrence (i.e., 1/6 for each number). To know the likelihood or probability that a certain number is thrown becomes complicated if we were told that the die is loaded. By rolling the die many times we can observe the fraction that each of the numbers turns up, and assume this is the true probability that we are looking for. However, even with a fair die the same number can be thrown many times in a row. Thus, if we depend on observations to estimate the loss distribution it will take many observations to be confident about our estimates. The problem of estimating the probability that a certain number will be thrown is even greater if we do not know whether we roll the same die each time, or if we do not know how many sides the die has. In the first instance, each throw of the die could be unique and earlier experiences are of little relevance. In the second instance, we do not know the range of possible outcomes. We have now reached the realm of uncertainty.

Few problems in risk management are like rolling a fair die. Seldom are the probabilities of possible events known *a priori*. As a result, we have to rely on observations to estimate them. These estimates are complicated by the fact that in business and economics there is continuous change. For example, technical progress and innovation change products and production techniques. Human behavior and social change influence consumer preferences.

In a broader perspective, the philosopher Karl Popper has made the point that the course of history is strongly influenced by the growth of human knowledge (e.g., political ideas, scientific knowledge).[4] Furthermore, he argues that, if human knowledge is growing, then we cannot anticipate today what we shall know only at a later time. For example, if we know today that we will know next year that a new type of medicine has been developed and will be introduced, then we already know today that a new type of medicine will have been developed and introduced next year. We can anticipate that event today, for example, by buying the stock of the relevant pharmaceutical company. In this case, knowledge is not growing because we already know today about next year's new type of medicine. However, if knowledge is growing, then we do not know today about the new type of medicine a year from now and, hence, we will not be able to anticipate that event today. Generalizing this line of reasoning implies that we cannot predict the course of human history because human knowledge grows. Nevertheless, Popper does not refute the possibility of every kind of social or economic prediction with this argument. For example, a prediction such as "the US dollar will depreciate if inflation in the United States increases" is still possible and can be tested. However, he does refute the possibility of predicting developments to the extent that they may be influenced by the growth of our knowledge. According to Popper, the growth of knowledge ultimately depends on the freedom of man: the diversity of individuals, their opinions, aims, and purposes.[5] Thus, it is the human factor that drives scientific discovery and social developments, and this factor is inherently uncertain.

G.L.S. Shackle has applied similar ideas to economic theory. He analyzed the role of uncertainty and time on decision making and human behavior. He argues that human decisions are driven by anticipation of the future and that this anticipation is inherently subjective and imaginative. Statistics can offer meaningful information provided that the universe stays the same. But when we imagine a universe of thought where new creative ideas can pour in, as Shackle and Popper argue is the case, then we do not have a stable basis for statistical analysis. According to Shackle, a decision maker cannot foreknow what future decisions he will make because future decisions will depend on choices made by others who are equally limited in their decision making. However, these unknown choices-to-come do provide the context for the decision to be made now. Consequently, "choice is a business conducted in the face of a void of knowledge."[6] Shackle concludes that predictions of human events and the economy are reliable only when relating to the immediate future, as the impact of the choices of others may only after some time have an appreciable effect on the economy.

Following Popper and Shackle we conclude that situations of uncertainty are closely associated with, and possibly inherent to, potential changes in human knowledge and behavior. Human behavior is also at the core of many economic theories. This received a strong impetus with the theory of rational expectations that was developed and applied in economic models in the 1960s and 1970s. The theory of rational expectations is the foundation of the efficient market hypothesis, which forms the starting point for many financial models. However, there are many situations in which observed human behavior is not rational. In response to this observation, a whole new branch of economics, behavioral economics, came into being, which studies human behavior and its impact on markets. Hence, significant progress has been made since the times of Popper and Shackle to incorporate human behavior in economic and financial theory. Nevertheless, there remain limitations, as identified by Popper and Shackle, to incorporate human behavior accurately in models. Managers therefore should be aware of the limitations of a model to measure risks in situations of uncertainty where changes in human behavior can have a significant impact on events.

The world of insurance provides some interesting examples of how risk and uncertainty are present and must be managed. In many forms of non-life insurance, human behavior influences the probability and severity of the insured event. Insurers manage this source of uncertainty by providing incentives for desirable behavior.

An example is auto insurance. At a basic level, an individual may not know the probability and associated cost of an auto accident. To the individual, this is uncertain. The individual can insure the (financial) loss due to an auto accident and thus reduce his uncertainty. Unlike the individual, the insurance company has access to loss data from many auto accidents and can estimate a loss distribution with a high level of precision. To the insurance company, the probability of an auto accident constitutes a risk with minimal uncertainty involved. The insurance company accepts the risk in return for a premium that will compensate it for the potential claims under the insurance policies. However, the risk transfer from the insured individual to the insurer also creates some uncertainty for the insurance company because a driver who has obtained insurance may change his driving behavior, thereby changing the probability of causing an accident. The insurer can manage this uncertainty by creating incentives for the driver to keep him from reckless driving, for example, through insurance deductibles and premiums that decrease the longer an individual has not caused an accident. When human behavior has a big impact on potential insurance claims, the insurance company can also limit the indemnifications in case the potential of loss is very high (e.g., liability claims in the United States), or ultimately by excluding the event from the insurance coverage (e.g., if no preventive measures are taken after many similar claims or in case of fraud).

We conclude that it is important for managers to realize when they are facing a situation of risk and when they are facing a situation of uncertainty. We will highlight in this book when we face situations of risk and situations of uncertainty. Mitigating options and actions will be different, as well as the extent to which we can rely on quantitative techniques. Nevertheless, even when we face uncertainty, it can be valuable to attempt to estimate the loss distribution because it helps to make explicit the sources of uncertainty. When more data becomes available over time, and with increasing knowledge and experience, the confidence in the estimated loss distribution may grow, specifically when this relates to short-term horizons. The level of confidence that we have in the estimated loss distribution and, consequently, in economic capital estimates, will depend on the nature of the losses that are modeled, our understanding of what may potentially cause the losses, the number of historic observations, and so forth. These factors all influence model risk, which we will discuss in detail in Chapter 4.

1.3.2   Coherent Risk Measures

In this section, we discuss a theoretical argument against the use of economic capital as risk measure. This theoretical argument relates to all value-at-risk (VaR) type risk measures, that is, risk measures that correspond to one particular realization from a probability distribution of many possible realizations. Such risk measures do not satisfy all properties of what have been called coherent risk measures. The properties of coherent measures of risk have been defined in a paper by Artzner, Delbaen, Eber, and Heath in 1999.[7] We will not review the properties of coherent risk measures here, but focus on the property that value-at-risk type risk measures, including economic capital as we have defined it, may violate.

The property that VaR measures may violate is the one called subadditivity. A risk measure satisfies subadditivity if its value for a combination of two entities never exceeds the sum of the values of the same risk measure for each of the individual entities. For example, suppose the value of a risk measure for one business unit equals 2, and its value for another business unit equals 3. If the value of the same risk measure for the combination of both business units equals 6 (or, more generally, any value larger than 5), then the risk measure is not subadditive. Subadditivity is desirable because of the intuition that a combination of multiple business units will be less risky as a result of diversification effects between them than the sum of the risk of all units considered in isolation. This is exactly the same argument behind the general investment advice not to put all eggs into one basket, but to diversify investments across multiple investment categories and titles.

Although it is possible to create examples in which VaR measures violate subadditivity, it is seldom experienced as a problem in practice. That is, in almost all practical situations, VaR-type risk measures (including economic capital estimates) do satisfy subadditivity.[8] That the potential violation of subadditivity of VaR is not a significant practical concern is exemplified by the long-run popularity of VaR as a risk measure for the trading activities of banks. Although there has been significant discussion in the wake of the sub-prime crisis about the limitations of VaR as a risk measure for trading activities, this discussion does not relate to the fact that it may not satisfy subadditivity. We will further elaborate on the potential and observed weaknesses of VaR in Chapter 4 when we discuss the calculation of economic capital for market risk.

A risk measure that satisfies all properties of a coherent risk measure is what is known as expected shortfall, expected tail loss, or conditional tail expectation. Expected shortfall is the average value of a subset of possible outcomes of a random variable (e.g., potential losses), where the subset is limited by the condition that the individual outcomes have to be greater than (or smaller than) some minimum (maximum) value. It is thus the expected value of a random variable, *conditional* on its realization being above (or below) some threshold value.

The threshold used for expected shortfall could be set at the high confidence level we use for economic capital. We are then measuring the expected loss conditional that we take only the losses equal to or larger than the amount of economic capital into account. By definition this expected shortfall number is higher than economic capital. If available capital is equal to economic capital then the difference between expected shortfall and economic capital is the expected deficit that debt and deposit holders will incur in case the institution becomes insolvent. This number is, thus, potentially meaningful for the creditors of a financial institution. Expected shortfall and variations thereof also are used by some institutions as the basis to allocate capital over business lines.[9] However, expected shortfall is not directly relevant for the institution's capital adequacy assessment because it does not indicate how much capital an institution should possess in order to avoid insolvency with a chosen level of confidence. That is indicated only by the amount of economic capital.

Expected shortfall will also show up in the next section when we review alternative risk measures that financial institutions use in practice.

1.4 Alternative Risk Measures

Many financial institutions monitor alternative risk measures in addition to economic capital. These alternative measures typically relate to less extreme events, and it is therefore easier to have some intuition for their values. They usually are linked more closely to the ability to continue operating on a going-concern basis. For this purpose, some institutions estimate the expected loss in case certain scenarios materialize to ensure that these losses remain within their risk appetite. For example, institutions may estimate how much their earnings and capital levels could decline in a next economic downturn. This provides insight into possible consequences for the dividend policy, as well as input for the institution's capital planning. As full economic cycles extend over approximately 10 years, it is easier to have an intuitive feel for such a number than for the extreme loss that economic capital represents.

If we derive a probability distribution of potential losses over a one-year horizon, the expected value of the largest loss that will be incurred once every 10 years can be calculated as the expected value of the 10% largest losses in the probability distribution. This is an expected shortfall calculation.

Alternative risk measures usually are derived in practice from the same methodologies that are used to estimate economic capital. In essence, these methodologies yield a probability distribution of potential changes in the net value of assets and liabilities of a financial institution over a chosen time period. Economic capital is then calculated from the tail of this probability distribution that corresponds to extreme and very unlikely unexpected losses. The alternative risk measures typically are related more to the body of the distribution, corresponding to less extreme and more likely outcomes. Hence, the underlying probability distribution is the same, but economic capital focuses on a different part of this distribution than the alternative risk measures.

Because economic capital has achieved such a central place as a risk measure in the financial industry during the past decade, we will focus this book on the important issues related to its calculation and use. Moreover, none of the alternative risk measures are of direct help in assessing how much capital a financial institution should have, which is a crucial question for both senior management and supervisors. The alternative risk measures also do not have a direct link to performance management and the creation of shareholder value, a purpose for which economic capital often is used, as we will see in the next chapter. Nevertheless, alternative risk measures can be useful in the broader risk and capital management of an institution, as we will illustrate in Chapter 2. Being based on the same methodologies as economic capital, many issues discussed in this book will also be relevant for the calculation of these alternative risk measures. We will often refer to the methodologies as economic capital methodologies in this book, but it should be understood that they can also be used to estimate alternative measures of risk.

1.5   Conclusion

In this chapter we introduced economic capital and a number of conceptual issues related to its definition and interpretation. We have defined economic capital as an estimate of the worst possible decline in the amount of capital at a specified confidence level, within a chosen time horizon. The confidence level and time horizon need to be set by the institution. Economic capital can be viewed as the amount of capital that a firm should possess if it wants to remain solvent with a probability that is equal to the chosen confidence level.

We distinguished between expected losses and unexpected losses, and explained how economic capital is related to large unexpected losses. Economic capital represents a potential extreme decline in the amount of capital, corresponding to the tail of the probability distribution of potential declines in capital. The aim is to reflect all material risks that can lead to a decline in capital in this probability distribution. Sometimes we may not have sufficient knowledge about the nature of specific risks to include them in such a probability distribution, however. We then refer to uncertainty instead of to risk. We presented situations in which financial institutions encounter uncertainty, often related to uncertainty about human behavior, and gave a few examples how they try to cope in practice with this uncertainty.

Many institutions use alternative risk measures in addition to economic capital. These alternative risk measures usually relate to less extreme events. The calculation of alternative risk measures is based mostly on the same methodologies as economic capital, but they refer to different points on the resulting probability distribution. Although the values of alternative risk measures may be easier to interpret because they relate to more likely events, none of the alternative risk measures is of direct help to determine how much capital an institution should have, or have a direct link with managing shareholder value. Hence, we focus this book on the use and calculation of economic capital. Many of the issues discussed will, however, also be relevant for the alternative risk measures. In the next chapter we elaborate on the purpose and use of economic capital in practice.

Endnotes

[1]Zaik E, Walter J, Kelling G, James C. RAROC at Bank of America: From theory to practice. *Journal of Applied Corporate Finance*. 1996;9(2):83–92.
[2]Basel Committee on Banking Supervision. Amendment to the capital accord to incorporate market risks, Bank for International Settlements. January. 1996.
[3]Knight FH. *Risk, uncertainty and profit*. Cambridge: The River Press; 1921.
[4]Popper KR. *The poverty of historism*. New York: Routledge and Kegan Paul; 1957.
[5]See also Popper's earlier monumental work: Popper KR. *The open society and its enemies*. Vols 1 and 2. New York: Routledge and Kegan Paul; 1945.
[6]Shackle GLS. Uncertainty in economics: Selected essays. In: Ford JL, ed. Aldershot: Edward Elgar; 1990.

[7] Artzner P, Delbaen F, Eber J-M, Heath D. Coherent measures of risk. *Mathematical Finance.* 1999;9(3):203–228.

[8] Daníelsson J, Jorgenson BN, Mandira S, Samorodnitsky G, de Vries CG. Subadditivity re-examined: The case for value-at-risk. Working paper. 2005.

[9] Venter GG. ERM for strategic management—Status report. Paper presented at the ERM Conference in Chicago, April. 2008.

2 Show Me the Money: The Purpose of Economic Capital

To establish an economic capital framework, which encompasses the total of models, systems, data, policies, knowledge, and applications related to economic capital, takes a significant investment. Hence, the natural question is what the return on the investment will be. Is investing in an economic capital framework a good investment?

The simplest answer would be that it is an accepted way to meet a regulatory requirement, whatever the other merits and costs may be. Under the Basel II Accord, regulators require banks to assess their capital position in relation to the risks to which they are exposed. This is referred to as the Internal Capital Adequacy Assessment Process, or ICAAP. In the ICAAP, economic capital is an accepted (and generally considered a best practice) measure to assess capital, but regulators have stopped short of making it mandatory. For example, the US regulators state explicitly in their guidance for Basel II that "economic capital is not the only means to meet the ICAAP requirement."[1] The European supervisors have worded it as follows: "Institutions will not be required to use formal economic capital (or other) models, although it is expected that more sophisticated institutions will elect to do so."[2] Hence, regulatory compliance may be an important reason but there may be more cost-efficient ways to become compliant if that is the only purpose of establishing an economic capital framework. The question thus remains why institutions choose to invest in an economic capital framework. We will provide reasons in this chapter.

If we want to assess the added value of an economic capital framework, we need to identify the stakeholders for whom we are creating value. Thus, we start in Section 2.1 by making an inventory of the stakeholders of financial institutions and their respective interests. Subsequently, we describe in Sections 2.2 and 2.3 the two major areas in which economic capital can add value to an institution's stakeholders: ensuring continuity and optimizing profitability. In Section 2.4, we discuss what management processes can make use of economic capital. Section 2.5 presents examples of how various institutions use economic capital in practice, and we conclude in Section 2.6.

2.1   A Round-up of Stakeholders

The first group of stakeholders comprises the institution's customers who want financial products that are valuable to them. Price, service, and product features are obviously important to the customer. Profitable organizations are at an advantage because they have the means to invest in innovation that can have a favorable impact on any of these aspects. However, a special feature for many financial products is that the institution's continuity should not be in doubt as discontinuity of the institution could cause a significant loss to the customer. For example, policy holders with outstanding claims on insurance companies and the beneficiaries of pension funds face losses in case the institution becomes insolvent. The insolvency or conservatorship of a bank will cause a loss to the customer in case he or she has deposits with the bank (ignoring any government deposit guarantee scheme) or has a claim on the institution related to derivative contracts. The customer may also face a loss in case he or she depends on the institution for funding or for processing money transfers. If customers are in doubt about the continuity of the institution, then they will quickly try to safeguard their interests, bring their business elsewhere, and a run on the institution may be the result.

A second group of stakeholders consists of bond investors and other debt holders who have an obvious interest in the continuity of the institution in order that the institution can fulfill its debt obligations as these come due.

A third group of stakeholders comprises the regulatory and supervisory authorities (central bank, bank supervisors, deposit insurers). They are interested in the continuity of the institution as financial difficulties at an institution may disrupt the (local) financial markets and have negative consequences for the broader economy. Furthermore, governments may have deposit guarantee schemes in place for banks, and insolvency of an institution may cause a direct loss to them.

The employees of the institution constitute a fourth group of stakeholders. There are many reasons why employees choose one employer over another, such as job content, wages, bonuses, social responsibility of the organization, and so forth. For their bonuses, bankers have an interest that the institution is profitable. Profitability in general is associated with growth and job opportunities. Once employees have found an attractive job and income, they will have a vested interest in the continuity of the organization as well.

A final group of stakeholders is formed by shareholders. Whereas social responsibility of the organization may be valuable to (some) shareholders, the primary value is the monetary return on the shares. Shareholders have thus a clear interest in the profitability of a financial institution. The return on shares is potentially unlimited upward, but the shareholder cannot lose more than he or she has invested. Because of the limited downside risk, a shareholder benefits from increased leverage as this increases the expected profit per share. However, increased leverage will also increase the probability of discontinuity.

In case the costs of discontinuity are significant, then the shareholders also have an interest that the continuity of an institution is not in jeopardy.

The advocates of "shareholder value" are of the opinion that the interests of the shareholders are the most relevant of all stakeholders. Without shareholders there is neither capital to invest nor capital to protect depositors and bond holders. As shareholders appoint the management of the institution they are indirectly in charge. Although these are valid arguments, equally valid is that an organization cannot flourish or even exist if not all stakeholders derive value in one way or the other to keep them engaged with the organization. Consequently, we believe that a viable institution has to take account of the interests of all stakeholders.

If we consider the interests that shareholders and other stakeholders have, we note that continuity and profitability are important to many. The challenge is to maintain the right balance between these objectives. This relates directly to the degree of leverage of the institution, as too little capital will endanger the continuity of the organization and too much capital will reduce the return for the shareholders. In the next sections, we will discuss in more detail how economic capital can help to ensure the continuity of an institution and how it can contribute to optimize its profitability.

2.2 Ensuring Continuity

Many stakeholders have an interest in the continuity of the institution. In this section we will discuss how economic capital can be used to realize this objective. However, we will first discuss the reasons why institutions have failed in the past and the role that capital plays in such failures, because this provides insight into the relevance of capital in general to ensure an institution's continuity.

2.2.1 Why Do Financial Institutions Fail?

There are many reasons why banks can fail. For example, in countries where the sovereign is in financial distress, many banks typically default as they often have large direct and indirect exposures on the sovereign of the country where they are domiciled. These sovereign-related bank defaults may be attributed to an external force that is difficult to control for banks. Bank defaults also have occurred in substantial numbers in mature economies without sovereign defaults. For example, between 1980 and 1994 the Federal Deposit Insurance Corporation (FDIC) in the United States closed or gave assistance to more than 1,600 banks it insured. The savings and loan crisis, the LDC (less-developed countries) crisis, and the fall of Continental Illinois, at the time the seventh largest bank in the United States and until the sub-prime crisis the largest bank failure, all occurred within this period.

Outside the United States there have been numerous countries that experienced a bank crisis as well at one time or another (e.g., Norway 1988–1993, Japan 1994–2002, Russia 1998), and the recent global sub-prime crisis has caused a number of bank casualties, in Germany, the United Kingdom, and the United States, among others. This illustrates that bank failures occur during all times, in both mature and emerging countries.

Banking supervisors have tried to understand and learn from these episodes of bank failures. Their reports make for interesting reading. For example, a study of the FDIC in 1997[3] observes that "although banks that failed had generally assumed greater risk before their failure, many other banks with similar risk profiles did not fail. In the case of these surviving banks, the effects of risk taking ... were apparently offset by other factors, including superior risk management skills." And further, "which banks failed and which banks survived in an increasingly demanding environment was largely determined by an individual bank's circumstances, particularly variations in the levels of risk it assumed, its success (or lack thereof) in operating with high levels of risk, the overall strength of management, good or bad fortune, and (in some cases) the presence ... of fraud and misconduct."

A study by the Basel Committee on Banking Supervision in 2004[4] cites an examination by the Groupe de Contact: "the majority of banking crises were manifest as credit problems and sometimes as operational risk. Management and control weaknesses were significant contributory factors in nearly all cases." The role of management and controls is emphasized further in research of Dziobek and Pazarbasioglu,[5] who find that "deficient bank management and controls were responsible in all cases [of bank default]." On the role of capital, the Basel Committee makes the following observation: "banking problems were more severe and/or difficult to resolve when they hit weakly capitalized institutions." Furthermore, "sufficient capital [to the prevalent standards at the time] did at least help the restructuring of banks as ongoing concerns."

Common themes that appear in all analyses and reports are the importance of the quality of management and controls, and the implementation of good risk management practices. The level of capital alone is seldom the cause for failures of institutions, but can contribute to it in combination with other factors. As Moody's states: "Banks typically fail because of losses in the loan portfolio, poor business models, or fraud. These factors ultimately lead to a decline in capital, but capital adequacy cannot truly be considered the cause of bank failure.... Capital is important, but is not a leading indicator of credit health, and therefore only rarely drives ratings.... That said, we [Moody's] do consider the current and expected level of capital in determining ratings." Moody's highlights the interrelation between profitability and continuity of an institution, stating that the "earnings power is a key determinant of the long-term success or failure of a financial institution."[6] FitchRatings states that "as the income earned by a bank may ultimately affect its solvency, this is another area to analyze. Fitch looks at the historic trend of a bank's earnings performance, the stability and quality of its earnings, and its capacity to generate profits."[7]

The importance of earnings and capital for the continuity of an institution shows up prominently in two studies that the rating agency A.M. Best published about failures of US property and casualty insurers and US life and health insurers.[8] The most important reason for insolvency that A.M. Best identifies is inadequate pricing or deficient loss reserves, which often coincided with strong growth of the insurance company. For life insurers, investment risk was the second most important reason for insolvency. Alleged fraud is the third most frequent cause of failure. A report by the CRO Forum concludes that spikes in insurance insolvencies were largely driven by insurers with highly concentrated risk profiles.[9]

Financial institutions typically are in distress well before they have lost all their capital. Consequently, it is important to determine at what capital level an institution would find it difficult to continue operations. In general it is assumed that banks should at least have an investment-grade rating to be able to operate, because otherwise the likelihood of discontinuity would become too high for many customers and debt providers. The Basel II regulations seem to confirm this line of thinking as the Basel II capital formula is based on a confidence level deemed consistent with an investment-grade rating.

The idea that the continuity of an institution is threatened long before capital is depleted also is reflected in the Solvency II proposal of the Commission of the European Communities. Solvency II specifies two capital requirements for insurance and reinsurance firms: a solvency capital requirement, which corresponds to a confidence level of 99.5%, and a minimum capital requirement, which corresponds to a confidence level of 80 or 90%. The solvency capital requirement is "the economic capital that insurance companies have to hold in order to ensure that ruin occurs no more often than once every 200 years." The minimum capital requirement is intended to reflect "a level of capital below which policyholders' interests would be seriously endangered if the [firm] were allowed to continue to operate."[10] If available capital falls below the solvency capital requirement, then management should take action to restore the available capital to a level above the solvency capital requirement. However, if available capital instead decreases further to a level below the minimum capital requirement, then the licenses to operate may be withdrawn if available capital cannot be restored within a short period of time. The Solvency II proposal thus makes the point of discontinuity for an insurer explicit by assuming that it corresponds to a probability of insolvency of 10 or 20%.

To determine to what extent a decrease in capital would negatively affect the continuity of a financial institution, we also should consider the funding and liquidity profile of the institution. For example, a bank with a stable retail funding base is more likely to survive a decline in capital than a bank relying on funding from professional counterparties in the short-term wholesale or interbank market. The demise of Bear Stearns in March 2008 and the subsequent takeover by JP Morgan was triggered largely by professional counterparties, who massively withdrew their funding in just a few days.[11] In a letter to the Basel Committee on March 20, just after Bear Stearns had been

rescued, chairman Cox of the Security and Exchange Commission (SEC) wrote
that the collapse of Bear Stearns was "due to a lack of confidence, not a lack of
capital."[12] Cox's assessment of the situation was that "notwithstanding that
Bear Stearns continued to have high quality collateral to provide as security
for borrowings, market counterparties became less willing to enter into collateralized funding arrangements with Bear Stearns. ... The market rumors
about Bear Stearns' liquidity problems became self-fulfilling." Some market
commentators disagreed that capital had nothing to do with the liquidity
problems of Bear Stearns. A commentator in the *Financial Times*[13] wrote that
Bear Stearns, after suffering losses early in the sub-prime crisis, should have been
aware that it needed capital well above the regulatory minimum set by the SEC in
order for its key clients to be comfortable with its financial soundness. Indeed,
with hindsight and considering later events with other institutions, there was
likely a solvency issue after all. But whatever the precise solvency position of Bear
Stearns, the event illustrates that a deteriorating capital position can endanger an
institution's continuity even if it is well above regulatory minimum levels. The
later demise of banks like Lehman Brothers and Washington Mutual confirm
the observation that capital may be above minimum regulatory levels, but that
concerns with respect to the capital position may trigger the withdrawal of funding and lead to the discontinuity of an institution.

2.2.2   *Economic Capital and Assessing Capital Adequacy*

With capital being an important factor for the continuity of the bank, the question arises, what is a sufficient level of capital for a financial institution? We
can take a regulatory, rating agency, and economic perspective to answer this
question.

National authorities have an interest in the continuity of (at least the largest)
financial institutions. To ensure this, they have issued regulations that require
institutions to have minimum amounts of capital available. These regulations
can range from simple leverage ratios (e.g., the ratio of capital to total assets)
to increasingly risk-sensitive ratios where a capital requirement is related to
the assets weighted by their relative risk (e.g., risk-weighted assets ratio). The
introduction of the Basel I Accord in 1988 already reflected the desire of the
regulators that banks hold more capital when they are exposed to higher risks.
This has gradually progressed with the Market Risk Amendment in 1996, the
Basel II Accord in 2004, and the Solvency II proposal for insurers in 2008. As
the regulations have to apply to all institutions being regulated, they necessarily
cannot be tailored to an individual institution. Consequently, institutions may
consider their own risk models more adequate to assess their risk profile, while
remaining in compliance with applicable regulatory capital requirements.

Assessments by rating agencies are relevant for the debt market perception of
the risk of failure of an institution. Many investors rely on the judgment of qualified experts at the rating agencies, as summarized in credit ratings, because

assessing the risk profile of an institution is complex and time consuming. Rating assignments are not purely based on capital adequacy assessments, but reflect general assessments with respect to the probability of failure of the rated institution to repay its debt. Capital is one of many factors considered, and there may be more than one solvency ratio that is incorporated into an agency's analysis.

During the sub-prime crisis, the rating agencies were criticized for their flawed risk assessments of structured credit instruments, and the ratings of financial institutions that were exposed to these instruments. They received much less criticism for their (more established) corporate ratings. Notwithstanding the criticism, rating agencies are likely to remain important providers of opinions on the creditworthiness of debt issuers. Hence, their rating criteria and use of solvency ratios, as well as the resulting ratings, remain relevant for financial institutions that fund significant parts of their debt in capital markets.

The economic assessment of capital adequacy compares the economic capital of an institution (viewed as an estimate of the amount of capital a firm should carry) with its available capital. The assessment is comprehensive in the sense that it also takes into account potential losses from exposures not on the balance sheet (e.g., off-balance sheet financial obligations, legal risk, and business risk). If material risks are not included, then there will be a gap in the capital assessment. This may seem obvious, but it requires the institution to assess whether it has identified and quantified all material risks to which it is exposed.

The regulatory and rating agency views of capital adequacy have played a dominant role in the capital assessment of institutions, in part as there is a well-defined audience for this assessment. Until recently, the economic assessment was performed mainly internally as external parties found it difficult to understand, assess, and interpret the numbers. However, this gradually is changing as a result of increased transparency of related risk and capital data. Stringent validation of risk parameters helped the acceptance of risk-based capital requirements by bank regulators and the use of internal models by the institution to assess its capital adequacy. Also, rating agencies are looking for ways to refine their risk assessments based on the new regulatory framework and the disclosure by institutions of additional risk and capital data.[14] In the end, the aspiration level of regulators and rating agencies is to have an economic view on capital adequacy. However, model risks and lack of comparability between institutions sometimes result in very different capital amounts for similar exposures. This can endanger the level playing field among institutions. Regulators, therefore, have reverted to the use of some simplifications and proxies in order to avoid (over)reliance on models developed by institutions.

In short, an institution needs to have capital in excess of the regulatory requirements, sufficient to support its desired credit rating as issued by the rating agencies, and in line with its chosen business model and risk profile. As each of these assessments aspires to take an economic view on risks, these assessments will gradually converge. However, at present there are still significant differences between the methods applied.

2.2.3   Economic Capital and Capital Management

Assessing capital adequacy is important, but it needs to be followed by management action to ensure that the bank has sufficient capital now and in the future. This requires a dynamic process of assessing the institution's capital adequacy against future plans and potential adverse events. The economic capital framework can be used to quantify the additional capital that the institution needs if its future plans are executed. Instead of the current assets, liabilities, and model parameters, the future expected values can be entered into the models to assess the capital required on a pro-forma basis. The same can be done for "what-if" scenarios to assess whether the bank has sufficient capital for eventualities. We will discuss this in Chapter 6 when we describe the role of stress tests in an economic capital framework.

If the outcome of the assessment is that an institution believes its capital to be insufficient, then the question arises what the most effective action is to ensure continuity. Attracting new capital and reduction of risk exposures can be contemplated. Risk reductions can occur in many ways; in each case, the amount of capital release needs to be weighted against the associated costs. Examples of risk reduction include the divestment of activities, sale of assets, buying credit protection or other forms of insurance, off-setting positions in the trading book, and asset securitizations.

In Section 2.2.1, we discussed that the continuity of an institution may already be at risk if its capital level decreases to a level below what is commensurate with an investment-grade rating. Hence, the institution may want to assess and manage this risk as well. However, the contribution of assets to the large potential decrease in capital that economic capital represents may differ from their contribution to a smaller potential decrease in capital that leads to a rating downgrade below investment grade. For example, assets with a low default probability contribute little to the risk of a rating downgrade, but they contribute significantly to economic capital. Hence, capital management and risk reduction require careful analysis for an optimal selection of assets to be sold, hedged, or securitized.

Besides managing the absolute level of capital, capital management also includes the optimal composition of capital. For example, what part of capital should be funded by subordinated loans, convertible debt, or preferred shares? The desired amount of each type of capital could be determined through the use of different confidence levels in the economic capital calculation. Each capital instrument or debt type may have its unique confidence level that corresponds to the tolerated probability of default on the specific type of capital instrument or debt. How these confidence levels can be set is discussed in Section 3.5.1.

The structuring of the liability side of the balance sheet on the basis of risk model considerations has been done in a very pure form for Structured Investment Vehicles (SIV) and special purpose vehicles (SPV) for securitization transactions. For SIVs and securitization SPVs, the entire liability side is tranched in several capital and debt instruments and titles, and each tranche has its own rating and unique confidence level. Many SIVs have been unwound during the sub-prime crisis when losses on the assets turned out to be much higher than expected, as a result of which investors were no longer willing to fund these vehicles. However, this does not invalidate the idea of explicitly dividing the liabilities in tranches with each a unique risk profile.

For companies whose cash flow profiles are not structured, the composition of capital and liabilities is less likely to be model-driven, but based on a combination of market, regulatory, and tax considerations. Economic capital is less suitable to take these factors fully into account.

2.2.4 Economic Capital and Risk Management

It may not be clear immediately how economic capital as a comprehensive risk measure can be used to actively manage risks. Rating downgrades, default rates, number of operational risk incidents, and duration of the portfolio can be observed directly by users, and give direct clues for risk management. Economic capital, however, is an abstract quantity, due to the fact that it is a single composite number. This is both its weakness and its strength. The weakness is that an increase of economic capital does not tell exactly which underlying risks are increasing. Are default rates increasing, are concentrations increasing, or something else? Further analysis needs to be performed in order to provide the answer. Hence, monitoring economic capital cannot replace the monitoring of the underlying drivers of risk.

The strength of economic capital is that it enables an overall assessment of a change in risk profile when risk exposures change in different directions, which could confuse an analyst. For example, if clients are downgraded and default rates are rising, but the loan portfolio is gradually shrinking and concentrations are reducing, is the portfolio becoming more or less risky? Economic capital provides an answer. As another example, if different risk types are changing in opposite directions (e.g., credit risk increasing, but market risk decreasing), then economic capital can help to provide insight whether the overall level of risk is increasing or decreasing.

One common risk management application of economic capital is to monitor concentrations in a portfolio of loans and other credit risk exposures. Concentrated exposures contribute more than proportionally to economic capital, and, hence, economic capital can provide a good indication of concentration risk per industry, geography, or single names. The typical argument to accept a concentration is that each of the individual exposures has a low risk. Economic capital can help to weigh the low-risk nature of the individual exposures with the overall size of the exposure, and provide an overall assessment of the risk. An important attention point is that exposures across the organization are combined in a single economic capital calculation. Otherwise concentrations may not be properly identified and aggregated. In the sub-prime crisis, many banks found out to their detriment that they had sub-prime exposure in their banking, trading, and investment books and had not considered all these related exposures in a single risk overview.

Risk management is not an activity that is performed in isolation in a financial institution. In practice, it starts with determining what the risk appetite is of the institution based on the business model and objectives of the institution. This is then further detailed in risk limits, guidelines, and policies throughout the organization. This approach may seem straightforward, but it is the number two recommendation in a report issued by the International Institute of Finance (IIF) on Best Market Practices published in July 2008.[15] (For the curious reader: the number one recommendation was that senior management, and in particular the CEO, is responsible for risk management.) The recommendation of IIF regarding risk appetite states that all relevant risks, comprising both quantitative and qualitative elements, should be included. As a quantitative risk measure that is comparable across risk types and across the organization, economic capital will have a prominent place. In this way, economic capital gradually is gaining a principal place in a financial institution's arsenal to manage its capital and risk profile and, thereby, ensure its continuity.

2.3 Optimizing Profitability

As discussed in Section 2.1, shareholders require that the institution optimize its profitability. In the next subsections we discuss how the return on economic capital can be a suitable profitability measure, and how it can be used for performance and portfolio management.

2.3.1 Economic Capital and Profitability Measures

From a shareholder perspective, the profitability measure that often is deemed the most relevant is return on equity (ROE). Most if not all investor reports provide this ratio in combination with one or more other profitability measures, such as cost-to-income ratio, return on assets, and price-to-earnings ratio. The drawback of ROE for shareholders is that it is not risk sensitive. The activist fund manager Eric Knight also pointed this out in an article in the *Financial Times* on June 19, 2008:[16] "Increases in ROE that come from increased leverage come with increased risk and do not necessarily represent improved performance." Knight argues that many banks have produced good ROE only because they have highly leveraged their investments. The investments themselves gave returns only slightly higher than their funding costs, which provided insufficient compensation for the risks involved. To make this investment strategy by banks transparent, Knight argues that banks should also publish divisional gross returns on assets to allow investors to assess the true performance of a bank. However, just like ROE, a gross return on assets does not take into account the risks associated with the assets.

Also other commentators have stressed the role played by the (over)lever-aging of banks and other financial institutions in the sub-prime crisis. The relevant question is what an appropriate amount of leverage is. What standard can be applied to determine a normative leverage for each investment or financial institution? A natural standard is economic capital, because it is a normative capital amount that is directly related to the underlying risk profile of the investment or institution. Thus, the return on economic capital is the performance measure that takes into account a normative, risk-based leverage of an investment portfolio or of an institution.

The return on economic capital is better known under the abbreviation RAROC, which stands for risk-adjusted return on capital. There are different ways in which it may be calculated, but the most common formula is:

$$RAROC = \frac{Revenues - Costs - ExpectedLoss - Tax}{EconomicCapital}$$

We introduced expected loss in Section 1.2.

RAROC can be calculated before or after tax. If it is calculated after tax, then the amount of tax included in the formula should correspond to the taxes that would be paid if actual losses are equal to expected losses. This may thus differ from the actual amount of tax paid, because this will depend on the actual losses incurred as opposed to expected losses.

A performance measure related to RAROC is economic profit (EP) or economic value added (EVA).[17] This measure is calculated as follows:[18]

$$EP = Capital\ Employed \\ * (Return\ on\ Capital\ Employed - Cost\ of\ Capital\ Employed)$$

If Capital Employed is set equal to the level of Economic Capital, and if Return on Capital Employed equals (Revenues – Cost – Expected Loss – Tax) divided by Capital Employed, then we can rewrite:

$$EP = (Revenues - Cost - Expected\ Loss - Tax) \\ - (Economic\ Capital * Cost\ of\ Capital\ Employed)$$

Rewritten in this way, economic profit equals the net profit, after the adjustment to replace actual losses by expected losses, minus the cost of capital. Economic profit can be calculated over multiple periods by discounting the economic profit amounts for each period. When economic profit is positive, the activity adds value to the shareholders, because the return is higher than the cost of capital. Projects or investments with a negative economic profit are expected to destroy shareholder value. In RAROC terms, investments with a RAROC above the Cost of Capital Employed generate value and vice versa. Critical in this comparison is how the Cost of Capital Employed, also known as the hurdle rate, should be determined. This will be discussed in Chapter 5.

An alternative performance measure that takes risk into account is the Sharpe ratio, named after its inventor, William Sharpe. The Sharpe ratio is used primarily to compare the performance of stocks or mutual funds, and is defined as follows:[19]

$$Sharpe\ ratio = \frac{E(R_i) - E(R_b)}{\sigma_{R_i - R_b}}$$

where:

$E(R_i)$ is the expected return on investment i.
$E(R_b)$ is the expected return on a benchmark investment. Often, the risk-free rate is taken as the benchmark.
$\sigma_{R_i} - R_b$ is the standard deviation of the difference between R_i and R_b. The standard deviation is the measure of risk.

The Sharpe ratio can be used to identify which investment gives the highest risk-adjusted return to the investor. It can also help to judge the performance of fund managers as it relates any excess returns over a benchmark to the additional risks taken. We could consider applying the Sharpe ratio within a business environment, thereby introducing a risk-return measure that is used by many investors. However, the standard deviation that acts as measure of risk in the Sharpe ratio only fully captures the risk if returns have a Gaussian (bell-shaped) probability distribution, also known as the normal distribution. In reality, returns are not always distributed according to a Gaussian distribution. A clear example is the return on a loan portfolio, which does not follow a Gaussian distribution because the upward potential of the returns is limited while the downward risk is the full investment amount in the event of a default. Contrary to the standard deviation, economic capital as a risk measure is sensitive to the actual shape of the probability distribution of potential returns.

A further advantage of RAROC as a performance measure compared to the Sharpe ratio is that RAROC can be viewed directly as return to the shareholders if we relate economic capital to shareholder capital. We will look into this relationship in Chapter 3.

2.3.2 *Economic Capital and Performance Management*

The aim of performance management is to determine to what activity or business line the institution should direct its resources in order to optimize its future profitability. Capital is one of the resources that have to be allocated. Typically, activities with a relatively high (prospective) return on capital will receive more capital than activities with a low return on capital. As we have seen in the previous section, RAROC and economic profit are useful performance measures in this context. Because economic capital is measured comprehensively and uniformly across the organization, it enables comparison between different business lines. Prospective or expected RAROC can be calculated per business line by using as inputs the estimated future revenues, costs, and risk exposures. This implies that the budget process should not only focus on financial numbers like revenues, but also on the associated risks to generate these revenues.

Performance management should also provide proper incentives and rewards for managers and business lines to add value to the organization. This requires a good *ex-post* measure for performance. The performance measure ideally should focus on items that can be influenced by the manager and are not the result of fortune or bad luck. The performance measure should take into account the risk during the full life of the transaction and avoid that returns are taken up-front while the potential losses fall in later performance periods. RAROC combines many of the desired features as it can take into account the risks over the full tenor of the exposure. A number of issues related to performance incentives are discussed in Section 5.2.6.

2.3.3 Economic Capital and Portfolio Management

Economic capital and RAROC were developed in the first instance to manage loan portfolios. RAROC is a practical measure to evaluate *ex-ante* whether the risk-adjusted return on a loan is deemed sufficient. Inputs to the calculation include default probability of the borrower, collateral, loan maturity, and the impact of loan covenants. Hence, the consequences of alternative loan structures on the expected profitability of the loan can be determined, which can help the relationship manager and credit officer to optimally structure and price the loan. In a similar way, economic capital and RAROC can be used in the product pricing process of insurers.

For a portfolio of loans, investments, or insurance contracts, we also would like to evaluate whether profitability and shareholder value can be enhanced by selling or securitizing parts of the portfolio, or by buying portfolio insurance in the form of credit derivatives or reinsurance contracts. In particular, if the capital management function in the institution demands that risk exposures are lowered, then the question arises how this can best be accomplished. In a situation of portfolio growth, the question to the portfolio manager is what exposures can best be added to the portfolio. The answers to these questions depend to a significant degree on the concentrations within the portfolio and the diversification effects. As economic capital is sensitive to these risk factors, the calculation of economic capital and RAROC for different scenarios can provide valuable guidance for these decisions.

2.4 Management and Economic Capital

Having discussed for what purposes economic capital can be used, we turn to the question of how this relates to the management of the institution in general. In which management processes can economic capital be used? Does economic capital have strategic or only operational value? For an answer, we need to have an overview of relevant management responsibilities and actions. We follow the structure provided by J. Magretta[20] (2002), as this summarizes the basic principles of management in a clear manner.

Magretta separately describes the design of the organization and the execution. The design of the organization comprises the following elements:

- **Value proposition.** This describes what value the organization will create for its customers. In a broader context, it is management's challenge to ensure that all stakeholders (such as shareholders, employees, and suppliers) choose to participate in the system that creates value for all of them.
- **Business model.** Magretta defines a business model as the set of assumptions about how an organization will operate to create value to all the players on whom it depends. Put more simply, a business model is a story of how the organization works, about the basic activities of producing and selling. Like a good story, it depends on characters, motivation, and plot. Characters must be delineated, their motivations must be plausible, and the plot must turn on an insight about value. By definition, a good business model represents a better way to deliver a product or service than the existing alternatives. Ideally, business models are relatively simple to understand. For example, eBay lowered the costs for small-business people to reach and supply potential customers in return for a small transaction fee. By choosing this business model, eBay has become the marketing and distribution arm for many small-business people. Another simple story as described by Magretta is about the PC-maker Dell, which looked at an existing value chain and took out one unnecessary and costly step from the process, thereby creating value to its customers in the form of cheaper PCs.
- **Strategy.** As organizations usually face competition, they must determine how they will differentiate themselves. This is the only way to produce superior returns. The aim of strategy is to move an enterprise away from a situation of full-fledged competition, in which excess returns are eliminated between competitors, and in the direction of monopoly, allowing for excess returns.
- **Organization.** What should the organization look like? This involves decisions on what is done inside and what is done outside the organization, how the organization is divided into working units and how they relate to each other, and finally, how the lines of authority are defined. Should the organization be centralized or decentralized? Should the organization own and control assets and employees or string together networks of suppliers and outsource selected functions? Typically, organization follows strategy, and as strategies change, so do organizations. A clear strategy thus becomes the blueprint of an organization's design.

What is the use of economic capital in these design elements? In deciding what value to create and to whom, financial institutions will need to think about the continuity risks for their customers. Furthermore, as part of their value proposition, financial institutions need to decide what the risk-return profile is that they are offering to their debt and shareholders. Business model and strategy will be related to these choices. All financial institutions have to make these choices, but few have done it so explicitly as Rabobank in The Netherlands. Rabobank has made it a key feature in its value proposition that, as one of the very few banks in the world, it wants to maintain a very low-risk profile to maintain its triple-A credit rating. Thus, its triple-A credit rating and financial soundness are prominently reflected in Rabobank's marketing expressions. The chosen value proposition has consequences for its business model and its strategy in the form of products offered and risk management practices.

As we have discussed before, economic capital is useful both to define and measure continuity risk and as a risk measure in profitability measures that trade off risk and return. Consequently, economic capital can play an important role in the value proposition of a financial institution. In the other design areas, economic capital has an indirect role only via the value proposition, because economic capital does not prescribe or indicate how an organization operates, how the institution can distinguish itself from its competitors, or how the organization should be set up.

While economic capital has a limited, although potentially important, role in the design of the business, does it have a larger role to play in the execution to translate plans into performance? Magretta distinguishes the following four key management activities related to execution:

- **Determine which numbers matter and why.** Numbers need to tell a story of how the company is doing in terms of value creation and strategy. The company's mission and measures need to be aligned with each other. This helps to determine whether the organization is successful and on track to achieve its objectives. It can also help to identify actions necessary to achieve its objectives. As the adage goes: what gets measured gets managed.
- **Manage innovation and uncertainty.** To protect the company's future profitability, managers need to consider innovation and the further development of their business. This requires dealing with uncertainty, which we discussed in Section 1.3. It involves activities like information gathering, listening, judgments about which bets to take, making trade-offs between risks and returns, and diversifying one's bets.
- **Deliver results.** Results will have to be delivered if the organization is to meet its objectives. This involves activities like prioritization and resource allocation.
- **Manage people.** All these activities are performed by people. It is the task of managers to hire the right people and to provide context and values to these people to do their job well.

The potential role of economic capital in financial institutions is apparent in all except the last activity. As a performance measure RAROC helps to allocate resources in an optimal manner (deliver results). By balancing risk and return of projects and investments, also the benefit of diversification is made transparent (manage innovation and uncertainty, or in our terminology, manage risk).

As economic capital and RAROC are important measures to ensure the continuity of the organization and to optimize profitability they are important numbers for an organization to measure, monitor, and manage. In short, economic capital can help management in various ways to execute its plans and deliver results.

2.5 The Actual Use of Economic Capital

Economic capital can be used for many purposes, but to what extent is it actually used by financial institutions? In a survey conducted in 2006 among 17 banks and 16 insurers, the IFRI/CRO Forum concluded that more than 90% of respondents use economic capital for capital budgeting, including capital adequacy assessments, and performance measurement.[21] Well above 50% of respondents use economic capital for target setting, compensation, portfolio management, and in the disclosure of information externally. Only 1 in 4 respondents use economic capital for M&A decisions. The latter probably reflects that a major acquisition is associated with significant uncertainty, in which case a quantification of the risks is more difficult if possible at all. A survey by the Society of Actuaries finds that US life-insurance companies use economic capital most frequently for the allocation of capital, followed by risk-adjusted performance measurement, making strategic and tactical decisions, and in product pricing and design.[22]

The diversity of institutions that use economic capital is illustrated by the following list. We summarize only the essentials that are disclosed in the 2007 annual reports, but the actual use by the institutions is not limited by what we describe:

- J.P. Morgan Chase, one of the biggest banks in the United States and the world, discloses its economic risk capital for credit, market, operational, and private equity risk, which is compared to its total common shareholders equity.
- Credit Suisse, active in investment banking, private banking, and asset management, uses economic capital for risk management, capital management, and planning and performance. It provides extensive disclosure of economic capital and RAROC numbers.
- Probably one of the most extensive disclosures of economic capital and RAROC numbers, including some explanation of the methodologies, is by the Dutch bank insurer ING.
- Allianz, a German bank insurer, and after the sale of Dresdner Bank in 2008 primarily an insurer, discloses economic capital in relation to available capital. It also mentions that it uses economic capital to identify and manage concentration risks.
- Barclays in the United Kingdom, one of the early adopters of economic capital, not only discloses economic capital and RAROC, but also expected loss per business line.

- Santander and BBVA, Spanish banks with significant emerging market exposure, disclose economic capital estimates in relation to available capital. Both banks also disclose performance-related measures like RAROC or Economic Profit.
- Nordea, a regional bank active in Scandinavia, discloses economic capital in relation to its capital adequacy.
- In Japan the Sumitomo Trust and Banking Group uses economic capital for capital adequacy and capital allocation.
- The Japanese Mitsubishi UFJ Financial Group reports that it uses economic capital for credit risk management and loan pricing.
- Rabobank, a cooperative bank in The Netherlands, discloses economic capital and RAROC per business line.
- Caixa Catalunya, a relatively small Spanish savings bank, calculates economic capital for credit, operational, market liquidity, structural interest rate, reputation, business, and concentration risk.
- One of the institutions using and disclosing expected shortfall for its capital adequacy assessment is Swiss Re. As discussed in Section 1.4 expected shortfall is derived from similar methodologies as economic capital.

In 2007, disclosure of economic capital was done more extensively by European institutions than by institutions in other parts of the world. Still, many institutions in North America and Australia are established users of economic capital, and in Asia the use is growing.

Not all institutions that use economic capital have come through the subprime crisis unscathed. For example, the US insurer AIG disclosed its approach to economic capital in early 2008, including the various ways it used economic capital for capital and risk management.[23] However, half a year later it faced significant credit losses and a funding crisis and, as a result, had to be bailed out by the US government. AIG was not the only institution that used economic capital and suffered large unexpected losses during the sub-prime crisis. The application of economic capital is, thus, no guarantee against large and unexpected losses. This does not disqualify the usefulness of economic capital, but emphasizes that risks need to be reflected accurately in economic capital models. In Chapter 4 we will discuss a few examples where the modeling of risks may have gone awry, such as the modeling of credit risk in the trading book, and the impact of correlations.

Notwithstanding the fact that economic capital is a comprehensive risk measure, we reiterate the point made earlier in Section 2.2.4 that monitoring of economic capital should not replace the monitoring of the underlying risk exposures and risk drivers. Monitoring these is necessary to understand the causes of the changes in economic capital, and because no single risk measure can identify all potential risks. This was also one of the key observations from the Senior Supervisors Group in March 2008: firms that avoided large losses had used a wide range of risk measures to measure and manage their risk profile. Consistent with this observation is the advice of the IIF in its

"Best Practices report" in 2008, that firms should not rely on a single risk measure and should take an integrated view on risks. This issue of combining economic capital with other risk measures will be taken up again in Chapter 6, when we discuss the interaction between economic capital and other risk tools and measures.

2.6 Conclusion

We started this chapter with an overview of important stakeholders of a financial institution and their main interests: customers, debt holders, supervisors, employees, and shareholders. We identified two interests that most of them share: continuity and profitability of the institution. We also noted the tension between these objectives with respect to the amount of capital that the institution should hold: too little capital will endanger the continuity of the institution, and too much capital will reduce the return for the shareholders. The focus of this chapter has been to clarify how the use of economic capital can help to achieve both objectives.

In the context of ensuring the continuity, we first reviewed why financial institutions have failed in the past. A conclusion from this analysis is that the quality of management and controls, and the implementation of sound risk management practices, are crucial to prevent failure. The level of capital is seldom the primary cause for failures, but can contribute to it in combination with other factors. Institutions typically get into financial distress well before they have lost all or even most of their capital. A prominent cause is funding liquidity problems. Such funding liquidity problems can often be attributed, however, to concerns of clients and funding providers about the capital position of an institution, triggering the withdrawal of funds. Hence, holding sufficient capital in relation to the risks to which an institution is exposed is crucial to avoid funding liquidity problems. Economic capital provides a means to assess what an adequate level of capital is for a financial institution. In addition, we discussed how economic capital can contribute to the management of the level and composition of capital, and support the overall management of risks.

With regard to optimizing the profitability of an institution, we first reviewed the most commonly used profitability measures. Although the return on equity is the most popular profitability measure in the financial industry, it does not take into account the underlying risks, and thus does not indicate whether the return provides sufficient compensation for the risks involved. A profitability measure that does take risks into account is the risk-adjusted return on capital (RAROC). We have discussed how RAROC and the related profitability measure economic profit can help to optimally allocate capital to business lines and transactions, and provide proper performance incentives to managers, thereby supporting the optimization of risk-adjusted profitability for the institution.

Subsequently, we reviewed what role economic capital and the related performance measures RAROC and economic profit can play in the general management of a financial institution. We concluded that they can help with the formulation of the value proposition for the institution's stakeholders and support management to execute its plans and deliver results.

In recognition of the wide range of benefits that the use of economic capital and related performance metrics can offer, many institutions have adopted or started to adopt an economic capital framework. In the next chapters we will discuss many choices, trade-offs, and challenges that institutions face when developing and implementing an effective economic capital framework.

Endnotes

[1]Department of the Treasury Office of the Comptroller of the Currency, Federal Reserve System, Federal Deposit Insurance Corporation, Department of the Treasury Office of Thrift Supervision. Supervisory guidance: Supervisory review process of capital adequacy (Pillar 2) related to the implementation of the Basel II advanced capital framework. July 2008.

[2]Committee of European Banking Supervisors. CP03, The application of the supervisory review process under Pillar 2. May 2004.

[3]Federal Deposit Insurance Corporation. The banking crisis of the 1980s and early 1990s. December 1997.

[4]Basel Committee on Banking Supervision. Bank failures in mature economies. Working Paper No. 13. April 2004.

[5]Dziobek C, Pazarbasioglu C. Lessons from systemic bank restructuring: A survey of 24 countries. IMF Working Paper 97/161. 1997.

[6]Moody's Investor Service. Bank financial strength ratings: Global methodology. February 2007.

[7]FitchRatings. Bank rating methodology. Criteria Report. May 25, 2004.

[8]A. M. Best's insolvency study, property/casualty US insurers 1969–2002. May 2004 and A. M. Best's insolvency study, US life/health insurers, 1976–2002. December 2004.

[9]The Chief Risk Officer Forum. A framework for incorporating diversification in the solvency assessment of insurers. June 10, 2005.

[10]Commission of the European Communities. Amended proposal for a directive of the European Parliament and of the Council on the taking-up and pursuit of the business of insurance and reinsurance (Solvency II). 26 February 2008.

[11]Congressional Research Service Report for Congress. Bear Stearns: Crisis and "rescue" for a major provider of mortgage-related products. Updated March 26, 2008.

[12]Christopher Cox, letter to Nout Wellink Chairman Basel Committee on banking supervision, Re: Sound practices for managing liquidity in banking organizations. March 20, 2008.

[13]Cohan W. The capital blunders that led to Bear's demise. *Financial Times*. April 9, 2008.

[14]Standard & Poor's. Request for comment: Standard & Poor's risk-adjusted capital framework for financial institutions. April 15, 2008.

[15]International Institute of Finance. Final report of the IIF committee on market best practices: Principles of conduct and best practice recommendations. July 2008.

[16]Knight E. Banks should be rewarded for transparency. *Financial Times*. June 19, 2008.

[17]Economic Value Added (EVA) is a registered trademark by its developer Stern Stewart & Co.

[18]Matten C. *Managing bank capital, capital allocation and performance measurement*. 2nd ed. New York: Wiley; 2000.

[19]Sharpe WF. The Sharpe ratio. *The Journal of Portfolio Management*. Fall. 1994.

[20]Magretta J. *What management is, how it works and why it's everyone's business*. New York: The Free Press; 2002.

[21]IFRI Foundation and CRO Forum. Insights from the joint IFRI/CRO forum survey on economic capital practice and applications. 2007.

[22]Society of Actuaries. Economic capital for life-insurance companies. February 2008.

[23]American International Group Inc. Economic capital modelling initiative & applications. February 2008 Update.

3 You Manage What You Measure: Defining Economic Capital

In Chapter 1, we introduced economic capital and defined it as an estimate of the worst possible decline in the amount of capital at a specified confidence level, within a chosen time horizon. In this chapter, we will discuss how we can make this definition operational, by considering how we can fill in the elements of this definition. In Section 3.1, we first address the issue of what value to assign to capital. As capital is the difference in value between assets and liabilities, this relates to how we value assets and liabilities. The value of capital will also be influenced by which assets and liabilities we choose to include. An important choice in this respect is whether to include intangible assets in the picture. We will discuss this in Section 3.2. In Section 3.3, we provide an overview of risks that could lead to a change in the value of capital, and should be included in the measurement of economic capital. The choice of the time horizon and how to reflect expected profits during this time horizon in the calculation of economic capital is the subject of Section 3.4. In Section 3.5, we focus on the choice of an appropriate confidence level and how this relates to economic cycles. We end this chapter by reviewing in Section 3.6 how the definition of economic capital and the related definition of available capital are a function of the main purposes for which economic capital is used: to ensure the continuity of a financial institution or to optimize its profitability. The conclusion is that we may end up with different definitions for the two different purposes. We will also discuss to what extent alignment of the definitions is possible.

3.1 Valuation Principles

When we measure the amount of capital and the amount by which it can potentially decline, the first issue to address is which valuation principles to apply. As capital is the difference in value between assets and liabilities, this relates to how we value assets and liabilities. Do we follow the accounting standards and consider book values, or do we value all assets and liabilities at fair value?

Book values have the advantage that they are audited and disclosed, and thus can be observed directly. The book value of financial assets and liabilities can be equal to the fair value or to the amortized cost, depending on their classification.

"Held-to-maturity investments" and "loans and receivables" are valued at amortized costs. This is defined in the International Accounting Standards (IAS) as "the amount at which the financial asset or financial liability is measured at initial recognition minus principal repayments, plus or minus the cumulative amortization . . . , and minus any reduction for impairment or uncollectibility." The definition implies that primarily the historic costs (amount at initial recognition) are considered and not any later market prices of the asset or liability. Consequently, the valuation is not susceptible to changes in market prices.

When an asset is classified as "held for trading" or "available for sale," then it is included at fair value in the financial accounts. Fair value is defined in IAS as "the amount for which an asset could be exchanged, or a liability settled, between knowledgeable, willing parties in an arm's length transaction." The best estimate of fair value is a quoted price in an active market. If no market exists, then a valuation technique must be used to establish what the transaction price would have been in an arm's length transaction motivated by normal business considerations. A common valuation method is the net present value of expected future cash flows, using an appropriate discount factor. The discount factor is the risk-free rate plus a risk premium that is related to the variability of the future cash flows. The higher the variability is, the higher the discount rate and the lower the fair value will be. Fair values are, therefore, sensitive to changes in risk.

When market values cannot be observed directly, the fair value must be estimated. During the sub-prime crisis, there have been many discussions between accountants and financial institutions how the fair value should be estimated in case of distressed and illiquid markets. In reaction, accounting bodies have issued further guidance for fair value measurement. For assets that originally were intended to be sold, but due to market circumstances this intention had to be changed to a hold-to-maturity strategy, several institutions argued that amortized costs would be the appropriate valuation principle because market values would not be representative for these assets. The counterargument is that a financial institution may be in need of funds and compelled to sell assets classified as loans and receivables or held-to-maturity before maturity. In that case, market prices would be obtained, and the difference between book and market value will potentially lead to a change in the amount of capital on the balance sheet. Such a compulsory sale not necessarily occurs only when a financial institution is close to bankruptcy, but may also be required in less extreme situations. For example, an institution may sell a noncore asset to finance a reorganization or an acquisition. Such a sale occurs against market prices, and if the noncore asset was booked as held-to-maturity, then any difference between book and market value will be reflected in the reported income and capital.

Because we want economic capital to be sensitive to changes in risk, the valuation method to be applied should also be sensitive to changes in risk. As a result, the fair value for assets and liabilities should be the leading valuation principle. The Solvency II proposal follows this principle; it stipulates that for capital adequacy purposes all assets and liabilities of insurers should be valued at fair value.

Goldman Sachs highlights the relationship between valuation principles and risk management in its 2007 Annual Report: "A large part of this discipline (i.e., risk management) is represented in the marking process, which assigns value to a position based on its currently traded market price. We believe that rigorous mark-to-market accounting for financial instruments is fundamental to prudent management because it facilitates a clear view of risk." Associated with the choice for fair values is the challenge to determine a fair value. If no traded market prices are available, fair values may be estimated using models. This gives rise to model risk, which we will discuss in Sections 3.3.1 and 4.1.5.

Even when all assets and liabilities on the balance sheet of a financial institution are represented at fair value, the corresponding accounting fair value of equity capital may differ from the market value of equity. The market value of equity equals the number of outstanding shares multiplied with the (market) share price. In theory, the market value of equity capital equals the discounted value of all expected future cash flows accruing to the shareholders. The difference between the market value of equity and the accounting fair value of equity capital can be attributed to the franchise value of the firm. We define the franchise value as the discounted value of all expected future cash flows that are not directly related to the current assets and liabilities included on the firm's balance sheet. The franchise value includes the value of contracts, brands, licenses, human and intellectual capital, and other intangible assets and liabilities that produce future cash flows for the firm. Some of these intangibles may be recorded on the balance sheet, such as paid goodwill and purchased licenses. Nevertheless, typically we would include these in the franchise value, and relate the accounting fair value only to tangible assets and liabilities. We note that the franchise value can also be negative, for example, in case there are no value-adding investment opportunities available and the company is facing high restructuring costs to continue operations or even liquidation costs.

We summarize the relationship between book value, fair value, and market value of equity capital as follows: The fair value of equity is the book value of equity plus adjustments for differences between the fair value and the book value of the assets and liabilities of the firm that are included on the firm's balance sheet. The market value of equity—that is, the market capitalization of the firm—is the fair value of equity plus the franchise value. For a consistent definition of the franchise value of the institution, all intangible assets should be included as part of the franchise value, regardless of whether they are recorded on the balance sheet or not.

3.2 Which Assets and Liabilities to Include in Economic Capital

As we discussed in the previous section, the fair value of an institution's available equity capital can be determined as the difference between the fair value of all tangible assets and liabilities on its balance sheet. As a consequence, value changes in these assets and liabilities can cause the value of the equity capital to change. Therefore, the potential value changes of all assets and liabilities have to be considered when measuring economic capital. In the previous section, we also discussed the franchise value of the firm, which typically is not included on the balance sheet of the firm. The question addressed in this section is whether the potential change in the franchise value of the institution should be included when measuring economic capital.

We defined the franchise value as the difference between the market value and the fair value of equity. However, the fair value of equity of an institution is usually not available, but only the book value. An indication of the franchise value of the firm can be obtained by looking at the difference between the market value and the book value of equity. This difference commonly is expressed using the market-to-book ratio. A ratio greater than one indicates a positive franchise value and a ratio smaller than one a negative franchise value. The market-to-book ratio varies considerably among financial institutions. At the end of 1994, for most European banks the ratio was between 0.6 (implying a negative franchise value) and 2. By the end of 2006, the ratio had increased to between 1.3 and 3.2. However, at the end of 2007, the ratio had decreased again, by 25% on average.[1] Although some of the changes in market value may be attributed to changes in the fair value of equity versus its book value, most variability in the market value of equity can be attributed to changes in the franchise value. For example, studies have shown[2] that the occurrence of large unexpected operational losses has an impact on the market value of financial institutions that is a multiple of the actual loss incurred. This multiplication effect can be attributed to the loss in confidence by investors in the management capabilities of the firm. As a result, investors expect more losses and lower cash flows in the future, causing the franchise value and the market value of equity to decrease by more than the actual loss incurred. We conclude that the franchise value can be material, that its value differs between institutions, and that its value can change significantly over time.

When the aim is to maximize the value for an institution's shareholders, then it is most consistent to define economic capital as an estimate of the potential decline in market value, which we will further elaborate on in Section 3.6.2. Hence, economic capital then also should include the potential decline in franchise value. However, to estimate the franchise value of the firm directly is difficult due to its long-term forward-looking nature and the uncertainty associated with human behavior over time that can have a significant influence on the franchise value. To attribute the franchise value to different business lines is not straightforward either. Therefore, in practice, many firms disregard the franchise value when managing their capital and performance. Managers should be aware of the consequences of such a choice, because in principle the franchise value should be included if the firm's objective is to maximize shareholder value. We will return to this issue in Sections 3.6.2, 5.2.7, and 5.2.8.

3.3   Which Risks to Include in Economic Capital

In this section we provide an overview of the main risk types for a financial institution. We distinguish three categories of risks: position risks, inherent risks, and model risks. We discuss each of these categories in turn. Subsequently, we consider the question, which of these risks can cause changes in the value of the institution's capital, and therefore should be included in the calculation of economic capital?

The estimation of economic capital for individual risk types will be covered in Chapter 4.

3.3.1   Position Risks

With position risks, we refer to the risks that a financial institution deliberately takes, and for which the exposure (position), in principle, could be reduced to zero. We include the following risk types under position risks.

Credit Risk

Credit risk is the potential loss of value on claims due to the reduced likelihood that the counterparty will fulfill its obligations or because the value of collateral securing the obligation decreases. The classic form of credit risk arises from lending money to counterparties (e.g., to private individuals, corporate clients, other financial institutions, government entities) who may not be able to pay interest on the loan or repay the principal as scheduled. Credit risk also arises when entering into derivatives transactions with counterparties who may not be able to honor their obligations, or when investing in securities whose value depends on the creditworthiness of one or more underlying entities (e.g., corporate and sovereign bonds, collateralized loan, or debt obligations (CLO/CDO)).

Market Risk

Market risk is the potential loss of value in assets and liabilities due to changes in market variables (e.g., interest and exchange rates, equity and commodity prices). This covers assets and liabilities in trading books, but also could include the market risk of assets and liabilities classified as available for sale, or even hold-to-maturity assets and liabilities. Banks often limit the scope of market risk to the assets and liabilities in their trading books, which is in line with the definition of market risk in the regulatory solvency regime for banks.

We will limit market risk to trading assets and liabilites in this book, and include the market risk for other assets and liabilities in asset-liability management risk. We note that the market risk for trading positions also includes market liquidity risk, that is, the risk that a firm cannot easily offset or eliminate a position without significantly affecting the market price because of inadequate market depth or market disruption.[3]

Asset-Liability Management (ALM) Risk

ALM risk is the potential loss in value of an institution's net asset value (the value of its assets minus the value of its liabilities) as a result of changes in market risk variables. For banks, this covers the interest-rate mismatch position between banking book assets and liabilities on the balance sheet, as well as the currency risk of any open currency position between assets and liabilities. For insurance companies and pension funds, ALM risk includes the risk that returns on the invested insurance premiums or pension contributions are less than expected and potentially insufficient to pay the expected insurance and pension liabilities.

A specific form of currency risk that is part of ALM risk is *foreign exchange translation risk*. This risk arises from an investment in a subsidiary that has revenues and costs primarily in a foreign currency. When reflecting earnings and capital of such a subsidiary in the financial accounts of the parent, changes in the exchange rate between the reporting currency of the parent and the foreign currency in which the subsidiary operates will change the subsidiary's contribution to earnings and capital.

Funding Liquidity Risk

Funding liquidity risk is the risk that an institution will not be able to meet expected and unexpected current and future cash flow and collateral needs.[3] For banks, it relates to the possibility that insufficient funds are available to repay maturing liabilities, including on-demand deposits that are withdrawn by their owners, or to provide funding under committed credit lines that are not yet fully drawn. This risk can lead to a default of the institution even if the value of its assets is still well above the value of its liabilities. Hedge funds and asset managers are also susceptible to funding liquidity risk, since clients may want to withdraw their money invested more quickly than assets can be liquidated. Insurance companies and pension funds are less susceptible to funding liquidity risk, because they are less likely to face an unexpected large increase in funding requirements.

The relevance of funding liquidity risk has been illustrated on several occasions during the sub-prime crisis. For example, the UK mortgage lender Northern Rock succumbed as a result of funding liquidity problems after a classic bank run, in which customers lined up outside bank branches to withdraw their deposits from the bank all at the same time. This event caused an overwhelming demand for cash that was well above the ability of the bank to raise. As another example, structured investment vehicles (SIVs) that some banks had established also experienced severe funding liquidity problems when they were no longer able to obtain funding in the commercial paper market. They were forced to revert to bank credit lines for their funding.

We include funding liquidity risk as position risk, because it can (largely) be avoided by matching the maturity of the assets with the maturity of the liabilities, by avoiding liabilities with undetermined maturities, and by restricting the amount of contingent credit lines under which the beneficiary can draw money at inconvenient times. However, given the fundamental role of banks to transform short-term deposits into long-term loans, they are almost inherently vulnerable to funding liquidity risk.

Pension Liability Risk

This is the risk of loss in case the institution has to make higher payments than expected to the pension fund of its employees. In many countries, there is a strong financial relationship between a firm and its pension fund, despite the fact that the latter will be a separate legal entity. For defined benefit pension plans (i.e., with pension benefits that are independent of the investment result), the investment risk is born by the pension fund. In these cases, a firm not only pays pension premiums to the pension fund for its employees to cover future pension benefits, but may also be liable to pay additional amounts in case a shortfall arises in the pension fund. This risk of having to cover a future shortfall in the pension fund is what we include as pension liability risk. We note that this risk is not present for defined contribution pension plans where the investment risk is borne fully by the pension beneficiary, and the only obligation of the employer is payment of the defined contribution.

Fixed Asset Risk

This is the risk that the value of the fixed assets owned by the institution (e.g., buildings, office equipment) will decrease below its expected value at the time horizon. Many institutions own fixed assets, but it is possible to avoid this risk by way of lease or rental of these assets. For that reason, we classify it as position risk. The risk associated with long-term lease and rental costs is captured under business risk.

Insurance Risk

This is the risk that insurance claims are higher than expected. These claims can relate to different forms of insurance, such as property, casualty, life, and catastrophe insurance. Measurement approaches can differ significantly between these different types of insurance, given the different statistical nature of the occurrence, timing, and size of the claims. We will elaborate on these differences in Chapter 4.

3.3.2 Inherent Risks

Next to position risks, financial institutions are exposed to risks that are inherent to being in business. Although some of these inherent risks may be reduced through mitigating actions and insurance policies, it is not possible to completely eliminate them for reasons that we discussed in Section 1.3.1. We list the main inherent risks.

Operational Risk

Following the definition in the Basel II Accord, operational risk is the risk of loss resulting from inadequate or failed internal processes, people, and systems or from external events. It includes legal risk such as the risk of losing the license to operate, or the risk of loss from legal fines or settlements. Although most firms strive to optimize their operational processes and thereby minimize operational losses, it will never be possible to fully eliminate these risks. As such, operational risk is an inherent risk of being in business.

Business Risk

Business risk is the risk of lower earnings than expected. This may be due to lower than expected revenues, higher than expected operating costs, or both. For example, competitive pressures, changes in the economic environment, or an overly optimistic assessment of the market potential for a specific product or service may cause actual revenues to fall short of expected revenues. Business risk is typically high for industries with volatile market prices and high fixed costs such as steel manufacturers. Business risk for financial institutions may be smaller than for steel manufacturers, but the risk is not negligible as seen in the sharp decline of revenues in many financial markets during the sub-prime crisis. Business risk is inherent in the chosen set of activities and the cost structure of the firm. As such, it is inherent to the strategy and business model chosen by the firm.

Strategic risk sometimes[4] is distinguished as a separate risk type, capturing the risk of losses on new activities such as specific large investments or acquisitions. We include this as part of business risk, however, and assume that the chosen set of activities includes any large investments or acquisitions that a firm plans to make.

Reputation Risk

Reputation risk is the risk of loss due to a negative external perception of the firm. A firm's sustainable relationships with clients, suppliers, and employees are built on trust, which is rooted in a positive perception of the firm. A dent in the reputation, therefore, can jeopardize a firm's continuity. Reputation loss can be the result of an action by the institution, changing attitudes in society, or a specific loss or event that relates to some other risk type.

An example of reputation loss is Bankers Trust. In 1994, Bankers Trust was sued by four clients for misleading information about the value and risk of certain derivatives. Eventually, the suits were settled, leading to a loss that could be classified as an operational loss. However, the incidents did lasting damage to Bankers Trust's reputation as an expert in derivatives trading and risk management. This reputation was important to clients who relied on the information provided by banks when entering into these relatively complex transactions. Although the precise impact of reputation loss is difficult to determine, it is likely that this incident cost Bankers Trust significant business.

Modeling reputation risk is difficult because the reputation of a firm is difficult to observe, let alone quantify. Nevertheless, the consequence of a loss in reputation is usually a decline in revenues, and we therefore discuss its quantification as part of business risk in Section 4.6.

Tax Risk

According to Benjamin Franklin, "In this world nothing can be said to be certain, except death and taxes."[5] Although paying taxes is thus an inherent part of life, the precise amount of taxes is uncertain. Tax risk is the risk of loss due to an unexpected change in the value of tax assets or liabilities. Tax costs can be higher than expected due to changes in tax laws, interpretation differences between the firm and the tax authorities, and compliance errors. Compliance errors related to taxes could also be included under operational risk.

3.3.3   Model Risk

Model risk is the risk that a model does not reflect the real world correctly in aspects that are essential to its purpose, as a result of which the outcomes from the model may deviate from reality. Model risk is inherent to the use of models as all models are abstractions from reality. Good models capture the essential features of the real world and help us to understand empirical relationships. Flawed models ignore essential features of reality, leading potentially to wrong model outcomes and subsequently to incorrect conclusions and decisions. Model risk arises because a model may be incomplete or incorrectly specified, uses wrong parameters values, or has a faulty implementation.

In the specific context of calculating economic capital, for which we have to estimate changes in the fair value of assets and liabilities, model risk arises from the fact that for many assets and liabilities the market values cannot be observed directly. For that reason, models are used to estimate fair values. These valuation models aim to capture the important factors and their interrelationships that influence the value of the assets or liabilities for which no market values can be observed. Market prices of similar assets or liabilities typically are used to estimate the parameters in the model. As a model is an approximation of reality, it may result in wrong estimates of market values, as well as wrong estimates of changes in value. Hence, economic capital may be under- or overestimated.

Since economic capital is concerned with the downside risk at a specific confidence interval, the possibility that economic capital is underestimated will increase with the level of model risk. Consequently, taking model risk into account will lead to a higher estimate for economic capital, where the extent of the increase depends on the degree of the model risk involved. In addition to the model risk arising from the valuation models used to calculate fair values, economic capital methodologies are also subject to model risk with respect to the way in which they include (or do not include) the factors that drive potential losses. For example, model risk arises from choices made regarding the probability distributions for the possible variation in default rates, changes in market variables, or the frequency of insurance claims, during the economic capital time horizon.

Model risk by itself is not a direct source of losses, which is the reason why we do not classify it as a position or inherent risk. Models can be an indirect source of losses, for example, in case a flawed model outcome results in wrong decisions being made. The consequence of the wrong decision typically will manifest itself as a credit, market, operational, insurance, or other type of loss.

In Chapter 4, we will discuss in greater depth the sources of model risk and the most important assumptions for each risk type that may lead to model risk. In the same chapter, we will also explore how model risk can be factored into the measurement of economic capital.

3.3.4 Choice of Risk Types

It follows from the definition of economic capital that all risks should be included as part of economic capital that can cause an unexpected loss and, consequently, a decrease of the firm's capital. This applies to most of the risk types described in the previous section, but is not as clear for reputation risk and liquidity risk. As mentioned in the previous section, we will discuss the contribution of reputation risk to unexpected losses as part of business risk in Chapter 4. In the remainder of this section, we will discuss to what extent liquidity risk should be included in economic capital. In the Basel II Accord, liquidity risk is mentioned as one of the risks that banks should consider when evaluating the adequacy of their capital. This raises the question whether capital can act as protection against liquidity risk.

We encountered market liquidity risk and funding liquidity risk in the overview of risk types in Section 3.3.1. Market liquidity risk in the context of trading portfolios is a source of price risk, and thus should be included in economic capital for market risk. Market liquidity risk is also present in relation to the funding of an institution, being the risk of higher than expected funding costs. Higher funding costs may arise from market disruptions that result in the unavailability of certain sources of funding. As a consequence, institutions may have to rely on a smaller set of more expensive funding sources. Higher funding costs may also result from a decline in the creditworthiness of the institution itself, driving up the cost of its funding in general. The risk of higher than expected funding costs should be included in economic capital. This risk can be modeled on a stand-alone basis, incorporated under ALM risk, or included as part of business risk. We will discuss it as part of ALM risk in Chapter 4.

Following the Joint Forum, we defined funding liquidity risk in Section 3.3.1 as the risk that an institution will not be able to meet both expected and unexpected current and future cash flow and collateral needs. The risk is often firm-specific since it relates to the risk that investors do not trust the repayment capability of the specific institution and, as a result, do not want to provide it any funding. With the interconnectedness of financial markets, this means that in such an event most funding markets are closed to the institution. Offering a higher price is no remedy anymore because beyond a certain threshold the higher price signals to the market that the institution is in a precarious situation, which only aggravates the problem. In these situations an institution may default on its obligations but still be technically solvent. It is this situation that the UK FSA seems to have had in mind when defining liquidity risk as "the risk that a firm, although balance-sheet solvent, cannot maintain or generate sufficient cash resources to meet its payment obligations in full as they fall due or can only do so at materially disadvantageous terms."[6]

It is important to understand the potential causes of firm-specific funding liquidity risk. The UK FSA mentions asymmetric information between institutions and investors as a potential cause, leading to investor uncertainty about an institution's net worth and creditworthiness. In this case, the typical solution is additional disclosure to remove the uncertainty about the institution's true net worth. However, this will take time and, therefore, the institution needs a sufficiently large liquidity reserve to survive this period. Liquidity reserves buy the institution time to improve its disclosure.

Nevertheless, there were several instances during the sub-prime crisis in which institutions suffered from funding liquidity stress where it is questionable whether additional disclosure would have solved the problem. In Section 2.2.1, we discussed the example of Bear Stearns. In this case, even statements from their regulators could not convince the markets that they were solvent. Consequently, when they ran out of liquidity reserves they had no option other than to be acquired by the larger and more solvent institution, JP Morgan Chase. Several other US banks that faced funding liquidity stress, like Wachovia and Washington Mutual, also found they had no other option than to be acquired by other, more solvent, institutions. In addition, the insurer AIG had to be rescued by the US Federal Reserve because of funding liquidity problems. In Europe and Asia, a significant number of banks received large capital injections from their governments to restore the confidence of investors and avoid funding liquidity stress. All this suggests that in many instances of funding liquidity stress there is a related problem with capital adequacy. The solution is then not further disclosure, but additional capital. In these circumstances the purpose of the liquidity reserves is to buy time to attract additional capital.

Is the fact that insufficient capital is often at the root of funding liquidity stress a reason to include funding liquidity risk in economic capital? Our answer is negative. First of all, as we have defined and described funding liquidity risk, it is not a *cause* for decreasing asset values or increased liabilities, and thus a decrease in capital, but a potential *consequence* of decreasing asset values. Second, if investors are concerned that capital is insufficient, then this implies that available capital would be lower than economic capital. This seems to be in conflict with the fact that some of the institutions that faced funding liquidity stress during the sub-prime crisis reported available capital well above their economic capital. The reason may have been that the economic capital numbers were not comprehensive (i.e., failed to take into account all risk types fully or adequately). Furthermore, the fair value of the assets, as estimated by investors, may have been much lower than the book value on which the amount of available capital was based. As a result, the reported economic capital may have been underestimated and the reported available capital overestimated. We therefore maintain that economic capital, provided it is measured comprehensively, is still the capital level that is needed to prevent funding liquidity risk to materialize. Additional capital will not reduce this funding liquidity risk in a material way. This conclusion is in conformity with the words of Nout Wellink, chairman of the Basel Committee, when he stated that "Liquidity risk cannot be mitigated with capital" and that "A strong capital buffer enhances a bank's creditworthiness and, from the market's perspective, reduces its counterparty risk. This helps to ensure continued access to funding."[7]

We conclude that market liquidity risk in the form of price risk of trading assets and liabilities, or in the form of higher funding costs than expected, should be included in economic capital. Funding liquidity risk does not correspond to a potential increase in funding costs, but to the unavailability of funding. We have argued that it should not be included in economic capital because it does not represent a cause for a decline in capital, but rather can be a consequence of such a decline.

3.4 Time Horizon and Expected Profits

In this section, we discuss the choice of time horizon for economic capital calculations. Related to this, we consider how to best account for the profit that an institution expects to generate during the time horizon, since expected profit forms the first buffer to absorb any unexpected costs or losses before capital will be affected.

3.4.1 Time Horizon

A possible choice for the calculation of economic capital is a liability run-off approach. In this approach, economic capital represents the amount by which the current value of all assets must exceed the current value of all liabilities, so that the cash flows from the assets are sufficient to fulfill all promised payments on the current liabilities plus associated expenses, at the chosen confidence level. As the maturities of an institution's liabilities vary, there is no clearly defined time horizon. It is also a static approach, as it ignores any changes in the composition of the assets and liabilities over time. A run-off approach to the calculation of economic capital is used regularly in the life-insurance industry, although a study of the Society of Actuaries[8] concludes that life-insurance companies increasingly use a fixed (one-year) horizon for economic capital calculations.

When choosing a fixed time horizon, the most natural choice from a capital adequacy perspective is to use the time period during which it will not be possible to substantially reduce risks or to attract additional capital if necessary. This does not suggest a concrete time period, however. Some exposures may be fairly easy to sell or to hedge to reduce risk, such as market risk for foreign currency trades. Other exposures, like business risk, may be difficult or impossible to reduce or hedge, and reducing risk may take a significant amount of time. For that reason, the choice of time horizon will necessarily be an average of the estimated time that is needed to reduce risk for different risk exposures. Moreover, the time needed in a situation of distress may be longer than in normal market circumstances, because market liquidity typically decreases in times of distress. This also applies to equity markets, which are the source of additional capital when needed. For example, in the beginning of the subprime crisis a number of institutions attracted new capital from investors, notably a number of sovereign wealth funds, in a matter of weeks. However, later during the crisis it became much more difficult to attract new capital, and it was sometimes only possible in the form of a capital injection by the government. It often came at the cost of significant dilution for existing shareholders. In conclusion, the time horizon from a capital adequacy perspective will be a compromise between different types of risk exposures, as well as assumptions about the liquidity of debt and equity markets.

For performance measurement, the natural time horizon coincides with the performance cycles that firms employ. These performance cycles normally include performance targets for a one-year period because this aligns with the financial reporting period, but many firms also set multiyear performance targets.

In practice, most institutions use a one-year time horizon for economic capital estimation. In the IFRI/CRO Forum survey on Economic Capital practices from 2007,[9] more than 75% of participants used a one-year time horizon. This seems a reasonable time horizon given the preceding discussion on what a natural time horizon would be for capital adequacy and performance measurement. This choice poses some challenges to measure economic capital for risk types with a natural horizon shorter or longer than one year. We will return to this in Chapter 4 when we discuss the assumptions regarding the dynamics of risk over time for each of the risk types.

3.4.2 Treatment of Expected Profits

An important choice is how to deal with the profit that an institution expects to generate during the period over which economic capital is estimated. Once expected profits are realized, they will increase the amount of capital that the institution has. Any shortfall of revenues below expectations, or unexpectedly high costs, will first lead to a decrease in profit before it leads to a decrease in the amount of capital below the initial amount. The higher the profit a firm expects to generate, the less likely it is that a shortfall of revenues or unexpectedly high costs will reduce the amount of capital below the level available at the initial date. This thus lowers the amount of capital that a firm has to hold initially. Hence, we expect economic capital to decrease when the level of expected profit increases if we use economic capital for capital adequacy assessment.

We have a different situation when we consider the use of economic capital in the context of optimizing the risk-adjusted profitability. The reason is that the market value of equity, on which the institution aims to provide an acceptable return, is based among others on the expected profit. In fact, the market value of equity will reflect the profit expectations over all future years. When economic capital is an estimate of the potential decline in market value of equity, it should measure the potential decline of those future expected profits. In other words, economic capital will constitute the potential decline of the net present value of future expected profits from the currently expected level, where the potential decline is measured over the chosen time horizon for economic capital. Consequently, economic capital should comprise the potential shortfall of earnings during the chosen time horizon in comparison to the expected earnings, plus the potential shortfall of profits from expectations beyond the horizon date. This is illustrated in Graph 3.1, which relates economic capital to expected profit and the time horizon.

On the initial date, the firm has a certain value as presented on the left side of the graph. Over time, this initial value is expected to grow by the expected profit until it reaches the expected value at the horizon date. The slightly upward-sloping line represents this expected growth over time. However, the firm value at the horizon date is uncertain and can be characterized by a distribution of values at the time horizon, represented by the curved line. This curve is similar to the one in Graph 1.1 in Chapter 1, where we discussed the concept

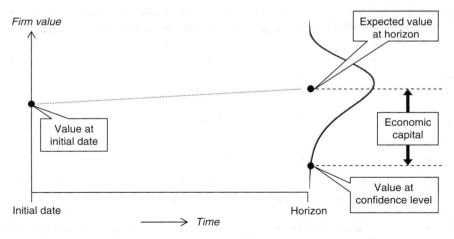

Graph 3.1 Definition of economic capital. The horizontal axis represents the time, the vertical axis, the value of the firm (being the market value of equity). The curved line at the horizon date represents the probability density function of the firm value at the horizon date.

of economic capital in relation to expected loss and unexpected losses. The point corresponding to the expected value at the horizon represents the average value of all points on the distribution. Economic capital is the difference between the expected value at the horizon and the value at the chosen confidence level. We note that there is no natural definition of expected loss when we consider a value distribution at the horizon, as we also discussed in Section 1.2. In this representation expected losses are already incorporated in the value at the initial date.

From this representation of economic capital, we can see what the impact of a higher expected profit is on economic capital. A higher expected profit leads to a higher expected value at the horizon date. However, the firm value at the chosen confidence interval also is likely to increase because the entire value distribution at the horizon date shifts upward. Consequently, economic capital may not change much in comparison to the increase in expected profit.

Higher expected earnings will, of course, increase RAROC because the numerator (the expected return) increases whereas the denominator (economic capital) remains approximately unchanged. In the context of calculating RAROC, it would also be illogical if an increase in expected earnings would both increase the numerator (the expected return) and decrease the denominator (economic capital), since it would give a double benefit to an increase in expected return (or a double penalty in case of a decrease in expected earnings). We note the similarity with the Sharpe ratio that is commonly used as risk-adjusted return measure for equity investments (see Section 2.3.1). This ratio is calculated as expected excess return divided by the standard deviation of returns. An increase in the expected excess return increases the numerator but does not change the standard deviation in the denominator.

This discussion suggests that the treatment of expected profits in the calculation of economic capital should depend on whether it is used for capital adequacy assessment purposes or for performance measurement purposes. For capital adequacy assessment we expect an increase in expected profits to lead to a decrease in economic capital, as the latter is an estimate of the potential decline in actual capital. For performance measurement, however, we have concluded that higher expected profits (*ceteris paribus*) should not change the amount of economic capital in a significant way. The divergent treatment of expected profits will lead potentially to two different economic capital quantities.

To avoid this, we can add expected profits to available capital rather than deduct it from economic capital when it is used in the context of capital adequacy assessment. This is also intuitive as profits will accrue to available capital and, thus, can be viewed as a source of available capital. Economic capital will then represent a potential downward deviation of the firm's value from the expected firm value at the horizon date. In this way, we can use the same definition of economic capital for performance measurement and capital adequacy purposes.

When adding the expected profits, or more precisely the expected change in the firm's value, to available capital for a capital adequacy assessment, there are a few practical issues to consider. First, we should decide what to do with planned or expected dividend payments, or planned share buybacks. To the extent that these are fixed and not affected by realized profits (e.g., if they have been announced, but not paid yet), they should be subtracted from the expected profit before it is added to available capital. Second, profits will only accrue to available capital over time, whereas unexpected losses may happen immediately. To be prudent, we can decide to include only a fraction of the total expected profit as part of available capital. Third, if unexpected losses are larger than pre-tax expected profits, then no taxes will be payable. Therefore, expected profits can be added on a pre-tax basis to available capital for the assessment of capital adequacy.

3.5 Confidence Level and Cyclicality

Economic capital measures the potential decline in capital at a certain confidence level. In this section, we will discuss how this confidence level can be determined. The discussion will address the relationship of the confidence level with the risk appetite of the firm and, in particular, the target credit rating of the firm. Thereafter, we will discuss how economic capital may fluctuate during an economic cycle, which is related to the question whether the outcomes of the underlying risk models and the target rating represent point-in-time or through-the-cycle values. We will argue that the choice of the confidence level should take into account whether the underlying risk models yield point-in-time or through-the-cycle outcomes.

3.5.1 Choosing the Confidence Level

The confidence level is derived from the generally very low probability that an institution is willing to accept that its available capital will decrease more than the estimated amount of economic capital. Specifically, it is the probability that the institution will remain solvent, that is, the value of capital remains positive. Although an institution will want to avoid insolvency, it can never reduce the probability of insolvency to zero. The more aggressive the risk profile of the institution, the higher the probability of insolvency for a given amount of capital. The choice of the confidence level thus relates directly to the institution's risk appetite. Different stakeholders may have different perspectives as to what is acceptable to them. For example, depositors and supervisors may have a relatively low risk appetite, whereas shareholders may have a higher risk appetite as higher risks may increase their expected returns. Management will have to find the right balance for the institution on behalf of these different stakeholders.

As we discussed in Chapter 2, many stakeholders have an interest in the continuity of the institution. However, these interests are seldom explicitly expressed in an acceptable probability that these stakeholders would suffer a loss. The exception to this rule is the debt holder, because he or she has based the investment decision, at least partly, on the credit rating of the institution and the debt issue. Many institutions, therefore, have specified a target rating of their debt as part of their risk appetite.

Once the institution has specified a target credit rating for its debt, we need to relate this to a confidence level. This often is done by considering the historic default frequencies of issuers and issues per rating category, as published by the rating agencies. The underlying assumption is that default, as defined by the rating agencies, is equivalent to insolvency. This may not always be the case since solvent institutions may default, as we observed when we discussed funding liquidity risk, and insolvent institutions may avoid default because they are supported by their governments. Sidestepping the potential difference between default and insolvency, the confidence level for the calculation of economic capital then equals one minus the probability of default associated with the target credit rating. For example, if the firm's target debt rating is single A and the chosen time horizon is one year then we can consider the one-year default frequency of debt issues with a single A rating. Looking at the historic default frequencies as published by Standard & Poor's, we observe that the historic default frequency for single A rated issuers is 0.06% (see Table 3.1). The associated confidence level is thus 99.94%.

Table 3.1 shows that there are sometimes significant differences between the published default frequencies of different rating agencies. For example, the observed default frequency for single-A rated debt is three times as high with Standard & Poor's (0.06%) than with Moody's (0.02%). This is caused by differences in the time period considered, differences in the universe of rated issuers, and differences in rating methodologies. Furthermore, the very low default rates associated with (high) investment grade ratings are the result of many years with no defaults and a few years with one or more defaults. This is illustrated in Graph 3.2 for the realized one-year default rate of firms with a Moody's single A rating. The average one-year default probability equals 0.02%, but only in a few years have actual defaults been observed. An extra

Table 3.1 Historic average one-year corporate default frequencies of Standard & Poor's and Moody's by investment-grade credit ratings (*Sources*: Standard & Poor's, *2007 Annual Global Corporate Default Study and Rating Transitions*; Moody's, *Corporate Default and Recovery Rates, 1920–2007*)

Standard & Poor's 1981–2007	AAA	AA	A	BBB
Average one-year default rate (%)	0.00	0.01	0.06	0.23
Moody's 1970–2007	Aaa	Aa	A	Baa
Average one-year default rate (%)	0.00	0.01	0.02	0.17

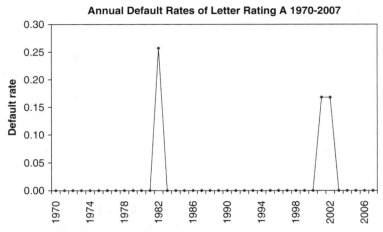

Source: Moody's, Corporate Default and Recovery Rates, February 2008

Graph 3.2 Observed annual default frequencies between 1970 and 2007 for Moody's corporate credit rating category A.

year of observations may have a noticeable impact on the average default frequency if in this extra year a few additional defaults have taken place. Cantor, Hamilton, and Tennant[10] also observe the relatively high uncertainty of one-year default rates for high-investment-grade ratings by considering the ratio of the mean default rate to its standard deviation. The uncertainty is much lower for speculative-grade ratings.

One way to decrease the uncertainty about the confidence level is to increase the number of default observations, for example, by considering the default information over a longer time horizon than one year. In their study, Cantor, Hamilton, and Tennant indeed observe that the uncertainty of multiyear default rates for high-investment-grade ratings is much lower than for the

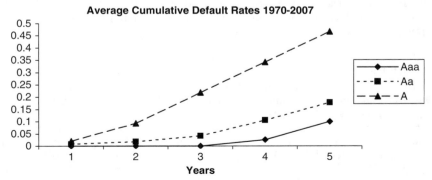

Source: Moody's, Corporate Default and Recovery Rates, February 2008

Graph 3.3 Average cumulative corporate default rates for Moody's investment-grade credit ratings categories Aaa, Aa, and A.

one-year default rate. In Graph 3.3, we depict the cumulative default rates up to five years and notice that they increase exponentially over time for investment-grade ratings. Taking this pattern into account, we can derive an implied one-year default rate from the respective cumulative default rates.

We conclude that if an institution wants to derive the confidence level from the published default frequencies by one of the rating agencies, then different choices and assumptions may lead to different confidence levels. In practice, confidence levels tend to lie between 99.95% and 99.98% for target ratings of A and AA of Standard & Poor's (A and Aa for Moody's). Thus, two institutions that apply the same target rating may use different confidence levels for the calculation of economic capital. These differences in confidence level have to be taken into account when comparing economic capital numbers across multiple institutions.

3.5.2 Cyclicality of Economic Capital

The credit ratings that rating agencies assign to debt issues and issuers are intended to reflect the fundamental credit quality, and therefore are not expected to change through an economic cycle as long as the underlying fundamentals of the issue or issuer remain unchanged. According to Standard & Poor's:[11]

> Standard & Poor's credit ratings are meant to be forward-looking, and their time horizon extends as far as is analytically foreseeable. Accordingly, the anticipated ups and downs of business cycles—whether industry-specific or related to the general economy—should be factored into the credit rating all along. Ratings should never be a mere snapshot of the present situation. Accordingly, ratings are held constant throughout the cycle, or, alternatively, the rating does vary—but within a relatively narrow band. [...] The ideal is to rate "through-the-cycle."

The consequence of this through-the-cycle rating philosophy is that observed default rates for a given credit rating are expected to vary over time, because a firm is more likely to default in bad than in good economic times. We expect a cyclical pattern in realized default rates for a given credit rating over time, corresponding to the cycles in the general economic situation. This cyclicality is indeed visible in the historic default rates for sub-investment-grade credit ratings of the rating agencies, as illustrated in Graph 3.4. For investment-grade ratings, this cyclicality is less conspicuous because of the very few defaults that occur in these rating categories and the consequently larger impact of firm-specific causes on realized default rates.

If we base the confidence level that is used in the calculation of economic capital on the *average* realized one-year default rate for the desired credit rating, then the calculated economic capital will be an estimate of the *average* potential decline in capital throughout an economic cycle in that respect. In other words, we calculate through-the-cycle economic capital.

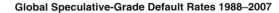

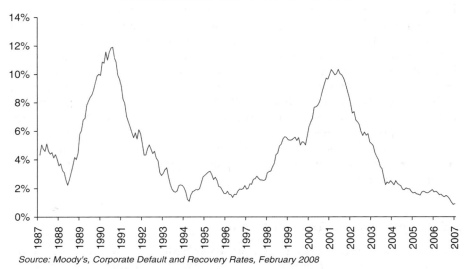

Source: Moody's, Corporate Default and Recovery Rates, February 2008

Graph 3.4   Cyclicality in realized default rates between 1988 and 2007 for sub-investment-grade credit ratings assigned by Moody's.

Alternatively, we can base the confidence level on an estimate of the *actual* probability of default for the target credit rating in the coming year. This probability will be higher than average in bad economic times and lower in good economic times. If we opt for this alternative, we calculate a so-called point-in-time estimate of economic capital, reflecting the minimum required amount of capital that is consistent with the expected one-year default rate of the firm's debt at the present point in time. Everything else being equal, such a point-in-time estimate of economic capital decreases in bad economic times (because the default probability will increase and hence the confidence level will decrease) and increases in good economic times (because the default probability will decrease and the associated confidence level will increase).

However, everything else does not remain equal throughout an economic cycle. For example, when economic conditions deteriorate, the actual probability of default of an institution's counterparties will increase. This will increase the economic capital estimate for credit risk when it is estimated on a point-in-time basis. Furthermore, the volatility of market variables may increase in a worsening economic environment, leading to an increase in market risk economic capital. Such changes will offset, in whole or in part, the decrease in economic capital that would be the result of a lower point-in-time confidence level in a deteriorating economic situation.

With a through-the-cycle economic capital calculation, the risk parameters of the model and the confidence level will remain relatively constant throughout the cycle. As a result, the estimated economic capital will remain relatively constant as well. With a point-in-time economic capital calculation, the risk parameters of the model will vary with the cycle. To be consistent, the confidence level should also vary with the cycle and this will compensate, to some extent, the pro-cyclical effects of the point-in-time model inputs.

In practice, it may be difficult to adjust the confidence level in both an accurate and timely manner in a point-in-time system since that requires insight into what phase the economy will be entering. For internationally diversified institutions, this is even more complicated, because the economic phase may differ per country or region. For pragmatic reasons, therefore, we may choose to keep the confidence level constant over time in a point-in-time economic capital calculation, but this is not entirely consistent with a capital objective that is expressed as a target through-the-cycle debt rating. The result is an economic capital estimate that behaves in a more pro-cyclical manner than it would be if the confidence level would be adjusted during the cycle.

Whether to choose a through-the-cycle or point-in-time calculation of economic capital may depend on the primary purpose of economic capital. If the aim is to perform an analysis of the long-run risk-adjusted profitability of different activities, then it would be appropriate to calculate a through-the-cycle economic capital. For capital adequacy purposes, a through-the-cycle economic capital generally is considered desirable, as it avoids the pro-cyclicality of capital requirements. Such pro-cyclicality creates uncertainty as to how much economic capital will increase during a downturn of a cycle and, thus, how much available capital is needed in those circumstances. The consequence of choosing for a through-the-cycle economic capital, however, is that it will not act as a warning signal of deteriorating economic circumstances because it will remain relatively insensitive to changes in the economic cycle. If managers and supervisors want economic capital to signal a deterioration of an institution's risk profile early, then a point-in-time economic capital is better suited. This enables an institution to take measures to reduce exposures or increase available capital early, when it is easiest and least expensive to do so. A point-in-time calculation of economic capital may be preferred as well if economic capital is used to evaluate the pricing of products in existing market conditions.

The choice between through-the-cycle and point-in-time economic capital not only should be reflected in the choice of confidence level but also in the way economic capital is calculated for each individual risk type. For example, if our aim is to calculate a through-the-cycle economic capital, then we should also use through-the-cycle default probabilities in the credit risk economic capital calculation. We will return to this requirement for consistency when discussing the methodologies to calculate economic capital for each of the individual risk types in Chapter 4.

In the context of the Basel II Accord, there has been much discussion on the potential for, and undesirability of, cyclicality in regulatory capital requirements. This discussion concentrates on the through-the-cycle or point-in-time nature of the credit rating models that are input to the credit risk regulatory capital calculations and not on the confidence level, which is fixed in the Basel II Accord. As emphasized earlier, we should not make a choice for one without considering the other, because there needs to be consistency between both. As we discussed, they have compensating effects.

3.6   Definition of Available Capital

In the previous sections, we have discussed the various elements in the definition of economic capital. Related to the definition of economic capital is the definition of available capital that is used to determine if the institution possesses sufficient capital. In this section, we will discuss how the definitions of economic capital and available capital are related to the purpose of economic capital: ensuring continuity and optimizing profitability. We will discuss if and how the definition for these purposes can be reconciled. Finally, we will discuss how to deal with hybrid capital in the definition of available capital.

3.6.1   Available Capital in Relation to Ensuring Continuity

In the context of ensuring the continuity of a financial institution, the objective is to avoid a situation of insolvency; that is, a situation in which the value of the assets is less than the value of the liabilities. As discussed in Chapter 2, this point of view relates most closely to the interest of debt holders and supervisors, and therefore is referred to as the debt holder view of capital.

The amount of loss-absorbing available capital from the point of view of a debt holder includes all equity and debt instruments that are junior to the debt holder's claim. Thus, the holder of subordinated debt will primarily be interested in the amount of equity capital that is available in the firm, as this is the capital buffer that protects him. A holder of senior debt will not only be interested in the amount of equity capital but also in the amount of subordinated debt, because both form a buffer against losses for the holders of senior debt. Supervisors of financial institutions have different stakeholders to protect and, for that reason, the relevant measure of capital differs between them as well. They even distinguish a number of different capital definitions to express different views on capital. For example, bank supervisors distinguish Tier 1, Tier 2, and Tier 3 capital, each including different types of equity and debt instruments.[12]

From a capital adequacy perspective, it is important to decide for which category of debt holders the amount of capital should be sufficient. Once this choice has been made, then the definition of economic capital should be aligned to that choice. The choice of confidence level, as discussed earlier, is closely related to the choice of which debt holders to protect and the target credit rating for that debt. Once it has been decided which category of debt holders should be protected, then available capital consists of all the equity plus debt instruments that are junior to the protected debt.

The value of available capital in a capital adequacy assessment normally is derived from an institution's financial accounts. As motivated in Section 3.1, however, it is desirable to value all assets and liabilities at fair value when estimating economic capital. The amount of available capital therefore has to be adjusted for any differences between book and fair value. Furthermore, the value of some assets such as deferred tax assets depends on the continuity of the institution and they should be consistently included in economic capital or deducted from available capital. Issues that require careful analysis to ensure economic capital and available capital are comparable quantities include the following:

- **Correction for fair value versus book value**
  If the valuation of assets or liabilities on the balance sheet does not concur with the valuation methods applied in the economic capital calculation, then we cannot just take the amount of capital that follows from the balance sheet as the available capital. For a numerical illustration, consider an institution that has a balance sheet consisting of assets of 100, liabilities of 90, and equity of 10. If we take equity capital as our choice of available capital, then the balance sheet information suggests available capital equals 10. In this example, suppose that the asset value on the balance sheet represents book value, and the fair value equals 102. If in our economic capital calculation we estimate that the value of the assets can decrease with 9 at the chosen confidence level and that liabilities are constant, then economic capital would be estimated as 9. However, this value of 9 should not be compared to available capital of 10; we should add the excess of market value to book value (2 in this example) to the amount of available capital that is determined from the accounting balance sheet. We should compare economic capital of 9 to available capital of 12 in this case.

- **Allowances**
  An issue related to the difference between fair and book values is that sometimes allowances are made for potential or expected declines in the value of specific assets. An example is an allowance for assets that are included at historic or amortized cost on the balance sheet but for which the market value is significantly below book value. This allowance is then part of the liabilities on the balance sheet, and offsets the book value of the assets on the asset side of the balance sheet. When economic capital includes the potential decline in the value of assets for which allowances have been made, then it should do so with respect to the book value minus the allowances made.

- **Franchise value, goodwill, and other intangible assets**
  The franchise value typically is not included on the balance sheet of the institution, but other intangible assets such as goodwill or trademarks may be included. For reasons of consistency, we have to ensure that either:
  - Economic capital includes the potential decline in value of these assets and consequently these assets are included in the definition of available capital.

- Economic capital does not include the potential decline in value of these assets and consequently these assets are excluded from available capital.

  The franchise value and many other intangible assets are likely to decrease in value significantly, if not completely, if the firm gets into distress. Consequently, the potential decline in value at the very high confidence levels used in most economic capital models is likely to be equal to the current value of these intangible assets. For the calculation of the capital surplus (i.e., the difference between available capital and economic capital), it may therefore be immaterial if the values of these assets are included in economic capital and available capital or not, as long as it is done consistently between economic and available capital.

- **Deferred tax assets**

  An asset that is likely to lose its value if the firm gets into distress is a deferred tax asset, since it can be effectuated only against future profits. In case of distress, these future profits are unlikely to materialize, and the claim loses its value. Like the intangible assets discussed earlier, the deferred tax claims should either be included in economic capital and available capital or be excluded from both.

- **Debt issued by the institution**

  The fair value of the debt of an institution may change as a result of changes in the creditworthiness of the institution. For example, if the creditworthiness of the institution decreases, then the risk premium that investors will demand increases and consequently the market value of the debt will decrease. If such fair value changes are included on the institution's balance sheet, then the available equity capital will change accordingly. An institution can take advantage of a decrease in the value of its own debt by buying the debt back in the market. However, in case the company defaults, then it will owe its creditors the amount legally due and not the lower market value. Consequently, any value gain by way of debt valued below par may be lost in case the institution defaults. To reflect this, available capital should be reduced by the amount by which the value of own debt on the balance sheet is lower than the par value. Potential increases in the value of own debt can then be ignored in economic capital. This is consistent with the Solvency II proposals, which prescribe that for regulatory capital calculations no adjustments shall be made to the valuation of liabilities that reflect changes in the own credit standing of the institution. Alternatively, economic capital can include the amount by which the value of own debt on the balance sheet is lower than the par value, and it can then be compared to the available capital on the balance sheet.

3.6.2 Available Capital in Relation to Optimizing Profitability

When optimizing profitability, the aim is to create value for the owners of a firm—the shareholders or the members of a cooperative. The capital relevant for the owners is the amount that they have invested in the firm, and it is on this amount that they hope to realize an attractive return. The value of their investment equals the market value of equity of the institution. The risk that they are exposed to is therefore that the market value of equity decreases in value. When used as risk measure in this context, economic capital should thus represent a potential decline in the market value of equity. This view on capital is referred to as the shareholder view on capital.

For economic capital to be an estimate of a potential decline in market value, it should reflect potential changes in the fair value of the assets and liabilities, as well as changes in the franchise value of the firm. Consequently, available capital is the value of common equity, calculated as the difference between all assets and liabilities valued at fair value, plus the franchise value.

Managers have found it difficult to manage and allocate their capital on the basis of the market value of equity, because this value changes on a daily basis. The market value of equity can be volatile and is susceptible to changing perceptions by investors. Also, in the short term, share price changes can overshoot, meaning that news can cause share prices to change more than the new information by itself warrants. As a result, the equity capital "available" to a firm can fluctuate significantly. This is not helpful when long-term investment decisions have to be made, since the firm has to decide whether it has sufficient capital available for the investment and whether the investment returns are higher than the costs of capital. In addition, institutions may prefer a measure of performance that does not depend on the franchise value of the institution because the franchise value is deemed to be outside the control of management in the short term.

On the other hand, ignoring the franchise value may lead to suboptimal decisions. The reason is that different business units contribute in different proportions to the franchise value. For example, the ratio of market-to-book value of equity is typically much higher for an asset management firm than for a corporate lending unit. This has been illustrated by Chris Matten, who compared the market-to-book ratios over the period 1992 to 1995 for various types of financial institutions.[13] The mean market-to-book ratio was 6.5 for asset managers (institutional), 2.6 for asset managers (private), and 1.3 for universal banks. More recently, at the end of 2007, the market-to-book ratios for most commercial banks were between 0.8 and 2.5,[1] and the same ratio for most asset managers at the time was approximately 3.0.[14] For the few private banks with publicly quoted shares, the market-to-book value was also around 3.0 at the end of 2007.[15] Therefore, if an asset management firm and a corporate lending unit are both part of one institution, then they will contribute in different proportions to a potential decline in the franchise value of the institution. Consequently, the amount of economic capital attributed to the asset management unit may be too low when compared to the economic capital attributed to the corporate lending unit if the franchise value is not reflected in economic capital. This is relevant when we discuss the use of economic capital for performance management and the determination of a hurdle rate of return in Chapter 5.

3.6.3   Aligning the Definition of Available Capital

From the discussion in the previous sections we conclude that the definition of available capital and economic capital differs depending upon whether we take a debt holder's view or a shareholder's view. Nevertheless, it is very inconvenient and confusing for users if two concepts of economic capital are calculated and used next to each other. The question is whether it is possible to align these two views.

To some extent, such an alignment is possible. As a first step, where the shareholder's view focuses on the market value of common equity, the debt holder's view could focus on protecting the debt holders that are just senior to (common) equity. In this way, the available capital for both approaches is equal to the common equity.

As a next step in the alignment, we have to decide whether to include the franchise value of the firm or not. When we express profitability as a return on economic capital with the aim to maximize shareholder value, the franchise value should be included in economic capital. When this definition of economic capital is also used to assess capital adequacy, we must also include the franchise value in available capital. Including the franchise value in economic and available capital requires that we are able to measure the franchise value directly. However, the measurement of the franchise value is difficult and uncertain. Furthermore, the amount of the franchise value may be volatile, which makes it more difficult to use for daily management decisions.

Alternatively, we can omit the franchise value from the economic and available capital calculations. For capital adequacy purposes, we can justify this choice if we are willing to assume that the franchise value will be zero in a distress situation. However, for performance management, we are then creating a potential bias that we need to take into account when assessing the performance of business lines and managers, and when making investment decisions. We touched upon this in the previous section, and we will discuss the practical implications further in Section 5.2.7.

3.6.4   Treatment of Hybrid Capital Instruments

An issue related to the definition of equity capital is the treatment of hybrid capital instruments that have gained popularity in recent years. These hybrid forms of capital have both debt-like and equity-like features. A debt-like feature is that they usually have a fixed or floating coupon. Equity-like features include provisions that an investor may be required to defer or forgo coupon payments in difficult times, lack of a fixed maturity date at which the claim must be repaid, and potential conversion rights to common equity. If the hybrid capital has a fixed or floating coupon, a firm will not include hybrid capital in available capital when it aims to maximize risk-adjusted profitability for its providers of equity capital. However, the equity-like features do achieve the goal that the money obtained through the issuance of these instruments provides protection against unexpected losses in the normal course of business. For regulatory capital purposes, banks are allowed to include hybrid capital instruments as part of the calculation of Tier 1 capital, although only up to a maximum percentage of total Tier 1 capital.

To set the confidence level, we should decide whether we include hybrid capital instruments in the definition of available capital. Because the choice of confidence level is driven mostly by debt categories that are senior to hybrid capital, many banks in practice do include hybrid capital in the definition of available capital. The fact that the Tier 1 capital of banks, which is an important regulatory capital measure, includes various types of hybrid debt is another reason for institutions to include it in their available capital. As long as the amount of hybrid capital is relatively small, the choice to include it in, or exclude it from, available capital will not cause a material difference in the choice of confidence level.

3.7   Conclusion

In this chapter, we have reviewed a number of choices that we face when deciding how to define economic capital. To provide the context for the next chapter, in which we discuss the calculation of economic capital for individual risk types, we summarize here the main conclusions from our discussion with respect to the definition of economic capital.

- **Fair value versus book value**
  We have argued that fair values should be used when measuring economic capital because only fair values reflect all changes in risk.
- **Coverage of risks**
  Economic capital should include all material risks to which a financial institution is exposed, and that can give rise to unexpected losses that may cause an impairment of capital. With respect to liquidity risk, we concluded that economic capital should include the risk of lower asset prices or higher funding costs due to illiquid markets (which we have considered part of market liquidity risk), but not funding liquidity risk, which relates to a complete absence of sources for funding.
- **Time horizon**
  For the choice of time horizon over which economic capital is estimated, we explained that a one-year horizon is a reasonable compromise considering the nature of the different risk types and the assumed liquidity of debt and equity markets. The one-year horizon is also consistent with the performance cycle that many institutions use. In practice most institutions use a one-year horizon.
- **Treatment of expected profit**
  Expected profits form the first buffer against lower than expected revenues or unexpected losses, before available capital is impacted. In the context of capital adequacy assessment, we therefore expect economic capital to decrease if the expected profit increases. However, for performance

measurement we have argued that changes in expected profits should not affect the economic capital estimate when using RAROC as a performance metric. To align the definition of economic capital between performance measurement and capital adequacy assessment, we advocate to include expected profits as part of available capital in a capital adequacy assessment, instead of deducting expected profits from economic capital.

- **Confidence level**
  The choice of confidence level is linked directly to the risk appetite of the firm. If the objective is to maintain the credit rating of a certain seniority of debt, then historic default frequencies published by the rating agencies provide guidance for what confidence level is consistent with the target debt rating.

  We elaborated on the implication of the choice between a through-the-cycle or a point-in-time economic capital. We argued that a through-the-cycle economic capital is best suited to assess capital adequacy and long-term profitability, and that point-in-time economic capital may be better suited to reflect the increasing risks due to a downturn in the economic cycle and for evaluation of prices in current market circumstances. The choice between a through-the-cycle and point-in-time economic capital has consequences for the value of the confidence level. If we choose to calculate point-in-time economic capital estimate, then the confidence level used in the calculation should vary over time for a given target debt rating. Besides, we must ensure that the calculation of economic capital for each individual risk type is consistent with the choice made.

- **Definition of available capital**
  The definition of available capital should be consistent with how economic capital is measured. Available capital consists of all equity and debt instruments that are junior to the debt type for which the target rating has been used to determine the confidence level. To determine the value of available capital, we have discussed some potential valuation adjustments and the inclusion or exclusion of a number of asset and liability categories.

  We have suggested to use common equity as the basis for available capital in order to align the definitions of economic capital and available capital for purposes of capital adequacy assessment and optimization of profitability. Ideally, the franchise value would be included in economic and available capital. However, given the difficulties in measuring the franchise value directly and its potentially volatile nature, many institutions do not include the franchise value in their definition of economic and available capital. If the franchise value is excluded, then this can create a bias for performance management, which has to be considered separately.

Whatever the choices made by the institution, it is important to make sure that the definition of available capital is consistent with the chosen definition of economic capital.

The suggested choices bring us to the following definition for economic capital:

> *Economic capital is an estimate of the maximum potential downward deviation of a firm's equity value from the expected equity value at a time horizon of one year, subject to a chosen confidence level.*

This definition of economic capital will be the starting point for the discussion in the next chapter, which covers the economic capital calculation for individual risk types.

Endnotes

[1]Thomas M, McManus R. Rallying value. www.financialworld.co.uk; February 2008.

[2]Cummins et al. find that the drop in market value within a time window around the disclosure of an operational loss is around four times as large as the operational loss itself for US banks, and around 2.5 times as large for US insurers (Cummins JD, Lewis CM, Wei R. The market value impact of operational loss events for US banks and insurers. *Journal of Banking & Finance*. 2006;30:2605–2634). Using longer time windows after a loss disclosure, Dunnett et al. find that losses in market value of banks exceed 10 times the size of the disclosed operational loss (Dunnett RS, Levy CB, Simoes AP. Managing operational risk in banking. *The McKinsey Quarterly*. 2005;1:9–11).

[3]The Joint Forum. *The management of liquidity risk in financial groups.* 2006. See also, Basel Committee on Banking Supervision. Principles for Sound Liquidity Management and Supervision. September 2008.

[4]See Crouhy M, Galai, D, Mark R. *The essentials of risk management.* New York: McGraw-Hill; 2006.

[5]Franklin B. Letter to Jean-Baptiste Leroy. 13 November 1789. From: "The Works of Benjamin Franklin," reprinted in 1817 and published by William Duane.

[6]UK Financial Services Authority. Review of the liquidity requirements for banks and building societies. December 2007.

[7]Wellink N. Responding to uncertainty. Speech at the International Conference of Banking Supervisors 2008, Brussels, 24 September.

[8]Society of Actuaries. Economic capital for life insurance companies. February 2008.

[9]Chief Risk Officer Forum and the International Financial Risk Institute. Insights from the joint IFRI/CRO Forum survey on Economic Capital practice and applications. 2007.

[10]Cantor R, Hamilton D, Tennant J. Confidence intervals for corporate default rates. *Risk*. March 2008.

[11]Standard & Poor's. Corporate Ratings Criteria. 2005.

[12]See Annex 1a in: Basel Committee on Banking Supervision. *Basel II: International convergence of capital measurement and capital standards: A revised framework.* Bank for International Settlements. June 2006 (can be downloaded from http://www.bis.org).

[13]Matten C. *Managing bank capital, capital allocation and performance management.* 2nd ed. New York: Wiley; 2000.

[14]Based on market-to-book ratios derived from the Web site of Reuters for Henderson, Schröders, MAN Group, Legg Mason, Janus, Invesco, T. Rowe Price, Aberdeen, Fortress, Ashmore, and F&C Asset Managers.

[15]Based on market-to-book ratios derived from the Web site of Reuters for Julius Baer, Vontobel, and Bank Sarasin.

4 Running the Numbers: Measuring Economic Capital

In Chapter 3 we arrived at the following definition of economic capital:

Economic capital is an estimate of the maximum potential downward deviation of a firm's equity value from the expected equity value at a time horizon of one year, subject to a chosen confidence level.

An important feature of this definition is that economic capital is derived from the probability distribution of equity values at the chosen time horizon. Hence, it does not measure the change in equity value between the current date and the chosen time horizon, but rather how much lower the equity value at the time horizon can be compared to the expected equity value, given the chosen confidence level.

We made the following specific choices in Chapter 3 to arrive at this definition:

- All risks that may give rise to unexpected losses, and thus a decrease in the value of a firm's equity value, should be included in the measurement of economic capital.
- For the assessment of potential changes in the equity value, we include potential changes in both earnings and value of assets and liabilities over the chosen time horizon.
- Expected profits are included as part of available capital in a capital adequacy assessment and do not reduce the amount of economic capital.
- The time horizon is set to one year.
- The confidence level is based on the target credit rating of an institution's most junior debt. As such, the amount of economic capital can be compared to the value of shareholder equity capital of the institution.

This definition will be the starting point for the present chapter, in which we discuss the calculation of economic capital for individual risk types. The purpose of this chapter is not to present a recipe for the calculation of economic capital for each risk type. Although we will describe the essential features of the main approaches, our emphasis will be on various choices that institutions will face when attempting to assess economic capital, and that need to be agreed between modelers and managers. Some of these choices are specific to a risk type, whereas others are relevant for all risk types. In the latter case, it is important that a consistent choice across risk types is made. In the endnotes to this chapter we have included suggestions for further reading that provide more details on specific approaches to calculate economic capital for individual risk types.

Before we start the discussion for each individual risk type, we first review some general considerations that apply to many risk types in Section 4.1. Sections 4.2 through 4.7 discuss economic capital modeling approaches for individual risk types, and Section 4.8 reviews methodologies for the aggregation of economic capital across risk types. The sections on the individual risk types can be read independently from each other, and the next chapters do not depend on the specific contents in these sections. However, the general topics covered in Section 4.1 will return in later chapters.

4.1 General Considerations

4.1.1 Incorporating Portfolio Dynamics

Economic capital is derived from the probability distribution of possible equity values of an institution at the chosen time horizon; that is, after one year. This probability distribution of equity values is determined by the value of all assets and liabilities that the institution has at the one-year time horizon, together with the earnings during the one-year period. The assets and liabilities at the one-year time horizon will likely differ from the current assets and liabilities, since new assets and liabilities will be added during the year, whereas existing assets and liabilities may be sold or may mature. For example, an institution will extend new loans or sell new insurance policies during the year. Trading positions will change over time, and can both increase and decrease in risk. An institution may even decide to acquire another company, or to sell a particular business. The question is how we deal with these changes in risk profile in an economic capital calculation.

Our starting point is the portfolio of assets and liabilities that exists today. The capital that an institution has must be sufficient to support the risks to which the institution is currently exposed, as well as the risks to which it cannot reasonably avoid becoming exposed in the future. The current amount of capital does not have to cater for major changes in risk profile that are the result of conscious decisions in the future by the institution's management. Hence, changes in risk profile as a result of potential acquisitions, divestments, or closure of businesses are not included in regular economic capital calculations. The capital consequences of such decisions should be considered separately at the time such a decision is made.

An institution may also have sold products or services to customers that cannot cause a loss today, but may cause losses to the institution in the future. For example, a bank may have provided a credit or money market line to a customer that is not used initially, but that provides the customer with the option to borrow money at future points in time. Because the decision lies with the customer, and not with the bank, we should take such potential increases in risk into account in economic capital calculations.

Less straightforward is what to assume about assets and liabilities that mature before the time horizon, such as loans to customers of which the remaining maturity is shorter than one year, bond issues that have to be repaid within one year, or insurance policies that end within one year. In a going-concern situation, these will typically be extended or replaced by new assets and liabilities with similar characteristics. However, in a distress situation, an institution may not be able or willing to extend or replace maturing assets and liabilities. A similar situation exists for trading or investment limits that institutions have put in place. In normal situations, traders and investment managers are free to change their positions within these limits, but in adverse scenarios the institution may lower the limits to reduce risks.

One possible choice is to restrict the economic capital calculation to the portfolio of exposures that is currently in place, and exclude potential future exposures if an institution can make a conscious decision whether to accept or reject these new exposures. In the insurance industry this is sometimes referred to as the liability runoff approach. At any point in time that an institution needs to make a decision whether to accept a new exposure, it must evaluate whether it wants to allocate part of its capital to the new exposures. This choice is in line with the principle that the current amount of capital has to be sufficient to support the existing portfolio of exposures only. For a capital adequacy assessment, when our aim is to ensure the continuity of an institution, this is a reasonable starting point. The expected earnings that are added to available capital then should reflect only the expected earnings from existing assets and liabilities.

However, for performance management purposes the expected earnings will be based on the assumption that maturing assets will be replaced, and even new assets will be added. The market value of equity also is based on this assumption. If economic capital represents a potential decline in market value, which we argued is an appropriate choice when the aim is to optimize profitability, then it is consistent to assume in the economic capital calculations that maturing assets and liabilities will be replaced. The potential shortfall in earnings from the expected value at the horizon date, because maturing assets and liabilities have not been replaced, should be captured under business risk. Because an institution will experience a shortfall in earnings most likely when the institution incurs large unexpected losses as a result of other risks to which it is exposed, this supports a positive correlation between business risk and other risk types.

Ideally, economic capital calculations reflect responses to changing circumstances. If we consider the probability distribution of the equity value at the economic capital time horizon (see Graph 3.1 in Chapter 3), then the scenarios in the middle (body) of the distribution correspond to a going-concern situation. For this part of the distribution it is reasonable to assume that maturing assets and liabilities will be replaced with new ones with similar characteristics, or even that the portfolio of assets and liabilities will grow in line with the planned growth of the institution. Similarly, trading and investment limits are likely to remain in place. In the part of the distribution (the tail) that corresponds to situations in which the institution incurs large unexpected losses, costs, or disappointing revenues, it is reasonable to assume that the institution will take measures to curtail its exposure to new risks. The further the scenarios are in the tail, the more restrictive the institution will be in accepting new risks, and the more actively it will pursue a reduction of existing risks and risk limits.

Incorporating the likely development of the portfolio composition over time in economic capital calculations requires that we specify how the bank's asset and liability portfolios will develop in normal situations, and how an institution's management will respond in adverse situations. Such behavioral assumptions are commonly made in asset and liability management (ALM) analyses in financial institutions, but are less common for other risk types. It is clear that these behavioral assumptions introduce uncertainty in the economic capital estimate because management responses to changes in circumstances are not arrived at in an automated fashion. Managers must, therefore, give guidance to modelers how they are likely to respond to large unexpected losses and a consequent decrease of available capital.

4.1.2 Capturing Dependencies

When financial institutions get into financial problems, in almost all cases multiple bad events happen at the same time. For example, a bank may incur unexpectedly large credit losses because many customers default at the same time. Insurance companies and pension funds may get into trouble when they experience losses across various investments at the same time, for example, when various stock markets drop in value at the same time. Or failures in a bank's control environment may coincide with adverse movements in market variables, leading to large trading losses as happened to Barings and Société Générale, for example. It is thus crucial for an accurate economic capital estimate to assess the likelihood that various bad events happen at the same time. For each individual risk type, we discuss this in subsequent sections. In this section, we will review some general issues with respect to the estimation of dependencies.

Causal Versus Statistical Relationships

First of all, we need to distinguish between causal and statistical relationships. In a causal relationship, one event causes another event. Although there may be uncertainty about the occurrence of the first event, if it occurs we know for sure that the second event will also occur. For example, if a country's government imposes a ban on the transfer of foreign currency out of the country, a bank knows that customers in that country will default on their foreign-currency loans. We do not know whether a country government will impose such a ban (we may estimate the probability that it will occur), but if it occurs we do know that all entities in the country will default on their foreign-currency loans. The reverse is not true: if a firm defaults on its foreign-currency loans, it is not necessarily the case that the government has imposed a ban on the transfer of foreign currency. The firm may default because of firm-specific reasons. This illustrates that causal relationships are not symmetric.

In statistical relationships, we do not know for sure that one event happens if another event has happened. It may be likely, but it is uncertain. For example, it may be likely that the three-year interest rate rises when the five-year interest rate rises, but it is not necessarily the case. When dealing with statistical relationships, we have to estimate the strength of the dependence between two events. A common measure of dependence is the correlation coefficient between two events. A correlation coefficient has a value between −1 and +1. A positive correlation between two events A and B means that if we know that event A will occur, then the probability that event B occurs will be higher compared to its probability if we do not know whether event A will occur. Hence, the *conditional* probability that event B occurs (i.e., conditional on event A taking place) is higher than the *unconditional* probability of event B. For example, a rise in the three-year interest rate is more likely if we would know that the five-year interest rate will rise, compared to the situation in which we do not know whether the five-year interest rate will rise or fall. The three-year and the five-year interest rates thus have a positive correlation. If there is a negative correlation between events A and B, then the probability that event B happens if we know that event A has happened is lower than the unconditional probability of event B. The closer the correlation coefficient is to +1 (or −1), the more the probability of event B increases (decreases) when we know that event A has occurred. We summarize this in Table 4.1, in which we assume that the unconditional probability that event B occurs equals 5%.

A correlation coefficient of zero indicates that there is no statistical dependence. A correlation coefficient of +1 or −1 corresponds to complete dependence; that is, the two events will always (correlation of +1) or never

Table 4.1 Interpretation of values of the correlation coefficient (the unconditional probability of event B is assumed to equal 5%)

If the value of the correlation coefficient between events A and B is ...	... and if event A has occurred, then the probability of event B is ...
−1	zero
between −1 and 0	lower than 5%
0	5%
between 0 and +1	higher than 5%
+1	100%

(correlation of –1) occur at the same time. Complete dependence is not the same as a causal relationship. For example, if two trading desks have exactly opposite positions, then they will never incur a loss at the same time. The correlation between changes in value of the positions of both trading desks is –1, but there is no causal relationship between the two. Correlation is a symmetric measure; that is, the correlation between event A and event B is the same as the correlation between event B and event A.

Use of Historical Data to Estimate Dependencies

Typically, the dependence between different events is estimated from historical data if sufficient historical observations are available. For example, correlations between changes in value of different stocks, or between stocks and interest rates, may be estimated from historical data. Value-at-risk calculations for trading positions are usually based on comovements of various market variables that have been observed in the past. Correlations between defaults of multiple companies may also be estimated from patterns of observed default rates in the past.

Although a reasonable, and often desirable, starting point, historical data may not always be a good guide for what can happen in the future. For example, the introduction of the Euro gave the countries in the Euro area a common monetary policy and, consequently, increased the correlation between the inflation rates in these countries. Hence, relations between different risk drivers may change over time, leading to changes in correlations. Furthermore, for many dependencies we have little or no historical information available on which to base statistical estimates. For example, for a young industry like the biomedical industry there is little historical data on defaults available from which we can estimate default correlations. In such situations, we have to base values of correlations, or other measures of dependence, on qualitative arguments or by using comparables.

Stress Correlations

A topic that often enters the discussion about economic capital is the presence of stress or tail correlations. Proponents of stress correlations argue that correlations are larger between events that correspond to large losses as opposed to small losses. The existence of stress correlations would imply, for example, that large trading losses coincide more often with large credit losses than small trading losses with small credit losses.

To prove the existence of stress correlations requires a time series of historical observations of large losses related to different loss events (e.g., trading and credit losses). For returns on stocks, research has shown that the correlation between large negative returns on different stocks is higher than between small returns.[1] This may point to the existence of stress correlations in stock returns. However, it is impossible to do a similar analysis for losses that contribute to economic capital. First of all, stock returns are available at daily or even higher frequencies, whereas financial institutions report losses on a quarterly basis at most. Second, the high confidence level used in the definition of economic capital implies that we should consider the correlation between very extreme losses for different loss events. Hence, we do not have the necessary data to study the presence of stress correlations in historical loss data that is relevant for economic capital estimates. This lack of data also causes problems for the empirical validation of economic capital estimates, as we will discuss in Section 4.1.6.

In discussions on the existence of stress correlations, the fact that a number of seemingly unrelated losses occur at the same time sometimes is used as indication that stress correlations are present. Clearly, we cannot perform statistics and draw conclusions from a single observation. Furthermore, to end up in the bad tail of a loss distribution, multiple loss events *need* to happen at the same time, even if the loss events themselves are uncorrelated. We therefore must be careful to conclude the existence of stress correlations from a single or a few bad events. Even if correlations are zero, multiple bad events can (and occasionally will) happen at the same time.

To illustrate this point, we can study blackjack players in a casino and analyze the big winners. We will find that they had an extraordinary sequence of lucky draws. This is the case by definition because otherwise they would not be big winners. However, does this mean that the correlation between lucky and unlucky draws was different than in other situations? That is highly unlikely—the winners were just lucky.

Although we cannot rule out the existence of stress correlations, the limited amount of historical loss data that we have at our disposal and the high confidence level that is used in the definition of economic capital makes it impossible to obtain statistical evidence in the context of economic capital estimates.

4.1.3   Estimating Parameters from Historical Data

When discussing the estimation of dependencies in the previous section, we remarked that historical data may not always provide a good indication of what can happen in the future. This applies obviously not just to the estimation of correlations, but more in general when we have to assign values to unknown quantities in economic capital calculations; for example, default probabilities of firms, expected returns on investments, the frequency and severity of insurance claims, or the life expectancy of pensioners.

It is not difficult to find situations in which there was a marked change in the behavior in certain market variables. As an example, in recent years we have seen an unprecedented rise and volatility in the price of oil and other commodities. The next graph shows the behavior of the oil price since 1947 in real (2008 USD equivalent) terms.

As the graph shows, there are long periods of relative tranquility in the oil price, interspersed with very volatile periods in which the oil price may also exhibit a large rise or fall. If we estimate the volatility of the oil price from a

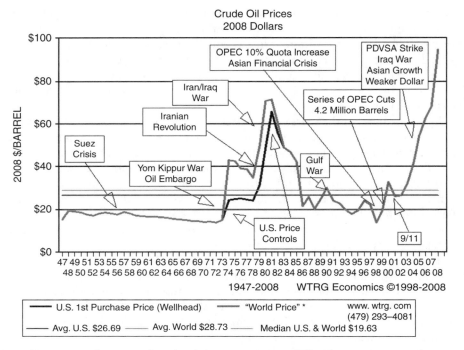

Graph 4.1 Development of crude oil prices in 2008 US dollars between 1947 and 2008.
Source: WTRG Economics, http://www.wtrg.com/prices.htm.

period with relatively small movements in the oil price, we will underestimate
the actual volatility if we enter one of the bumpy periods. The graph also indicates specific historical events that have had an impact on the behavior of the
oil price. If we are aware of such events, then we can take these into account
when estimating the values for parameters in economic capital calculations.
Often, however, events will come as a surprise, and we can only react to them
once they have occurred. This is clearly the case for many of the events in
Graph 4.1.

During the sub-prime crisis of 2007 and 2008, credit spreads have risen to
unprecedented levels, and volatility has increased significantly. This is illustrated by the spreads on the iTraxx credit default swap indices that are
maintained by Markit, which are displayed in Graph 4.2.

An estimate of the spreads on these indices based on historical data up to the
summer of 2007 would have seriously underestimated the level of the spreads
that materialized in 2008. Based on the volatility of the spreads up to the summer of 2007, the levels attained during 2008 were extremely unlikely. Only a
fundamental analysis of the market situation in 2007 could possibly have given
clues for the rise in the spreads that actually occurred.

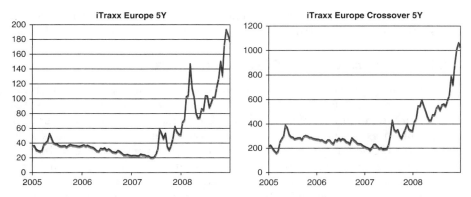

Graph 4.2 Historical development of spreads on various iTraxx credit default swap indices between 2005 and 2008. The iTraxx Europe 5Y represents the premium (in basis points) for a five-year CDS contract on an index consisting of 125 investment-grade European reference entities (100 non-financial and 25 financial companies). The companies in the index are selected as the ones with the most actively traded single-name CDS contracts. The iTraxx Europe Crossover 5Y represents the premium (in basis points) for a five-year CDS contract on an index consisting of 35 sub-investment grade European reference entities.
Source: Markit.

Another example of a situation in which the past was not a guide for the future relates to payment behavior of homeowners in the United States. As described in the *Financial Times*:[2]

> *When American households have faced hard times in previous decades, they tended to default on unsecured loans such as credit cards and car loans first— and stopped paying their mortgage only as a last resort. However, in the last couple of years households have become delinquent on their mortgages much faster than trends in the wider economy might suggest. That is particularly true for the less creditworthy sub-prime borrowers. Moreover, consumers have stopped paying mortgages before they halt payments on their credit cards and automotive loans—turning the traditional delinquency pattern on its head. As a result, mortgage lenders have started to face losses at a much earlier stage than in the past.*

These changes in consumer behavior not only increase actual delinquency rates, but also decrease the (market) value of all residential mortgage loans on a bank's balance sheet.

These examples are not intended to suggest that historical data is never useful. In fact, historical data is usually the best starting point for estimates when such data is available. The point that we want to highlight is that the use of historical data should be supplemented by fundamental analysis of the environment. This analysis can point to changes in patterns or behavior in the future, which in turn require adjustment of values of parameters in economic capital models from the ones that were valid in the past. Such changes in behavior obviously also present a significant source of uncertainty for economic capital models.

4.1.4 Calculating Economic Capital Contributions

To manage economic capital for both capital adequacy and performance measurement purposes it is important to know how much an existing or prospective activity, or even a single transaction, contributes to economic capital of an institution as a whole. The economic capital contribution measures how much a specific activity or transaction (exposure) is expected to contribute to the decline in equity value of the firm when this decline equals economic capital. In other words, for the large loss in equity value that economic capital represents, we aim to determine how much each exposure is expected to contribute to that loss. A number of alternative methods have been suggested in the literature and are used in practice.[3] Different methods can lead to different economic capital contributions, which in turn can lead to different conclusions and decisions. It is thus important for managers to understand the differences between the different methods.

There are several properties that we could look for when choosing a method to calculate economic capital contributions:

1. The sum of the economic capital contributions of all exposures of a firm should equal the total economic capital of the firm. This property ensures that the full economic capital is allocated to individual exposures.
2. The calculated economic capital contribution for an exposure should equal the decline in the economic capital of the firm as a whole if we would eliminate the exposure. If this property is satisfied, we have a direct measure of the marginal impact of an exposure on total economic capital.
3. The method should take into account correlations with other activities and transactions. If it satisfies this property, we expect the economic capital contribution to be positive for an exposure that is expected to show an unexpected loss if the firm as a whole incurs an unexpected loss equal to economic capital. Conversely, we expect the economic capital contribution to be negative for an exposure that is expected to show an unexpected gain when the firm as a whole incurs an unexpected loss equal to economic capital. The higher the correlation between the loss on an individual exposure and the loss on the total portfolio, the higher we expect the economic capital contribution of the exposure to be (and vice versa). This property thus ensures that the method is risk sensitive.
4. The method should allow for quick and reliable calculation, given the desire to base decisions about individual transactions on the economic capital contribution.

We will see that none of the methods to calculate economic capital contributions fully satisfies all these properties. Hence, it is necessary to make a trade-off between these properties when choosing a method.

Component Economic Capital

The method that is most closely aligned to how we defined economic capital contributions is the component economic capital calculation. It is based on a direct evaluation of how much each exposure contributes to the economic capital for an institution as a whole. More formally, the component economic capital contribution equals the unexpected loss (or gain) of an exposure in the particular extreme scenario in which the institution as a whole incurs an unexpected loss equal to economic capital. The calculated economic capital for the institution as a whole is thus decomposed to individual exposure level. In the general value-at-risk (VaR) literature the contribution determined in this manner is referred to as the component VaR, and we follow the analogous terminology here for economic capital.

As an example, suppose the current value of the firm is 100, its expected value at the one-year horizon is 110, and the minimum firm value at the chosen confidence level for economic capital equals 10. Then economic capital for the firm equals 100 (the difference between 110 and 10). Suppose further that the firm consist of two business units A and B, each valued at 50 initially, and that business unit A is expected to be worth 54 at the horizon, and business unit B, 56. If the value of business unit A drops to 7 in the extreme adverse scenario corresponding to a firm value of 10, and business unit B is worth only 3 in that scenario, then the economic capital contribution equals 47 for business unit A (calculated as 54 minus 7) and 53 for business unit B (56 minus 3).

By construction, the sum of the economic capital contributions over all exposures equals the total economic capital of an institution (property 1) when using the component economic capital method. It clearly also takes into account diversification effects between potential losses resulting from different exposures if the overall economic capital calculation for the institution does so (property 3). Economic capital contributions calculated in this manner will not exactly equal the change in overall economic capital when an exposure is eliminated from the overall economic capital calculation (property 2), but it will be quite close if the exposure is a relatively small part of the institution as a whole. For large exposures, we would need to perform a separate calculation using the incremental economic capital contribution method as described later to derive a more precise estimate of the decrease in economic capital if these exposures would be eliminated.

The difficulty with using the component economic capital contribution method primarily lies with property 4, a quick and reliable calculation. In most practical situations, economic capital for an institution cannot be calculated using analytic methods, but simulation methods are necessary to determine the value distribution at the horizon. When simulation methods are used, it is computationally quite difficult to obtain reliable estimates of component economic capital contributions. The reason is that economic capital as a risk measure represents the single point on the value distribution that corresponds to the chosen confidence level. In a simulation, this corresponds to one particular simulated scenario. The simulated loss in this single scenario, and in particular, the simulated losses and gains on individual exposures in this scenario that add up to the total loss, are subject to significant simulation noise. That is, if we repeat the simulation to derive the value distribution, the simulated losses and gains on individual exposures can differ significantly in the particular scenario corresponding to economic capital, although their sum may not be that different.

This is easiest to see when calculating credit risk economic capital for a large portfolio of similar loans using simulation of default events of individual loans. Although overall economic capital can be estimated quite reliably using simulation, the individual loans that default in a simulated scenario that corresponds with a certain level of unexpected losses can vary substantially between different simulations.

A considerable amount of research has been performed on methods to arrive at reliable estimates for component economic capital contributions, using, for example, kernel estimators,[4] the saddle-point approximation method,[5] and importance sampling.[6] In addition, the component economic capital contribution can be calculated more reliably if we use an expected shortfall risk measure, because an expected shortfall risk measure is based on an average of realizations in the tail of the distribution, instead of a single realization.[7] These methods have enabled the calculation of component economic capital contributions in practice, at least up to a certain aggregated level of exposures. An increasing number of institutions therefore have adopted this method, to replace some of the computationally simpler methods that we review next.

Standard Deviation Contribution

Instead of calculating the contribution to economic capital itself, as the component economic capital contribution method does, we can estimate what the contribution of an exposure is to the standard deviation of the value distribution at the horizon. This standard deviation contribution can be calculated more easily and more reliably than the component economic capital contribution (property 4). The reason is that the standard deviation contribution is a function of the whole distribution of possible values, instead of being based on one particular point (scenario) in the tail of this distribution.

The standard deviation of the value distribution will be much smaller than economic capital. The sum of the standard deviation contributions over all exposures will therefore be smaller than the overall economic capital of an institution (property 1). To satisfy property 1, we need to multiply the calculated standard deviation contributions with a scaling factor. This scaling factor must be set equal to the economic capital of the institution, divided by the sum of the standard deviation contributions over all exposures. For a Gaussian (bell-shaped) distribution, the scaling factor will be around 3, whereas for a distribution with fat tails that we often encounter in the context of economic capital calculations the scaling factor will be substantially larger than 3.

The scaled standard deviation contribution may differ substantially from the economic capital contribution that we intend to measure, because individual exposures may have very different contributions to the standard deviation and to the tail. For example, in a portfolio of loans with low and high default probabilities, losses on loans with a low default probability will have a relatively small contribution to unexpected losses in scenarios in the body of the value distribution, which receive significant weight in the standard deviation. The reason is that typically only few loans with a low default probability will default during a mild recession, which is associated with the body of the value distribution, whereas many loans with a high default probability are likely to default during a mild recession. However, loans with a low default probability have a relatively large contribution to scenarios in the bad tail of the value distribution, which are most relevant for economic capital, because in very severe recessions more loans with an initially low default probability start to default, whereas the number of defaults of loans with an initially high probability of default increases to a lesser extent. Hence, economic capital contribution estimates based on standard deviation contributions may differ substantially from the actual economic capital contributions of individual exposures. As a consequence, properties 2 and 3 may be violated. In a recent evaluation of economic capital modeling practices,[8] the Basel Committee characterizes the calculation of economic capital contributions based on the contribution to the standard deviation as "simple, but not very meaningful."

Incremental Economic Capital

An alternative method to calculate economic capital contributions is based on an incremental economic capital calculation. Incremental economic capital of an exposure equals the decrease in economic capital if the exposure is excluded from the calculation. As such, it satisfies property 2 by definition. Property 3 will also be satisfied, because the incremental economic capital calculation will take the dependence of a specific exposure with the other exposures into account. Property 1 will not be satisfied. In fact, it can be shown that the sum of the incremental economic capital over all exposures will be lower than the economic capital for the firm as a whole. To correct for this, we would need to scale up each of the calculated incremental economic capital amounts. If the scaling factor is significantly larger than one, then the scaled incremental economic capital amounts may differ materially from the actual contribution to economic capital. This will be the case if there are a few dominant exposures (concentrations) in the portfolio.

The determination of incremental economic capital for each exposure is daunting if we need to repeatedly calculate economic capital for the firm as a whole, but each time with a different exposure removed. For any reasonable granularity of exposures that are distinguished within a firm, this is practically impossible. Furthermore, if simulation methods are used to calculate economic capital, the incremental economic capital calculation for relatively small exposures may suffer from significant simulation noise. It will thus only be feasible, and thereby satisfy property 4, only if we can use accurate and fast approximation methods.

Although less suitable as a general method to determine economic capital contributions across an institution as a whole, an incremental economic capital calculation is the method of choice to evaluate the impact on economic capital of a significant change in exposure of an institution, for example, as result of a contemplated acquisition, divestment, or significant growth of a specific activity. When using it in this setting, the method will yield a precise indication of the impact of such a significant change on overall economic capital.

Stand-alone Economic Capital

A feature of all methods discussed so far is that the resulting economic capital contributions may be negative for exposures that have a negative correlation with the majority of other exposures, or for positions or transactions that offset part of the risk of other positions and transactions. A negative economic capital contribution is intuitive for transactions or positions that are intended to reduce the risk of an institution. Examples are hedges of a bank's interest-rate risk on the balance sheet using interest-rate swaps, or credit risk hedges using credit default swaps. However, assigning negative economic capital to positions that are not intended to be risk mitigating may not be intuitive, or even desirable. It may occur if two trading desks happen to take (partially) offsetting or negatively correlated positions, or if two business units in a bank have offsetting interest-rate risk positions on their balance sheet (ALM risk). If we use one of the earlier methods to calculate economic capital contributions, one of the trading desks or business units may be attributed a negative amount of economic capital. For performance management purposes, this will be undesirable and potentially provide wrong incentives.

To avoid negative economic capital contributions, we can allocate economic capital on the basis of stand-alone economic capital estimates. Stand-alone economic capital equals the amount of economic capital for each exposure in isolation. Although this method avoids negative economic capital contributions, using stand-alone economic capital as an estimate of economic capital contributions has the drawback that it ignores diversification effects with other exposures. Hence, it will overestimate how much a specific exposure contributes to economic capital for the firm as a whole. Consequently, the sum of the stand-alone economic capital amounts over all exposures will be higher than overall economic capital of an institution (property 1). We can correct for this by scaling down the stand-alone economic capital of exposures so that the sum of the scaled stand-alone economic capital amounts equals the overall economic capital of the firm. The scaling factor equals the total economic capital of the firm, divided by the sum of the stand-alone economic capital estimates of all individual exposures. However, economic capital contributions that are calculated in this way will still not capture the actual diversification effects of an exposure with the other exposures (property 3). As such, the calculated economic capital contribution can also differ substantially from the change in economic capital that would occur if the exposure would be removed (property 2).

We note that stand-alone economic capital may not be a meaningful number for individual exposures, such as a single loan. It is sensible to apply it only for the allocation of economic capital to aggregate sets of exposures. From a computational perspective (property 4), calculating stand-alone economic capital estimates can usually be done quite efficiently since only a small set of exposures is considered for each calculation. Stand-alone economic capital estimates may even be derived directly from simulation results of the overall economic capital calculation, by considering only the losses simulated for the relevant subset of exposures, and deriving economic capital from the results for this subset. An issue that warrants attention when calculating stand-alone economic capital for a business unit or activity is how to deal with transactions with other parts of the institution, such as hedge transactions and internal guarantees. These transactions can be ignored for institutionwide economic capital calculations, but they should be taken into account for a realistic stand-alone economic capital calculation.

Comparison of Methods

We have summarized the strengths and weaknesses of the various methods with respect to the properties outlined at the start of this section in Table 4.2.

It is clear from the preceding discussion, summarized in Table 4.2, that none of the reviewed methods to calculate economic capital contributions satisfies all properties that we outlined at the start of this section. Each of the methods can be useful in specific situations.

Component economic capital is best aligned with what the economic capital contribution is intended to measure, and as such is the preferred general method. It has serious computational challenges, however. Stand-alone economic capital and standard deviation contribution in contrast are much easier to implement, but may seriously violate some or all of the other properties.

Table 4.2 Overview of properties of different methods to calculate economic capital contributions (++ fully satisfies, + approximately satisfies, − may not satisfy, − − does not satisfy)

	Property			
	1	2	3	4
Component economic capital	++	+	++	−
Standard deviation contribution	− −	− −	+	+
Incremental economic capital	+	++	++	− −
Stand-alone economic capital	− −	− −	− −	++

As a compromise, we can combine these methods for practical implementa-
tions in two steps. In the first step, we can use the component economic capital
calculation to determine economic capital contributions for sufficiently large
groups of exposures (e.g., exposures related to the same business unit or credit
rating). Further subdivision of economic capital to individual exposures within
each group can then take place in the second step by applying the standard
deviation contribution or stand-alone economic capital methods. Where we
draw the line for the use of the component economic capital method depends
on the complexity of the economic capital calculation itself, and to what extent
it allows for the application of some of the advanced methods that can be used
to improve the accuracy of calculating component economic capital.

When the aim is to assess the impact on economic capital of a significant
change in exposure of an institution, the incremental economic capital method
is the natural choice. In that case we would not use the method to attribute economic capital to all existing exposures of an institution, but only to assess the
contribution to economic capital of the exposures that change significantly.
The stand-alone economic capital contribution method can be used in situations
that other methods lead to very low or even negative economic capital contributions for an activity or transaction, if this presents undesirable incentives for
excessive risk taking. Obviously, we should be aware of the limitations of this
method in other respects.

4.1.5 Model Risk

We introduced model risk in Section 3.3.3 as the risk that a model does not
reflect the real world correctly in aspects that are essential to its purpose, as
a result of which the outcomes from the model may deviate from reality. This
can potentially lead to wrong decisions and unexpected losses. Because any
model is an abstraction from reality, there will always be some model risk
when models are used. The question is therefore how to minimize and manage
model risk. In the context of economic capital, we also need to consider how to
account for model risk in economic capital estimates. We discuss these issues in
a general sense in this section, and include a more detailed discussion for individual risk types in subsequent sections. As background to these discussions,
we first review potential sources of model risk.

Sources of Model Risk

We can distinguish several sources of model risk, as described next.

Model Misspecification

Any model is an abstraction from reality, and as such will not fully capture all
real-world relationships. If a model does not incorporate an explanatory factor
or relationship that is essential to its purpose, or incorporates it incorrectly,
then we say that the model is misspecified.

Any forecasting model based purely on historical data runs the risk of being misspecified, since the environment from which the historical data stem may differ in important aspects from the current situation. That is, some factors that were important in the past may no longer be important today, and vice versa. In addition, the relationships between different factors may have changed over time. An example of such changes in relationships was given in Section 4.1.3 regarding the mortgage repayment behavior of house owners in the United States. The assumptions that mortgage lenders made about the repayment behavior for the extension and valuation of mortgages turned out to be out of line with the actual behavior in recent years, because the assumptions did not reflect the fundamental change in the situation of many homeowners.

Alan Greenspan has pointed to the incorporation of human behavior as an important missing element in many statistical risk management models. When evaluating the performance of such models in the wake of the sub-prime crisis, he commented:[9]

> The most credible explanation of why risk management based on state-of-the-art statistical models can perform so poorly is that the underlying data used to estimate a model's structure are drawn generally from both periods of euphoria and periods of fear, that is, from regimes with importantly different dynamics.

To include these different dynamics, Greenspan sees the need to explicitly incorporate human behavior in risk management models:

> But these models do not fully capture what I believe has been, to date, only a peripheral addendum to business-cycle and financial modeling—the innate human responses that result in swings between euphoria and fear that repeat themselves generation after generation, with little evidence of a learning curve. Asset-price bubbles build and burst today as they have since the early 18th century, when modern competitive markets evolved. To be sure, we tend to label such behavioral responses as non-rational. But forecasters' concerns should be not whether human response is rational or irrational, only that it is observable and systematic.

This presents a clear challenge to risk modelers.

We note that a simplifying assumption does not constitute a model misspecification *per se*. For example, the Black-Scholes model for stock options assumes that interest rates are constant. This is clearly not a realistic assumption. However, the influence of including volatility of the interest rate on calculated prices is so small compared to the influence of other factors that the assumption of constant interest rates is acceptable for the valuation of stock options. As such, we would not classify it as a misspecified model. Clearly, the assumption of constant interest rates would not be acceptable for a model that is used to price interest-rate options. Any such interest-rate option valuation model would clearly be misspecified.

Parameter Uncertainty

Even if a model comprises all essential variables and relationships, we may not know exactly what the correct values of all model parameters are. Choosing wrong values for the parameters in a model may result in wrong outcomes and conclusions. The more uncertainty exists about the parameter values, the greater this risk, and the more we are exposed to model risk.

Examples of parameter uncertainty are abundant. For trading value-at-risk models, we need to estimate the volatility of and correlation between market variables. For portfolio credit risk models we need to estimate default probabilities of, and default correlations between, individual counterparties. For insurance risk capital models, we need to estimate the likelihood of, and correlation between, insured events.

In practice, there is usually a trade-off between a realistic but complex model with many parameters whose values are difficult to determine precisely, and a simple parsimonious model with a few parameters that can be estimated more reliably. Hence, we often have to trade off parameter uncertainty on one hand with model misspecification and incompleteness on the other. Striking a good balance requires insight into the magnitude of the various types of model risks.

Faulty Implementation

A model may be an adequate description of reality and have the correct parameter values, but if there are errors in its implementation, then it will yield the wrong outcomes. Given the complexity of today's models, both for the valuation of financial products and for risk management purposes, it is no easy task to ensure that there are no mistakes in the numerical implementation.

That incorrect implementation is a serious risk was illustrated by an error that has been discovered in the computer coding of a model used by Moody's to assign ratings to Constant Proportion Debt Obligations (CPDOs).[10] The error reportedly had the effect of assigning ratings that were up to four notches better than they would have been if the model had been implemented correctly.

Managing and Mitigating Model Risk

Many institutions subject models to validation to reduce model risk. Validation of a model can take place *ex-ante* (i.e., before a model is used) or *ex-post* (i.e., after a model has been used).

In an *ex-ante* validation, the model can be evaluated on all sources of model risk that have been distinguished earlier: its specification, choices for the values of the parameters, and the correctness of the implementation. The evaluation can be both qualitative and quantitative. The qualitative part of the validation, for example, would review the conceptual soundness of the assumptions underlying the model and its specification, based on general economic and financial theory as well as the actual market environment. In doing so, the review should focus on the choices and assumptions to which the model outcomes are most sensitive, and that are most relevant for its intended use. The quantitative part of an *ex-ante* validation, for example, can test whether postulated relationships in the model held up in the past (backtesting) or whether parameter estimation methods were sound and the data used for the estimation sensible. It will also include checks on the correctness of mathematical derivations and the model's implementation as computer code. Furthermore, quantitative *ex-ante* validation can include a comparison of the model to alternative models, possibly those used by other institutions (benchmarking), and an evaluation whether the performance of the model on hypothetical portfolios is in line with expectations.

An *ex-post* validation examines a model after it has been used for some time. With the actual experience obtained, we can evaluate whether the model has performed satisfactorily. If the model under investigation is a valuation model of a financial product, we can evaluate whether changes in value that have occurred in reality during the period can be explained by changes in factors in the valuation model. If not, then this may point to a misspecified model. Another example of *ex-post* validation is the backtesting of a bank's VaR models for the trading books. Using daily profit-and-loss (P&L) data, we can evaluate whether the number of times that the actual P&L exceeds the calculated VaR is in agreement with the chosen confidence level of VaR. If the confidence level is 99%, we expect to observe one excess on average in every hundred trading days. An *ex-post* validation can also assess whether choices and assumptions made in the setup of the model are still valid, or if they need to be adjusted in response to changes in the market. Such an evaluation can have both quantitative and qualitative aspects.

Validation is very common for models that are used to value and hedge traded financial products within banks. In many banks, products cannot be traded, or only to a very limited extent, until the model that will be used to value and hedge positions has been validated successfully. Until recently, formal validation has been much less common for other models used within financial institutions. For banks, the Basel II Accord stipulates that risk management models also need to be subjected to validation by qualified persons who are independent from the model developers and the model users. This includes economic capital models.

Accounting for Parameter Uncertainty in Economic Capital Calculations

Model risk enters economic capital estimates at two levels. First, it is present in the models that are used to value individual assets and liabilities. Economic capital calculations assess potential changes in value of assets and liabilities, and thus depend on the correctness of these valuation models. Second, the economic capital models are subject to model risk themselves in how they translate potential changes in the values of individual assets and liabilities into changes in the value of the firm as a whole, and from that derive an economic capital estimate.

Whereas all sources of model risk will be tested as part of a validation, parameter uncertainty in principle can also be included in the economic capital calculation. The simplest way is to choose conservative parameter values. This is how the Basel II Accord prescribes to deal with parameter uncertainty for the minimum capital requirement calculations under the internal-ratings-based (IRB) method for credit risk. However, choosing each of the parameters in a conservative manner (e.g., each of probability of default, loss given default, and exposure at default in the IRB context) may result in an overly conservative capital estimate. This may lead to an understatement of RAROC as a result of which the institution may forgo profitable investment opportunities. It is, therefore, important for managers to be aware how conservative choices for parameter values can affect business decisions.

Moreover, in economic capital calculations it may not always be clear how to choose a conservative value for a parameter. For example, choosing a higher default probability for an entity than the value that results from statistical estimation will not be conservative if we have bought CDS protection on the entity, because a higher default probability will increase the value of the CDS protection. As another example, increasing a correlation will be conservative if we only consider positively correlated positions (e.g., different loans in a loan portfolio, or trading positions that all benefit from a rise in interest rates), but not if we also allow for short or negatively correlated positions (e.g., a loan portfolio hedged with a position in a CDS index, or a long position in the 10-year interest rate combined with a short position in the five-year interest rate). Hence, what is conservative may depend on the specific exposures for a financial institution.

A more attractive way to deal with parameter uncertainty is to embed the parameter uncertainty directly in the economic capital calculations. For this approach, it is necessary that uncertainty about parameter values can be quantified by means of a probability distribution. How this can be embedded is easiest to see when we use simulation methods to estimate economic capital. To begin with, we have to establish a probability distribution for each parameter value, which specifies by how much the parameter value can deviate from the estimated value, and with what probability. Subsequently, for each simulated scenario, we randomly draw one realization from the probability distribution of each parameter value, and use these specific values for the calculation of the unexpected loss (or gain) in the particular scenario. For each simulated scenario, we draw new realizations for all parameters from the respective probability distributions. In this way, parameter uncertainty is explicitly incorporated in the economic capital calculation. As economic capital represents a worst-case unexpected loss, it will in such a calculation also correspond to a combination of worst-case parameter values. Explicitly including parameter uncertainty in economic capital calculations will thus result in a higher economic capital estimate when compared to fixing the parameters to their best-estimate values. The approach cannot only be applied to uncertainty around the input parameters of an economic capital model (e.g., default probabilities of counterparties, volatility of interest rates, correlation estimates) but also to uncertainty about the potential changes in value of individual assets and liabilities (which will be a function of other variables in the economic capital model).

It may not be practical or computationally feasible to explicitly include parameter uncertainty in this manner in regular economic capital calculations. However, such a calculation could be performed occasionally, possibly using a stylized portfolio of exposures if computation time is a bottleneck. The results of this calculation can then be used to establish fixed values for the parameters that, when used in the regular economic capital calculations, yield a correct estimate of economic capital reflecting the parameter uncertainty. This approach to reflect parameter uncertainty in economic capital calculations also rewards resolution of uncertainty over time. That is, if additional experience over time diminishes the uncertainty around the value of parameters, and thereby the width of the probability distribution of the parameter values, then the previous calculation will lead to a lower value of economic capital.

Correctly accounting for parameter uncertainty is also important in the trade-off between specialization and diversification, which we will discuss in Section 5.2.9.

4.1.6 Validation of Economic Capital

Although subjecting economic capital models to validation may establish a level of comfort with the choices and assumptions underlying the model and its correct implementation, there will still be uncertainty around the actual economic capital estimate. It is impossible to backtest the calculated amount of economic capital itself using actual unexpected loss realizations, given the high confidence level at which it is calculated and the one-year horizon. We would need thousands of years of observations, while keeping the model unchanged, to be able to perform a formal backtest on the calculated amount of economic capital directly. This is clearly an impossible requirement to satisfy.

In Chapter 1 we reviewed a number of alternative risk measures that relate to much less extreme points on the value (or loss) distribution that economic capital models generate. But even if such an alternative risk measure would relate to an event that is expected to occur once every 10 years, we would need at least a few decades of observations to perform an actual backtest on the calculated values for the alternative risk measure. In addition, the economic capital models that are used to generate values for the alternative risk measure should not change in any material manner during these decades to perform a proper backtest. Hence, also a backtest of less extreme risk measures than economic capital is practically impossible.

If economic capital models do not change much for a number of years, we could evaluate whether realized unexpected losses (or value changes) are statistically consistent with the loss (value) distribution that the models have generated. For example, we can track to which percentile an unexpected loss (value change) at the end of a year relates on the loss (value) distribution that was generated at the beginning of the year. We expect the percentiles to be distributed evenly between zero and 100%. Although the statistical power of such analysis will not be very high if we have only a few observations, it will provide some comfort if the generated loss distribution is reasonably aligned with observed losses or value changes. The situation is more difficult if there is misalignment. Should we conclude that the models are wrong based on a few observations? A further analysis to trace the reasons for the misalignment is necessary.

We can perform a partial backtest for some of the parameters in economic capital models by comparing the expected loss to realized loss amounts. Because expected loss is typically a function of several parameters, this is a check on the correctness of the joint values of these parameters. For example, expected credit losses are calculated by multiplying the default probability, loss-given-default, and exposure-at-default. Doing such a backtest on the joint values of parameters avoids that each of the parameters individually would be set to a too-conservative value. By comparing expected losses to realized losses, we will not get any information on the correctness of the modeled dependencies, however, that form the heart of economic capital models.

As a formal backtest of calculated economic capital amounts is practically not possible, we have to resort to more subjective ways to evaluate the outcomes of the models. Besides the various analyses that can be performed as part of a model validation, like benchmarking and hypothetical portfolio comparisons, outcomes of stress tests can also play a useful role to increase the comfort level. Usually, an estimate is made how likely it is that a certain stress test will occur, and we can then evaluate whether the expected loss in the stress scenario is consistent with the loss distribution as generated by the economic capital models. The use of stress testing is discussed further in Chapter 6.

4.1.7 Aggregation of Risk Types Versus Risk Drivers

In the following sections we discuss economic capital calculations for individual risk types. Our presentation in this way may suggest that calculating economic capital for each risk type individually, and then aggregating the calculated amounts across risk types to obtain an overall economic capital estimate, is the best route to follow. Although it certainly is the most common way to calculate economic capital in financial institutions, it does not necessarily yield the most accurate overall estimate. A potentially more accurate, but computationally demanding way to calculate overall economic capital is to aggregate exposures across *risk drivers* instead of *risk types*.

When estimating economic capital for an individual risk type, we first identify which factors (risk drivers) play a role in the realization of unexpected losses (or value changes). Examples of such factors for credit risk are default rates, loss-given-default and exposure-at-default. For market risk economic capital, relevant factors are interest rates and exchange rates in different currencies, equity prices, and commodity prices. For operational risk, we can think of the frequency and severity of various types of potential operational losses. The most natural way to obtain an overall picture of risk that encompasses all risk types is by aggregating exposures per underlying risk driver, and assessing dependencies between all risk drivers across risk types. For example, this would involve modeling and estimating correlations between default rates, interest rates, and frequency of operational loss events.

Because there are many risk drivers per risk type, an overall economic capital calculation model based on aggregating exposures across risk drivers for all risk types will be very large and therefore computationally very demanding. Furthermore, it requires the estimation of dependencies between all risk drivers across risk types, for which historical data may not be readily available. These are the main reasons why this approach is not used in practice. Instead, exposures to risk drivers are aggregated only for each risk type to arrive at an economic capital estimate per risk type. Subsequently, the economic capital estimates per risk type are aggregated to end up with an overall economic capital estimate. This is also how we will present it in the rest of this chapter. Modeling and estimating dependencies is, however, more natural between risk drivers than between risk types, because each risk type represents a complex composite of exposures to multiple risk drivers. We will elaborate on this when we discuss aggregation across risk types in Section 4.8.

Another choice is at which level in the organization to calculate economic capital for a risk type. That is, we can choose to calculate credit risk economic capital in one go for the bank as a whole, or calculate it for each business unit separately and then aggregate it across business units. We will discuss the implications of a centralized versus decentralized calculation of economic capital in Section 5.1.1. The issues we discuss in the remainder of this chapter for the calculation of economic capital per risk type do not depend on whether we choose to calculate economic capital for an institution as a whole at once, or first for each business unit individually and then aggregate the results across business units.

4.2 Credit Risk

Credit risk is the potential loss in value of claims on counterparties because of a reduced likelihood that the counterparty will fulfill its payment obligations, or because the value of collateral securing the obligation decreases. The claims can consist of interest and principal payments on loans that a financial institution has provided to its customers, or bonds in which it has invested. Claims can also arise from derivatives transactions in which the institution has entered with a counterparty, or from guarantees that the institution has obtained from third parties. The term *counterparty* is used most commonly in trading book transactions to indicate the contract party, but we will use it going forward as a general term to include all types of contract parties on which an institution may have a credit exposure, including borrowers, guarantors, and issuers.

The importance of credit risk arising from derivatives transactions and guarantees has been demonstrated with the bankruptcy of Lehman Brothers in September 2008 and the consequences for the credit default swap (CDS) market.[11] At the time of bankruptcy, the total notional value of CDS trades referencing Lehman Brothers was about USD 72 billion. This resulted in bilateral payments of USD 21 million between buyers and sellers of CDSs that referenced Lehman Brothers based on auction-determined payouts. For the sellers of the CDSs, this was their credit loss due to the Lehman bankruptcy. For the buyers, this amount represented their combined credit exposure on the CDS protection sellers; that is, the amount they lose if the sellers of the CDS contracts that reference Lehman Brothers would not fulfill their obligation to pay under the contracts. Next to being a reference entity for billions of dollars of CDSs, Lehman Brothers was also a CDS dealer, providing significant amounts of credit protection by selling CDS contracts that referenced other entities. Moody's has estimated that Lehman's CDS book size in notional terms was between USD 2 and 3 trillion. On top of that, Lehman was also counterparty in many other types of derivative trades in the equity, interest rate, and FX markets. The default of Lehman meant that many financial institutions and corporates who had hedged their exposures with Lehman had an open risk position again and had to replace their hedges. These replacement costs resulted in significant losses for a number of dealers.

Credit risk is the single most important reason why banks fail, as we have seen in Chapter 2. In line with this, credit risk often contributes more to the total economic capital of a bank than any of the other risks to which the bank is exposed. The core function of banks is to intermediate between those with surplus money (savers) and those who need money (borrowers), and consequently lending should be among the core competencies of a bank. Despite this core competency, what is it that makes managing credit risk so difficult that it is the major cause of bank failures? Stated in a different way, what are the risk drivers that credit risk models should focus on in order that an institution can successfully manage its credit risk?

In Section 2.4 we noted that successful organizations often have an underlying business model that can be told simply. Warren Buffett formulated three key principles for insurance underwriting, which seem simple and general enough to also form a sound basis for a successful business model when accepting credit risk.[12] According to Warren Buffett, the winners (in the insurance underwriting business) unfailingly stick to three key principles:

1. They accept only those risks that they are able to properly evaluate (staying within their circle of competency) and that, after they have evaluated all relevant factors including remote loss scenarios, carry the expectancy of profit. These insurers ignore market-share considerations and are sanguine about losing business to competitors that are offering foolish prices or policy conditions.

2. They limit the business they accept in a manner that guarantees they will suffer no aggregation of losses from a single event or from related events

that will threaten their solvency. They ceaselessly search for possible correlation among seemingly unrelated risks.

3. They avoid business involving moral risk: No matter what the rate, trying to write good contracts with bad people does not work. While most policyholders and clients are honorable and ethical, doing business with the few exceptions is usually expensive, sometimes extraordinarily so.

When translating these principles to a lending business, principles 1 and 3 are about sound credit analysis and judgment when granting a loan. To stay within your circle of competency is sometimes at odds with ambitions to grow and diversify, and we will discuss this trade-off in Section 5.2.9. However, also when you stay in your circle of competency it is part of doing business that the repayment capacity of a debtor can be misjudged. Having competent credit analysts helps to minimize these errors. The principle that brings down seemingly competent banks is principle 2. A bank will not fail because a single loan or a few loans default, but only when many loans default. This basic truth has been at the root of such diverse bank defaults as Continental Illinois in 1984, Nippon Credit Bank in 1998, and the Danish Roskilde Bank in 2008. Hence, the key to credit risk management at a portfolio level is the search for joint defaults or correlations. How to search for, assess, and model correlations will be a recurrent theme in the sections hereafter.

4.2.1 Fundamental Choices and Assumptions

In this section we review choices and assumptions that an institution faces when developing an economic capital model for credit risk. For the interpretation of the outcomes of economic capital models it is important to be aware of these choices and assumptions, because they can have a material impact on the results. They also determine how an institution can use the results when comparing economic capital to available capital in the context of ensuring continuity, and when comparing returns to economic capital in relation to optimizing profitability.

Portfolio Dynamics

In Section 4.1.1 we discussed different choices that can be made with respect to the evolution of the portfolio of assets and liabilities during the economic capital horizon of one year. At the extremes, we can choose between a constant portfolio, in which assets and liabilities that mature within one year are not replaced, and a constant level of risk, in which case maturing assets and liabilities are replaced by new assets and liabilities with comparable risk characteristics.

This choice is relevant for many types of credit-sensitive assets when calculating economic capital for credit risk. Loan underwriting commitments constitute one important example. Such commitments often are related to financing mergers and acquisitions, and therefore have a large size. Due to the large size, they can have a substantial impact on concentrations in the portfolio, and thereby economic capital. Once a client accepts a loan underwriting commitment, the bank will usually try to sell (syndicate) a large part of the commitment to other banks in a short period of time. The primary risk is that parts of the commitment can only be sold at a loss compared to the price at which the bank has committed itself to the client. The decline in price can be due to a deterioration of the client's financial prospects. In an extreme situation, the client may default during the syndication period. This risk obviously increases the longer it takes to find other banks that are willing to share in the commitment. When including loan underwriting commitments in economic capital calculations, we must thus make a choice about the time horizon over which the risk of a price decline as well as default are modeled. This time horizon may well be longer than the bank expects it needs for the syndication when entering into the commitment. In the sub-prime crisis, the market for syndicated loans completely dried up, and banks had no choice but to hold on to the remaining positions. As a consequence, they were exposed to price declines on these positions over a much longer period than initially expected, and many banks incurred significant market value losses. Furthermore, we must decide whether to measure the risk only on the actual commitments in the portfolio, or whether to assume that there will be an ongoing stream of loan underwriting commitments during the year.

The choice about the evolution of credit risk in the portfolio is also relevant for money market and derivatives trading lines. In normal times, new transactions typically replace maturing transactions, thereby maintaining approximately a constant level of risk. However, money market and derivatives trading lines are not always communicated to the client. In that case, a bank has the option not to enter into new transactions when transactions mature and in this way reduce the credit exposure when the creditworthiness of the client deteriorates, or when the bank itself is in distress. What choice is made about the evolution of the exposure over time will depend on how likely it is that the bank will reduce the credit exposure in times of distress.

Including Value Changes

Losses due to credit risk can result from actual defaults on required payments by counterparties, or from declines in their creditworthiness. A decline in the creditworthiness lowers the fair value of the claim that a financial institution has on the counterparty, because the counterparty is more likely to default on required payments in the future. A change in the creditworthiness of a counterparty can be reflected by changes in its credit ratings or credit spreads. In Section 3.1, we provided the motivation why it is relevant for financial institutions to take changes in fair value of an institution's assets into account when calculating economic capital. This implies that changes in credit rating and credit spreads should be taken into account in the economic capital calculation for credit risk.

Point-in-time Versus Through-the-cycle

The input data and parameters that are used to calculate economic capital for credit risk may depend on whether the calculated economic capital should represent the best estimate of the potential decline in equity value during next year (point-in-time), or whether it should represent an estimate of the potential decline on average during an economic cycle (through-the-cycle). This choice was discussed in general in Section 3.5. As credit losses tend to vary with the economic cycle, this choice is especially relevant for credit risk. The choice will have particular relevance for the nature of the probabilities of default and rating migration probabilities that are input to the models, and for the other parameters to the extent that they vary with the economic cycle (exposure at default, loss given default, correlations, credit spreads). We will specifically elaborate on this choice when discussing the estimation of probabilities of default in Section 4.2.3.

4.2.2   Modeling Approaches

In this section, we sketch the main modeling approaches that financial institutions use to estimate economic capital for credit risk. The models used typically are referred to as credit risk portfolio models. Our focus will be on the important features of such models that determine their applicability and influence the outcomes, and which are therefore important to understand for managers of financial institutions and other users. Various books and many papers can be consulted for technical details of the various modeling approaches that we discuss, several of which we refer to in the endnotes to this chapter. We distinguish four classes of models:[13] structural models, rating migration models, actuarial models, and reduced-form models.

Structural Models

Structural models have their roots in the valuation method that Nobel laureate Robert Merton developed for the pricing of corporate debt.[14] Structural models start from the capital structure of a firm; that is, how the assets are financed by debt and equity. The uncertainty about the development of the value of the assets over time determines how likely it is that the firm will default. This in turn determines the current value of its debt and equity. We describe how structural credit risk portfolio models can be used to derive economic capital for loan or bond portfolios of a financial institution. In Section 4.2.4, we discuss how other types of credit exposures can be included in credit risk portfolios.

   The loans that a financial institution has provided to firms are part of the debt of these firms. To estimate economic capital for the loan portfolios of a financial institution, structural credit risk portfolio models thus need to assess potential changes in the value of the debt of each firm to which the institution has lent money. This requires that we model potential changes in the value of the assets of each firm, as well as the evolution of its capital structure over time. Using Merton's ideas, this enables a derivation of a probability distribution of potential debt and equity values at the one-year economic capital horizon for each firm. Structural credit risk portfolio models amalgamate these probability distributions of debt and equity values for individual firms into a joint probability distribution covering all firms. From this joint distribution, economic capital for the institution's loan portfolios can be derived as the largest potential decline in the debt value of all firms combined at the appropriate confidence level. Structural credit risk portfolio models can similarly be applied to portfolios of bond investments, in which case they are based on a description of the potential evolution of asset value and capital structure of each bond issuer. Because structural models not only yield values for the debt but also for the equity of firms, this approach can also be used to evaluate potential changes in (private) equity investments of a financial institution in other firms. We will elaborate on this in Section 4.2.4.

The central idea behind the Merton model is that equity holders own a call option on the assets of the firm, with a strike price that equals the amount of debt that has to be paid to the debt holders at its maturity. Because the value of the equity and the debt together equals the value of the assets of a firm, the debt holders by implication own the assets of the firm but have sold a call option on the assets (to the equity holders). In its simplest version, the model of Merton assumes that debt has a fixed maturity date and no coupons are paid on the debt. If the value of the assets at the debt maturity exceeds the amount of debt to be repaid (the strike price), equity holders will exercise their option by repaying the debt to the debt holders. They will then own the remaining assets of the firm. If the value of the assets at the debt maturity is below the strike price, equity holders will let the option expire worthless. The debt holders can then divide the value of the assets between them, but this is lower than the amount they were promised to be repaid. Merton uses the Black-Scholes option pricing formula to determine the value of the call option, and thus the firm's equity value, at the initial date. The value of the debt can then be calculated as the value of the assets of the firm minus the value of the call option. The setup can be generalized to include various kinds of debts with multiple maturities and coupon payments, rendering the equity a more complex call option on the assets of the firm. However, the essential idea of the equity being a call option on the assets of the firm remains the same.

Taking the view that debt holders have sold a call option on the assets of the firm to the equity owners helps to clarify the different interests that both stakeholders have with respect to the properties of the assets in which the firm invests. Specifically, an increase in the volatility of the assets will increase the value of the call option that the equity holders own, and thereby decrease the value of the debt. This is intuitive: the increase in volatility will increase the probability that the value of the assets falls below the amount of debt to be repaid. As a consequence, the default probability increases. Moreover, the loss-given-default increases because the higher volatility increases the probability of large losses for the debt holders. For the equity investors, the increase in volatility increases both the potential payoff from the option and the probability that the option expires worthless, but due to the limited liability of equity investors the former consequence dominates the latter, thereby increasing the value of the call option. This asymmetry between equity and debt holders is at the heart of the debate that originated during the sub-prime crisis about the incentive that exists for managers of financial institutions to increase the risks that the institution takes if they want to maximize the value to its shareholders, to the detriment of the debt holders (as well as the government to the extent that the government protects debt holders, which include deposit holders).

There are a number of challenges for the implementation of structural credit risk portfolio models in practice:

1. We need to specify a process for the potential evolution of asset values of firms over time. However, this asset value cannot be observed in practice. For publicly listed firms, equity values can be observed; for other firms we may have only accounting information.
2. We need to describe the evolution of the capital structure (i.e., the proportion of debt and equity used to finance the assets) as a function of the value of the assets for each firm.
3. We need to capture the dependence between the changes in value of the assets of multiple firms. Because asset values cannot be observed directly, we cannot derive this dependence structure directly from empirical data.

The most widely used structural credit risk portfolio model is the Portfolio Manager model developed by KMV (part of Moody's Investor Services). It makes a number of choices to address the challenges just listed:[15]

- The default threshold for the assets (i.e., the strike price of the call option that the equity holders own) is set equal to the short-term debt of the firm plus half its long-term debt. Short-term debt is the debt that matures before the one-year economic capital horizon, and long-term debt matures after that. The default threshold is assumed to be constant into the future. The equity is treated as a call option with an indefinite maturity, but which ceases to exist as soon as the asset value falls below the default threshold (*down-and-out* call option).
- Potential changes in the value of the assets adhere to the assumptions of the Black-Scholes option pricing formula; that is, the asset value is assumed to follow a random walk (formally, a geometric Brownian motion). For firms with observed historical equity values, the initial value and volatility of the assets are derived from the equity returns. The equity volatility can be estimated from historical equity values. The volatility and the current value of the assets are then derived from the calculated equity volatility and the current value of the equity. This derivation is based on writing the equity value as the value of a down-and-out call option on the assets (see previous bullet).
- Using the chosen default threshold and the derived asset value and volatility, one-year and multiyear default probabilities, in principle, can be derived directly. To control for the impact of the assumptions made for the derivation of the asset and debt value, KMV instead estimates the default probability

(called the expected default frequency (EDF) by KMV) using an extra step. With the estimates of the initial value and volatility of the assets, KMV calculates a distance-to-default. This distance-to-default equals the number of standard deviations that the expected asset value at the horizon is above the default threshold. Using the results of statistical analysis on the relationship between observed default rates and calculated distances-to-default, using historical data pooled for many firms, it translates the calculated distance-to-default for an individual firm to an EDF. This procedure was found to result in more reliable probability of default (EDF) estimates. KMV performs such EDF estimates for both one-year and multiyear time horizons.

- To value loans at the one-year economic capital horizon as a function of the realized asset value at this time, KMV uses the derived term structure of default probabilities, together with an assumed loss-given default.
- For firms without listed shares, the derivation as described previously cannot be directly applied. For such "private firms," the EDF term structure is derived from the term structure of public firms that are comparable with respect to industry, geography, and other risk characteristics.
- To model the dependence between changes in asset values of different firms, KMV again uses historical equity values. Using the procedure just described, KMV translates historical equity values into asset values, and uses the latter to estimate correlations between asset value changes of different firms. Instead of estimating correlations between each pair of firms directly, however, KMV writes changes in the asset value of a firm as a function of a global, a regional, an industry, and a firm-specific factor. These factors are identified using statistical (principal component) analysis on the comovements of historical asset values of all firms. Correlations between different firms then arise through the dependence on the same global, regional, or industry factors. Using such a factor model substantially reduces the number of correlations to be estimated. Furthermore, it provides an intuitive framework to include firms without listed equity values in the correlation structure. By assuming a certain probability distribution for the changes in the global, regional, industry, and firm-specific factors, we can efficiently simulate changes in asset values of all firms.

The KMV Portfolio Manager model, and structural credit risk portfolio models in general, provide an intuitive approach to model the credit risk of a financial institution that results from exposures to corporate counterparties. They incorporate changes in the creditworthiness of firms as reflected in changes of their equity prices. For its implementation in practice, a number of choices and simplifying assumptions need to be made, as outlined for the KMV Portfolio Manager model. How well structural models can capture the credit risk of portfolios of credit exposures depends largely on how realistic these choices and assumptions are. Being centered around equity prices, the application of structural credit risk portfolio models is not so intuitive for the modeling of credit risk arising from retail credit exposures.

Rating Migration Models

Rating migration models link potential changes in the value of credit exposures to changes in the credit rating of the counterparties to which the financial institution is exposed. When a firm to which a financial institution has extended a loan, or from which it has invested in a bond, is downgraded, this will decrease the value of the loan or bond to the financial institution because there is now a larger probability that the firm will not be able to honor its payments on the bond or loan in the future. The starting point for rating migration models is a transition matrix that contains the probabilities that a firm with a given credit rating migrates to a different rating in the course of a certain time horizon (typically one year). Table 4.3 depicts a one-year transition matrix, based on historical rating transitions from Moody's. It indicates, for example, that a firm with rating A at the beginning of a year has, on average, a probability of 87.532% of still having rating A at the end of the year, and a probability of 4.926% of having rating Baa at the end of the year.

A well-known rating migration model is CreditMetrics, which was developed in the 1990s by J.P. Morgan,[16] and has been adapted by many institutions for internal use. To model rating migrations, CreditMetrics introduces a variable for each firm that represents the credit quality of the firm. We will refer to this variable as the "credit-quality variable." If the credit-quality variable has a low value, a firm's creditworthiness (rating) is low, and vice versa. In fact, the realizations of the credit-quality variable can be bucketed, where all values in a certain bucket correspond to a certain rating at the end of the period. For a certain initial rating, the buckets are chosen such that the probability of drawing a realization of the credit-quality variable in each bucket equals the corresponding rating transition probability from a transition matrix. CreditMetrics assumes a Gaussian probability distribution for each credit-quality variable.

The CreditMetrics approach has some apparent similarity to the structural models described earlier. The role of the credit-quality variable in Credit-Metrics resembles the asset value in the structural models, and the default threshold in the structural models corresponds to the default bucket in the CreditMetrics approach. The important difference is that structural models are based on (estimates of) actual values of assets, debt, and equity for firms, whereas CreditMetrics only employs rating migration probabilities. The credit-quality variable in CreditMetrics is simply a modeling construct to be able to efficiently simulate rating migrations of multiple firms.

To model potential rating migrations of multiple firms, realizations need to be drawn for the credit-quality variables for all firms at the same time. In doing so, we need to account for dependencies between credit-quality variables of different firms, reflecting to what extent changes of the credit-quality variables of different firms move together. To model these dependencies, CreditMetrics suggests the use of a factor model, which relates the change in value of the credit-quality variable of a firm to changes in value of indices that correspond to the region and industry in which the firm is active. The idea is similar to the use of factor models

Table 4.3 Average one-year rating migration rates, 1970–2007 (the column WR reflects firms for which ratings have been withdrawn)
(*Source*: Moody's Investor Services)

Cohort rating	Aaa	Aa	A	Baa	Ba	B	Caa	Ca C	Default	WR
Aaa	89,066	7,146	0,611	0,000	0,014	0,002	0,000	0,000	0,000	3,161
Aa	0,991	87,369	6,825	0,253	0,055	0,017	0,000	0,000	0,007	4,483
A	0,069	2,710	87,532	4,926	0,499	0,091	0,025	0,003	0,020	4,125
Baa	0,048	0,224	4,797	84,341	4,324	0,781	0,223	0,022	0,170	5,070
Ba	0,008	0,055	0,395	5,660	75,730	7,672	0,534	0,047	1,096	8,802
B	0,012	0,041	0,154	0,369	5,497	73,580	4,868	0,635	4,488	10,355
Caa	0,000	0,032	0,032	0,192	0,683	9,878	58,129	3,554	14,705	12,794
Ca-C	0,000	0,000	0,000	0,000	0,401	2,630	8,513	38,667	29,975	19,813

in KMV's Portfolio Manager. The factor model requires that sensitivities of the credit-quality variable of a firm to the industry and regional indices are specified. These sensitivities, for example, can be based on the relative shares of the firm's revenues from different regions and industries. Historical equity index returns often are used to estimate the correlations between the regional and industry indices. The sensitivities of each firm's credit-quality variable to the regional and industry indices and the correlations between the regional and industry indices together determine the correlation between the credit-quality variables of individual firms. For firms with listed equity prices, we can backtest the modeled correlations in the factor model to the historical equity correlations.

A question is whether the use of equity correlations as a proxy for the correlations between the credit-quality variables of different firms in the CreditMetrics approach results in realistic rating migration and default correlations between firms. De Servigny and Renault have investigated this question using equity return data as well as Standard & Poor's rating migration data of US firms over the period 1980 to 2001.[17] They conclude that the level of default correlation as implied by equity correlation is *on average* only slightly higher than directly estimated default correlation from rating migration information. This alignment on average masks, however, that the default correlation that is implied by the equity correlation can differ substantially from directly estimated default correlation when they are compared at industry level. De Servigny and Renault find large positive as well as negative differences at industry level. Hence, they conclude that default correlations as implied by equity correlations are not a reliable estimate of directly estimated default correlations. They attribute this to the fact that equity returns are influenced by factors that do not directly relate to the financial soundness of individual firms, such as changes in risk premiums and liquidity in financial markets. In conclusion, using equity correlations as correlations between the credit-quality variables in the CreditMetrics approach may yield a reasonable economic capital estimate for portfolios that are well diversified over different industries and geographies. It may, however, over- or underestimate the actual level of correlation, and thereby economic capital for portfolios that are concentrated in one or a few industries or geographies.

Another question is whether the correlations between asset values that are used in structural models differ significantly from equity return correlations, which the CreditMetrics approach suggests to use. As described earlier, KMV's PortfolioManager derives asset value correlations from equity return correlations for publicly listed firms. De Servigny and Renault analyze the difference between asset value correlations and equity return correlations. They derive asset value correlations from estimated joint default probabilities for firms in the same and in different industries, and conclude that they are very similar to equity return correlations of the same firms. Separately, Mashal, Naldi, and Zeevi[18] reach a similar conclusion. Conceptually, this is also what we would expect. As we saw in the discussion of structural credit portfolio models, equity can be viewed as a call option on the assets of the firm. Because the default probability of most firms is small, this option is typically deep in-the-money. As a consequence, a change in asset value leads to a change in the equity value of (nearly) the same amount. Therefore, we could expect that correlations between changes in equity values are comparable to correlations between changes in asset values.

The final element of rating migration models is that loans or bonds need to be revalued at the economic capital horizon, as a function of the rating that a firm has at that point. CreditMetrics suggests to do this by discounting promised future cash flows at a rating-specific discount curve that is derived from the credit spread curve per rating category at the initial date, in combination with a risk-free (government) yield curve. Although the credit spread curves, and thus the discount factors, differ per rating grade, no uncertainty about credit spreads per rating grade is included, although it is possible to extend the model in this direction.[19] As a consequence, potential declines in market value as a result of spread changes may be underestimated in CreditMetrics (and rating migration models in general).

Another rating-migration credit risk portfolio model is CreditPortfolioView, which has been proposed by McKinsey. It starts by describing speculative-grade default rates as a function of macro-economic variables, such as GDP growth and unemployment rates. The statistical relationship can be estimated from observed historical data, using regression analysis. This can be done for individual sectors in a country if speculative default rates are available at that level. Thomas Wilson reports[20] that results of such regression analyses for industry sectors in the United States, United Kingdom, Germany, and Japan yield very high explanatory power for realized speculative-grade default rates, using data from 1960 to 1992. If we can furthermore establish a forecasting model for the macroeconomic variables employed, we can simulate values for these macro-economic variables into the future, and as a function of these values determine speculative default rates. Based on the simulated default rates, CreditPortfolio-View adjusts the rating migration matrix in such a way that rating downgrades and defaults become more likely if the simulated default rate is above its long-term average, and vice versa. The adjustment of the rating migration probabilities in this manner embeds correlation between rating migrations and defaults of different firms in the model, because the increase or decrease applies to all firms at the same time. Conditional on the adjusted transition matrix, rating migration probabilities of different firms are assumed to be independent.

As a function of the simulated end-of-period rating of each firm, using the adjusted rating migration matrix, the loss or gain in value of the relevant credit exposures can be estimated using a similar approach as described earlier for CreditMetrics. Although appealing in principle, the CreditPortfolioView model does not seem to be widely used in practice. This is probably due to the difficulty of establishing the required relationship between default rates and macro-economic variables for all relevant geographies and industries in which a financial institution is active.[21]

In its basic and most frequently implemented form, a rating migration model assumes that all firms with the same initial rating are subject to the same rating migration probabilities and credit spread curve. This is a drawback compared to structural credit portfolio models, which calculate firm-specific default probability term structures based on individual equity prices. Equity prices are also more responsive to changes in credit quality than rating migrations, thereby potentially providing a more accurate reflection of credit losses if a point-in-time calculation of economic capital is desired. However, in a typical bank portfolio, a small minority of firms has equity that is publicly traded. For other firms, assumptions need to be made in structural models on the parameters of the asset value process. As most banks have internal ratings for all firms to which they have credit exposure, rating migration models can more readily be applied to a bank's credit portfolio. For insurance companies and pension funds, which invest primarily in bonds of publicly listed companies, the latter may be less of an issue.

As we observed for structural credit risk portfolio models, it is less intuitive to apply rating migration models to the modeling of credit risk for retail portfolios. Although most banks assign a credit rating to individual retail clients, the use and estimation of rating migration matrices for retail clients are less common. Furthermore, simulating rating migrations and defaults for individual retail clients will make the overall calculation very time-consuming. To cope with this, sometimes a loss distribution for a retail portfolio is calculated on a stand-alone basis, and then the loss distribution as a whole is linked to a credit-quality variable in the rating migration model. The realization of the credit quality variable is then related to a point on the loss distribution for the portfolio as a whole. The credit-quality variable for the portfolio has to be embedded in the dependence structure of the rating migration model, for example, by linking it to the factor representing the country in which the retail portfolio resides.

Actuarial Models

Actuarial models have their origin in the insurance industry, where they are used to assess the size of potential payouts on insurance policies. Depending on the type of insurance policy, actuarial models describe the uncertainty around mortality, morbidity, and disability rates in a population, or the incidence rate of accidents. The outcome of the models is a probability distribution of potential insurance claims. We can also apply the statistical techniques used in actuarial models to model the uncertainty in default rates. This has been done in the CreditRisk+ model of Credit Suisse,[22] which is the most popular model in this class of credit risk portfolio models. An important advantage of the CreditRisk+ model is that the probability distribution of potential credit losses can be calculated very efficiently, without resorting to simulation. A number of choices in the model have been made to achieve this, which also determine its limitations. We will describe the essential characteristics of the CreditRisk+ model, and highlight its advantages and potential limitations.

If we know the default probability of each obligor in a portfolio, we still do not know which obligors in a portfolio will actually default, and thus how large the loss on the portfolio will be. In reality, we also do not know exactly what the default probability of each obligor is, as we have no perfect model to predict this. For example, the default probability will depend on the general economic situation that will prevail in the coming year, which is inherently uncertain. CreditRisk+ captures both sources of uncertainty in the determination of the loss distribution. To do so, it requires as input for each obligor in the portfolio both a best estimate of the default probability and the standard deviation of the default probability. The standard deviation measures the uncertainty around the expected default probability. The loss in case an obligor defaults is assumed to be known, and also needs to be provided as input.

Because the creditworthiness of all obligors is at least to some extent influenced by the general economic situation that will prevail, it is likely that the default probability of all obligors will at the same time be higher (in case of a bad economic situation) or lower (in case of a good economic situation) than the best estimate. The CreditRisk+ model captures this by writing the default probability of each obligor as a function of a number of common factors, called sectors. The idea is similar to the use of factor models in the modeling of correlations in the structural and rating migration models, the difference being that the factor model in CreditRisk+ relates to default probabilities instead of to asset values (in structural models) or credit-quality variables (in rating migration models). If the realization of a common factor is higher than its expected value, then this will increase the default probability of all obligors that have a positive weight to this common factor, and vice versa. The standard deviation of each common factor is determined by the standard deviation of the default probability of each obligor that has been provided as input, together with the weights of each obligor to each of the common factors. These weights also need to be specified as input for each obligor. Consequently, the common factors in CreditRisk+ are constructed on the basis of the model inputs, and cannot be identified directly with observable factors.

To enable efficient calculation of the loss distribution, CreditRisk+ assumes that each of the common factors follows a particular probability distribution (a Gamma distribution), and furthermore that all the common factors are mutually independent (i.e., there is no correlation between the realizations of the common factors). The latter assumption makes it difficult to interpret these common factors directly as representing industry sectors or geographic regions, because default rates in different industry sectors and geographic regions typically have a positive instead of zero correlation through their common dependence on the general economic situation. The assumption of zero correlation between the common factors makes it difficult to specify the weights of each obligor to each of the common factors (sectors). Generalizations of the CreditRisk+ model have been developed that allow for nonzero correlation between different sectors.[23]

The efficient calculation further necessitates that losses in case of default of all obligors are grouped in buckets, where each bucket contains exposures that are assumed to have the same size. The loss distribution in CreditRisk+ can then be expressed in terms of the default rate per bucket, instead of modelling defaults of all exposures individually. The more buckets are distinguished, the smaller the impact of this approximation will be, but the longer the calculation of the loss distribution will take. Other limitations of the CreditRisk+ model as originally described are that it captures only losses due to default, and not losses due to changes in creditworthiness separate from default. As we have argued in Chapter 3, including general changes in value and not only default losses is preferred for the determination of economic capital. Moreover, CreditRisk+ does not allow for uncertainty in the amount that will be lost in case of default of an obligor. Extensions to the CreditRisk+ model have been developed that relieve some of these restrictions.[24] It is not clear how to include hedges and portfolio management transactions, such as securitizations, in CreditRisk+ without sacrificing the analytic tractability of the loss distribution calculation.

Besides calculating the probability distribution of potential losses, from which economic capital can be derived, CreditRisk+ enables the analytic calculation of the contribution of each obligor to the loss at a particular point of the loss distribution, and thereby to economic capital, as well as to the standard deviation of losses.[25] This is important for the allocation of economic capital and performance measurement.

In conclusion, the CreditRisk+ portfolio model is attractive because it allows for an efficient, analytic calculation of the credit loss distribution. To achieve this, it imposes a number of restrictions on the correlation structure in the model, and on the characteristics of the credit exposures in the portfolio. Whether these restrictions are acceptable for a specific practical application requires evaluation on a case-by-case basis. Although more general versions of the CreditRisk+ model have been proposed in the literature that relax some of the original assumptions of the model, it remains less flexible with respect to the incorporation of nonstandard credit exposures and hedges than the credit risk portfolio models presented earlier, which make use of simulation methods to calculate a loss distribution.

Reduced-form Models

Reduced-form credit risk portfolio models have been developed primarily for the valuation of credit-derivative products, of which the value depends on the value of multiple other instruments that are subject to credit risk (such as bonds, loans, and credit default swaps). Examples of such multiname credit-derivative products are first-to-default credit default swaps, tranches of collateralized debt obligations (CDOs), or total return swaps on a basket of credit-sensitive instruments. Credit-derivative products may be used in the context of credit portfolio management to modify the risk profile of an institution, and as such have a clear link with economic capital calculation. Reduced-form models are not commonly used, however, to assess economic capital for an institution as a whole.

Reduced-form models are similar to CreditRisk+ in the sense that they model the default process of individual firms (names) and combine them to assess potential gains and losses on a portfolio of exposures to these firms. To value credit-derivative products, it is important in many cases to know not only whether a particular firm defaults before a certain time horizon, but also at what point in time default occurs. Taking a single-name credit default swap (CDS) as an example, in case the reference entity of the CDS defaults, then the protection buyer will receive a payout only if the seller of the CDS has not defaulted prior to the reference entity. Furthermore, the seller of the CDS will receive premiums from the buyer of the CDS only until the default date of the reference entity. We therefore need to know not only what the default probability is between two points in time, but also how the default probability changes between these time points.

Reduced-form models extract information on this behavior over time from the term structure of credit spreads or credit default swap premiums in the market. The credit spread or CDS premium is a compensation for the credit risk borne on a reference entity that may default—for example, a firm or sovereign. Its level depends not only on the default probability but also on the loss in case of default. To distill information on the default rate from a credit spread or CDS premium, it is necessary to make an assumption about the amount of loss in case the reference entity defaults. Given such an assumption on the loss in case of default, and if in addition we assume that the credit spread equals the product of default probability and loss-given-default, we can derive an estimate of the term structure of default probabilities.

The default rate that is obtained from credit spreads in this manner, often referred to as the *risk-neutral* default rate, is typically substantially higher than the actual probability of default, however. This is due to the fact that the credit spread not only contains a compensation for the expected credit loss on the instrument, but also a risk premium to compensate for potential unexpected losses (comparable to a cost of capital). In addition, the credit spread may contain a compensation for other risks, for example, liquidity risk.[26] Although risk-neutral probabilities of default are central to the pricing of credit-derivative products, for the calculation of economic capital we need actual default probabilities. To obtain an estimate of the actual default probability from credit spreads or CDS premiums, we need to correct for the risks that are not related to expected credit losses. Alternatively, we could use term structures of default rates derived from historical rating agency information, but then we lose the link with the specific reference entity of the credit-derivative product, as well as with the actual market situation.

Correlation between defaults of different firms can be embedded in different ways. In the model developed by David Li,[27] which has become the market standard for the valuation of multiname credit-derivative products, first a probability distribution of the time until default (survival time) of each firm is estimated. This can be derived from credit spreads or historical default rate information as described in the previous paragraph. Correlation between the survival times of different firms is embedded in this model through a copula function, which ties the individual probability distributions of the survival times together using a dependence (correlation) structure. Various choices for such a copula are possible in principle. The one most often used in practice is the Gaussian copula, for which David Li shows that there is a one-to-one correspondence with the CreditMetrics model that we discussed earlier. Copulas are discussed further in Section 4.8.2 on risk aggregation.

Other reduced-form models embed correlation directly in the default rate processes of individual firms by including one or more common factors in these processes. These common factors typically are assumed to cause jumps in the default rate of all firms at the same time, thereby inducing correlation, but the timing of such jumps is random.[28] When used for the pricing of credit-derivative products, the parameters in the correlation structure (i.e., correlations in the Gaussian copula model, or the probability and size of jumps in the default rate processes) usually are estimated from available market prices of standardized credit-derivative products.

If the credit portfolio of an institution contains credit derivative instruments with multiple reference names, whether as a hedge against other exposures or not, then we face the challenge of assessing potential gains and losses on these products when estimating economic capital. Whichever credit risk portfolio model the institution has chosen to use for the estimation of economic capital for its credit portfolio, it then also needs a consistent valuation model for these credit-derivative products. As reduced-form models can provide analytic valuation formulas under simplifying assumptions, they can fulfill a useful role in this context even if they are not frequently used to estimate economic capital itself.

The fact that reduced-form models are not commonly used for economic capital calculations is due primarily to the difficulty to calibrate the models, because market data on credit spreads or CDS premiums is available only for a small set of firms in the credit portfolio of a typical financial institution. Even if available, extracting information on actual default probabilities from credit spreads or CDS premiums is not straightforward, as mentioned earlier. The availability of market data for a relatively small set of firms also complicates estimation of the parameters that drive the default rate correlations between different firms. For economic capital calculations, it is more important to model the event of default than the timing of default, while reduced-form models are aimed at modeling the timing of defaults because this is often crucial for the valuation and hedging of credit-derivative products. Although reduced-form models can thus fulfill a useful role to assess potential value changes of credit-derivative products in the context of a credit risk economic capital calculation, they are less suitable to calculate economic capital for an institution's total credit portfolio.

Comparison of Different Model Approaches

In this section we have reviewed the main approaches that are used in practice to calculate economic capital for credit risk, and emphasized their attractive features as well as potential limitations. We have summarized the main attractive features and potential limitations in Table 4.4. Which type of model is most suitable in a particular setting depends on the specific portfolio of credit exposures under consideration, and which characteristics of the model are most important in relation to its use.

Table 4.4 Summary comparison of credit risk portfolio models

Model type	Attractive features	Potential limitations
Structural models	• Use counterparty-specific information on equity prices and balance sheet composition. • Responsive to changes in market view on creditworthiness of counterparties.	• Not directly applicable to counterparties without public equity. • Not applicable to retail credit portfolios.
Rating migration models	• Based on institution's own assessment of creditworthiness (rating) of counterparties. • Applicable to wide variety of credit exposures.	• All counterparties with same credit rating exhibit same migration and default dynamics. • Less amenable for retail credit portfolios.
Actuarial models	• Efficient calculation of loss distribution. • Based on institution's own assessment of creditworthiness (PD) of counterparties.	• Restrictive assumptions with respect to correlation structure, incorporation of fair value changes, and inclusion of complex credit products.
Reduced-form models	• Use counterparty-specific information on credit spreads and CDS premiums. • Responsive to changes in market view on creditworthiness of counterparties. • Explicitly model timing of defaults.	• Not directly applicable to counterparties without quoted credit spreads or CDS premiums. • Developed for pricing of credit derivatives, not directly applicable to calculation of economic capital.

Although the various credit risk portfolio models appear to be quite different, it is not clear whether these differences also result in different outcomes when they are applied to a given credit portfolio of loans or bonds.

Several studies have analyzed the similarities and differences between different types of credit risk portfolio models in terms of both the mathematical formulation and the outcomes that the models yield for hypothetical portfolios.[29] These studies show that simplified versions of these models can be written in mathematically equivalent form. They also derive how parameters can be chosen so that the resulting default rate and its potential variation (standard deviation) over time are equal in the various models. Several of the studies also show, however, that matching the average default probability and its standard deviation can still result in significant differences between estimates of potential losses in the tails of the distribution. The percentage differences in economic capital estimates can be 10% or more. These differences arise from the different probability distributions that are assumed for the common factors that drive correlation between defaults in the different models, and how these common factors influence the default probability of all obligors in the portfolio. Additional differences may result from the use of different sources of data to estimate the parameters in each model (e.g., use of equity returns compared to variability in observed default rates to estimate correlations). Using different data sets to estimate parameters may yield different values for the variability of default rates in each of the models, thereby contributing to differences in economic capital estimates.

In practice, it is often not easy to estimate precise values for the default probability and its variability (or more generally, the correlation between defaults) for a given portfolio of credit exposures. This is true in particular for portfolios of obligors of high credit quality, as few actual defaults have happened for such firms in the past to which the results of any estimates can be benchmarked. It is even more difficult to obtain evidence on the shape of the tail of the credit loss distribution from which economic capital estimates are derived. This was discussed earlier in Section 4.1.6 on the validation of economic capital estimates. Which of the portfolio models that we have reviewed provides the most realistic estimate of the tail of the credit loss distribution therefore is hard to tell. For any chosen type of model, it is advisable to benchmark the model to other models occasionally, and compare the results with those of independently developed stress tests (see Section 6.1).

The International Association of Credit Portfolio Managers (IACPM) and the International Swaps and Derivatives Association (ISDA) jointly have conducted a benchmarking study of credit risk portfolio models that banks use for internal purposes.[30] In this study, 28 banks participated, some of which used Moody's KMV PortfolioManager, CreditMetrics, or CreditRisk+ directly, whereas others used variants of these models that were developed internally. If input (portfolio) data and model parameters are aligned between the internal models used by banks, the study shows that the expected loss and economic capital outcomes are similar. However, some of the standard settings differ between the models, for example, with respect to how loans are valued at the one-year horizon, and whether coupons during the first year are assumed to be lost in the event of default or not (affecting the effective loss-given-default). Such differences can lead to significant differences in economic capital estimates. The study further indicated that banks use different methods to calculate economic capital contributions for subportfolios and individual loans, which can lead to substantial differences. This illustrates the importance of making a conscious choice for the method used to calculate economic capital contributions (see Section 4.1.4).

The various comparisons conducted between credit risk portfolio models indicate that the mathematical formulation, choice of probability distributions for the factors that drive correlations, definition of input data, and calibration of model parameters can all influence the amount of economic capital that results from the models in a significant way. It is therefore important to understand the consequences of particular choices made, and, as there is often no conclusive evidence on the best choice, to conduct comparative analyses on the impact of different choices.

4.2.3   Determination of Model Parameters and Inputs

In this section, we review a number of important issues related to the determination of inputs to and parameters of credit risk portfolio models. Key inputs and parameters are the probability that a counterparty will default (probability of default, PD), the exposure that the institution will have on the counterparty at the moment of default (exposure at default, EAD), the loss that the institution will suffer in the event that the counterparty defaults (loss given default, LGD), and the correlations between changes in the creditworthiness of different counterparties.

We will not elaborate on techniques that can be used to determine these inputs and parameters, since that is beyond the scope of this book. Rather, we highlight properties that may have a significant impact on the outcome and use of credit risk portfolio models in practice and therefore are important to be aware of when applying the available techniques and interpreting the outcomes of the model. The endnotes contain references to some of the literature on techniques that can be applied to determine model parameters and inputs.

Whatever method is used to estimate model parameters and inputs, they will be subject to estimation uncertainty. In Section 4.1.5, we discussed in general how we can account for parameter uncertainty in economic capital estimates. For credit risk portfolio models specifically, Gunter Löffler[31] has investigated the impact of uncertainty in estimates of default probabilities, recovery rates, and the dependence structure on resulting economic capital estimates for credit risk. He concludes that the impact can be material.

Estimating Default Probabilities

The starting point in credit risk analysis is the creditworthiness of a counterparty. In credit risk portfolio models this is reflected in the probability that the counterparty will default within a specific time horizon. The probability of default (PD) may be a direct input into credit risk portfolio models (as in rating migration and actuarial models), or derived from other information on the counterparty (e.g., using equity prices and debt values in structural models, and credit spreads in reduced-form models).[32] The probability of default usually relates to a one-year time horizon in practice, which is consistent with the time horizon used for economic capital.

To estimate a probability of default, we first need to define what constitutes a default. Basel II defines that default occurs at "the moment that the bank considers that the obligor [counterparty] is unlikely to pay its credit obligations to the banking group in full, or the moment that the obligor is past due more than 90 days on any material obligation to the banking group." The probability of default depends on how narrow or broad the chosen definition of default is. The broader the definition of default (i.e., the more extensive the list of events that constitute a default), the higher the corresponding probability of default. This will be compensated, however, by a lower average loss given default, which we will discuss later.

The default definition under Basel II implies that a counterparty defaults on all obligations to a financial institution at the same time. As a consequence, all exposures to a counterparty have the same probability of default. The only exception is lending to sovereigns. They can default on one obligation and not on another because bankruptcy laws do not apply to sovereigns. Consequently, different exposures on a sovereign can have different default probabilities. Basel II allows banks to estimate different default probabilities for foreign and local currency claims on sovereigns, but in principle it is possible to differentiate default probabilities further between different types of sovereign claims. For example, default probabilities may differ between sovereign exposures related to export finance, co-lending with multilateral organizations, central bank exposures, bonds, and loans.

A counterparty may also default on its obligations because the government of the country in which it resides imposes restrictions on the transfer of money abroad, or the convertibility of local currency into foreign currency. We will refer to this as a transfer and convertibility (T&C) event. T&C events are outside the control of the counterparty and unrelated to its creditworthiness, but can force it to default on its foreign currency obligations. It is possible to include the probability of default due to a T&C event in the overall probability of default of a counterparty. This is not desirable, however, because default due to a T&C event is very different in origin and consequences from default due to insolvency:

- A T&C event will cause the counterparty to default on its foreign currency obligations, but not on its local currency obligations.
- The loss to the institution in a T&C event is likely to be very different from the loss in the event that the counterparty defaults because of insolvency.
- In a T&C event all counterparties with foreign currency obligations in a country will default at the same time, and hence the correlation between defaults of such counterparties in T&C events is +1.

As a consequence, an institution may choose to assess and model the risk of a T&C event separately from the counterparty-specific default risk. We will return to this when we discuss the inclusion of country risk in credit risk portfolio models in Section 4.2.4.

Estimating default probabilities poses additional challenges if there are covenants in place that require a counterparty to post additional collateral if the covenant is breached. For example, loan agreements may stipulate that a counterparty has to deposit additional collateral in case its credit rating is downgraded. When the rating downgrade occurs, it will cause a deterioration of the liquidity situation of the counterparty, which may trigger a negative spiral of diminishing trust of lenders, creditors, and customers, and a further deteriorating liquidity situation that can ultimately lead to default. This nearly happened to the insurance company AIG when it was required to post additional collateral to its counterparties in September 2008 after its credit rating was downgraded. The US Federal Reserve prevented default of AIG by extending a loan of USD 85 billion that enabled AIG to make the required collateral postings (later, additional loans were provided to AIG to avoid default). This illustrates the importance of taking contingent obligations into account when estimating the default probability of a counterparty.

A choice needs to be made whether the PD should represent a point-in-time or a through-the-cycle estimate. We introduced this distinction in Section 3.5 for the calculation of economic capital itself, and there is obviously a direct relation to the character of the probabilities of default. A point-in-time estimate reflects the best estimate of the probability of default during the coming period, which generally is either the tenor of the loan or one year. It takes the current economic environment into account and thus will increase in economic downturns and decrease in favorable economic times. Because PD estimates in structural and reduced-form credit portfolio models usually are derived from current market information (equity prices or credit spreads), they will be point-in-time estimates. The resulting economic capital estimate will then also have a point-in-time character.

In Section 3.5.2 on the cyclicality of economic capital, we noted that rating agencies strive for through-the-cycle credit ratings. To associate a PD with a through-the-cycle credit rating, institutions usually take an average of the realized default rate for the credit rating class in question during one or more full economic cycles. We noted in Section 3.5.1 that such estimates are subject to statistical uncertainty, especially for good credit ratings. As realized default rates vary over time with the economic cycle, there is a difference between an estimated through-the-cycle PD and the realized default rate. The size of the difference depends on the phase of the economic cycle. When financial institutions calibrate their internal ratings to those of rating agencies, they will inherit the through-the-cycle nature of the rating agency ratings. If the probabilities of default associated with the internal ratings are subsequently input to rating migration or actuarial credit risk portfolio models, the resulting economic capital estimate thus also will have a through-the-cycle character.

In practice, the ideal of through-the-cycle ratings is hard to achieve and ratings do change due to cyclical effects because, as S&P states, "rating through the cycle requires an ability to predict the cyclical pattern [which is] difficult to do." In fact, credit rating agencies typically put somewhat more weight on the short-term perspectives than on the longer-term ones when assigning credit ratings for counterparties with a low creditworthiness, which brings a point-in-time element into their through-the-cycle philosophy. To what extent point-in-time features are embedded in the ratings and related default probabilities can be assessed by looking at the number of rating upgrades and downgrades that occur over time. In deteriorating economic circumstances, the number of rating downgrades by rating agencies tends to exceed the number of rating upgrades, and vice versa when the economic environment improves. The higher this variation, the more the ratings are point-in-time.

Banks often use point-in-time methodologies in consumer lending. In corporate and commercial lending, both point-in-time and through-the-cycle systems are used. To understand the variability of economic capital over time we need to know whether point-in-time or through-the-cycle default probabilities are used. Although financial institutions often use different types of default probabilities next to each other in economic capital models, ideally a consistent choice for either point-in-time or through-the-cycle default probabilities is made. The choice of point-in-time or through-the-cycle default probabilities should align with the intended purpose of economic capital to represent a point-in-time or a through-the-cycle estimate of the potential decline in the institution's equity value.

Estimating Exposure at Default

The second credit risk parameter that we need to estimate is the size of the exposure on a counterparty at the moment of default. For term loans and bonds this exposure at default (EAD) will depend on the size of the loan or bond, the coupon rate, and the redemption schedule. For revolving loans the exposure may be anywhere between zero and the loan limit, and potentially even higher if the limit is overdrawn. Typically, companies in distress have negative cash flows and finance this by drawing on their credit lines. Data from rating agencies confirms that outstanding amounts under revolving loans tend to increase in the run-up to default.[33] The ability of the counterparty to draw upon existing credit lines will depend on loan covenants and the credit monitoring practices within a financial institution. To the extent that these covenants and practices have a significant influence on realized EAD, institutions will have to rely on internal data to estimate EAD.

The Basel II regulations stipulate that institutions must incorporate a margin of conservatism if there may be a positive correlation between EAD and default rates. In general, we would expect that closer monitoring of credit exposures takes place during an economic downturn. This would cause a negative correlation between EAD and default rates. Ultimately, the actual relationship between EAD and default rates depends on the actual credit management practices of an institution.

Correlation between default rates and EAD can also be a function of the nature of the credit products involved. As an example, we consider the exposure arising from derivatives transactions. The size of this exposure will vary with changes in market variables, such as interest rates, credit spreads, equity prices, foreign exchange rates, or commodity prices. If these changes in market variables are correlated with changes in the creditworthiness of the derivatives counterparty, then this causes a correlation between the likelihood of default and the size of the exposure at default. For example, interest rates and equity prices tend to decrease when economic circumstances deteriorate and default rates rise. Whether there is a negative or a positive correlation between the likelihood of default of a counterparty and its exposure from derivatives transactions will depend on the nature of the transactions, for example, whether the counterparty has a long or a short position in interest rates and equity prices through the derivatives transactions.

When there is a positive relationship between the level of exposure and the likelihood of default of a counterparty, we speak of wrong-way exposures. Wrong-way exposures are risky for institutions, because the exposure may be at an acceptable, low level during good times, but the institution may in fact lose a much larger amount if the counterparty experiences financial difficulties. Wrong-way exposures can arise in various ways, and often are related to derivatives transactions. We present a few examples.

The first example is a cross-currency swap with a counterparty in a country with a weak currency, in which the counterparty receives its home currency and pays a strong currency. A weakening of the home currency will lead to an increase of the exposure on the counterparty, and this is likely to coincide with a deterioration in the credit quality of the counterparty. To illustrate, suppose a US institution entered in April 2008 into a six-month cross-currency swap with an Icelandic bank, in which the US institution would receive USD 100 million and pay 7.2 billion Icelandic Krona at maturity. As long as the actual forward exchange rate remains close to the exchange rate agreed upon in the swap, then the net exposure of the institution on the Icelandic bank will be close to zero. However, when the crisis hit the Icelandic banks in October 2008, the exchange rate had changed from 72 to 127 Krona per US dollar. As a consequence the net exposure on the Icelandic bank increased from nearly zero to USD 43.3 million. This increase would occur at the worst of moments, namely, when the counterparty was in distress.

Another example of potential wrong-way exposure can be found in derivatives transactions between banks and hedge funds. Hedge funds often execute derivatives transactions with only a few banks (prime brokers). As a consequence, if a hedge fund faces large losses on its derivatives positions, this is likely to correspond to a large positive exposure of a prime broker on the fund. If the losses are large enough for the hedge fund to default, the claim of the prime broker on the hedge fund will be at its maximum. To reduce the risks stemming from such potential wrong-way exposure, prime brokers have collateralization agreements in place with hedge funds. As a consequence, hedge funds must offset exposure increases by posting additional collateral with the bank. When large unexpected market moves occur that lead to large losses on the hedge fund positions, the fund may not be able to liquidate sufficient assets in a timely manner to post the additional required collateral to the prime broker. The prime broker may thus incur a loss that is equal to the uncollateralized part of the exposure if the hedge fund subsequently defaults.

Wrong-way risk can also arise from credit derivatives positions if there is significant correlation, or even a direct relationship, between the creditworthiness of the counterparty and the value of the underlying security in the transaction. If we buy protection from a counterparty for potential losses on a bond, a loan, or some other security (reference security) through a credit derivative, then the value of this protection will increase if the risk of loss on the underlying security increases. If the creditworthiness of the counterparty decreases at the same time, however, it becomes less likely that the counterparty will be able to provide protection just when we would need it. This type of wrong-way exposure may be of a statistical nature (e.g., when the counterparty and the reference security relate to the same industry or country), but there may also be a direct relationship.

An example of the latter situation is the large amount of protection that a number of insurance companies, in particular monoline insurers, had provided up until 2007 on structured credit products with mortgage-related assets as reference assets. When losses on the mortgage-related assets increased significantly, and much more than expected, it became more likely that these insurers would have to pay out on the protection they had sold. The market value of the protection bought from the insurance companies thus increased. Some insurance companies had sold such large amounts of protection on similar assets, that their own future had become closely linked to the performance of the mortgage-related assets. For example, AIG had sold USD 440 billion of credit protection to other market participants. The default of some, and the severe credit rating downgrades of several other monoline insurers during the subprime crisis, was a direct consequence of this dependence. Financial institutions that had bought credit protection from the monoline insurers incurred significant losses as a result, either because the protection fell away (when the insurer defaulted) or because the fair value of the protection dropped significantly (when creditworthiness of the insurer decreased).

Identification of wrong-way risks requires an in-depth analysis of the nature of the credit exposure and the counterparty. In credit risk portfolio models the exposure at default is often a fixed number. An underestimation of this input parameter will obviously lead to an underestimation of economic capital. If the exposure at default of a material part of an institution's portfolio depends on the realization of specific risk drivers or the occurrence of a specific event, then we would ideally include this dependence explicitly in the portfolio model. Examples of risk drivers that may influence the exposure at default of many counterparties at the same time are market variables for the exposure resulting from derivatives exposures, or country-specific events for cross-border exposures.[34]

Estimating Loss Given Default

The third credit risk parameter that we discuss is the loss given default (LGD), representing an estimate of the amount that a financial institution will lose if a counterparty defaults. The loss given default usually is expressed as a percentage of the outstanding amount at the time of default. The recovery rate is the part of the exposure at default that is repaid in case of default, and is thus the complement of the LGD. The LGD can depend on many factors, such as the seniority of the claim, the collateral available, and the applicable jurisdiction(s). The way in which a financial institution handles the work-out of distressed loans may also influence the realized losses. For example, some institutions sell the defaulted exposure immediately after default or outsource the work-out process, whereas other institutions have their own work-out departments.

The level of the LGD estimates furthermore has a dependence on the definition of default used. The broader the definition of default, the more events of default will be triggered, including some that ultimately may not result in a loss. As a consequence, the LGD will be lower with a broad definition of default than with a narrow definition. Since the expected loss of a loan, which is the product of PD and LGD, is independent of the definition of default, a lower estimated LGD will be accompanied by a higher estimated PD.

Empirical studies of realized losses on traded debt typically measure the realized LGD as the difference between the nominal value of the debt and the market price of the debt one (or more) month(s) after default. This is the market-LGD. Alternatively, a work-out LGD can be calculated on the basis of the discounted value of the cash flows received after default. As the work-out period can sometimes take several years, establishing the work-out LGD takes considerably more time than is required for the market-LGD, and moreover may be complicated if payments in kind (e.g., equity) are received. However, the work-out LGD is not subject to market sentiments or the (temporary) illiquidity of the market for distressed assets. The potential unavailability of market prices is also a restricting factor for the use of market-LGDs. Most financial institutions therefore estimate LGD values from internal experience, based on the actual recovered amounts on defaulted loans and other credit exposures.

Empirical data shows that realized LGD values vary widely between 0 and 100% of the exposure at default.[35] Realized losses are often zero, because the defaulted company may have been restructured successfully and can continue its operations without the need for a write-off by its debt providers. At the other extreme, losses may be very high as collateral is not available, has not been properly documented, or has lost its value. In fact, LGD distributions often have two peaks, one near the 0% loss and a second one at a loss rate close to 100%.[36] This is illustrated in Graph 4.3 with Moody's loss data. There is thus considerable variation around an estimated average LGD, and the realized loss in individual cases is likely to differ significantly from the average LGD. The graph also illustrates the differences between bonds and loans, which may be related to their relative seniority. Moody's observes that the uncertainty of the LGD assessments is higher for debt in the middle of the debt structure of a company than for very senior or very junior types of debts. The reason is that very senior and very junior debt will in general experience very low and very high losses, respectively. For debt types that are in the middle of a company's debt structure, the losses will be more dispersed around their average.

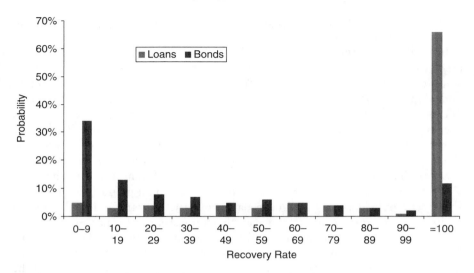

Graph 4.3 Loan and bond work-out recovery rate distribution.
Source: "Back-testing Moody's LGD methodology," Moody's Investor Services, June 2007.

Several studies have investigated whether LGD realizations are related to economic downturns and realized default rates.[37] The studies mostly focus on bonds and loans for which traded market prices are available, and compare the market price before and after default. They typically find a positive correlation between realized LGD and default rates. The intuition behind this positive correlation is that a high number of defaults will lead to a high supply of assets to be liquidated. Hence, the value of these assets will decrease, which will result in lower recovery and higher LGD. However, we should be careful to apply the conclusions from these studies directly to an individual institution because the relevant work-out practices, types of exposures, and collateral may differ substantially from the setting in the studies. For example, an institution with a work-out practice that avoids forced liquidations in an illiquid market, but waits until markets have become more favorable, may show higher than average LGD that is less correlated to default rates.

Basel II captures the potential correlation between LGD and default rates by way of a "downturn LGD." This is an estimate of the LGD that would be realized in an economic downturn. It requires an estimate of the relation between the LGD and the default rate, as well as an estimate of the default rate that is applicable in an economic downturn. The downturn LGD is expected to be higher than the average LGD, resulting in a higher minimum regulatory capital requirement. If the same downturn LGD is used in economic capital models, also a higher economic capital will result. We can achieve a more precise impact of the variability in LGD on economic capital by using the actual probability distribution of the LGD in combination with an estimated correlation with default rates.

In addition, correlation may exist between the value of collateral and the creditworthiness of the counterparty. A typical example is a loan to a shipping company secured by a mortgage on its ships. A depressed freight and shipping market is likely to both increase the probability of default and decrease the value of the collateral. The estimated value of the ships in the hypothetical situation that the counterparty is in default will thus be lower than expected ship prices in nonrecessionary times. To reflect this, the LGD should be higher than the loss based on current ship prices.

Some financial institutions reflect the presence of guarantees in the LGD value of the exposures that are guaranteed. A loss on a guaranteed exposure will occur only if both the counterparty and the guarantor default, and in addition the guarantor defaults before the counterparty. In that case, the loss equals the loss on the exposure without a guarantee. In all other cases, the loss is zero. It is impossible to reflect this binary situation through an adjustment of the LGD. The only way to capture the dependence of the loss on the default of both the counterparty and the guarantor is by explicitly including the default risk of both counterparty and guarantor in the economic capital calculations. In this way, it is also possible to capture the dependence between counterparty and guarantor default properly, as well as wrong-way risk, if present. We will return to the modeling of this double-default risk in the next section, when we discuss credit risk hedges.

Estimating Correlations

The central part of an economic capital model for credit risk is how dependencies between changes in creditworthiness of different counterparties are included. Correlations have a large influence on the estimate of economic capital. To illustrate this, we consider a portfolio with a large number of one-year loans that all have the same size, a uniform probability of default of 1%, and a uniform LGD of 60%. The expected loss of this portfolio thus equals 0.60% of the exposure-at-default of the portfolio (60% of 1%). We have used the simplified credit risk portfolio model that forms the basis of the formula to calculate the minimum capital requirement for credit risk in the Basel II Accord (see Section 4.2.6) to derive the one-year loss distribution for this portfolio. This loss distribution considers only potential losses due to default during the one-year horizon and ignores the income on the loans as well as changes in fair value. Graph 4.4 displays the loss distribution for three different assumptions about the asset correlation (the Basel II Accord prescribes correlation values between 12 and 24% for corporate, sovereign, and bank exposures, depending on the probability of default; 15% for residential mortgage portfolios; and between 3 and 16% for other retail exposures, again depending on probability of default).

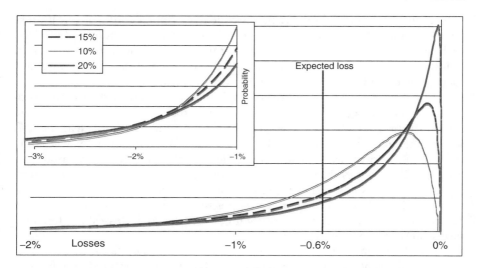

Graph 4.4 Credit loss distribution for different values of the asset correlation, using the capital requirement formula in the Basel II Accord. The insert shows the distribution of losses between −1% and −3%.

Although the expected loss is the same in all three cases, the distribution of potential losses differs substantially. For all three correlation values, the probability that actual losses will be smaller than the expected loss is more than 50% (between 60 and 70%, depending on the correlation), but there is a small probability that they will be much larger. The higher the correlation, the larger the probability is of either very small or very large losses, as visible in the graph. The insert in the graph shows more clearly how the probability of large losses increases with the asset correlation. Economic capital will therefore also increase with the correlation. At a confidence level of 99.9% (which is the confidence level used in the Basel II Accord), the largest potential loss equals 4.65% when the correlation is 10%, 6.62% when the correlation is 15%, and 8.73% when the correlation is 20% (we need to subtract expected loss of 0.6% to derive economic capital at a confidence level of 99.9%). Hence, the estimate for the correlations in a portfolio of credit exposures will have a significant impact on economic capital.

As we observed in Section 3.5, defaults occur in waves related to the general economy. Hence, the first source of correlation is the general state of the economy. Although defaults rise across the whole economy in an economic slowdown, the extent and the timing of a rise in default rates will vary between industry sectors. This is caused by the nature of the industries, and the way in which the effects of a slowdown are transmitted through the economy. When modeling correlations between defaults, it is important to take such economic relationships into account.

In a typical economic slowdown, a decline in consumer confidence will cause people to hold off on purchases of luxurious and expensive goods and services, such as cars, other durable goods, and travel. A slowdown in these cyclical industries in turn will affect industries that supply parts and raw materials, such as steel and plastics. Furthermore, manufacturers of capital goods will be affected, as companies hold off on replacing or expanding the existing production facilities. Over time, the slowdown forces companies to restructure their operations and lay off employees. Higher unemployment (or fear thereof) will further reduce expenditures by individuals and companies, exacerbating the economic downturn. The longer and deeper the downturn is, the more also noncyclical industries that produce basic consumer goods will be affected. Such a pattern explains how defaults rise gradually over time in an economic downturn, and how different industries are affected at different points in the cycle and to a different extent. This directly influences the credit losses that financial institutions will experience.

The fact that industries may be affected at different points in the cycle suggests that the time interval over which correlations are measured may be relevant for the value of the correlation. For example, if weekly or monthly default or equity return data is used to estimate correlations, then the correlation between cyclical and noncyclical industries may appear low as firms in these industries default or change in value in different periods. However, if quarterly or annual data is used, then more firms in both types of industries may default or experience similar changes in value. The estimated correlation will then be higher. It is, therefore, advisable to analyze how sensitive the estimated correlations are for different time intervals, and determine what the most appropriate time interval is.[38]

A sector that often has been at the source of a general economic downturn, and frequently caused problems for financial institutions, is the real estate sector. The sub-prime crisis is no exception to this. When the economy is doing well, demand for new houses and commercial real estate by individuals and companies tends to increase. As construction of new real estate to satisfy the increased demand takes a significant amount of time, a shortage may persist over an extended period, driving up prices and thereby mortgage costs. The increase in prices encourages additional real estate development, and increases the demand for loans to finance this. Once supply catches up with demand, prices will stabilize, or may even drop in case an oversupply arises. If the oversupply increases and persists over some time as a result of the completion of real estate development that was originated in the past, prices may fall further. Together with a slowdown in real estate development, this typically causes financial problems for real estate developers, construction companies, and suppliers. The effect on the economy is exacerbated as real estate constitutes a significant part of the net worth of companies and individuals, and lower prices will reduce their net worth. This may hurt consumer and investor confidence, which may trigger an economic downturn, causing demand for real estate to fall and contributing to the decrease in prices. For individuals that are heavily indebted because of a high mortgage, the lower prices may result in a negative net worth. If they also experience a decrease in income or an increase in mortgage payments, they may default on their mortgages. Firms may get into financial distress because of the economic downturn, and become unable to fulfill their mortgage payments. Banks often have significant direct exposures to real estate: they finance real estate developers and construction companies, provide residential mortgages to private individuals, and commercial mortgages to firms. When individuals default on their mortgages, they may simultaneously default on other obligations such as credit cards and personal loans. Firms that default on a commercial mortgage will also default on other loans. A real estate crisis thus potentially induces correlations across different loan portfolios. The correlations that are embedded in credit risk portfolio models should ideally reflect such general economic dependencies and interrelationships.

When we described the various types of credit risk portfolio models in the previous section, we discussed that default dependencies can be estimated from different sources of data: directly from observed default rates, from observed equity returns, or from asset returns (with asset values typically derived from equity prices). For portfolios of credit exposures to consumers and small companies, financial institutions often use historical default and loss data to estimate correlations. Ideally, internal data is used for this purpose, as it captures the specific nature of the credit exposures and the institution's risk management practices, but many institutions supplement this with an analysis of industrywide data. Industrywide data is usually available for longer periods of time, and may therefore contain the loss experience during one or more economic downturns. Including such periods is important to provide a good estimate of correlations in bad economic times. To estimate dependencies between defaults of corporate counterparties, financial institutions often use equity or asset return data, and distinguish geographical and industry dimensions.

A complication is that correlations tend to vary over time.[39] Hence, correlations may have been low during a period in the past, but may be higher in the future. Especially when aiming for a point-in-time calculation of economic capital, we should take this time dependence into account. For a through-the-cycle estimate of economic capital, we may be tempted to use a long period of historical data from which to estimate correlations, so as to average over periods of high and low correlation. When doing so, however, we must be sure that no structural break has occurred that causes correlations to be permanently higher or lower than in the past. As an example, since the formation of the European Union the correlation between equity returns of firms in different countries has gradually increased.[40] Estimates of correlations that are based on a long period of historical data may then be significantly lower than actual correlations. It is thus important to analyze the time dependence of correlations, and combine the results from a statistical analysis with a more fundamental one on potential shifts in the overall level of correlation from the past due to changes in the economic environment or the structure in a particular industry.

Correlations may also depend on factors other than industry and geography. For example, a number of studies have found that equity prices and asset values of large firms are more highly correlated to general market circumstances than small firms.[41] The common explanation is that large firms typically comprise a variety of activities, and thereby are internally more diversified than small firms. As a consequence, a significant deterioration in the financial position of a large firm requires that several of its activities perform poorly, which is most likely to happen because of a downturn in general market circumstances. The difference in correlations that is found thus is attributed to the size of the firm, but the actual explanation relates to differences in the breadth of activities between different firms. Although correlations can be differentiated according to the size of counterparties in a credit risk portfolio model, ideally it would relate directly to the extent to which a company is specialized or diversified in its activities.

If large firms are assigned a higher correlation with the market in general in a credit risk portfolio model, this does not mean that we will observe relatively more defaults of large firms than small firms in economic downturns. The reason is that large firms also typically have a better credit rating than small firms, and therefore, a lower probability of default. The default probability is lower precisely because of their typically larger internal diversification of activities. Although the *asset* correlation thus may be higher between large firms and the market in general, this is not necessarily the case for the (implied) *default* correlation.

In the formula for the minimum credit risk capital requirement in the Basel II Accord under the internal-ratings-based (IRB) approach, the asset correlation is a decreasing function of the probability of default for corporate exposures. Although in an indirect manner, this aims to incorporate the higher correlation for large firms with the general state of the economy because large firms tend to have better ratings than small firms. Gordy and Heitfeld[42] have analyzed whether implied asset value correlations are a function of the credit quality of firms in general, but do not find a statistically significant relation. A general dependence of the asset correlation on the probability of default is also not intuitive. If a firm increases its leverage, thereby increasing its default probability, it would imply that the asset correlation decreases. However, without a change in assets, the asset correlation should remain unchanged. In general, it is important to explore the underlying rationale for any correlations found through statistical analysis, as an economic explanation may help to point to the actual source of the correlations found, and thereby provide clues to how correlation risk can best be measured and managed.

In conclusion, when estimating correlations for credit risk portfolio models, it can be important to differentiate between credit portfolios in different sectors of the economy and different geographic regions, as they may exhibit different default and loss dynamics. Various data sources can be used to estimate correlations, including historical default and loss data, as well as equity prices. The history should be long enough to reflect experience in bad economic times, as this is especially relevant for economic capital estimates. Furthermore, we should be aware that correlations may change over time as a result of structural changes in the economy or industry sectors. Hence, historical data may not always be a good guide. Correlations between counterparties may also depend on other factors, for example, to what extent they specialize in a particular activity, or comprise a variety of different activities.

Individual Versus Aggregated Exposures

Ideally, we take the specific risk characteristics of each individual loan or other credit-sensitive asset into account in economic capital calculations. For large portfolios of small exposures, such as retail portfolios of loans to private individuals or small companies, it is practically not possible to do this. Institutions usually subdivide such portfolios in groups of homogeneous exposures (e.g., with comparable size and default probability), and then treat such a group as one aggregate exposure. Because counterparty-specific risks have no material impact on economic capital estimates in portfolios that contain a large number of exposures of similar size and risk characteristics, treating them as an aggregate exposure will not impact the calculated amount of economic capital in a significant way. If there are single exposures that are significantly larger or riskier than the bulk of a portfolio, it is important to include them individually in the calculations to adequately capture the impact of such a risk concentration on economic capital. This will often be the case for portfolios of loans to large companies. Many financial institutions therefore include loans or other credit exposures to large companies on an individual basis in credit risk economic capital models.

4.2.4   Special Topics

In this section we review a number of topics that require special attention in the modeling of credit risk.

Short Maturities

In Section 4.2.1, we discussed the choice of what to assume about loans or other credit-sensitive assets (credit exposures) that mature within the one-year capital horizon. If we assume that a maturing asset will not be rolled over into a new one, then a loss can arise only if the counterparty defaults before or at the maturity of the exposure. It is then necessary to determine the timing of default in a credit risk portfolio model.

For some types of credit exposures, such as loan underwriting commitments that we discussed in Section 4.2.1, it is not clear beforehand what the actual duration of the exposure will be. This duration may well be longer than initially expected if the counterparty, or the financial institution itself, gets into distress. As economic capital represents stress losses, it is important to take this potential longer duration of the exposures into account.

Very short maturities apply when including settlement risk in a credit risk portfolio model. Settlement risk represents the credit risk that arises in the settlement of transactions. For example, it can be present when buying or selling a security from a counterparty in exchange for cash, or in case of an exchange of two cash amounts in different currencies in relation to a foreign-exchange transaction. The risk is that the institution performs its part of the exchange by transferring money or a security to the counterparty, but the counterparty fails to perform his or her part of the exchange. Although the risk may exist for only a few days, the amounts involved can be large. To include settlement risk in a credit risk portfolio model, we need to assess the settlement risk profile per counterparty during the one-year horizon as a function of the outstanding transactions. In addition, an assumption can be made on additional settlement risk that arises from future transactions during the coming year.

To mitigate settlement risk, settlement of transactions can be carried out through a clearing house. Each party in a transaction then transfers the money or security to the clearing house, and the clearing house transfers this to the other party only when both parties have fulfilled their obligations. Although this eliminates the settlement risk on a counterparty, it replaces it with credit risk on the clearing house. The remaining credit risk is usually much smaller, however, due to the high credit quality of most clearing houses and the fact that transactions with different counterparties that are executed through the same clearing house can typically all be netted.

Defaulted Assets

For defaulted assets, there is clearly no default risk anymore, but there still exists risk with respect to the ultimate recovery on a defaulted asset. When a counterparty defaults, an institution makes a provision for the loss that it expects to incur on the claims outstanding on the counterparty. This is usually a best estimate of the loss that will be incurred. The realized loss, however, may turn out to be higher than the provision that has been made. This recovery risk should be included in the economic capital calculation. If correlation exists between recoveries on different defaulted counterparties, then this correlation can be embedded in the credit risk portfolio model as well. This can be done by introducing an additional factor in the correlation model that drives recoveries on all defaulted assets, or by linking the recovery realization per defaulted asset to existing (geographic and industry) factors in the correlation structure. In the latter case, this enables inclusion of a negative correlation between the recovery on defaulted assets and default rates in the model.

Credit Risk Hedges

In the past, financial institutions reduced the exposure to credit risk primarily by obtaining third-party guarantees. In the past decade, they also have obtained the possibility to manage credit risk through credit default swap (CDS) transactions and by securitizing pools of assets on the balance sheet. We will describe the features of these credit risk management tools in this section, and highlight the challenges they pose for economic capital modeling.

Companies and financial institutions can reduce credit risk by paying a third party to guarantee future counterparty payments or insure potential credit losses. The guarantee usually relates to specific assets that the financial institution owns. In the past decade, an active market in CDSs has developed, which allows participants to buy protection against credit losses on predetermined (reference) assets. These reference assets may be different from the specific assets that a financial institution owns. For example, the CDS could reference a bond, while the institution has extended a loan to the counterparty on which it buys credit protection through the CDS (the reference name). The institution is then exposed to the risk that the loss on the loan in case of default may differ from the loss on the reference asset in the CDS.

A guarantee or CDS does not fully eliminate credit risk, since the possibility exists that both the counterparty of the original credit exposure and the party that provides protection against losses on this exposure default. This usually is referred to as double-default risk. Only when the protection provider is deemed to have no default risk, as may be the case for some government guarantees, may credit risk be considered as fully eliminated. To include double-default risk accurately in economic capital calculations, we need an estimate of the probability of default for both the counterparty and the protection provider. In addition, we need to assess the dependence between changes in creditworthiness of the counterparty and the protection provider. The probability of a double-default event is lower than both the probability of default of the counterparty and the probability of default of the protection provider, provided that default of one does not automatically imply default of the other.

When assessing the dependence between counterparty and protection provider, we need to take into account that through the protection itself there is a direct relation between counterparty and protection provider, and not just a statistical correlation, because default of the counterparty will have direct financial consequences for the protection provider. As a result, it may be prudent to set the modeled correlation between the counterparty and protection provider in credit risk portfolio models higher than the statistical correlation estimated from past data.[43] In case the protection provider has sold significant amounts of protection on the same or similar securities, then this may lead to wrong-way risk, as we discussed for monoline insurers in the previous section.

We further need to decide to which party the economic capital contribution resulting from the double-default risk will be allocated: to the original counterparty or to the party providing the protection? There is no clear answer to this question, as the remaining exposure is a function of the joint default probability. Whatever choice is made for the allocation, it is worth monitoring the exposure as part of the total exposure to both original counterparty and protection provider, because credit exposure concentrations in a portfolio can exist with respect to each of them.

In case credit protection is bought through a CDS, the maturity of the CDS may differ from the maturity of the credit exposure that is hedged. A financial institution may choose a shorter horizon for a CDS hedge on purpose, but a maturity mismatch can also arise because a liquid market for CDS contracts exists only for certain standard maturities. In addition, a mismatch between the size of the credit exposure and the notional amount of the CDS may exist, for example, because the credit exposure has become larger or smaller since the CDS hedge was put in place. Furthermore, a financial institution may not be able to buy protection in the CDS market on a specific counterparty, but only on a related entity (e.g., the parent company or a firm that is active in the same sector). However, changes in the creditworthiness of the related entity may not move in parallel with those of the counterparty to be hedged. If such imperfect hedges make up a material part of the portfolio, we must decide how much benefit to give to such hedges in economic capital calculations, and how they can be included in a chosen credit risk portfolio model.

Financial institutions also increasingly have used securitization transactions to reduce credit risk. In a traditional securitization, the institution sells loans on its balance sheet to a separate legal entity that typically is set up solely for the purpose of the securitization (a special purpose vehicle; SPV). To buy the loans, the SPV attracts funds from outside investors and divides the revenues from the loans, but also the losses due to defaults, between the investors. In almost all securitizations, the funding is divided into various tranches that differ in seniority and, therefore, risk profile. Investors have a choice to invest in one or more tranches. The most junior tranche is called the equity and will absorb the first losses on the pool of loans. The size of the equity tranche is usually a few times the expected loss on the pool of loans, and in normal circumstances it will absorb all losses on the pool of loans. On top of the equity, there are typically a number of successively more senior tranches. Investors in a particular tranche will incur losses on their investment only if actual losses on the pool of loans have exceeded the size of all tranches that are more junior. The coupon of each tranche obviously decreases with the seniority of the tranche. Almost always, the institution retains a large part of the equity in a securitization. It may thus still absorb most losses on the pool of loans, but it has capped its potential (unexpected) loss. By retaining part of the equity, the bank maintains an economic interest in monitoring the quality of the counterparties of the loans and minimizing losses on the pool of securitized loans.

Instead of the traditional securitizations as just described, banks also increasingly have engaged in synthetic securitizations in which loans are not actually transferred to a SPV, but protection is bought on pools of loans through credit derivative transactions. These credit derivatives usually provide protection against losses on the pool between a certain minimum and maximum amount, comparable to a tranche in traditional securitizations. In such a synthetic securitization, the bank will be exposed to counterparty risk on the party that sells the protection, which needs to be accounted for in economic capital calculations.

It is a challenge to capture securitization transactions that extend over multiple years properly in credit risk portfolio models with a one-year horizon. In principle, we can accomplish this by including potential market value changes during the one-year horizon, as we have advocated should be done in general for exposures that mature beyond the one-year horizon. Calculating and embedding market value changes of securitization transactions in credit risk portfolio models is no mean feat, however, given the complexity of these transactions.[44] This complexity is increased by additional features that many securitization transactions incorporate in practice beyond the basic structure just described. Examples of such features are reserve accounts, the ability to change the pool of loans over time subject to certain substitution criteria, requirements to maintain a minimum overall credit quality and diversification within the pool, and maintenance of minimum overcollateralization and interest-coverage clauses.

Most of the securitizations that banks have carried out in the past in fact have not materially reduced economic capital, due in large part to the losses that banks have tended to retain through the equity tranche. An important motivation to enter into securitization transactions has been to obtain regulatory capital relief under the Basel I Accord. The Basel II Accord has removed the incentive to enter into securitization transactions for regulatory capital purposes alone. Securitization transactions will therefore increasingly be evaluated for their economic capital consequences. In addition, securitization of assets may continue since it provides an alternative source of funding.

Trading Book Exposures

As we discussed in the context of the estimation of exposure at default, derivatives transactions pose a specific challenge because the market value of derivatives, and thereby the credit exposure, varies with changes in market variables such as interest and exchange rates, equity prices, and commodity prices. Ideally we would include the variability of the relevant market variables, and the resulting variation in credit exposure, directly in credit risk portfolio models if credit risk from derivatives transactions forms a material part of an institution's overall credit risk.[34] However, such models quickly become rather unwieldy. Most institutions therefore represent credit exposure arising from derivatives transactions as a loan-equivalent exposure, and then effectively treat it as a loan in economic capital calculations.

The loan-equivalent exposure is determined per counterparty, taking into account all outstanding derivatives transactions with the counterparty. It usually is calculated as the average expected exposure (AEE)—that is, the expected level of credit exposure, averaged over all points in time during the one-year time horizon. If there is significant correlation between the level of credit exposure and the creditworthiness of the counterparty, with wrong-way risk as the extreme situation, then this must be accounted for in the AEE calculation. The Basel Committee refers to the AEE as the expected positive exposure (EPE), and allows banks to use it as the basis for minimum regulatory capital requirements for credit risk arising from trading books.[45] Just taking the AEE as loan-equivalent exposure ignores the additional risk posed by the variability in the level of exposure over time, however. To compensate for this, the AEE is usually increased by a certain percentage. Empirical analyses for typical trading portfolios within banks indicate that an increase of the AEE with 10% or less is sufficient to avoid an underestimation of economic capital.[46] Such a small percentage is sufficient because there tends to be no systematic relation between changes in the level of credit exposure on different counterparties and changes in their creditworthiness. For banks, this is intuitive because for any long position of a counterparty in one market variable, there will be another counterparty with a corresponding short position, assuming that the bank hedges itself against market risk. The Basel II Accord specifies a default value of 1.4 for the scaling factor that needs to be applied to the EPE, but allows a bank to estimate the scaling factor itself based on its specific counterparty trading portfolios, subject to a minimum value of 1.2.

The calculation of the AEE should also reflect the choices made about the dynamics of the trading portfolio with a counterparty, in particular if trades that mature within one year are assumed to be replaced by similar trades. In addition, banks often have collateralization agreements in place with counterparties to mitigate credit risk arising from derivatives transactions. When the net market value of derivatives transactions with a counterparty increases, and thereby the credit exposure, a collateralization agreement requires the counterparty to post collateral to reduce the credit exposure. The actual credit exposure on the counterparty is then the difference between the net market value of all derivatives transactions and the value of any collateral posted. When calculating a loan-equivalent exposure, it should relate to the exposure net of any collateral posted. This net exposure may increase to the next point in time that a counterparty can be requested to post additional collateral. If negative correlation exists between changes in the credit exposure and the value of the collateral posted, this can be taken into account. A specific consideration is the presence of gap risk; that is, the risk that sudden large market moves cause a large increase in exposure. This would require the counterparty to post a lot of additional collateral at one time, possibly increasing the probability of default. Although a collateralization agreement clearly reduces credit risk, it introduces some additional operational risk, as the credit exposure with the counterparty needs to be monitored closely, and collateral has to be requested or posted when necessary.

Country Risk

There are several country-specific events that have a direct or indirect impact on the credit losses that a financial institution may incur. In this section, we discuss sovereign defaults, maxi-depreciation events, and transfer and convertibility events. These events are important because they typically impact a large number of counterparties at the same time. We will elaborate how this can be embedded in economic capital calculations.

The first type of country event that we consider is default of the sovereign of a country. When this happens, an institution suffers a credit loss on its direct exposure to the defaulting sovereign. When discussing the estimation of default probabilities in the previous section, we noted that sovereign counterparties may be selective in the types of liabilities on which they default. For example, a sovereign may choose to default on foreign currency but not on local currency obligations, or vice versa. To reflect this, credit rating agencies as well as many financial institutions assign both a foreign-currency and a local-currency rating to sovereign counterparties, and associate different default probabilities with each. Although separate events, there will be a strong correlation between them, which must be taken into account in credit risk portfolio models.

Sovereign defaults are seldom isolated events, and history has shown that sovereign defaults often have occurred in waves. When looking back over the past few centuries, the latest peak in sovereign defaults occurred during the 1980s and 1990s when a large number of less developed countries defaulted on debts that had accumulated during many years. Earlier peaks in sovereign defaults occurred during the Great Depression of the 1930s, the period after 1870, and during the Napoleonic War. Thus, sovereign defaults exhibit clear correlation.[47] Estimating the correlation between different sovereigns is, however, difficult as there are no equity prices available and historical default data may be limited and not representative of current circumstances. Changes in credit spreads on sovereign bonds and CDS premiums are sometimes used to estimate the dependence between potential default events of different sovereigns.

Sovereign defaults can have significant contagion effects. For example, local banks are often highly exposed to the sovereign and governmental entities, and may become insolvent as a direct result of a sovereign default. Furthermore, a sovereign default will typically lead to higher inflation and reduced government spending. As a result, many firms and individuals may go bankrupt. A sovereign default, therefore, will lead to significantly higher default probabilities of many counterparties in the local economy.

A second country event that can have a significant effect on many firms and individuals is a large depreciation (maxi-depreciation) of the local currency. For example, after the fall of the Thai baht in August 1997, 65% of Thailand's companies had severe liquidity problems and nearly 25% were insolvent. These figures were even worse for Indonesia in 1997 and 1998, when nearly 80% of all firms had severe liquidity problems and 65% were insolvent after a maxi-depreciation of the rupiah.[48]

The case of Indonesia was remarkable as government finances were relatively sound and most macro-economic indicators were favorable when compared to other countries. An important cause of the crisis was the fact that many Indonesian firms and banks had borrowed in foreign currencies, because of the prevailing lower interest rate on foreign currency loans. When the

Indonesian rupiah began to depreciate after the fall of the Thai baht, these firms had to hedge their open positions to avoid severe losses, and these hedging activities led to a further depreciation of the rupiah. As a consequence, inflation increased to 50% and the value of the corporate debt measured in rupiah increased significantly, resulting in defaults on a large scale. Furthermore, 16 banks became insolvent and had to be closed by the government.[49]

What emerges from the Indonesian example is that a maxi-depreciation of the currency can have significant consequences for many private firms and banks. This is particularly the case if they are exposed to currency risk, which is the case when their revenues and (debt) costs are denominated in different currencies. In the recent past, maxi-depreciations occurred in Turkey (2001) and Argentina (2001–2002), and caused many banks and private firms to default. In the case of Argentina, not only private firms, but also the sovereign was exposed to currency risk as most public debt was denominated in US dollars. On top of that, the Argentinean government had significant debts outstanding with local banks and residents. As a result, after the maxi-depreciation of the peso, the Argentinean government defaulted on its debt, which caused the insolvency of the local banking system and the ensuing severe economic crisis in the years thereafter.[50]

These cases illustrate that contagion effects can be severe in the event of a maxi-depreciation or a sovereign default. The contagion effects may be very different and more severe than during a regular economic downturn upon which the model correlations may be based. As a consequence, it may be necessary to include the potential occurrence of a maxi-depreciation and of a sovereign default explicitly in credit risk portfolio models. When such en event occurs, then the default probabilities of all counterparties exposed to such an event will increase at the same time. This increase in the probability of default in these circumstances can be embedded in the estimate of the overall probability of default of a counterparty, by specifically assessing its vulnerability to, respectively, a maxi-depreciation and a sovereign default. The default probability of the counterparty is then constructed as a function of three parts: a part that represents the default probability in case of a maxi-depreciation event, a part that represents the default probability in case of a sovereign default event, and a part that represents the default probability in case neither of these events occur. The overall default probability is a weighted average of these parts with the weights reflecting the probability of a maxi-depreciation, the probability of a sovereign default, and the probability that neither event occurs. By explicitly accounting for country events in credit risk portfolio models, and by reflecting them in the default probability estimates of counterparties, we avoid that the impact of this type of low-probability/high-severity event is disregarded or underestimated. Such underestimation could be the result if the default probabilities are based only on historical default rates.

In the discussion on the estimation of default probabilities, we argued that a transfer and convertibility event also is best included as separate event in a credit risk portfolio model. Including it as a separate event enables us to properly reflect the immediate impact on counterparties with foreign currency obligations in the relevant country, and apply a suitable loss given default amount. Because transfer and convertibility events are temporary, if a counterparty is able to survive the duration of the event, the actual loss will be limited to the time value of money on the payments in foreign currency that could not be made on time during this period. Given the direct impact that a transfer and convertibility event has on all foreign currency obligations in a country, we argued that the probability of such events should be modeled separately, and not be included in the default probability of individual counterparties.

Private Equity

Many financial institutions have units that specialize in private equity investments. A significant part of these investments comprises so-called leveraged buy-out transactions. By taking a large equity stake in the firm, the intent is usually to force a management change and increase the efficiency of the firm in question. The equity investment then typically is combined with an increase in the leverage of the firm, so that an improvement in the operating efficiency has a larger impact on the value of the equity investment. The aim is to sell the equity investment after a number of years with an attractive profit.

Many financial institutions estimate the price risk of such equity investments using market risk methodologies. Because often no market values are available for these equity participations themselves, the price risk is derived mostly from the price risk of what are deemed comparable equities for which market values are available. In leveraged buy-outs, however, the specific capital structure of the firm may have a large influence on the potential gains and losses on the equity participation. As such, structural credit risk portfolio models provide an intuitive starting point to model the risk of the equity participation more directly.[51] The parameters of the model, and in particular the asset volatility, may still need to be derived from information on comparable listed companies, after correcting for differences in leverage. The firm also needs to be embedded in the overall dependence structure of the credit portfolio model, which may be intuitive if this dependence structure has industry and geographic dimensions.

Private equity investments also take place in start-up companies. The participations then are commonly referred to as venture capital. For venture capital investments, the hope is that the companies will be successful and profitable in a number of years, after which the participation can be sold with a handsome profit. A majority of venture capital investments may not be successful, but the losses on these often are compensated by large increases in the value of the successful ones. The price risk of venture capital investments is less amenable to include in one of the credit risk portfolio models discussed, because there is often no historical information available on which to base risk parameters. Moreover, it is difficult to find comparable firms for a start-up company, which can provide guidance with respect to the choice of risk parameters. To model the risk of a portfolio of venture capital investments, we can look at the historical performance of venture capital investments in general and its variability, and extrapolate that to the venture capital portfolio under consideration. This type of analysis is closer to the approaches that usually are applied for market risk than for credit risk modeling.

A company in which a financial institution has a private equity participation may be consolidated on its balance sheet if the institution has a controlling stake in the company. In that case, the participation usually is included at book (historical cost) value instead of market value, unless the market value is lower than the book value. When comparing estimates of potential changes in value for such participations with available capital, both need to be measured on a comparable basis, as discussed in Section 3.6.1.

Structured Credit Products

Large losses on structured credit products, and in particular those based on sub-prime mortgages, were at the root of the sub-prime crisis that started in the summer of 2007. The actual losses on these products far exceeded potential loss estimates that resulted from the risk management models that banks and insurance companies had been using. To understand the reasons behind these unexpectedly large losses, we start by describing briefly the origins of the sub-prime crisis.[52] Subsequently, we provide an overview of "lessons learned," which not only relate to the representation of the risk of structured credit products, but also highlight issues that became apparent during the sub-prime crisis and which are relevant for a proper representation of risks in general in economic capital models. For structured credit products specifically, we present a numeric example to illustrate the difficulty of representing the risk using traditional credit ratings, and the high sensitivity of potential losses on structured credit products to errors in the estimates of credit-risk-related parameters.

In the years before 2007, US mortgage originators gradually relaxed underwriting standards for new mortgages, and increasingly provided mortgages to less creditworthy (sub-prime and Alt-A) borrowers. These relaxed underwriting standards were driven by a large demand from a variety of investors (including pension funds, hedge funds, insurance companies, and investment banks) for residential mortgage-backed securities (RMBS) and other structured credit assets. In the low interest rate environment that prevailed, these securities promised attractive yields while carrying seemingly little risk. The RMBS were issued by special-purpose vehicles (trusts) that bought mortgages from banks and other financial institutions, and allocated the cash flows and losses from the pool of mortgages into various tranches that differed in risk profile and yield, similar to what we described earlier for securitization transactions in the context of credit risk hedges. Senior tranches with high ratings from rating agencies often were sold to investors directly, while riskier (mezzanine) tranches were in demand by arrangers of collateralized debt obligations (CDOs). The institutions that had originated the mortgages usually kept a stake in the equity of the pool, and thus remained exposed to the first losses on the pool.

Arrangers of CDOs, often investment banks, bought lower-rated tranches of various RMBS, together with tranches of securitizations of other asset types (e.g., credit cards and auto loans), and used these as an underlying pool for new securitization structures. The senior tranches of these CDOs again received high ratings from the rating agencies and could be sold to institutional investors, whereas the riskier tranches often were kept by the CDO arrangers or sold to hedge funds. In some cases, investors invested in tranches in combination with an insurance (wrap) by a monoline insurer against losses on the tranche, which gave the investments an ostensibly very secure triple-A status. This business was lucrative for all parties involved: for the institutions that originated the mortgages and sold them to the RMBS trusts at attractive prices; for the financial institutions that acted as arranger and servicer of the RMBS and CDOs for the fees this generated; and for the investors because of the seemingly attractive yields relative to the risk involved.

The high demand for securitized assets and the attractive fees that could be earned provided a strong incentive for mortgage originators to originate as many mortgages as possible. As a consequence, they became increasingly accommodating toward prospective clients by reducing documentation requirements, relaxing borrower due diligence, and providing additional incentives to take out new mortgages. Often no, or only a small, down payment was required from new clients who applied for a mortgage. Less creditworthy borrowers were offered mortgages with low teaser rates for the first two or three years. The idea was that the anticipated rise in house prices would enable the borrower to refinance his mortgage at a cheaper rate before the end of this period, and thus before the mortgage rate would increase substantially. However, when the rise in house prices stalled in 2006 and turned to a decline in 2007, the new homeowners were not able to refinance their mortgages. In addition, information from mortgage brokers on the creditworthiness of new mortgage applicants proved to be incomplete or inaccurate in many cases. The actual credit quality of the new mortage owners turned out to be worse than represented.

As a consequence, losses on sub-prime mortgages underlying securitization transactions were much higher than originally envisioned, especially for the pools of sub-prime mortgages (vintages) that were originated between 2005 and 2007. As a result of the high losses on sub-prime mortgages, losses on the equity pieces of the RMBS and CDO structures that financial institutions had retained were also higher than expected. In addition, they incurred fair value losses on investments in more senior tranches in their trading books, due to the increased probability that actual losses would be incurred some time in the future. Being essentially leveraged securities, the RMBS and CDO tranches are much more sensitive to changes in the value of the credit risk parameters than the underlying mortgage pools, as we will illustrate with a numerical example later. Fair values were further depressed by a general increase in risk aversion in credit markets.

That the losses spread so widely through the financial system can be attributed partly to the fact that all parties relied heavily on the ratings that the credit rating agencies assigned to the RMBS and CDO tranches. Investors usually did not have sufficient information about the underlying assets to perform an independent credit analysis. There was thus an industrywide dependence on the assessments and models of the rating agencies. When rating a new structure, rating agencies rely heavily on the historical performance of the specific underlying assets, or pools of assets that are deemed similar in risk characteristics. They further relied on information provided by the mortgage originators and servicers that proper due diligence had been performed with respect to the credit quality of the underlying mortgages. As the quality of the mortgage pools for new CDO structures significantly decreased over time, losses were much higher than experienced on older pools. As a consequence, the rating agencies had to lower the credit ratings of a large number of structured credit products, often not long after they had assigned the initial rating. For example, by July 2008 Moody's had downgraded at least one tranche from 90% of all asset-backed-security (ABS) CDOs it had rated. For Fitch and Standard & Poor's, this was 85% and 82%, respectively.[53] Not only did each individual investor in, and guarantor of, structured credit products thus have significant exposure to model risk related to the rating-agency models, there was also a common dependence (correlation) across the industry on these models. This common dependence negatively affected all financial institutions, as the large losses caused a shortage of capital for many institutions and an industrywide reluctance to lend money to other institutions, thereby increasing the funding costs for all. For several institutions, this led to acute liquidity problems and the necessity for governments to provide liquidity or funding guarantees, and to prop up the capital of the institutions involved.

A clear lesson from the sub-prime crisis is that it is dangerous to rely on someone else's credit analysis and models, especially when assuming credit exposure to unfamiliar and complex products. For economic capital modeling, the experiences during the sub-prime crisis highlight various issues with respect to the inclusion of structured credit products, and the reflection of correlations. Without pretending to be exhaustive, we outline a number of important "lessons" here.

- A financial institution can be involved with structured credit products in any of the roles that we encountered: as originator of the underlying assets, as arranger and servicer of an RMBS or CDO trust, as investor, and as seller of credit protection on specific securities. Although each of these activities may reside in a different part of the organization, it is important to aggregate the exposure across all activities to properly reflect correlations and concentration risk in economic capital calculations. A particular challenge exists if exposures to structured credit positions reside in both banking and trading book, as potential changes in market values for trading book positions are captured under market risk instead of credit risk. To properly capture the dependence between losses on the underlying pools of assets requires an economic capital calculation that integrates market and credit risk.
- As a result of their complexity, it is difficult to assign an accurate fair value to structured credit products. Quoted market values are usually not available, and financial institutions therefore have to rely on internal models to

estimate fair values. Given the lack of market prices, especially during a crisis, it is difficult to determine reliable values for the parameters in these models. When financial institutions had to sell structured credit products during the sub-prime crisis, the realized market value was often well below the estimated fair value. There is thus substantial model risk involved in estimating potential changes in fair value during the economic capital horizon, which is important to include explicitly in economic capital estimates. Even though it may not be possible to determine precisely how large the valuation uncertainty is, it is still much better to include an estimate of the valuation uncertainty in the economic capital calculation than to completely ignore it. We note that there will also be a positive correlation between model errors for different products if there is correlation between potential losses on the underlying assets, increasing the impact of model risk on economic capital.

- The deterioration of the performance in the pools of sub-prime mortgages occurred more uniformly across the United States than was the experience in previous periods of increased default rates. This can be attributed at least partly to the change in the mortgage industry from an originate-to-hold to an originate-to-sell model. Due to the incentives that this presented for increased mortgage origination, as we discussed earlier, this led to an increase in house prices across the country. When losses on the mortgages started to increase beyond earlier expectations, and investors became wary, fewer newly originated mortgages could be sold for securitization purposes, and house prices were affected across the country. This illustrates that correlations may change over time in response to structural changes in an industry, which we highlighted in Section 4.2.3 when discussing the estimation of correlations for credit risk portfolio models in general.

- As direct exposures to different types of credit products tend to be correlated, structured credit products based on different types of underlying credit products will be correlated as well. For example, if private individuals default on their mortgage payments, there is also a higher probability that they will default on credit cards and personal loans (e.g., auto loans). This contributes to a positive correlation between losses on mortgages, credit cards, and personal loans, which should be reflected in credit risk portfolio models. It would be natural to use these correlations also as the basis for assessing correlation between different structured credit products that are based on pools of mortgages, credit cards, and personal loans.

- The large losses incurred on investments in RMBS and CDO tranches based on pools that included sub-prime mortgages had the effect that investors lost confidence in structured credit products in general. As a consequence, financial institutions had to reduce the estimated fair value of their holdings of structured credit products in general, even though asset categories like corporate loans had not experienced significant increases in default rates. Correlations derived from historical loss data may thus underestimate correlations between fair value changes of products based on different asset categories.

- Different structured credit products may be based in part on the same underlying assets, thereby increasing correlation and concentration effects in the overall portfolio. For example, CDOs on pools of corporate exposures (or reference names in case of a synthetic CDO, based on credit default swaps) tend to include a limited set of a few hundred large international companies. Tranches of two or more different corporate CDOs may thus well have an overlap in the names involved. To properly account for the resulting single-name concentrations in economic capital calculations, it is necessary to "look through" the structure of the transactions and identify the overlap in the underlying pools.

As we noted in the description of the sub-prime crisis, financial institutions heavily relied on the credit ratings that rating agencies assigned to structured credit products. The credit ratings assigned by rating agencies aim to reflect the probability that a loss will be incurred. Rating agencies have used the same rating scale for structured credit products as for corporate bonds. This gives the impression that the risk of a structured credit product with a certain rating is comparable to the risk of a corporate bond with the same rating. Although the probability that a loss is incurred may be the same for both, the risk profile of structured credit products is quite different from corporate bonds. We will use a numerical example to illustrate this. Specifically, we illustrate that credit ratings that are based on the default probability do not provide an adequate picture of the risk profile of structured credit products. That is, two structured credit investments with the same probability of default can have a very different risk profile. In addition, we will show that an estimate of potential losses on structured finance assets (and thereby the economic capital required) is much more sensitive to parameter misestimation (model risk) than losses on the underlying pool. As a consequence, for economic capital purposes it is important to monitor closely the performance on the underlying asset pool, and adjust the risk parameters of structured credit products in a timely manner when the actual performance differs from the assumptions used in the initial risk assessment.

Our numerical illustration starts with a pool of sub-prime mortgages that has a total size of USD 50 million, and we assume that each individual mortgage in the pool has a probability of default (PD) of 10% and a loss-given-default (LGD) of 20%. These parameters are roughly equal to historically observed values for sub-prime mortgages. The expected loss on the pool then equals USD 1 million. We assume that the pool of mortgages is the basis of an RMBS structure, and we consider the tranche of the RMBS structure that bears the losses on the mortgage pool when they exceed USD 5 million (attachment point) and are smaller than USD 6.5 million (detachment point). We calculate potential losses on the pool of mortgages using the model that underlies the minimum capital requirements for credit risk in the Basel II Accord (see Section 4.2.6), and assume a correlation of 15% in this model. This is the correlation parameter that the Basel II Accord prescribes for residential mortgages.

We note that the following illustrations do not depend on the assumption that the underlying pool of assets consists of sub-prime mortgages. The conclusions drawn are equally valid if we would consider a pool that consists of other assets like prime mortgages, credit card receivables, auto loans, or corporate bonds and loans.

The Deficiency of Credit Ratings Based on Default Probability

If we perform the calculations as described, we find that the probability that losses on the pool will exceed USD 5 million within a one-year horizon, and thus that the RMBS tranche under consideration experiences a loss in the first year, equals 0.046%. According to historical default rate statistics from rating agencies (see Table 3.1), this would correspond to a rating of approximately single A. Due to the small probability of incurring a loss at all, the expected loss on the RMBS tranche is negligible (equal to USD 200). To calculate a stand-alone capital requirement for an investment in the RMBS tranche (or, equivalently, for providing a guarantee against losses on the RMBS tranche as many monoline insurance companies have done), we use a confidence level of 99.98%. Such a high confidence level corresponds roughly to the triple-A credit ratings to which monoline insurance companies aspired. With a probability of 99.98%, losses on the mortgage pool will not be larger than USD 5.39 million. The capital requirement for the RMBS thus equals USD 390 thousand (= 5.39 mln – 5 mln – 200). This is 26% of the RMBS tranche notional of USD 1.5 million.

From this calculation it is clear that the probability of losses on the RMBS tranche does not change if we change the detachment point of the tranche from USD 6.5 million to some other value. If a rating of the RMBS tranche is based purely on the probability of incurring a loss on the tranche (which many rating agencies state as being their rating philosophy), then the credit rating would not change when we change the detachment point. The absolute amount of economic capital also would not change (remaining at USD 390,000) if the detachment point is changed, but as a percentage of the RMBS tranche notional the economic capital decreases (increases) if the detachment point increases (decreases). Hence, relative to the size of the RMBS tranche, the risk decreases if the tranche width increases, while the credit rating remains the same.

The deficiency of using the probability of loss as a risk measure for structured credit products can be illustrated further if we consider a second pool of sub-prime mortgages with the same size and characteristics as the pool we just described, except that we assume a correlation of 5% instead of 15% within the pool. If we consider an RMBS on this pool that covers losses on the pool between USD 2.9 and USD 4.4 million, then the probability of incurring a loss on the RMBS is also approximately 0.046%. Based on the default probability only, this would yield the same credit rating as the RMBS we considered on the first pool. The maximum loss on this second RMBS at a confidence level of 99.98% is only USD 186,000 instead of USD 390,000 on the first RMBS, however. The lower correlation in the second pool of mortgages reduces the likelihood of extreme losses in the pool, and hence the risk for the second RMBS. This illustrates the effect that the correlation within the underlying pool of assets has on the risk of an investment in a RMBS tranche, which is not captured by a rating based on the probability of loss.

The Sensitivity of Losses on Structured Credit Products to Parameter Misestimation

Suppose we have misestimated the probability of default of the mortgages in the pool, and it is 11% instead of 10%. In that case, the maximum unexpected loss on the pool at a confidence level of 99.98% increases by 3%, and for the RMBS tranche it increases by 61%. This illustrates that the size of potential unexpected losses on the RMBS tranche is much more sensitive to misestimating the default probability for the assets in the underlying pool than the size of potential unexpected losses for the pool itself. It is important to reflect this larger model risk for structured credit products in economic capital estimates.

We have performed a similar sensitivity analysis for a change in LGD from 20% to 21%, and for a change in correlation within the mortgage pool from 15% to 16%. The results of these sensitivity analyses are reported in Table 4.5. In each case the size of potential unexpected losses for the RMBS tranche increases by an order of magnitude more than the unexpected losses on the underlying pool.[54] This further illustrates that potential losses on the RMBS security are much more sensitive to misestimation of risk parameters in the underlying pool than a direct investment of equal size in the underlying pool of mortgages. This effect may be even larger if we consider tranches of CDOs that have a pool of RMBS securities as underlying instead of a pool of mortgages.

4.2.5   Allocation of Economic Capital

As described in Section 4.1.4, the generally preferred method to calculate the economic capital contribution of subportfolios and individual counterparties is the component economic capital contribution method. When applied to credit risk economic capital, the method will result in negative economic

Table 4.5 Sensitivity of unexpected losses on a pool of mortgage assets and on a RMBS tranche to changes in risk parameters of the mortgages in the pool

		Unexpected loss at 99.98% confidence	Change from base
Base	Pool	4.39	
	RMBS	0.39	
PD = 11%	Pool	4.52	+ 3%
	RMBS	0.62	+ 61%
LGD = 21%	Pool	4.61	+ 5%
	RMBS	0.66	+ 70%
Correlation = 16%	Pool	4.58	+ 4%
	RMBS	0.58	+ 51%

capital contributions for credit risk hedges if these hedges are included separately in the credit risk portfolio model. Because they are hedges, this is reasonable. The main challenge is a computational one, namely, to obtain reliable estimates of component economic capital contributions at a granular level in the portfolio. Several computational approaches have been developed that improve the precision with which component economic capital contributions can be calculated, as more extensively referred to in Section 4.1.4.

4.2.6 Regulatory Capital for Credit Risk

The Basel II Accord distinguishes a standardized approach and an internal-ratings-based approach to calculate minimum required regulatory capital for credit risk. In the standardized approach, the capital requirement is a function of the type of counterparty, the product type, and the external rating of the counterparty (among others). For credit exposures without an external rating, the capital requirement in the standardized approach is independent of the creditworthiness of the counterparty, and therefore not risk-sensitive. In the internal-ratings-based approach, the capital requirement is determined using a formula that takes values for the probability of default (PD), exposure at default (EAD), loss given default (LGD), and maturity (M) as input. The capital requirement increases if any of these risk parameters increases. The internal-ratings-based approach has two variants, the foundation and the advanced approach. In the foundation approach, a bank can use its own estimates for PD and has to apply values for EAD, LGD, and M that are prescribed by the regulator. In the advanced approach, the institution can use its own estimates for each of PD, EAD, LGD, and M.

The formula that is prescribed to determine the minimum regulatory capital requirement in the internal-ratings-based approach is a simplified version of the CreditMetrics model. The simplifications are the following:[55]

- Only losses due to default are considered in the formula. Market value declines due to credit rating migrations are not explicitly included. However, the capital requirement that results from the formula needs to be multiplied by a factor that depends on the maturity and the PD of the credit exposure. This factor has been calibrated to capture the impact of potential market value declines due to rating migrations.
- Correlations are included through a single common factor. This factor can be interpreted as representing the general economic situation. All credit exposures are assumed to have a positive correlation with this common factor, with the value of the correlation depending on counterparty PD, as well as product type for retail products.
- The portfolio of credit exposures of a bank is assumed to have no single-name concentrations (or more technically, consists of an infinite number of infinitely small loans to different counterparties).

These simplifications have the effect that the capital requirement for a portfolio of credit exposures can be calculated analytically, and, moreover, that the capital requirements for individual credit exposures are additive. In other words, the capital requirement for an individual credit exposure can be calculated independently from the characteristics of the rest of the portfolio. A consequence is that the capital requirement is insensitive to concentrations in the credit portfolio. For example, the regulatory capital requirement for an exposure of 100 on a counterparty is twice as large as the capital requirement for an exposure of 50.

The Basel II Accord also distinguishes a standardized and an internal-ratings-based approach for the calculation of regulatory capital requirements for credit exposures arising from securitization transactions. The internal-ratings-based approach is based on an extension of the simplified CreditMetrics model that underlies the capital requirements formula for ordinary credit exposures.[56]

The advanced internal-ratings-based approach is a step toward a more risk-sensitive framework because capital requirements increase with higher PD, LGD, and maturity. The correlations used in the regulatory capital formula are, however, a simplification of the large variation in correlation values that are applicable to an institution. Although the simplifications are understandable in order to avoid too much complexity in the regulatory framework, they do present serious shortcomings for a risk-sensitive framework in light of our earlier observation that bank failures due to credit risk have been caused primarily by (undetected) correlations and concentrations within the credit portfolio. The Basel II Accord leaves the monitoring of credit risk concentrations to national supervisors as part of the supervisory review process.

4.3 Market Risk

As defined in Chapter 3, market risk is the potential loss in value of assets and liabilities due to changes in market variables. Market variables include interest and exchange rates, equity and commodity prices, and credit spreads. We restrict our discussion of market risk to the trading books of banks, in line with the scope of market risk regulation in the Basel II Accord. Many banks include the interest-rate mismatch position on the balance sheet when reporting economic capital estimates for market risk, but we include this mismatch position as part of asset-liability management (ALM) risk in Section 4.5.

Large trading losses figure prominently in the news when they occur. Table 4.6 lists a number of large trading losses that have occurred in the past 15 years.[57] In the case of Barings and Long-Term Capital Management, the losses led effectively to insolvency of the firm. Many others were forced to attract new capital to maintain their desired or required level of capital. In addition to institution-specific trading losses included in the table, many institutions incurred large losses on trading positions in structured credit products during the sub-prime crisis, as we discussed in the previous section on credit risk.

In many cases, the large trading losses in Table 4.6 occurred because traders exploited weaknesses or failures of control procedures, systems, and management oversight to take positions that far exceeded their limits. As such,

Table 4.6 Large historical trading losses

Institution	Loss	Reported	Position
Deutsche Bank	USD 1 billion	December 2008	Corporate bonds vs. CDS
Citic Pacific	USD 2 billion	November 2008	Currency forwards
Société Générale	EUR 5 billion	January 2008	Equity index futures
National Australia Bank	USD 360 million	January 2004	Currency options
Allied Irish Bank	USD 700 million	February 2002	Currency forwards
LTCM	USD 4.4 billion	September 1998	Bonds
Sumitomo	USD 2.4 billion	June 1996	Copper futures
Barings	USD 1 billion	February 1995	Nikkei options and futures
Metallgesellschaft	USD 1.4 billion	January 1994	Oil futures

most of these losses usually are classified as operational losses as opposed to market-risk-related losses. The pattern underlying many of these losses is illustrative of the nature of market risk, however, and therefore relevant to consider when developing models to assess economic capital for market risk. In many of the cases listed in Table 4.6, the traders involved had pursued a trading strategy that had been very profitable over an extended period, often a number of years. This increased confidence in their ability, and trading limits were increased over time as their stature in the respective firms grew. Profits turned to losses, however, when market behavior suddenly changed from the patterns in the past on which the trading strategies had been based, and this change persisted over a prolonged period. In trying to make up for the losses, often bets were increased, and loopholes in procedures and systems exploited, to mask the losses in the hope that markets would revert to "normal" and the loss would change into a profit. For the cases listed in Table 4.6, it clearly did not.

This pattern illustrates two important aspects of market risk. First, losses often occur when markets behave differently from what has been observed in the (recent) past. And second, market risk may be highest in areas where the largest profits are made.

Banks assess market risk usually by means of the value-at-risk measure. VaR is an estimate of the maximum decline in value of a bank's trading portfolio at a certain confidence level over a chosen time horizon. For a bank's internal risk measurement, the chosen confidence level is mostly between 95 and 99%, and the time horizon is one to 10 business days. For economic capital, we need an estimate of potential losses at a confidence level that is consistent with a bank's credit rating objective, which will be significantly higher than the one used in VaR, and during a time horizon of one year. To assess this, we need to make a number of choices and assumptions, which we review in the next section.

4.3.1   Fundamental Choices and Assumptions

Portfolio Dynamics

As trading portfolios can change quickly over time, a question is what to assume about the size of trading risk exposure during the one-year economic capital horizon. Assuming that the actual trading position is the best estimate for the coming year may not be reasonable, especially if the current position is relatively large or small compared to historical positions. Moreover, it can make economic capital estimates quite volatile when trading positions change over time. To avoid this, many banks choose to calculate potential changes in value of the trading portfolio as an average of potential value changes on a variety of positions. It is easiest to select a variety of trading positions from the past, but in principle they could also be hypothetical ones. When taking trading positions from the past, we need to decide how far to look back. The important consideration is to what extent past trading positions are representative for the future. If a certain growth or shrinkage in trading activities and positions is expected, we can scale the positions from the past up or down.

Estimating Potential Value Changes

Given assumptions about the level of trading exposure during the year, we need to decide whether the economic capital estimate for market risk should represent a point-in-time or a through-the-cycle estimate. Although the link between trading losses and the economic cycle may not be as clear as for credit risk, the volatility of market variables that drive changes in the value of trading portfolios often is influenced by events that also have an impact on the general economy. We illustrate this in Graph 4.5, which depicts daily returns on the S&P

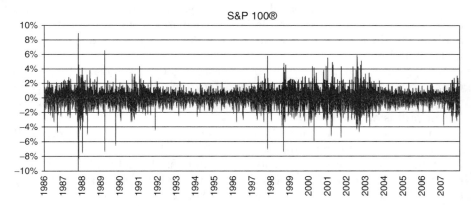

Graph 4.5   Daily returns on the S&P 100 stock market index, from January 1986 to December 2007. The loss of −21% on the index on October 19, 1987 (Black Monday) has been truncated in the graph.
Source: CBOE.

100 stock market index. It is clear that periods of higher and lower volatility alternate. If we compare Graph 4.5 to Graph 3.4 in Chapter 3, which depicts default rates on sub-investment-grade debt issues from 1987 to 2007, then it is clear that the calm periods for the S&P 100 index coincide with periods of relatively low default rates. Major market events and economic crises are visible in the volatility of the S&P 100 index: the stock market crash in October 1987, the savings-and-loan crisis in the United States between 1986 and 1991, the Asian crisis that started in the summer of 1997, default of Russia on its debt in August 1998, the bursting of the dot-com bubble in 2000 and the ensuing economic slowdown, the surprise defaults of Enron in late 2001 and Worldcom in July 2002 as a result of accounting fraud, and the terrorist attack on the World Trade Center in New York in September 2001. In the second half of 2007, the increase in volatility as a result of the sub-prime crisis is visible. The graph illustrates that changes in market variables can easily be twice as high in turbulent and uncertain periods compared to those in calmer and economically prosperous periods. This directly translates to higher volatility in trading results if positions are not adjusted.

The impact of market events is even clearer when we look at the implied volatility of options, which reflects the uncertainty among investors about the future development of stock prices. Graph 4.6 depicts the VXO index, which is a measure of the implied volatility of short-term options on the S&P 100 index. The peaks in the implied volatility coincide with the major market events just mentioned. If trading portfolios contain options, then such increases in volatility can have a significant impact on the value of these options, and even more so if the increase in volatility coincides with large changes in the underlying market variables.

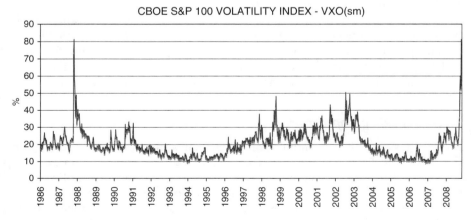

Graph 4.6 VXO index values from January 1986 to November 2008. The VXO index measures the implied volatility of short-term options on the S&P 100 stock market index.
Source: CBOE.

If the aim is to arrive at a best estimate of potential trading losses for the next year, it may be tempting to base such an estimate on a relatively recent history of observed changes in market variables. Because we are interested in the size of potential losses at a high confidence level when estimating economic capital, however, it is questionable whether recent history provides sufficient information on such extreme events. If a bank incurs a very large trading loss in the coming year, it is likely that it has been caught by surprise by an unexpected market event (abstracting from large trading losses as a result of operational failures and fraud). Taking a longer history into account, which includes periods of stress events in the relevant market variables, may provide a better basis to estimate extreme trading losses that correspond to the economic capital confidence level. If the aim is to arrive at a through-the-cycle estimate of economic capital for market risk, the use of a long history is a natural choice.

Management Intervention

Since trading positions are monitored continuously, traders are able to react to changes in markets and thereby reduce the susceptibility of the positions to large losses. Furthermore, a bank's senior management may reduce trading limits when market circumstances deteriorate, or when losses on trading positions have accumulated. Many banks therefore make assumptions about the impact that management of trading positions has on the size of potential trading losses. These assumptions can reduce the estimated economic capital substantially. When a marketwide stress event occurs, however, the liquidity in certain trading products may dwindle or even disappear completely. In that case, it may not be possible to reduce positions, or only at a high cost. Banks experienced this during the sub-prime crisis, when markets in structured credit products dried up completely and there were no parties willing to enter into hedging transactions. Banks had no choice but to stick to their trading positions in these products, which over time experienced significant losses. Hence, the effectiveness of management intervention in a general crisis situation may be limited, in particular for complex trading products. When making assumptions about management intervention, this should be taken into account.

4.3.2 Modeling Approaches

Most banks base their economic capital estimates for market risk directly on their VaR calculation. As mentioned earlier, VaR differs from economic capital because it represents potential changes in value of the trading portfolio over a time horizon of one to 10 business days instead of one year, and uses a lower confidence level. Furthermore, banks usually measure VaR for their trading portfolios as the maximum decline in value at the chosen confidence level from the current portfolio value. As we argued in Chapter 3, however, for economic capital we should consider the potential downward deviation in value from the expected value at the horizon. Graph 4.7 illustrates the difference.

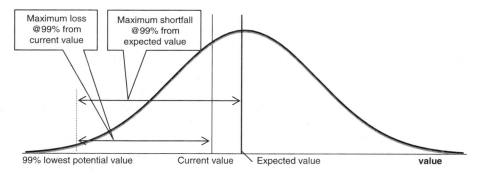

Graph 4.7 Difference between the maximum loss from the current value, and the maximum downward deviation (shortfall) from the expected value, assuming a confidence level of 99%.

Although the difference between the change in value at a chosen confidence level from the current or from the expected value will be small for the short time period over which VaR is measured, over the one-year horizon that is used to calculate economic capital it can be substantial. This is because the expected change in value of a portfolio increases linearly with the length of the time horizon, whereas the potential loss in the tail of the distribution at a given confidence level increases proportional to the square root of time if gains and losses on successive trading days are uncorrelated (which is the usual assumption). To illustrate the impact, suppose the current value of a trading portfolio is 1,000, the expected value after one day is 1,001, and the 99% worst-case value after one day is 975. The 99% one-day VaR then equals 25, and the difference between the expected value after one day and the 99% worst-case value equals 26. If trading gains and losses on successive trading days are sampled randomly from the probability distribution of potential one-day value changes, then the expected portfolio value after one year (approximated as 256 trading days) equals 1,256, and the 99% worst-case portfolio value after one year equals approximately 600 (calculated as the current value (1,000) – 16 × 25, where 16 is the square root of 256). Hence, over the one-year horizon, the 99% worst-case loss compared to the current portfolio value equals 400, while the 99% worst-case shortfall from the expected value at the one-year horizon equals 656. This is a difference of 64%, whereas the difference between both risk measures over the one-day horizon is only 4%. This shows the significance of measuring economic capital as the difference from the expected value at the one-year horizon instead of the current value.

Value changes considered for VaR usually relate only to potential changes in market value of the current position, assuming that the position is left unchanged. They do not include earnings from bid-ask spreads, or results from intraday trading and adjustment of the position. Intraday trading and adjustment of positions may reduce the risk of losses for a position, but has the potential of increasing risk. This is usually not explicitly included in VaR or economic capital calculations for market risk. Actual trading income will obviously include both the income from bid-ask spreads, and reflect the results from intraday trading and adjustment of positions.

The simplest way to arrive at an economic capital estimate is by multiplying the VaR with a scaling factor. The VaR multiplied by the scaling factor should thus yield an estimate of the difference at the one-year horizon between the expected value of the trading portfolio, and the worst-case value at the chosen economic capital confidence level. To avoid too large a dependence on a particular trading position, it is often more representative to apply the scaling factor to the average VaR during a certain time period (e.g., one month) instead of the VaR at a specific point in time. To arrive at a proper scaling factor we must make an assumption about the probability distribution of trading gains and losses in successive one-day or 10-day periods, and whether trading gains and losses in successive periods are correlated. If trading results over successive periods are assumed to be uncorrelated, then the probability distribution of potential values of the trading portfolio at the one-year horizon will resemble much closer a Gaussian (bell-shaped) distribution than the one-day or 10-day probability distribution. This feature may be used to arrive at a scaling factor. The scaling factor can further embed an assumption about the impact of management intervention.

Many banks calculate VaR using historical simulation. In this method, potential changes in value of the current trading position are derived by applying historical changes in market variables to the current trading position. For example, if we apply changes in market variables during the past 500 business days to the current trading position, we obtain 500 possible one-day changes in value of the current trading position. The VaR for the current trading position can then be estimated as the maximum simulated loss at the relevant confidence level. With a 99% confidence level and 500 potential changes in value, the VaR would correspond to the fifth-largest loss of the 500 potential value changes.

If we have a collection of potential one-day or 10-day changes in value of the current trading position derived from historical simulation, then a one-year loss scenario can be constructed by sampling from these potential value changes and summing the results. A one-year scenario thus would consist of a sequence of 26 periods of 10 business days each (or 256 single business days), where the profit or loss for each 10-day period (respectively, single business day) is sampled randomly from the available historical simulation results. To avoid too large a dependence on the current trading position, we can extend the collection of potential one-day value changes from which we sample by including the historical simulation results of trading positions during a recent period (e.g., the last month). By generating many one-year loss scenarios in this manner, we obtain an empirical distribution of potential value changes over a one-year horizon. Economic capital can then be estimated as the difference between the expected simulated change in value, and the worst-case value corresponding to the economic capital confidence level. When considering the loss in each scenario, we can account for management intervention assumptions if desired. For example, we can assume that trading positions (and thus potential value changes) will be reduced once cumulative losses during the year have exceeded a certain threshold. In addition, we can take account of autocorrelation of value changes over time if it is observed that bad trading days and good trading days cluster over time.

An advantage of historical simulation is that correlations between changes in different market variables are automatically taken into account. A potential drawback is that the history may not contain the stress events that in reality often cause large trading losses. When simulating one-year scenarios from historical simulation results as described earlier, we could embed stress events by allowing for a certain probability that a stress event occurs. These stress events and their probability of occurrence can be based on historical stress events, or on hypothetical ones. We will return to the inclusion of stress events in the next section.

Some firms use Monte-Carlo simulation to calculate VaR. In that case, a probability distribution of potential changes in all relevant market variables needs to be specified, as well as correlations (or more in general, the dependence structure) between them. The parameters of the probability distributions, as well as the correlations, usually are estimated from historical data. The same qualifications apply with respect to the use of historical data as made earlier for the historical simulation method. The Monte-Carlo simulation method in principle can be used also to estimate economic capital by simulating one-year changes in market variables instead of one-day or 10-day changes. In doing so, it is possible to take into account autocorrelation or mean-reverting behavior in market variables, and reflect the effect of management intervention if desired. Furthermore, stress events can be included within this simulation approach.

The advantage of the Monte-Carlo simulation method compared to the historical simulation method is that it offers more flexibility to include potential changes in market variables that deviate from (recent) historical experience. Furthermore, it enables incorporation of longer-term dynamics of market variables. A drawback is that the method requires explicit specification of the dependence structure and tail behavior of all market variables, whereas this is included automatically in the historical simulation method.

4.3.3 Special Topics

In this section we elaborate on a few topics that are relevant for the estimation of economic capital for market risk for each of the general approaches that we described in the previous section. We will touch upon certain elements of the VaR calculation since it usually forms the basis for arriving at an economic capital estimate, but we will not provide a comprehensive overview of issues related to the VaR calculation in general.[58]

Accounting for Extreme Market Moves

Historical changes of market variables usually form the starting point for a bank's VaR calculation, either by applying historical simulation directly or by using this data to estimate distributions of, and correlations between, market variables in the Monte-Carlo simulation method. In addition, banks employ a variety of stress tests on trading portfolios that consider large movements of important market variables for each portfolio. Such stress tests can serve to highlight the consequences of extreme moves in relevant market variables for a trading position that exceed the changes observed in the past (see Section 4.1.3 for illustrations regarding the oil price and credit spreads). Another purpose of stress tests can be to examine potential losses as a consequence of basis risk in a trading portfolio that may not be fully captured in the regular VaR calculation. Basis risk is present if the portfolio contains a long position with respect to one market variable, and a short position with respect to another, where both market variables usually move in tandem so that the long and the short positions act as hedges. The risk is that changes in value of the long and short positions may not offset each other as much as expected when the position was established. Examples of basis risk are a long position in the 9-year swap rate and a short position in the 10-year swap rate, or a long position in a portfolio of individual stocks and a short position in an equity index (e.g., by means of a futures contract). A stress test can illustrate the potential losses if both market variables do not move in tandem as expected, or even in opposite directions.

Large trading losses have often resulted from significant and persistent changes in the level or the behavior of market variables compared to the past. For example, LTCM got into problems in 1998 because of the basis risk to which its trading positions were exposed, combined with the high leverage that it employed. Its trading positions involved a long position in illiquid instruments of which the prices were deemed to be below their fundamental values, and a short position in similar but different liquid instruments of which the prices were deemed to be at or above their fundamental values. The bet was that these instruments would gradually converge in price as had been observed in the past. However, during the flight to quality that followed the unexpected default of Russia on its debt, the liquid instruments increased in price while the illiquid instruments fell in price. As a consequence, LTCM's trading position incurred large losses, which were exacerbated by the high leverage that LTCM employed.[59]

Because large trading losses are often the result of such changes in behavior of certain market variables, we would like to capture the possibility of such changes and the consequences for trading losses in economic capital estimates. However, it is impossible to foresee what the next market dislocation will be, and by how much precisely market variables will change as a consequence. It will therefore only be possible to include the impact of such market stresses on trading gains and losses in a stylized way. It is nonetheless important to do so to obtain a more accurate estimate of the capital needed to support a trading business.

Inclusion of Specific Risk

For the market risk VaR calculation, it is practically impossible to simulate changes in value of each individual trading position. This is due to the sheer number of market variables that would need to be considered, as well as the fact that for some market variables no, or only little, historical data is available from which we can estimate potential future value changes of a transaction. As a consequence, trading positions usually are mapped to a large but limited set of common market variables, and the impact of changes in these market variables on the value of the trading position is modeled. For an individual transaction, however, actual changes in value may differ from the simulated changes in value if transaction-specific market variables are not present in the overall VaR calculation. For example, potential value changes of nonlisted equity positions may be approximated in the VaR calculation by applying value changes that are derived from seemingly similar listed equities. As another example, value changes of an interest-rate-dependent instrument may be approximated by applying potential changes in a swap curve, while the instrument in fact depends on a similar but slightly different interest-rate curve.

A further example relates to the incorporation of credit-spread changes and potential default events for transactions whose value depends on the credit quality of a specific firm, sovereign, or retail segment (referred to as "name" in the following discussion). This usually is referred to as specific risk. Specific risk has increased in importance because of the tremendous growth in the trading of credit derivatives during the past decade. Market risk VaR calculations typically have not included name-specific changes in creditworthiness or credit spreads due to the lack of data and the computational challenges this poses. Instead, value changes in credit-sensitive transactions usually were related to movements in general credit spread levels, instead of to name-specific spreads. For example, value changes of structured credit products often were estimated from changes in the general corporate credit spread curve that corresponded to the credit rating of the structured product, without taking the nature of the specific underlying exposures into account. As a result, the models missed the risk of significant losses on structured credit products as the specific risk characteristics and the high correlations between these products were not adequately captured. Regulators have started to amend the regulatory capital rules for market risk, requiring banks to incorporate all credit-related risks in much more detail in their VaR models.[60]

Inclusion of Liquidity Risk

Banks' VaR models usually employ a short time horizon of one to 10 trading days because trading positions can change quickly, and it is often possible to neutralize an open position within a short time horizon. How easy it is to sell or hedge a trading position depends on the nature of the products. For simple products in which there is a large market (e.g., standard interest-rate swaps and currency forwards) the time needed to sell or hedge a position can be very short, usually less than a day. However, for complex products it may be possible neither to sell nor fully hedge. These differences in market liquidity can influence the size of potential losses on trading portfolios. When one-year scenarios are constructed as a sequence of gains and losses during (say) 10-day periods for economic capital calculation purposes, illiquidity of products could be reflected by including an illiquidity discount in the estimated price changes for these products. The potential illiquidity of positions may also reduce the possibility of management intervention, as mentioned in Section 4.3.1.

Model Risk

The calculation of changes in value of a trading portfolio makes use of valuation functions for derivatives products in the portfolio. Especially for complex derivatives products, the valuation functions are based on a number of assumptions that may be hard to validate empirically. As a consequence, the actual change in value of a derivative product when market variables change may differ from the change in value as predicted by the valuation model. In the daily profit-and-loss reconciliation, such a difference would show up as unexplained profit or loss, and reflect the model risk of the product's valuation. Most banks maintain an income reserve for such model risk by setting aside part of the initial profit on a transaction. If any errors in the model lead to losses at a later point in time, then the money in the income reserve can be used to cover these losses.

This model risk will also enter into the VaR calculation, as it is based on estimates of changes in value of trading positions as a function of changes in market variables. Moreover, many banks do not explicitly revalue all derivatives products using their specific valuation functions when simulating changes in market risk variables as part of the VaR calculation, because this is computationally extremely demanding. Instead, many firms approximate the resulting value changes of a trading portfolio by deriving the sensitivities to changes in the market variables (usually referred to as the Greeks, because they are denoted with Greek letters) for each product from the product-specific valuation function, aggregating sensitivities to the relevant market variables over many trading positions, and then applying changes in market variables to these aggregated sensitivities. Because the sensitivities may change when underlying market variables change, the change in value of the trading portfolio that is estimated in this way may differ from the true value change corresponding to the move in market variables that is considered. The use of aggregated sensitivities instead of full revaluation of each individual transaction therefore introduces another source of model risk in the VaR calculation, even if the underlying valuation functions were perfect.

We can account for this model risk in the economic capital calculation for market risk. To estimate the potential size of this model risk, we could look at historical time-series of unexplained profit-and-loss for the specific products involved. Alternatively, we can try to estimate the size of the model risk for a derivative product by analyzing hedging errors in a hypothetical hedge test. Such a test considers market value changes during a historical period, and evaluates how well a specific derivative product could be hedged through hedging positions in the underlying market variables or assets, based on the sensitivities as calculated by the valuation model for the derivative product. If a bank maintains an income reserve for model risk, and if model risk is explicitly accounted for in economic capital, then the income reserve can be included as part of available capital when comparing it to economic capital.

4.3.4   Allocation of Economic Capital

The VaR for all trading books in a bank combined is typically much smaller than the sum of the VaR for each trading book in isolation. This diversification of risk between trading books can result from offsetting positions between different trading books (e.g., one trading book is positioned to benefit from a rise in US interest rates, whereas another trading book is positioned to benefit from a decline), as well as from low or even negative correlation between the major risk drivers of different trading books (e.g., low correlation between changes in commodity prices and exchange rates). The presence of offsetting positions or negative correlation between risk drivers can lead to economic capital contributions that are negative for specific trading books if some of the methods from Section 4.1.4 are used. That is, in scenarios that correspond to large trading losses for the bank as a whole, some desks may actually show a profit if they tend to perform well when the trading activities as a whole perform poorly. When considering stylized situations, such negative economic capital contributions are not intuitive.

For example, consider two trading desks that have exactly offsetting positions. Then economic capital for the two trading desks combined will be zero. When applying the component economic capital contribution method, one desk may be allocated a positive economic capital amount, and the other desk a negative amount of the same absolute size. It will be arbitrary, however, which desk to assign the positive and the negative economic capital amount. If the positions of the desks are only partially offsetting, then the desk with the largest position in absolute size will have a positive economic capital contribution, and the other desk a negative contribution. If during the next month, the desk with the largest position has reduced its position to below the position of the other desk (in absolute size), then it will suddenly receive a negative economic capital contribution, and the other desk a positive one. Hence, economic capital contributions can appear quite arbitrary, and fluctuate significantly over time, when using the component economic capital contribution method. Similar issues plague the standard deviation and incremental economic capital contribution methods.

The stand-alone economic capital contribution method circumvents this problem, and will always lead to positive economic capital contributions for individual trading desks and business areas. This method, however, may understate the risk contribution of desks that have a large influence on the total amount of economic capital for market risk. In a risk-adjusted return analysis, these desks may then look more attractive than they really are. Whichever economic capital contribution method is chosen, the potential undesirable effects that each of them can have need to be taken into consideration.

4.3.5   Regulatory Capital for Market Risk

Banks are allowed to use their internal VaR calculation also for the determination of regulatory capital for market risk. In principle, regulatory capital for market risk equals three times the VaR that is calculated over a 10-day horizon at a 99% confidence level. The multiplication factor of three can be viewed as translating the 10-day 99%-VaR to a one-year horizon and a higher confidence level, but no explicit confidence level and time horizon are mentioned in the regulatory rules. Banks are required to backtest their VaR methodology by comparing the calculated one-day 99% VaR at the start of each trading day with the trading profit-and-loss during that day. If the number of days on which the trading loss exceeds the one-day VaR is higher than what is consistent with the 99% confidence level, then the supervisor can increase the VaR multiplication factor to a value above three, with four as maximum.

In January 2009, the Basel Committee issued a proposal in which the capital requirement for market risk not just depends on the results of a bank's regular VaR calculation, but also on the VaR that results when inputs are calibrated to "historical data from a period of significant financial stress relevant to the firm's portfolio."[60] The proposal suggests that a 12-month period relating to significant losses in 2007/2008 could constitute such a period of stress. The role of such a stress-VaR in the capital requirement for market risk aims to capture the impact of potential extreme market moves that we discussed in Section 4.3.3.

In proposed rules for the inclusion of name-specific spread, credit migration, and default risk in the VaR calculation, the Basel Committee has specified a time horizon of one year and a confidence level of 99.9% for models that are developed by banks for this purpose.[61] Although the capital horizon for regulatory capital is thus set to one year, banks are allowed to specify different holding periods (liquidity horizons) for different products. If the holding period is chosen shorter than one year, banks must assume that the risk during successive holding periods within the one-year capital horizon is identical. In other words, the regulatory capital calculation assumes that positions are rolled over during the one-year capital horizon if the liquidity horizon is shorter than one year. It is expected that banks need to implement the proposed rules for name-specific risk by December 31, 2010, although some national regulators may require earlier implementation.

4.4   Operational Risk

As we saw in Section 2.2.1, operational risk is mentioned in a study by the Groupe Contact as the second-most important reason for banks to fail, after credit risk. Hence, operational risk is likely to contribute significantly to the total economic capital of an institution. In the Basel II Accord, the Basel Committee on Banking Supervision defines operational risk as "the risk of loss resulting from inadequate or failed internal processes, people, systems or from external events." It adds that this definition includes legal risk, but excludes strategic and reputation risk. Some institutions include business risk under the banner of operational risk, and denote the operational risk as referred to in the previous definition as event risk. We will discuss business risk separately in Section 4.6, and follow the definition in the Basel II Accord for operational risk.

The Basel II Accord distinguishes seven categories of operational loss event types, which we include in Table 4.7. Each level 1 event-type category is subdivided into one or more level 2 categories that provide more detail on the types of loss events included.

As the overview in Table 4.7 shows, operational losses can result from both internal and external events. When managing operational risks, institutions can aim to reduce both the probability that events occur (frequency) and the impact of an event if it occurs (severity). The probability of occurrence will be more difficult to influence for external than for internal events. For external events, the focus, therefore, may be primarily on limiting the potential impact. By its very nature, it will not be possible to eliminate operational risk completely. When spending money to reduce operational risk, an institution will trade off the cost against the reduction of future operational risk losses. Some investments may be primarily aimed at reducing expected losses (e.g., improvements to an institution's systems infrastructure and processes) whereas others may be directed to contain potential unexpected losses (e.g., establishing business continuity plans in case of natural disasters or terrorist attacks).

An important difference between operational risk on the one hand, and credit and market risk on the other hand, is that the full set of exposures is not clearly defined. For credit and market risk, and more generally for position risks, an institution knows exactly what the set of exposures is on which it can incur a loss. For operational risk, the complete set of possible events is limited only by the imagination. As a consequence, institutions typically do not just consider their own experience of operational risk losses when estimating economic capital for operational risk, but also those experienced by other institutions. To enable this, several organizations have started to collect industrywide information on operational loss events, either by gathering information from public sources (such as the OpData database of Algorithmics), or by combining internal loss data from individual institutions (as the ORX consortium does).

When modeling economic capital for operational risk, two types of operational events usually are distinguished: high-frequency/low-severity events, and low-frequency/high-severity events. High-frequency/low-severity events are events that happen frequently, but each one individually tends to result in a relatively small loss. Often, both the frequency and the severity of these events can be estimated with reasonable precision based on available loss data. High-frequency/low-severity events contribute primarily to expected losses. Low-frequency/high-severity events occur infrequently, but may result in large losses when they occur. Because of the low probability of occurrence, the associated expected loss may be small, but it can contribute heavily to

Table 4.7 Basel II Accord detailed operational loss event type classification. (*Source:* Annex 10 in Basel Committee on Banking Supervision (2006), "International convergence of capital measurement and capital standards: A revised framework")

Event-type category (Level 1)	Definition	Categories (Level 2)
1. Internal fraud	Losses due to acts of a type intended to defraud; misappropriate property; or circumvent regulations, the law, or company policy, excluding diversity/discrimination events, which involves at least one internal party.	Unauthorized activity (e.g., transactions not reported, intentional mismarking of positions); Theft and fraud
2. External fraud	Losses due to acts of a type intended to defraud, misappropriate property, or circumvent the law, by a third party.	Theft and fraud; Systems security
3. Employment practices and workplace safety	Losses arising from acts inconsistent with employment, health, or safety laws or agreements; from payment of personal injury claims; or from diversity/discrimination events.	Employee relations; Safe environment; Diversity and discrimination
4. Clients, products, and business practices	Losses arising from an unintentional or negligent failure to meet a professional obligation to specific clients (including fiduciary and suitability requirements), or from the nature or design of a product.	Suitability, disclosure, and fiduciary; Improper business or market practices; Product flaws; Client selection, sponsorship, and exposure; Advisory activities
5. Damage to physical assets	Losses arising from loss or damage to physical assets from natural disaster or other events.	Disasters and other events (e.g., terrorism, vandalism)
6. Business disruption and system failures	Losses arising from disruption of business or system failures.	Systems (e.g., hard- and software failures, utility outage)
7. Execution, delivery, and process management	Losses from failed transaction processing or process management, from relations with trade counterparties and vendors.	Transaction capture, execution, and maintenance; Monitoring and reporting; Customer intake and documentation; Customer/client account management; Trade counterparties; Vendors and suppliers

unexpected loss and thus economic capital. In principle, we could also have high-frequency/high-severity events and low-frequency/low-severity events. However, institutions exposed to high-frequency/high-severity events are probably not viable, and the class of low-frequency/low-severity events is not material for economic capital modeling purposes.

Estimating potential losses from low-frequency/high-severity events is the big challenge in operational risk modeling. Due to the low frequency, there are few observations on which to base statistical analysis. Moreover, if institutions get into trouble as a result of operational risk, it is usually as a result of a single large loss instead of an accumulation of many small losses. This differentiates operational risk from credit risk, for example. The essence of operational risk modeling is, therefore, to estimate how large a large operational loss can be at the chosen confidence level of economic capital. Operational losses that arise from external events like earthquakes, diseases, and terrorist attacks are often difficult to predict, both with respect to the probability of occurrence and the likely damage they inflict if they occur. Operational losses caused by human behavior may be even more difficult to predict, but they are highly relevant because the largest operational losses in the past resulted from human (mis) behavior. It is clear that we are mostly in the realm of uncertainty rather than risk when estimating economic capital for operational risk.

In the previous section on market risk we reviewed several large trading losses caused by traders who took large unauthorized positions. These losses would be classified as resulting from internal fraud in the classification of Table 4.7. Large operational losses also have occurred in the category "Clients, products, and business practices." For example, the Belgian bank Dexia agreed to a settlement of more than 1 billion Euros with clients of its "legio-lease" product, which Dexia inherited as a result of the takeover of the Dutch Banque Labouchère in 2000. Clients had experienced significant losses on this leveraged equity investment product in the declining stock markets after the tech-bubble burst in 2001. Dutch judges ruled that Banque Labouchère had not provided sufficient information about the risks of this product to the private investors. Large settlements as a result of improper business practices also occurred in the United States after the defaults of Enron and Worldcom. Investors sued several large banks for helping the firms to manipulate their financial statements (e.g., by assisting with the establishment of off-balance sheet entities that enabled the firms to hide a substantial part of their liabilities and flatter their income statements), and for providing materially misleading financial information when they sold investors securities of the two firms. Among others, J.P. Morgan agreed to pay USD 2 billion in the Worldcom settlement and USD 2.2 billion in the Enron settlement, and Citibank settled for USD 2.6 billion in the Worldcom and for USD 2 billion in the Enron case.[62]

In general, investment banking operations seem more vulnerable for major operational risks than other activities in banks. The *Financial Times* gave a vivid description of the different behavioral patterns, and hence operational risks, associated with commercial and investment bankers in its commentary on February 23, 2008:[63]

> Commercial and retail bankers are like battery hens. You [...] pressure them with tough sales targets, but provide a decent salary, and they will produce a steady stream of returns. Most are conservative, somewhat harassed souls, who seldom think to bite the hand that feeds them. An investment bank is more like a zoo, full of bizarre, prideful and sometimes dangerous animals. The job is to keep the animals in their cages, so they do not savage the paying customers, while understanding their individual behavior patterns. What does it mean, for example, when a derivative trader refuses to take a holiday?

In Section 4.4.2 we will review the main modeling approaches that financial institutions use: the loss-distribution approach and the scenario approach. Before doing so, we first discuss a few important choices and assumptions that we face when embarking on modeling operational risk.

4.4.1 Fundamental Choices and Assumptions

We consider three dilemmas that we face when developing models for operational risk economic capital: when to classify losses as operational losses, what to do with operational errors that result in a gain, and how to treat expected operational losses in the context of economic capital.

Boundary Problems: When to Classify Losses as Operational Losses

Many times, operational errors come to light only when an institution incurs losses as a consequence of some other risk to which it is exposed. In the previous section on market risk we saw that many of the large trading losses experienced by banks in the past could happen only because of failures in the adherence to operational procedures and the lack of proper internal controls. As such, they are classified as operational losses in a bank's internal operational loss databases. Furthermore, when a counterparty defaults, it may become clear that the documentation of the transaction on which the counterparty defaults contains errors or omissions, which may have the effect that a bank cannot levy a claim on the counterparty's assets that it had envisioned it could. Hence, at least part of the loss can be classified as an operational loss instead of a credit loss. When and to what extent losses should be classified as operational losses may not always be clear-cut, but it is important to ensure as much consistency as possible. However, some element of judgment in specific cases will be unavoidable.

Inclusion of Gains

Operational errors do not always result in losses, but sometimes in gains. For example, an unauthorized investment may end up being profitable for the institution, or a bank may have carried out profitable business with a client that does not conform to the internal client acceptance criteria. The question is whether to take such potential gains into account when estimating economic capital for operational risk. If gains are included, they have the effect of reducing the amount of economic capital needed to support operational risks. This potentially creates perverse incentives, since errors could be rewarded. Therefore it may be decided not to take gains from operational errors into account. In that case, the corresponding events also should be excluded from frequency estimates of operational risk events.

Accounting for Expected Losses

As we argued in Chapter 1, expected losses should be compensated by the margin that a financial institution earns on its assets. Capital serves as a buffer against (large) unexpected losses, and economic capital should thus be a function of unexpected losses only. This is valid in general, and therefore also for operational risk losses. When assessing forward-looking RAROC for business activities or new investments, many institutions do not estimate expected operational losses explicitly, however. Instead, they often decide to calculate economic capital for operational risk without subtracting expected losses from the extreme loss that corresponds to the economic capital confidence level. This is also how the Basel II Accord prescribes that regulatory capital for operational risk should be calculated if banks use internal models, unless expected operational losses are explicitly accounted for in the bank's internal business practices. If expected operational losses are included in the economic capital estimate for operational risk, the expected loss should not be diversified with other risks when aggregating operational risk with other risk types to arrive at an overall economic capital estimate, in contrast to the part representing unexpected losses. Furthermore, the inclusion of expected operational losses in the economic capital estimate overestimates RAROC when RAROC is smaller than 100%, as it usually is. The reason is that the positive impact of ignoring expected loss in the numerator of the RAROC formula is larger than the negative impact on RAROC from the inclusion of expected loss in economic capital in the denominator of the RAROC formula.

For an internal capital adequacy assessment, the inclusion of expected losses in economic capital does not matter as long as the expected profit is included as part of available capital to which economic capital is compared (as we advocated in Section 3.4.2), and if expected profit is not reduced by expected operational losses. We note that the Basel II Accord does not allow that expected profits are included as part of available capital, and thus the inclusion of expected operational losses in the regulatory capital requirement for operational risk is conservative.

4.4.2 Modeling Approaches

The main approaches used in practice to estimate economic capital for operational risk are the loss distribution approach and the scenario approach. Some firms also use a combination of both. We will review both approaches in this section, with a focus on the aspects that are crucial to their successful implementation and use, and the interpretation of their outcomes. We will refer to operational losses in our discussion, but this can include operational errors that result in a gain.

Loss Distribution Approach

The loss distribution approach (LDA) derives a probability distribution of operational losses by estimating from empirical loss data separate probability distributions for the frequency and for the severity of operational losses. The frequency distribution describes the variability in the number of operational loss events per year, and the severity distribution the variability in the potential size of the loss for an operational loss event. An aggregate loss distribution can be obtained through simulation: the number of operational loss events in a year is drawn randomly from the estimated frequency distribution, and for each of the simulated number of loss events a severity is determined by repeated sampling from the estimated severity distribution. After doing this many times (in practice, often a million aggregate annual losses are simulated in this way), we obtain a simulated one-year loss distribution from which we can estimate economic capital.[64] There are several issues that we encounter when following this approach.

A first question is at what granularity to estimate probability distributions for frequency and severity. This can be done for the full set of operational losses combined, separately for individual types of operational loss events (e.g., for the event types listed in Table 4.7), or for individual lines of business. Provided that enough data is available at such lower levels of granularity to estimate a frequency and severity distribution, it makes sense to differentiate frequency and severity distributions if they are distinctly different between event types or business lines. For example, some event types may occur relatively infrequently, but if they occur they tend to lead to relatively large losses (e.g., power outages or terrorist attacks), whereas other event types could occur frequently but with generally small losses (e.g., processing errors). The severity distribution of such event types will thus be distinctly different. Combining the event types when estimating a frequency and severity distribution may lead to a poor fit of the combined empirical loss data, and also to a significant error in the estimation of economic capital.[65]

To illustrate differences in characteristics of losses per business line and event type, Graphs 4.8 and 4.9 show the composition of reported losses per business line (Graph 4.8) and per Basel II event type (Graph 4.9) in the ORX database from 2002 to 2006.[66]

It is clear that some business lines have more exposure to large losses than others. For example, corporate finance nearly exclusively experiences large operational losses, whereas retail banking and retail brokerage experience a large number of relatively small losses. The distribution of losses is also markedly different between event types, with "Internal fraud" and "Clients, products, and business processes" including relatively many large losses, and

Loss amount (€ millions)

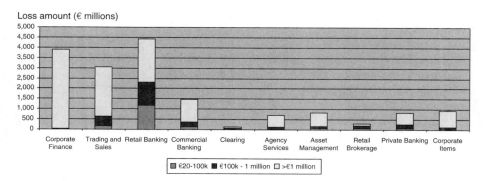

Graph 4.8 Distribution of loss severity per business line from the ORX database comprising submitted losses from 2002 to 2006.
Source: ORX Operational Risk Report 2007.[66]

Loss Amount (millions)

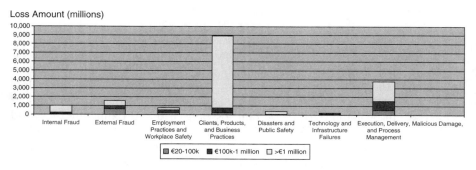

Graph 4.9 Distribution of loss severity per Basel II event type from the ORX database comprising submitted losses from 2002 to 2006.
Source: ORX Operational Risk Report 2007.[66]

"External fraud" and "Execution, delivery, and process management" containing many small ones. These observations may well be related: Corporate finance tends to be heavily exposed to loss events related to "Clients, products, and business processes," whereas retail banking and retail brokerage have a large exposure to "Execution, delivery, and process management" events. Hence, it may not be necessary to include granularity in both event type and business line dimensions when introducing granularity in an economic capital model for operational risk.

A second challenge that we encounter when fitting a severity distribution to observed operational losses is that the probability distribution tends to have very fat tails; that is, the probability of incurring large losses only decreases slowly with the size of the potential loss. This can be seen from Graph 4.10, which depicts various percentiles of the empirical distribution of losses for the different Basel II event types as submitted to the ORX consortium by the participating banks between 2002 and 2006.

Loss amount (€ millions)

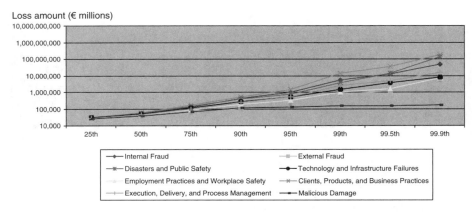

Graph 4.10 Percentiles of the empirical distribution of loss severity per Basel II event type from the ORX database comprising submitted losses from 2002–2006.
Source: ORX Operational Risk Report 2007.[66]

Graph 4.10 shows that the event category "Clients, products, and business processes" has the highest probability of large losses. The graph also shows how slowly the probability of large losses decreases when the size of the loss increases. For the event category "Clients, products, and business processes" there is a tail probability of 0.1% that losses exceed approximately EUR 100 million (corresponding to the 99.9th percentile), and a tail probability of 1% that losses exceed approximately EUR 10 million (the 99th percentile). Hence, the tail probability decreases with a factor of 10 if the loss size increases with approximately a factor of 10. We see a similar effect if we compare the EUR 10 million loss at the 99th percentile with the loss of (a little below) EUR 1 million at the 90th percentile. In fact, if the tail probability decreases at the same rate as (or slower than) the size of the loss increases when we move into the tail of the probability distribution of experienced losses, then the expected value of the loss severity is infinitely large (a so-called infinite-mean distribution). As Graph 4.10 shows, the empirical distribution of observed operational losses (close to) exhibits this behavior. This feature of the empirical data is fully consistent with the earlier observation that institutions get into problems as a result of a single, very large operational loss instead of a series of small losses. When fitting probability distributions to this type of data, and using these in a loss distribution approach, the estimated economic capital may become very large and will be subject to considerable uncertainty. As a consequence, the calculated economic capital is very sensitive to changes in the fit when additional loss data are incorporated.

Institutions have dealt with this modeling challenge in various ways, for example, by capping the loss that can be incurred for any given event type in the economic capital calculation, or by fitting a distribution to the data that does not exhibit the infinite-mean behavior. This is not as unreasonable as it may sound.

When estimating economic capital for operational risk we extrapolate from the domain of observed losses to a domain of unobserved, very large potential losses that drive the economic capital estimate. The shape of the distribution is inherently unknown for such large losses. Moreover, for some types of operational loss events, it is reasonable to assume that there is some level of loss beyond which the probability of experiencing even larger losses decreases more quickly than in the domain of observed losses. For example, large settlements related to the event category "Clients, products, and business processes" are bounded in practice by what an institution can reasonably afford without jeopardizing its immediate continuity. Moreover, the value of transactions with clients that would fall in this event category is naturally bounded, and thus the damage cannot be unlimited. As another example, if a fraudulent scheme is executed that consists of the repetition of a "trick," each of which results in only a small gain for the person executing it and thus a small loss to the institution, then large losses occur only if the scheme remains undetected over an extended period. However, the probability of being detected may increase exponentially with the length of time that it is executed, and the amount of loss that is accumulated. At what level to cap a severity distribution, or what distribution to use that does not exhibit the infinite-mean property, is a difficult choice, but one that has a large impact on the economic capital estimate. Because there is little or no data to support the choice, it will have to be based primarily on qualitative arguments.

A third issue with the implementation of a loss distribution approach is that internal loss data will include few low-frequency/high-severity losses, which tend to drive operational risk capital estimates. Furthermore, internal loss data may not contain specific types of events, for example, when an institution decides to enter a new market or activity. Financial institutions therefore often combine the internal loss data with loss experience from other financial institutions. When doing so, however, the question is how relevant the loss data from other institutions is, both in terms of the nature of events that have led to the losses and the size of losses. Rogue trader losses will not be relevant for a regional retail bank, and losses experienced by a large international retail bank may overestimate the potential loss size for the regional retail bank. Moreover, the control environment can differ significantly between institutions. Although the use of external loss data can help with the estimation of the severity distribution, a careful selection needs to be made with respect to the nature and the size of losses that are included from other institutions. Furthermore, operational loss data that is pooled by individual institutions can be subject to survival bias because the pool will not include loss data from institutions that ceased to exist as a result of large operational losses. Survivorship bias will not be present in collections of operational loss data that are gathered from public sources.

A fourth issue relates to the use of historical data in general. Typically, if an institution suffers a large operational loss it will review and improve its internal controls. More in general, the internal controls and operating environment are not constant, but change over time. This reduces the relevance of historical loss data. We can attempt to reflect this by incorporating the impact of changes in the operating environment on the loss distribution, but such an impact may be difficult to determine precisely and is likely subject to a high degree of uncertainty. We will return to this in Section 4.4.3.

A fifth issue that we face when implementing a loss distribution approach is what to assume about correlations between the occurrence and severity of events. It is not difficult to think of reasons why a positive correlation can exist between the occurrence of operational losses, as well as between the frequency and severity of operational losses. For example, a reduction in the number of persons exercising controls in an institution can lead to an increase in both the number and the size of operational losses. However, due to the feature that economic capital for operational risk typically is caused by a single large event instead of a series of smaller ones, correlation between multiple loss events will have a much less pronounced impact on the economic capital estimate for operational risk than it has, for example, for credit risk.

Scenario Analysis Approach

In recognition of the fact that large operational losses tend to arise from single, high-severity events for which there is little empirical data, some institutions have adopted a scenario approach to operational risk. In this approach, a number of scenarios that would lead to large operational losses are specified, and a loss distribution is constructed from these scenarios. The economic capital estimate can be derived from this loss distribution.

In its simplest form, each scenario is assigned a certain probability and a certain severity. For example, a scenario related to internal fraud could state that there is a 5% probability that the institution incurs a loss of $10 million as a result of internal fraud. If multiple scenarios have been specified, an overall loss distribution can be derived through simulation. In a simulation run, it is determined at random which of the specified scenarios occurs (taking into account the specified probability of occurrence for each), and the loss in a simulation run is calculated as the sum of the losses associated with the scenarios that have been simulated to occur. By simulating many different runs (e.g., one million), we obtain a simulated loss distribution, from which economic capital can be derived at the chosen confidence level.

A question is what correlation to assume between the occurrences of different scenarios in the simulation runs. Usually, institutions employ a broad definition for each scenario in the sense that it comprises all direct and indirect losses related to an event. Hence, if it is likely that one event happens in conjunction with, or as a consequence of, another event, then the losses of these events would be included as part of the same scenario. Consequently, institutions typically assume zero correlation between the occurrence of different scenarios in the scenario simulation.

In the simple scenario approach just described, there is a trade-off between the probability and the size of the potential losses. The choice made can influence the economic capital estimate significantly. For example, there may be a 5% probability of a USD 10 million loss due to internal fraud, and a 1% probability of a USD 50 million loss. Although the expected loss is the same in both cases (USD 500,000), including the latter more extreme scenario in the scenario simulation will lead to a higher economic capital estimate.

A more sophisticated and less arbitrary approach associates a frequency and severity distribution with each scenario, instead of specifying a single probability and severity. Such a frequency and severity distribution can be based on a number of statements for each scenario of the form, "once every d years, the loss associated with this scenario will be x or higher." The different statements per scenario can relate to increasingly unlikely events; for example, the loss that may be exceeded once every 10, 50, and 100 years. The information contained in these statements can be used to estimate the parameters of the frequency and severity distribution for the particular scenario.[67] In a simulation algorithm that is used to calculate the overall loss distribution, we randomly draw in each simulation run the number of events per scenario from the fitted frequency distribution, and for each event the severity from the fitted severity distribution. This procedure thus closely resembles the simulation performed in the loss distribution approach. In the scenario analysis approach, however, each of the scenarios is intended to represent a low-frequency/high-severity event, and thus the likelihood that an individual scenario occurs in a simulation run will be small.

As the specified scenarios typically represent low-frequency/high-severity events only, it will be necessary to supplement it with an analysis of high-frequency/low-severity events. Although the impact of these high-frequency/low-severity events on the unexpected loss, and thus on economic capital, will be small, they can significantly contribute to the expected loss. Certainly if economic capital includes expected losses in its definition for operational risk (see the discussion in Section 4.4.1), this may have a significant impact. To estimate potential losses from high-frequency/low-severity events, internal loss data may be used as the basis, in a way that is similar to the use in the loss distribution approach.

There is clearly subjectivity involved in specifying the scenarios. On the one hand, this allows for the incorporation of the specific nature of the business activities and the robustness of the control environment in an institution. On the other hand, there may be a tendency to underestimate the likelihood of very large losses. History has shown that realized large operational losses often exceed the amount that was deemed to be possible. To avoid an underestimation of large potential losses, financial institutions may use information about large historical operational losses from both internal and external sources as input into the specification of the scenarios.[68]

4.4.3 Special Topics

In this section we discuss how to account for the impact of operational risk management, and for insurance against operational losses, in economic capital models for operational risk. These topics are relevant irrespective of whether a loss distribution or a scenario analysis approach is chosen.

Accounting for Operational Risk Management

A common complaint from business management about capital assigned for operational risk is that it is not responsive to actual measures taken to reduce operational risk. In principle, some measures could be reflected directly in the assessments of the probability and size of operational losses in the loss distribution and scenario approaches that we discussed. For example, the implementation of a new system or new procedures that will remedy a particular source of operational losses can be reflected directly in the frequency or severity assessment of the specific type of loss event. Often, however, it may not be immediately transparent to what extent specific actions will reduce the frequency and severity of particular types of operational losses. It may then be desirable to first await the effect of the measures on the actual number and size of operational losses that will be incurred in the future. Furthermore, low-frequency/high-severity events tend to show up in unexpected places, and it may be difficult to devise measures of which it is clear beforehand how they influence the occurrence and severity of low-frequency/high-severity events.

In general, it is easier to estimate how management action impacts losses from high-frequency/low-severity events, and thereby expected loss. Because these losses form a recurring item in the income statement of an institution, and are therefore very visible, there is a clear incentive to manage them. If it is deemed desirable also to create incentives to mitigate low-frequency/high-impact operational risk events, then risk-mitigating actions may be reflected in an economic capital calculation even if their precise impact is difficult to estimate. These actions may relate to changes in the business environment and internal controls. For the reasons provided, we would advocate a cautious approach to recognize the risk-mitigating (i.e., capital-reducing) effects of these actions.

Including Operational Risk Insurance

A direct way to mitigate the impact of unexpected operational losses is through insurance policies. Institutions in general will have insured themselves against the financial consequences of external events like flooding and fire. Furthermore, many firms have insurance policies in place to provide protection against the financial consequences of legal litigation cases. A number of insurance companies also have started to provide insurance against financial losses from more general operational risk events. Given the substantial uncertainty about the size of potential operational losses and the ability of management to influence them, these insurance policies will have a maximum coverage, and often require the institution to share in the losses to align its incentives with the provider of the insurance (see also our discussion in Section 1.3.1 on risk and uncertainty). The benefits of operational risk insurance can be embedded easily in the simulation of the overall loss distribution that we described earlier. In each simulation run, the simulated loss can be reduced by the benefits from all insurance policies in place.

We note that obtaining insurance from external parties gives rise to counter-party risk, which should be reflected in the economic capital calculations. This is best done in the economic capital calculation for operational risk directly, by including a probability that the insurance policy will not pay out. There is wrong-way risk on the insurance provider if its creditworthiness is closely related to required payouts under the policy. See also our discussion on wrong-way risk in Section 4.2.3.

4.4.4 Allocation of Economic Capital

As we highlighted in our discussion, economic capital for operational risk tends to be driven by a single large operational loss. If we follow the component economic capital contribution method to attribute economic capital to business units, which we argued in Section 4.1.4 is the preferred method conceptually, economic capital will be allocated largely to the business unit or units that contribute to this single large loss. Other business units may be allocated hardly any economic capital. Given the unpredictability of the nature and size of future large operational losses, this may not result in a fair allocation of risk. As a consequence, many institutions choose to apply an alternative allocation method.

A simple way to allocate operational risk economic capital is to do so in proportion to a business unit's share of expected operational losses. An advantage is that it provides an incentive to manage operational risk, in particular the high-frequency/low-severity events. However, a business unit's exposure to high-frequency/low-severity events (which drive expected losses) may not have a strong relation to the unit's susceptibility to low-frequency/high-severity losses (which drive unexpected losses, and thus capital requirements). Alternatively, economic capital can be allocated on the basis of the contribution to realized losses. However, this allocation may change significantly if one business unit incurs a large operational loss. Its allocation of operational risk economic capital will increase as a result, and it will decrease for the other units, despite the fact that their operational risk profile may not have changed.

Another alternative is to attribute economic capital on the basis of stand-alone economic capital per business unit. This requires that there is sufficient information to estimate economic capital for individual business units in an organization. Especially for the estimate of a severity distribution in the loss distribution approach, this may not be the case. As a compromise, we can keep the severity distribution(s) the same for all business units, and vary only the frequency distribution.

We note that the use of an allocation key, whether it is expected losses, realized losses, or stand-alone economic capital, has the drawback that a change in value of the measure that is used as allocation key for one business unit has an impact on the amount that is allocated to the other business units, even if their risk profile does not change. To avoid this, we could leave the allocated amount of economic capital to the other business units unchanged, but then the sum of the allocated economic capital amounts no longer sums to the total amount of economic capital. Consequently, a choice between different allocation methods requires a trade-off between various strengths and weaknesses, and may also reflect incentives that management wants to provide to the business lines.

4.4.5   Regulatory Capital for Operational Risk

The Basel II Accord introduced an explicit capital requirement for operational risk for banks. In the Basel II Accord, banks can choose among three methods to calculate the capital requirement: the Basic Indicator approach, the Standardized Approach, and the Advanced Measurement Approach (AMA). The AMA allows banks to develop internal models for operational risk, and base the regulatory capital requirement on the 99.9 percentile of the one-year loss distribution that is calculated. Requirements that the Basel II Accord imposes on qualification for the AMA are that the operational risk measurement system makes use of internal as well as relevant external data, employs scenario analysis, and includes factors that reflect the business environment and internal controls. The Basic Indicator and Standardized approaches are simpler but less risk sensitive, and determine the capital requirement as a percentage of gross income, averaged over the past three years. The Basic Indicator approach uses a flat percentage (15%), whereas the percentage in the Standardized Approach varies between 12, 15, and 18%, depending on the type of business line.

The Solvency II proposal also includes a capital requirement for operational risk for insurance companies. Insurance companies may either apply their internal risk models based on a confidence interval of 99.5%, or they can use a standard formula. The proposed standard formula multiplies the technical provisions and the earned premiums with percentages varying between 0.2 and 3%, and adds 25% of the amount of annual expenses of the unit-linked business. The total capital requirement for operational risk under the standard formula is capped at 30% of the Basic Solvency Capital Requirement, which includes capital for market risk, counterparty default risk, and underwriting risk for life, non-life and health insurance.[69]

4.5   Asset-Liability Management Risk

Asset-liability management (ALM) is the discipline in financial institutions to monitor and control the potential mismatch in size and timing of cash flows between assets and liabilities. Financial institutions typically allow for a mismatch as they expect to generate higher returns as a result. For example, banks often fund long-term assets (e.g., mortgage loans) with short-term funding (e.g., customer deposits or money market loans) to profit from the positive difference between long-term and short-term interest rates. Life insurance companies and pension funds typically invest a substantial part of the premiums they receive in equity markets with the expectation that this will yield higher returns in the long term than fixed-income investments, although this creates a mismatch between assets and liabilities because the value of their liabilities depends largely on interest rates instead of equity prices.

ALM risk is the potential loss in value of an institution's net asset value (the value of its assets minus the value of its liabilities) as a result of changes in market variables. We exclude assets and liabilities in the trading book from ALM risk, since they are captured under market risk. The value of assets and liabilities will not only change as a result of changes in market variables. For example, loans and bonds will change in value if the creditworthiness of the borrower, respectively issuer, changes. This risk is captured under credit risk, and we therefore do not consider it part of ALM risk. Furthermore, liability cash flows on insurance policies are uncertain as a result of insurance risks. We will cover these risks in Section 4.7.1 under insurance risks.

For banks, ALM risk primarily relates to differences in interest-rate sensitivity between assets and liabilities in the banking book. In addition, banks may be exposed to exchange rate risk if there is a currency mismatch between assets and liabilities. Because of interest-rate and exchange-rate mismatches between assets and liabilities, banks may need to attract external funding in the future when cash flows from the assets are insufficient to make required payments on the existing liabilities. This exposes them to the risk of increased funding cost in the future. In an extreme situation, funding may not be available at all, potentially leading to liquidity problems. Because of the close relation with interest-rate and exchange-rate mismatches between assets and liabilities, we will discuss funding cost and liquidity risk in this section on ALM risk as well (in Section 4.5.3).

The importance of ALM risk for banks was demonstrated in the Savings & Loan crisis in the United States, which unfolded during the 1980s. The primary function of Savings & Loan associations (thrifts) was to take in savings from private customers, and lend this money as residential mortgages. They performed a central role in the government's aim to promote home ownership. During the late 1970s and early 1980s, interest rates in the United States rose strongly as a result of a sharp increase in inflation after the second oil crisis in 1979 (see Graph 4.11). At the same time, money market mutual funds were introduced that offered higher interest rates to customers than the Savings & Loan associations. To maintain sufficient funds, the associations were forced to increase the interest they paid on savings accounts. This put severe pressure on earnings, because their assets largely consisted of long-term fixed-rate mortgages that had been extended when interest rates were lower. The economic value of the mortgage assets dropped significantly as a result of the strong rise in interest rates, and many Savings & Loans associations had become *de-facto* insolvent due to their large interest-rate mismatch position.

With the aim to improve their financial situation, and helped by a relaxation of federal rules, many Savings & Loan associations subsequently started to lend money to real-estate development and construction companies because

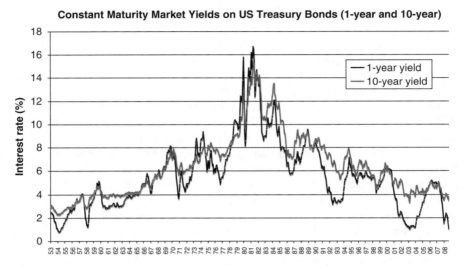

Graph 4.11 Development of yields on one-year and 10-year US Treasury bonds from 1953 to 2008.
Source: US Federal Reserve (www.federalreserve.gov)

this promised higher returns than their traditional residential mortgage lending. When the property market in many regions in the United States collapsed in the second part of the 1980s, defaults of the real-estate development and construction companies soared, and losses mounted for many Savings & Loan associations. Between 1989 and 1993 more than 1,000 Savings & Loan associations were closed, and the total cost of the bailout of these institutions has been estimated at USD 153 billion.[70] The Savings & Loan crisis not only illustrates the potential consequences of a large interest-rate risk mismatch position, but also the relation between interest-rate, funding cost, and liquidity risk.

For life-insurance businesses and pension funds, interest-rate risk is also an important component of ALM risk because it directly influences the net present value of future liabilities. Due to the long-term nature of life-insurance policies and pension plans, their economic value is very sensitive to changes in interest rates. As life-insurance companies and pension funds often invest a substantial part of their assets in equities, whereas their liabilities typically are not directly related to the performance of equity markets, they have significant equity market exposure. The risk of this exposure became clear in the second half of 2008, when many equity markets worldwide dropped by more than 40% in value. The OECD reported that pension funds in all OECD countries together had lost nearly 20% of their asset value, or USD 3.3 trillion, in 2008 up to October.[71]

In addition, ALM risk arises from guarantees that some insurance products offer. The risk of such guarantees is illustrated by the fate of Equitable Life Assurance Society in the United Kingdom, once the country's oldest mutual insurer. From the 1950s onward, it had sold guaranteed annuity rate (GAR) policies, which guarantee investors a minimum annuity rate when they retire. This constituted a substantial part of its business. When interest and inflation rates declined significantly in the 1990s, Equitable Life was not able to uphold these guarantees, and it proposed to reduce the benefits to its policy-holders. After a number of sessions in court, the House of Lords ruled that Equitable Life had to honor its obligations to the policyholders. As a conse-quence, it had to close its doors to new business in December 2000, and put itself up for sale.

For life-insurance companies and pension funds, ALM risk is often the larg-est contributor to total risk. For banks, it usually is significantly smaller than both credit risk and operational risk, and many institutions report it together with market risk economic capital.

Asset managers may also be exposed to ALM risk if they have sold investment products with certain guarantees. An example is capital-protected investments that promise clients to receive at least the originally invested amount back at maturity. In addition, they are exposed to liquidity risk if a large number of cli-ents demand their money back at the same time, and the asset manager is unable to liquidate its investments in the market. This happened to a number of hedge funds toward the end of 2008, and several large hedge funds decided to suspend redemptions by investors to avoid liquidity problems.[72]

In the next section we review some important choices and assumptions to consider when estimating economic capital for ALM risk in a financial institu-tion, before we discuss economic capital modeling approaches for ALM risk in Section 4.5.2.

4.5.1 Fundamental Choices and Assumptions

We review a number of issues that warrant consideration when developing a methodology to assess economic capital for ALM risk.

Earnings-at-risk or Value-at-risk

Most banking book assets and liabilities are included at amortized cost on a bank's balance sheet as a consequence of which their book value does not change with changes in interest rates. Banks therefore focused on earnings-at-risk when managing interest-rate risk in the banking books. Earnings-at-risk measures the risk to one-year (accounting) earnings as a result of interest rate changes. It results from timing mismatches between interest-rate resets on floating-rate assets and liabilities, and between refinancing of assets and liabilities that mature within one year. Changes in fair value of assets and liabilities with a maturity date beyond one year are not included in earnings-at-risk measures.

In Chapter 3 we have argued that economic capital should include poten-tial changes in fair value. Hence, value-at-risk should be considered in addi-tion to earnings-at-risk. Value-at-risk is also most closely related to the market value of equity. In its principles for the management and supervision of interest-rate risk in the banking book,[73] the Basel Committee on Banking Supervision also emphasizes the importance of an economic value perspective: "Since the economic value perspective considers the potential impact of interest rate changes on the present value of all future cash flows, it provides a more comprehensive view of the potential long-term effects of changes in interest rates than is offered by the earnings perspective. This comprehensive view is important since changes in near-term earnings—the typical focus of the earnings perspective—may not provide an accurate indication of the impact of interest rate movements on the bank's overall positions." The Savings & Loan crisis illustrates the practical relevance of an economic value perspective, since an adoption of this perspective would have shown the need for a strengthening of the capital levels at a much earlier stage.

When estimating potential value changes, we need to take into account whether economic capital is intended to be a point-in-time or through-the-cycle estimate. Similar to what we discussed in the section on market risk, this may determine how much history to take into account for the estimation of potential changes in the relevant market variables. Graph 4.11 clearly shows that both the level of interest rates and the shape of the yield curve (the difference between the 10-year and the one-year interest rates) can change dramatically over time. However, even for point-in-time estimates it is important to ensure that sufficient volatility in market variables is included, because the extreme potential changes in value that we consider for economic capital purposes will likely correspond to extreme changes in market variables.

Portfolio Dynamics

When evaluating the risk to earnings of the interest-rate mismatch position in the banking books, banks typically assume that maturing assets and liabilities are replaced by similar ones. Such assumptions also feed through when the earnings-at-risk assessment is extended to a value-at-risk assessment. It is important to ensure that assumptions made in this respect are consistent with the assumptions made for the other risk types, in particular credit and market risk.

As pension funds have a contractual agreement to accept additional pension liabilities that arise in the coming year, they have to take these into account when assessing ALM risk. For insurance companies and asset management firms, an explicit choice needs to be made whether to include expected future liabilities and assets in the evaluation of ALM risk for economic capital assessment purposes.

Management Intervention

Asset-liability mismatch positions usually are taken with a long-term view, and are therefore less frequently adjusted than trading positions. However, when time passes and market variables change, the mismatch position may change as well. An assumption can be made in the economic capital calculations for ALM risk how frequently the mismatch position is brought back to the target mismatch position. In addition, when the market situation changes significantly from earlier expectations, there is clearly the possibility to adjust the position and reduce risk. A further assumption can be made about a reduction of the size of the mismatch position in case losses reach a certain level. However, it may be costly or impossible to reduce positions in a distressed market.

4.5.2 Modeling Approaches

Following our general definition of economic capital in Chapter 3, economic capital for ALM risk should be calculated as the potential downward deviation of an institution's net asset value from the expected value at the one-year horizon, where the size of the potential shortfall is calculated at the confidence level chosen for economic capital. The expected (positive) change in net asset value will be included as expected return in a RAROC calculation, and can be included as part of available capital when assessing capital adequacy. We elaborated on this point in more detail in Section 4.3.2 when describing economic capital modeling approaches for market risk.

Since the nature of the ALM risk in banks is quite different from the one for insurance companies and pension funds, we describe modeling approaches for them separately.

ALM Modeling Approaches for Banks

Many banks include economic capital estimates for the ALM mismatch position under the reported figure for market risk economic capital. They also often arrive at this estimate by applying a market risk VaR calculation, and extrapolating the results from this VaR calculation to an economic capital estimate in the same or a similar way as described under market risk. In the VaR calculation, the banking book positions usually are represented as sensitivities to changes of interest-rate yield curves and exchange rates, instead of considering assets and liabilities individually.

In the section on market risk we described how a simulated one-day or 10-day profit-and-loss distribution that forms the basis for the VaR calculation can be extrapolated to an annual profit-and-loss distribution. From the annual distribution, economic capital can be derived. Instead of assuming a constant trading position, we have thus assumed that the one-day or 10-day profit-and-loss distribution remains relatively stable over time. For trading books this is a practical and defendable approach since trading positions can change quickly, whereas the characteristics of the profit-and-loss distribution may be more stable over time because of existing trading limits. For the interest-rate mismatch position, it may be most realistic to assume that the mismatch position is held constant because of the longer-term nature of this position. The resulting profit-and-loss distribution will then vary over time with changes in market circumstances.

As an alternative to a market risk VaR-based calculation of economic capital for interest-rate risk in the banking books, we therefore can model explicitly longer-term movements in interest rates (and other relevant market variables), and apply these to the mismatch position. In this way, longer-term characteristics of changes in market variables can be accounted for, such as mean-reverting behavior of interest rates and longer-term dependency patterns between different market variables. Nonlinear changes in the values of assets and liabilities as a result of embedded options (e.g., mortgage prepayment options) can also be incorporated more adequately. Furthermore, it provides better insight into which interest-rate scenarios pose the largest risk for a chosen mismatch position. When assessing the change in net asset value over longer horizons, we need to reflect the choice with respect to the inclusion of portfolio dynamics, as discussed in Section 4.5.1. In addition, rules reflecting management intervention as a function of changes in market circumstances can be embedded.

ALM Modeling Approaches for Insurance Companies and Pension Funds

According to a survey by the Society of Actuaries and Towers Perrin,[74] insurance companies increasingly use stochastic models to calculate economic capital for the major risks to which they are exposed. In these stochastic models, important risk factors are simulated into the future over a one-year or a multi-year horizon, and the impact on the value of assets and liabilities is assessed. By performing a large number of simulation runs, a probability distribution of the future net asset value is obtained, from which economic capital can be derived. The effect of relevant risk factors on the net asset value may be assessed for individual risk factors, and then aggregated across risk factors, or the simulation may include a joint evolution of the risk factors, taking dependencies between them into account. The stochastic models are thus comparable to the ALM modeling approach described earlier for banks, when long-term movements in interest rates and exchange rates are simulated. A larger set of market variables may be included in a stochastic model for an insurance company, however, depending on the types of assets in which it invests and the nature of its liabilities. Also pension funds often use such stochastic simulation models to assess ALM risk, and estimate how much the value of the pension fund assets should exceed the value of its liabilities to prevent insolvency with a sufficiently high probability.

4.5.3   Special Topics

In this section we review a number of issues that relate to the implementation and use of economic capital models for ALM risk.

Funding Cost Risk

As a consequence of mismatches in the timing and size of cash flows between assets and liabilities, financial institutions are also exposed to funding cost risk (i.e., the risk of increased cost of funding). Funding cost risk is most prevalent for banks, due to the reliance of many banks on short-term funding sources to invest in long-term assets. Due to the typical long-term nature of insurance policies and pension contracts, funding risk is typically not a major risk for insurance companies and pension funds. Managing funding cost risk is complicated by the fact that the timing of a substantial part of the cash flows on assets and liabilities may be uncertain. This can be an important source of model risk, as we discuss later in this section.

Increased funding costs as a result of increases in the general level of interest rates will be captured in the quantification of ALM risk. However, the cost of funding may also increase because liquidity disappears from specific markets from which the institution obtains a significant part of its funding. As a consequence, the institution has to rely on other, potentially more expensive markets for funding. Funding costs may also increase because of a deterioration in the creditworthiness of the institution itself, resulting in a higher compensation that providers of funding require from the institution. These reasons for potentially higher funding costs usually are not included in the modeling approaches for ALM risk, and would then need to be included separately or as part of business risk.[75]

Instead of attracting funding from external sources when needed, an institution can also decide to sell part of its assets. The risk is then that the assets can only be sold at a discount to the value at which the institution has included them on its balance sheet, resulting in a loss. To mitigate the risk of incurring losses when having to sell assets for funding purposes, institutions normally have a portion of their funds invested in liquid assets, which can easily be sold when a need for funds arises. The opportunity cost of investing part of an institution's funds in liquid assets, which usually have a lower yield than other assets, needs be balanced with lower funding cost risk.

Funding Liquidity Risk

As introduced in Section 3.3.1, funding liquidity risk represents the possibility that no funding is available at all. This is usually due to a complete lack of confidence by investors in the financial situation of the specific institution.

An institution's investments in liquid assets that reduce funding cost risk also help to mitigate funding liquidity risk, since these assets can be sold quickly in normal circumstances without a significant impact on price, or be placed with central banks as collateral for loans. These liquidity portfolios only provide relief for a certain period of time, however. If the source of the lack of confidence by investors is not resolved in the meantime, for example, by a capital injection to restore confidence in the financial soundness of the institution, then the institution may default on its obligations due to a lack of funds, even though it is technically still solvent.

Default resulting from a lack of funding will be accelerated if existing providers of funding are able to withdraw funds on short notice. This happened to Northern Rock in the fall of 2007, at the time the fifth largest mortgage lender in the United Kingdom, when retail depositors queued on the street to withdraw their deposits in a classic bank run. As recounted in Section 2.2.1, it also happened to Bear Stearns in March 2008 when professional counterparties withdrew their funds *en masse* from the bank when doubts about its solidity arose. Default can also be accelerated when rating agencies lower the official credit rating of a firm, and if this triggers contractual provisions that require the institution to post large amounts of additional collateral with its counterparties. AIG experienced this, and had to be rescued by the US Federal Reserve in August 2008 to prevent default.

Although an actual or perceived shortage of capital is often the source of liquidity problems, we argued in Section 3.3.4 that funding liquidity risk itself should not contribute to economic capital. To prevent a firm-specific liquidity crisis, available capital should be commensurate with all risks that can lead to unexpected losses, and consequentially a decrease in available capital. It is also important that providers of funds perceive that the level of capital is adequate and thus active external communication about the risk profile in relation to an institution's capital position is crucial.

Model Risk

It is often not easy to determine precisely the sensitivity of the value of certain classes of assets and liabilities to market variables. Estimates of the sensitivity usually are derived from models, and we therefore have exposure to model risk. We will give a few examples.

Customer deposits of a bank have no fixed maturity, and can in principle be withdrawn at any given time. This would argue for assuming a very short maturity. The experience is, however, that the bulk of the customer deposits stays with the bank for a long time, and this core part of customer deposits effectively has a long maturity. The interest rate that is paid on customer deposits may therefore not only depend on short-term but also on (typically higher) long-term interest rates, especially in situations of strong competition between banks for customer deposits.

Banks use statistical models to estimate what part of the customer deposits will be withdrawn at future points in time, and how sensitive the interest rate that is paid on customer deposits is to short-term and long-term interest rates. These statistical models may have short-term and long-term interest rates as explanatory variables, but also other ones, like the difference in interest rate paid by different banks, and macro-economic variables. These statistical models can be embedded in simulation models from which economic capital for ALM risk is derived, provided the explanatory variables in the statistical models are explicitly part of the simulation.

Institutions are exposed to the risk that these models do not correctly represent the behavior of customers in the future, or that the bank changes the way in which it sets interest rates on customer deposits. In an extreme situation, all customer deposits may be withdrawn simultaneously in a bank run. Ideally, we would include the model risk from using such statistical models explicitly in the economic capital calculation. This is especially relevant if a breakdown of the statistical models results in losses to the bank precisely when the bank is likely to experience other unexpected losses. A clear example is that withdrawals of customer deposits will be higher than has been experienced in the past in case the bank in general goes through difficult times (with a bank run as extreme situation).

Model risk is also present when estimating the interest-rate sensitivity of residential mortgage portfolios. Although mortgages often have long (e.g., 30-year) maturities, people may repay them earlier when they move to a different house, or when interest rates have declined, as this provides an incentive to redeem the existing mortgage and take out a new one at a lower interest rate. How strong the incentive is depends on the penalty that financial institutions charge when the mortgage is repaid early, which differs from country to country. Financial institutions use statistical models to estimate how many of the outstanding mortgages will be repaid at different points in the future, based on past experience. These statistical models usually take into account important factors that influence mortgage repayment rates, such as the age of mortgages, and the difference between the interest rate paid on mortgages and the prevailing market rate. To the extent that these statistical models incorrectly predict the level of repayments, the estimated interest-rate mismatch position and the interest-rate sensitivities that enter into the ALM models will be incorrect.

Model risk further exists with respect to the valuation of assets and liabilities at the end of the one-year economic capital horizon, as a function of the evolution of market variables during the year. There is no liquid market, nor are there generally accepted valuation formulas, for many of the assets and liabilities on the balance sheet of financial institutions, including customer deposits, residential mortgages, insurance contracts, and pension benefits. Hence, there is typically substantial model risk involved when attaching a value to such assets and liabilities, in particular because they often contain various complex embedded options. Although it is difficult to quantify the valuation uncertainty precisely, we can obtain insight into the effect of the valuation uncertainty on economic capital estimates for ALM risk by including at least a rough estimate of the valuation uncertainty in the modeling approach used (e.g., by imposing a probability distribution of possible valuations around the best estimate, and sampling from this distribution in an overall simulation approach for ALM risk).

In the management of ALM risk, institutions often make use of the concept of a replicating portfolio to estimate sensitivities and potential value changes for classes of assets and liabilities of which the timing, size, or duration of cash flows are uncertain. A replicating portfolio represents such classes of assets and liabilities as a portfolio of financial instruments for which the cash flows are clear, and for which sensitivities and changes in value can be calculated relatively easily. ALM risk management uses these replicating portfolios when managing the mismatch between assets and liabilities of the institution, and to assess how this mismatch can result in adverse changes of the institution's net asset value in the future. Model risk is present in the representation of the actual assets and liabilities by such a replicating portfolio.

4.5.4 Allocation of Economic Capital

How economic capital for ALM risk, as well as for funding risk, should be allocated within an organization largely depends on how these risks are managed. If these risks are managed at a central (group) level, and resulting revenues and costs are not allocated to the business units, then economic capital for these risks should also be held at group level. Financial institutions take mismatch risk and the associated funding risk with the expectation to generate higher returns, and hence a proper risk-adjusted profitability analysis can be performed at the level of the group from taking a mismatch position.

Some organizations allow business units to assume mismatch positions on their own. In this case, it is consistent to allocate to the business units an amount of economic capital that is commensurate with the level of ALM risk assumed. Similar to what we described for the allocation of market risk in Section 4.3.4, allocation of ALM risk economic capital based on the component economic capital contribution method can result in somewhat arbitrary, and potentially volatile, contributions for business units. This can happen, for example, if a business unit takes a mismatch position that the ALM unit at the group level decides to reduce, or even offset completely. To prevent counterintuitive and volatile allocations of economic capital, it can be allocated on the basis of stand-alone calculations of ALM risk, just as we described for market risk. As we noted there, this may have the effect that business units that largely drive the economic capital for ALM risk at the group level receive a relatively low allocation of economic capital.

4.5.5 Regulatory Capital for ALM Risk

For banks, there is no capital requirement for ALM risk in Pillar 1 of the Basel II Accord, which specifies the calculation of minimum capital requirements, but it is explicitly mentioned as part of the supervisory review process, which is part of Pillar 2 of the Basel II Accord. In fact, the Basel II Accord states:[76]

> The Committee remains convinced that interest rate risk in the banking book is a potentially significant risk which merits support from capital. However, comments received from the industry and additional work conducted by the Committee have made it clear that there is considerable heterogeneity across internationally active banks in terms of the nature of the underlying risk and the processes for monitoring and managing it. In light of this, the Committee has concluded that it is at this time most appropriate to treat interest rate risk in the banking book under Pillar 2 of the Framework.

It is suggested to test the necessity for an additional capital charge on the basis of a simple stress test:

> *Supervisors should be particularly attentive to the sufficiency of capital of "outlier banks" where economic value declines by more than 20% of the sum of Tier 1 and Tier 2 capital as a result of a standardized interest rate shock (200 basis points) or its equivalent [. . .].*

As we remarked in the introduction, ALM risk is a major source of risk for insurance and reinsurance companies, which is reflected in the proposed Solvency II regulations: "The Pillar I requirements are based on an economic total balance sheet approach. This approach relies on an appraisal of the whole balance sheet of insurance and reinsurance undertakings, on an integrated basis, where assets and liabilities are valued consistently." With respect to the reflection of market risks in the Solvency Capital Requirement, the proposal states: "It shall properly reflect the structural mismatch between assets and liabilities, in particular with respect to the duration thereof." The Solvency II proposal allows for the use of internal models to determine the size of the minimum solvency capital requirement.

4.6 Business Risk

Business risk is the risk of lower revenues and/or higher operating costs than expected. Inherent to being in business is that revenues and costs are uncertain because they depend on many factors, including market circumstances, actions of competitors, and the way in which the firm is managed. A flexible cost structure can mitigate the impact of lower revenues, because it enables firms to reduce costs when revenues decrease.

Business risk sometimes is regarded as a given for a firm, but in actual fact business risk is the result of several management choices. These choices can have an operational character such as the marketing strategy and the operational efficiency of the firm. They can also have a more strategic character when it comes to decisions on large investments, acquisitions, in what markets the firm operates, and the organizational design. Reversing such management choices takes time, but that does not imply that business risk cannot be managed.

In the booming financial markets between the early 1990s and the start of the sub-prime crisis it may have seemed that business risk was hardly a relevant risk for financial institutions. However, the sub-prime crisis brought an end to that boom period in many financial markets. For example, the activity in the markets for syndicated loans, initial public offerings, and advisory on mergers and acquisitions all decreased significantly. Investment banks are particularly active in these markets and, as a consequence, their revenues declined sharply. The relatively flexible cost structure of investment banks allowed them to shed costs quickly as well, but the materialization of business risk cast doubt in the eyes of some observers on the viability of their entire business model.[77] Although business risk may not have been the direct cause of many bank failures, it has been at the root of the restructuring and acquisition of many financial institutions. Consequently, management of business risk is closely related to the continuity of an institution.

Business risk can differ materially between financial institutions and activities. Typically, financial institutions with (volatile) fee business have higher business risk than institutions with relatively stable interest income. The difference in business risk between business lines is illustrated nicely by the change in revenues of Deutsche Bank, which combined investment and commercial banking activities, from 2007 to 2008 (Table 4.8).

The revenue changes show that trading and fee-related advisory and asset management businesses were most vulnerable to the slowdown of the financial markets, while interest income and transaction fees were relatively stable and even increased. Not all revenue changes are a reflection of business risk. Sales and Trading revenues were significantly negatively affected by losses from proprietary trading, which should be attributed to market risk rather than business risk. Furthermore, the increase in revenues of Loan Products was largely driven by mark-to-market hedge gains on credit exposures. However, these qualifications do not change the observed pattern. The decline in overall revenues was mitigated to some extent by a 15% decrease in non-interest expenses. To complete the picture, the economic capital for business risk of Deutsche Bank on December 31, 2007, was EUR 0.3 billion.[78] This amount appears low, but may be the result of netting economic capital with the expected profit, which we will discuss in the next section.

Table 4.8 Revenue per business line of Deutsche Bank in 2008 compared to 2007. The revenues exclude the markdowns on investments as these markdowns relate to credit and market risk. (*Source*: Interim report Deutsche Bank, "Deutsche Bank reports net loss of EUR 3.9 billion for the year 2008," and 4Q 2008 Financial Data Supplement [5 February]).

Business line	Revenue 2007 (billion Euro)	Revenue 2008 (billion Euro)	Growth %
Sales and Trading—Debt	10.0	5.4	−46%
Sales and Trading—Equity	4.6	(0.6)	−113%
Origination and Advisory	3.4	1.9	−44%
Loan Products	1.0	1.3	+29%
Transaction Banking	2.6	2.8	+7%
Private Banking	5.8	5.8	+0%
Asset Management	4.4	3.5	−20%
Corporate Investment	1.5	1.3	−15%
Adjustments + Other	(0.1)	(0.6)	Not meaningful
Total Revenues	33.1	20.7	−37%

4.6.1 Fundamental Choices and Assumptions

There are two fundamental choices to make when estimating economic capital for business risk: whether or not to deduct expected profits from economic capital, and whether or not to take the franchise value into account. We also discuss how the measurement of business risk relates to the choice made for other risk types regarding the dynamics of the portfolio of assets and liabilities during the economic capital horizon.

Treatment of Expected Profit

We listed in Section 3.4.2 the arguments for whether or not to deduct expected profits from economic capital. We argued that for capital adequacy purposes such a deduction can be justified. Expected profit is then typically deducted from economic capital for business risk. The supporting argument is that only an actual operating loss, and not a deviation from the expected operating profit, will decrease the amount of available capital. Economic capital for business risk must then be defined as the risk of a negative operating result. However, as we showed in Section 3.4.2 as well, the deduction of expected profit is not correct when economic capital is used for performance measurement. To align the capital adequacy perspective and performance measurement perspective, we suggested not to deduct expected profits from economic capital, but to include it in available capital. As a consequence, expected profits should not be deducted from business risk economic capital. This is consistent with our original definition of business risk in Section 3.3.2, to which we will continue to adhere.

Franchise Value

In Section 3.2 we considered the franchise value of an institution and stated that the potential decrease of the franchise value may be reflected in economic capital for business risk. To substantiate this statement, we will further explain in this section the relationship between business risk and the franchise value.

The cash flows related to the assets and liabilities that are on the balance sheet of the institution are known, and the risk that these cash flows change is taken into account with one or more of the risk types other than business risk. Hence, business risk primarily originates from expected cash flows related to future assets and liabilities that are not on the balance sheet yet, to avoid an overlap with these other risk types. The franchise value of the institution relates to the same cash flows, following our definition of the franchise value in Section 3.1 as the discounted value of all expected future cash flows that are not directly related to the assets and liabilities included on the institution's balance sheet. Thus, the franchise value is the expected value of the future cash flows not related to assets and liabilities currently on the balance sheet, and business risk is the risk that these cash flows are lower than expected.

The current franchise value of an institution can be split between the value of the expected cash flows from new business during the period up to the economic capital horizon date, and the value of the expected cash flows from new business in the period thereafter. The value of the expected cash flows from new business after the economic capital horizon date defines the franchise value at the horizon date. Hence, economic capital for business risk consists of two parts: the risk that the fair value of equity at the horizon date is lower than expected due to lower revenues from new business and/or higher costs than expected during the one-year economic capital horizon, and the risk that the franchise value of the firm at the horizon date is lower than expected. If we exclude the franchise value at the horizon date from the definition of available and economic capital, then economic capital for business risk represents only the risk that the fair value of equity at the horizon date is lower than expected due to lower revenues from new business and/or higher costs than expected up to the economic capital horizon.

Many institutions in practice ignore the risk of a potential decline in the part of the franchise value that relates to expected cash flows beyond the economic capital horizon in their measurement of business risk. They focus on the extent to which revenues will be lower or costs higher than expected during the economic capital horizon, and the impact on the fair value of equity at the horizon. Clearly, available capital should be defined consistently in the context of a capital adequacy assessment. In particular, the expected profit that is added to available capital should also only relate to the period up to the time horizon of economic capital, and not beyond that. Available capital defined in this way likely differs from the market value of equity, which we argued is most relevant for performance measurement, because the market value takes expected profits beyond the economic capital time horizon into account.

Portfolio Dynamics

The measurement of business risk also interacts with the choices made for other risk types regarding the extent to which assets and liabilities that mature before the economic capital horizon are assumed to be replaced, and expected business growth is accounted for. To the extent that this is assumed, then the other risk types (credit risk, market risk, ALM risk) will reflect potential changes in value of these future assets and liabilities. If the economic or competitive environment changes in such a way that maturing assets and liabilities will not be (fully) replaced, then the earnings consequences will be reflected in business risk. The corresponding decrease in the potential for losses from the other risk types is ideally incorporated consistently. This requires an integrated model of business risk with the other risk types.

4.6.2 Modeling Approaches

There are various approaches to model business risk and, according to the 2007 IFRI/CRO Forum survey,[79] there is no dominant approach among financial institutions. However, most institutions include under business risk only the risk that the fair value of equity at the time horizon is lower than expected due to lower revenues from new business and/or higher costs during the economic capital time horizon. Hence, potential changes in the franchise value at the economic capital horizon date usually are not included. We present a few methods that are applied in practice to estimate economic capital for business risk, and discuss at the end of this section how the risk of a lower franchise value can be addressed.

The first method is to benchmark with other financial institutions. Economic capital is then based on an average of business risk economic capital estimates that are disclosed by similar financial institutions. Alternatively, if business risk is the major risk type to which another financial institution is exposed (e.g., asset managers), then benchmarking can be based on the actual capital position of that institution minus the estimated economic capital deemed to cover the other risk types. Economic capital for business risk can be expressed as a percentage of revenues or (fixed) costs in order to scale economic capital based on the firm's size. Although this approach is simple and pragmatic, it assumes that the estimates of other institutions are correct and applicable. Furthermore, it is not very risk-sensitive since internal actions and changes in the cost structure do not have an immediate influence on economic capital.

The second method is to derive economic capital for business risk by using expert judgment to estimate (points on) the probability distribution of the operating result by business line. Management and budget experts are asked to provide the expected operational result, as well as the operational result in one or more downward scenarios, each associated with a certain confidence level. If the confidence levels are all lower than the confidence level that is used for overall economic capital, for example, because it is difficult to make realistic estimates based on such very high confidence levels, then extrapolation is necessary to derive the operating result corresponding to the economic capital confidence level. To do this, it is often assumed that the uncertainty about the operating result at the one-year economic capital horizon can be described using a Gaussian distribution. Economic capital for the business line is the difference between the expected operational result and the (extrapolated) operating result corresponding to the economic capital confidence level.

The next step is that we aggregate these economic capital estimates across business lines, which requires that we know the correlations between the operating results of different business lines. Expert judgment may be used as an input again, but ideally this would be complemented with historically observed correlations. This approach to calculate economic capital provides results that are directly recognizable for managers. However, it requires many subjective inputs, which makes it difficult to ensure consistency between the different business lines.

The third and more objective method to measure economic capital for business risk is to estimate the probability distribution of the operating result by using as input the expected revenues and the historically observed volatility of these revenues. Again, a certain probability distribution function has to be assumed for revenues (e.g., a Gaussian distribution) in order to derive the downward level of revenues corresponding to the economic capital confidence level. The expected operating costs are modeled as a combination of fixed costs and variable costs (i.e., costs that vary with revenues) and are deducted from the expected revenues to derive the expected operating result. Economic capital is the potential downward deviation of the operating result that corresponds to the economic capital confidence level from the expected operating result. This method can be applied for the institution as a whole and for an individual business line. When the method is applied to calculate economic capital for each business line, then combining these economic capital numbers requires that we estimate the correlations between the operating profits of these business lines. If costs are modeled as the sum of a fixed part and a variable part, and if the variable part changes proportionally to the revenues, then the correlation between the operating profit of different business lines equals the correlation between their revenues.

An attention point with this method is that we have to ensure that there are no overlaps with the other risk types. In particular, the historical revenue volatility may also be caused by other risk types, such as credit, market, ALM, and insurance risk. The measured historical revenue volatility may also be influenced by acquisitions, divestments, and internal reorganizations, and this will complicate the calculations further. Although this third approach is more objective than the second approach, there are significant challenges to measure the volatility of the revenues to the extent that they pertain to business risk, and the correlations between the business lines.

The fourth method is based on a specification of the relationship between revenues and internal and external factors. Examples of external factors that may influence the level of future revenues are growth of gross domestic product (e.g., for consumer lending), real interest-rate levels (e.g., for savings accounts and insurance), equity indices (e.g., for asset management), and number and amount of corporate acquisitions (e.g., for corporate finance). Revenue volatility and correlations between business line revenues can be derived from the volatility of these factors, the correlations between them, and the sensitivity of revenues to these factors. This approach avoids the risk of overlap with other risk types, and correlations do not have to be estimated separately. The costs can be modeled as in the third method (i.e., by specifying fixed and variable costs per business line).

This fourth method is the most objective of all approaches and is reasonably risk-sensitive because it can accommodate changes in business mix and cost structure. However, the method is demanding because it requires modeling of the relationship between revenues and the identified revenue-driving factors, and the availability of sufficient historical data for the underlying revenue-driving factors. Moreover, internal reorganizations, large divestments, and acquisitions may necessitate a review of the relationships specified between revenues and the external and internal factors, and historical data on which to base such relationships may not be readily available.

If we want to include the risk of a lower franchise value at the economic capital horizon date in the economic capital estimates, we have to extend the revenue and cost estimates over multiple years and discount them to the horizon date to derive the expected franchise value at the horizon date. In addition, downward estimates of future cash flows have to be made to determine the distressed franchise value at the stipulated confidence level. Obviously, these estimates are uncertain as there are many factors that can influence future revenues and costs. The simplest solution is to assume that the distressed franchise value at the horizon corresponding to the economic capital confidence level will be zero. This assumption is supported by the observation that during the sub-prime crisis many companies wrote down the activated goodwill from earlier acquisitions. In some cases, the franchise value of firms even became negative (i.e., the market value of equity was lower than its book value). An explanation can be that the reported value of assets and liabilities of distressed firms were not adjusted yet to reflect their fair value. In that case, the book value of equity at the time of distress was overstated.

To summarize, economic capital for business risk consists of two parts: the risk that the fair value of equity at the horizon date is lower than expected due to lower revenues from new business and/or higher costs than expected, and the risk that the franchise value of the firm at the horizon date is lower than expected. There are a number of methods to estimate the first part—the risk of a lower fair value of equity at the horizon date, each with its strengths and weaknesses. To estimate the second part of economic capital for business risk requires modeling the variability of revenues and costs over a long period of time into the future. Given the uncertainty involved in such an analysis, it may be just as accurate to assume that the franchise value at the horizon date is zero in the distress scenario corresponding to the economic capital confidence level.

4.6.3   Special Topics

Reputation Risk

We concluded in Chapter 3 that reputation loss typically leads to a decline in revenues. As reputation risk has an impact on future revenues and costs, we have argued that it should be included in business risk. In Section 3.2 we also referred to research that showed how large unexpected operational losses that damage the institution's reputation can lead to decreases in the franchise value. Modeling reputation risk should, therefore, be aligned with how business risk is modeled. For example, if the franchise value is excluded from the definition of available and economic capital and thus also excluded from business risk, then the impact of reputation risk on the franchise value should be disregarded. The possibility to reflect reputation risk in the economic capital calculation for business risk depends on the way in which economic capital for business risk is modeled. If revenues and costs are modeled explicitly, then an attempt can be made to include the potential impact of an event that leads to reputation loss.

Modeling reputation risk is challenging because there are many potential causes of reputation damage. Causes can be internal and external, and the impact may be influenced significantly by management action. Hence, there is substantial uncertainty involved when we model reputation risk. Including it in economic capital models requires that explicit thought is given to the potential origins and consequences of reputation risk. If done successfully, it can provide directionally correct risk management incentives. We review some general characteristics that may be taken into account when modeling reputation risk.

First, at the root of a loss of reputation is almost always another loss or event that has materialized. One illustration forms the consequences of the theft of client data in 2008 from LGT, a small bank in Liechtenstein. The client data came into the possession of the German tax authorities, who used it to prosecute German citizens for tax evasion. The result for LGT was that clients no longer trusted that their records would be kept confidential. Consequently, a steady inflow of client funds in the previous years changed into a net outflow in the months after the theft and the subsequent actions by the German tax authorities.[80] Thus, the theft of client information resulted in a reputation loss, which in turn led to a loss of revenues.

As another example, the reputation of Bankers Trust was seriously damaged as a result of a legal dispute with a number of clients about derivatives transactions that resulted in a large settlement (operational loss), which we described earlier in Section 3.3.2. More recently, the Swiss bank UBS suffered large losses on structured credit products during the sub-prime crisis, and was subsequently confronted with negative press coverage and with negative perceptions by their shareholders, clients, politicians, and the Swiss public at large. Reputation risk, therefore, typically is correlated positively with the other risk types.

Second, a loss of reputation affects the entire organization. Although an error may have occurred in a small department or branch, clients and the public perceive the organization as one entity with a single brand and a single management team ultimately in charge. Just as the benefits of the brand name are shared across the organization, so are the reputation risks shared as well. A clear example is the Anglo Irish Bank. Its financial situation was already precarious as a result of bad property loans, but its fate was sealed after it was revealed in December 2008 that its directors had secretly received loans up to EUR 179 million from the bank, of which EUR 84 million was for its chairman. The reputation of the bank's senior management, and consequently of the bank itself, was irreparably damaged. It was faced with severe funding problems, as a result of which the bank was nationalized in January 2009.

If the volatility of revenues is modeled using a factor model, as in the fourth modeling approach that we described, then reputation risk can be represented by a factor that is common to all business lines to reflect the observation that reputation risk affects the whole organization at the same time. The positive correlation of reputation risk across business lines, and between reputation risk and other risk types, implies that economic capital for reputation risk is unlikely to be diversified away when aggregated with economic capital for the other risk types.

4.6.4   Allocation of Economic Capital

How to calculate economic capital contributions for different business lines depends first on the modeling approach chosen. In case the benchmark approach is used, then the contribution can be calculated by using simple proxies, such as the share of the business line in total revenues or (fixed) costs. In case the distribution of operating profit has been estimated per business line, which subsequently has been combined to a distribution at group level, then the methods from Section 4.1.4 can be applied. The generally preferred method is the component economic capital contribution method, for reasons that we described in Section 4.1.4. Revenues often are assumed to follow a Gaussian distribution in the models used for business risk. In that case, the standard deviation contribution method is equivalent to the component economic capital contribution method, and the economic capital contributions are then straightforward to compute.

4.7   Other Risks

In this section, we review economic capital methodologies for a number of additional risk types. Although the description of economic capital methodologies for the risk types in this section is less extensive than for the risk types in the previous sections, this should not be interpreted as implying that these risks are less material than the risk types covered thus far.

4.7.1   Insurance Risks

Insurance companies assume risk through the insurance contracts that they underwrite. They run the risk that the insurance claims are higher than expected, which is known as insurance risk or underwriting risk. Within insurance risk, a distinction typically is made between life insurance and non-life insurance (the latter is also called general insurance, or property and casualty insurance).[81] Life insurance policies are related to the occurrence of death, disability, or critical illness. The policies may specify single payments at the occurrence of such an event, or a sequence of payments (annuities) up to or after the event. Life-insurance policies usually extend over long periods, often one or more decades. Non-life-insurance policies cover the losses or costs related to damages incurred or caused by the insured persons. They include property insurance, liability insurance, motor insurance, accident insurance, and health insurance. Typically, non-life-insurance policies are renewable every year. Within non-life insurance, a distinction often is made between premium and reserve risk. Premium risk relates to the uncertainty about the number, timing, and size of claims related to potential future events, and reserve risk to the uncertainty about the size of claims related to events that have occurred already.

In addition to the uncertainty about the occurrence of insured events and the size of the resulting claims, insurance risk also comprises lapse risk and surrender risk. A lapse is the expiration of all rights and obligations under an insurance contract if the policyholder fails to comply with certain obligations required to uphold those, such as the premium payment or the proper care of an insured property. Lapse risk constitutes the risk that the number of lapses deviates from the expected level. A surrender is the termination of an insurance contract by the policyholder, in which case the insurance company must pay the cash value that is contractually agreed or legally prescribed. Life-insurance policies may contain surrender options for the policyholder. Surrender risk is the risk that the number of surrenders, and the size and timing of associated payments, differs from expectations.

The value that insurance companies attach to an insurance liability is called the technical provision. This technical provision is the present value of all expected future payments arising from the insurance contract, and a risk premium that reflects the cost of the capital that needs to be set aside to cover larger than expected payments. The risk premium is thus a function of the uncertainty in the timing and size of the cash flows arising from the contract. For example, for life-insurance contracts this relates to the uncertainty about mortality or morbidity (disability) rates.

The Solvency II proposal prescribes that the technical provision should equal the fair value of the insurance contract—that is, the amount that the insurance company would expect to pay if it transfers its contractual rights and obligations to another party. This is in line with our choice in Chapter 3 to use economic values of assets and liabilities in the calculation of economic capital. Market prices for insurance liabilities are, however, not readily available in most cases. Actuarial models therefore are used to establish the size of technical provisions for insurance liabilities in practice. These actuarial models may differ from firm to firm, and there is significant model risk involved in establishing values (technical provisions) for insurance liabilities. This model risk increases when the insurance contract embeds guarantees or options. Furthermore, given the long tenors of many life-insurance contracts, unknown future events may cause a structural change in the frequency or severity of claims. For example, a medical breakthrough (e.g., a cure for cancer) or new diseases (e.g., AIDS) can significantly change the mortality rate in a population. As discussed in Section 2.2.1, model risk has been one source of insurance company failures, when insurance companies underestimated technical provisions for a significant part of their insurance business.

Another source of potential large losses for insurers is the occurrence of extreme events, also called catastrophe events, which have a low-frequency/high-severity character. They represent one-time events that cannot realistically be estimated from events that are experienced regularly (high-frequency/low-severity events). Examples of extreme events are contagious diseases that affect many insured persons at the same time, and natural catastrophes. To illustrate the frequency and severity of catastrophe events, Swiss Re reports 335 catastrophe events in 2007, of which 193 were man-made (e.g., shipping, aviation, and mining accidents) and 142 were triggered by natural forces (e.g., earthquakes, flooding). The insured losses are typically higher for natural catastrophe events, as illustrated in Graph 4.12. The graph also shows that the insured losses as a result of man-made disasters have been fairly stable, with the exception of the consequences of the terrorist attacks on September 11, 2001. The weather-related events, in contrast, have produced very volatile losses for insurers. To illustrate the risks related to life insurance, Swiss Re estimates that catastrophes cost the lives of more than 21,000 people in 2007, and this number increased dramatically to 238,000 in 2008. Primary causes of this large increase are a tropical storm in Myanmar that cost the lives of 138,400 people, and an earthquake in China's Sichuan region that killed 87,400.[82] Most casualties from these two events were not insured, and hence did not lead to insurance claims.

To mitigate insurance risk, insurers can reinsure part of their insurance policies. The reinsurance can be in the form of proportional or nonproportional protection. In proportional protection, the reinsurance company shares for a fixed percentage in the premiums and losses of a pool of insurance policies. Nonproportional protection can have many forms, such as excess-of-loss or stop-loss, where the reinsurance company assumes the losses above a certain threshold amount. Proportional reinsurance reduces equally the expected loss and the loss in the tail of the loss distribution, whereas a stop-loss primarily reduces losses in the tail of the loss distribution. By buying reinsurance,

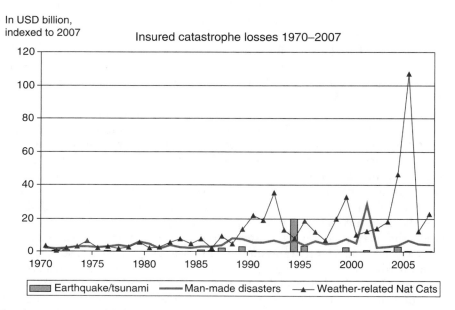

Graph 4.12 Insured losses 1970–2007 (property and business interruption losses). *Source*: Swiss Re sigma No 1/2008.

the insurer has a contingent exposure on the reinsurance company and, hence, is exposed to counterparty risk. Reinsurance buyers should be aware of wrong-way risks, which may be present if the reinsurance company is already heavily exposed to the risk that the reinsurance buyer wants to reinsure. Counterparty risk and wrong-way risk were discussed earlier in Section 4.2.3 on credit risk.

Modeling Approaches

There are two main approaches to model insurance risk: a scenario-based approach and a stochastic factor approach.[83] For both approaches, a choice must be made whether to include new insurance policies that the institution expects to originate during the economic capital horizon (see Section 4.1.1).

In a scenario approach, the firm defines a number of adverse scenarios and calculates for each of them the impact on the insurance liabilities, in particular, by how much they will be higher than in the expected scenario. The liabilities relate to both the actual claims incurred during the economic capital time horizon, and the change in value of the outstanding insurance policies at the horizon. For insurance risk, we only take into account the changes in value of the liabilities that are caused by changes in insurance-specific factors, such as mortality and casualty rates. The value of liabilities can also change because of changes in market variables, such as interest rates and equity prices, but these changes are included under ALM risk. The likelihood of the scenarios that are considered in the scenario-based approach must be consistent with the chosen confidence level for economic capital. Ideally, each scenario is a comprehensive description of a potential future state of the world and stresses the values of the relevant risk factors jointly (e.g., combine stressed mortality rates and morbidity rates). Alternatively, each risk factor is stressed separately and the respective impact on the insurance liabilities is summed (static factor model) or aggregated using a variance-covariance matrix (covariance model). Aggregation methods are discussed separately in Section 4.8.

A stochastic factor model generates a full probability distribution of potential insurance liabilities. To do so, first the functional dependence of the insurance liabilities on each risk factor must be estimated. As in the scenario-based approach, this should relate to both the actual claims incurred during the economic capital time horizon, and the change in value of the outstanding insurance policies at the horizon. The risk factors may represent the variables that directly drive insurance claims (e.g., mortality rates), but also catastrophe events that may affect several of such variables at the same time (e.g., mortality rates as well as morbidity rates and loss rates on properties). Subsequently, the joint distribution of all risk factors is simulated, taking their dependencies into account. Given the substantial role that model risk with respect to the valuation of insurance liabilities can play, this model risk preferably is included directly in the stochastic factor model. This can be done by specifying a probability distribution of potential liability values at the economic capital horizon date, reflecting the valuation uncertainty. For any given simulated realization of the stochastic factors in the model, this probability distribution is imposed on top of the expected liability value in that simulated scenario. A random realization is then drawn from it. If liability values of different insurance contracts are driven by the same factors, then we can incorporate positive correlation between valuation errors. Such positive correlation is likely to exist, for example, between insurance contracts that relate to the same insured event and geographic region.

According to a survey by Towers Perrin, most large life insurers use the stochastic factor modeling approach.[74] Besides being more flexible in general, this approach also allows them to capture better the nonlinear aspects of reinsurance contracts and the resulting counterparty risk, for which a scenario-based approach is less suitable.

A main challenge for either approach is to assess the potential impact of catastrophe events, as there will be few data available that can be used as a guide. Even if data on losses as a result of catastrophe events is available, there is the question of whether the data is still relevant. For example, to estimate potential losses as a result of pandemic influenza, often the 1918 pandemic is used as a reference point. However, this pandemic had several unique features, among others that it occurred in the aftermath of the First World War, and that it is therefore less suitable to be used to assess a potential loss that is applicable for the first decade(s) of the twenty-first century.[84] Hence, an in-depth analysis of all relevant aspects is necessary to model such an event. As an example, Swiss Re developed a tailor-made model for pandemic influenzas. To calibrate the model, Swiss Re uses data from the latest four pandemics. This small number of observations unavoidably leaves significant uncertainty about the value of the estimated risk parameters. The model produces a loss distribution on the basis of which it is possible to calculate economic capital and the expected tail loss at confidence levels set by Swiss Re and its regulators.[85]

Another example that illustrates that we must be careful to use historical data for estimating the potential impact of catastrophe events is the risk of flooding. Graph 4.13 shows that the number of flooding incidents was relatively low in the 1960s to 1980s but increased sharply thereafter. Hence, models that attribute too much weight to observations in these earlier years underestimate the risks. It is believed that global warming is causing the increased number of floods. Since heavy rainfall is brought on by certain weather conditions, and if these weather conditions are likely to persist, then a series of flooding events may occur. This gives rise to a positive correlation between flooding events.[86] Models of catastrophic events should account for these underlying risk drivers and associated correlations. Identifying these drivers requires expert judgment and depends on the state of scientific knowledge. Consequently, model risk will be high. As such, we end up in a situation that is comparable to operational risk, where low-frequency/high-severity events have a significant impact on economic capital but their measurement is subject to a high degree of uncertainty and, hence, model risk.

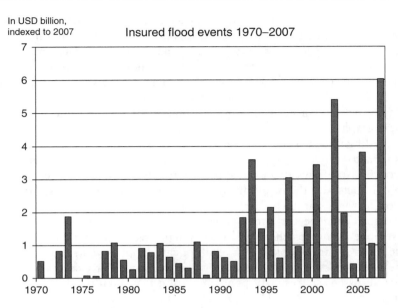

Graph 4.13 Global insured flood losses 1970–2007.
Source: Swiss Re sigma No 1/2008.

Allocation of Economic Capital

The prominence of low-frequency/high-severity events in economic capital calculations for insurance risk complicates the calculation of economic capital
contributions for business lines. Large losses in any specific scenario may be
due to a catastrophic event in a particular business line. However, in different
large-loss scenarios the catastrophic event and associated losses may relate to
different business lines. If economic capital for insurance risk is driven largely
by single catastrophic events, although they may occur in different business
lines, then the contribution to total economic capital of a business line can be
based on the probability that a catastrophic event will occur in that business line
relative to other business lines. In that case, the economic capital contribution
would be directly related to how prone each business line is to catastrophic
events. The estimated size of the loss may also be taken into account in case this
varies considerably across different types of catastrophic events. Allocation
is then done on the basis of the expected loss of catastrophic events.

If economic capital is determined by high-frequency/low-severity losses that
are not caused by a single catastrophic event, then any of the contribution
methods discussed in Section 4.1.4 can be used. As we discussed, the preferred
method is the component economic capital contribution method. This contribution method considers the contribution of each business line to the higher
than expected insurance claims and changes in value of insurance liabilities.

Any reinsurance contract in place would receive a negative economic capital contribution, where the size of the negative contribution can take the counterparty risk into account.

4.7.2 Pension Liability Risk

The pension risk that we discuss in this section takes the point of view of the institution that is liable to make contributions (i.e., acts as a sponsor) to a pension fund. It is not the point of view of the pension fund itself. We define pension liability risk as the risk that the institution has to make higher payments than expected to the pension fund of its employees. The risk is primarily relevant for defined-benefit pension plans, in which the pension benefits for the employees are contractually defined. The pension fund, and indirectly the employer, then bears the investment risk. The agreement between the pension fund and the sponsoring company may specify that the sponsoring company has to pay additional funds to the pension fund if the value of the pension fund's assets falls below a certain threshold. This threshold is usually a certain percentage of the value of the liabilities, representing the fair value of the existing pension obligations. The institution may be allowed to spread the additional payments that are due, within limitations, over multiple years.

Changes in the net asset value of a pension fund are driven by the return on its assets, and by changes in the value of its liabilities. The latter is subject to, among others, longevity risk (lower mortality rates will increase the pension obligations) and interest-rate risk (lower interest rates lead to lower discount rates that will increase the fair value of the pension obligations). The value of the obligations may also be subject to inflation risk if the pension obligations are increased each year with the realized inflation rate (indexation). In many cases, however, the pension fund has the right to forego the indexation if the financial situation of the fund warrants this. Consequently, indexation is usually not an unconditional obligation of the pension fund and, indirectly, the sponsoring firm.

The impact of pension liability risk on a company's earnings, and thus potentially capital, can be significant. This was illustrated in a study by the consulting firm Hewitt Associates,[87] which calculated in early 2008 that the net profit for all companies quoted on the Amsterdam Exchange would decrease with 15% over the next 10 years if share prices would fall by 33%, interest rates would decrease with 1%, and the life expectancy would increase with 5% (most Dutch companies have defined-benefit pension plans).

The annual contribution that the sponsoring firm must pay to its pension fund is based on assumptions about expected investment returns. The higher these expected returns are, the lower the required contribution to the pension fund is. However, if the assumptions turn out to be too optimistic, then future pension costs will increase for the sponsor. In his 2007 letter to the shareholders of Berkshire Hathaway, Warren Buffett pointed to the optimistic average investment return of 8% assumed by the 363 companies in the S&P 500 that have pension plans. This assumed return is much higher than the historical returns on bonds and equities. Buffett, skeptical of so-called experts being able to outperform the market, warned that actual returns are likely to be much lower than 8% and, hence, that many of these firms will be faced with significantly higher future pension costs.

International accounting rules[88] require that changes in the net asset value of a defined-benefit pension plan are reflected in the equity value of the sponsoring company. However, such changes in net asset value do not have to be included in the income statement of the sponsor. Only when the accumulated unrecognized gains or losses exceed 10% of the value of the pension plan assets (or the fair value of the pension liabilities, if higher), will part of the excess need to be recognized in the income statement. These unrecognized gains and losses are calculated with respect to the actuarial assumptions about the expected investment returns. This approach is intended to largely insulate a company's reported profit and loss from the volatility of changes in the net value of its pension plans.

As discussed in Chapter 3, economic capital is preferably based on the valuation of all assets and liabilities at fair value, and we apply this to pension liability risk as well. This definition of economic capital thus aligns with the way in which defined-benefit pension plans are included in the capital position of the sponsor. The fair-value approach implies that it does not matter for the capital position of the sponsoring firm whether it can replenish a shortfall in its pension funding gradually over time, or whether it needs to pay the shortfall immediately. However, being able to spread the required payments over time does decrease the liquidity risk for the institution.

Modeling Approaches

There are two basic approaches to calculate economic capital for pension risk, one aligned with the way in which pension plans are included on the balance sheet of the sponsor (value approach), and one that is based on the contractual obligations of the sponsor (earnings approach).

The value approach essentially consolidates the pension assets and liabilities on the balance sheet of the sponsor. Economic capital for pension liability risk is derived from the probability distribution of possible net asset values of the pension plans at the economic capital horizon. To determine this probability distribution requires modeling of ALM risk and insurance risk, as well as potentially other risks. The methods that we described earlier for financial institutions in general can be applied for this purpose to the pension plan assets and liabilities.

Although the net asset value (surplus) of a pension fund is thus considered in combination with the equity value of the sponsoring firm in the value approach, a positive surplus cannot absorb general losses of the sponsor. Hence, we cannot treat a positive surplus of the pension fund as part of the available capital of the institution for a capital adequacy assessment. However, a negative net asset value of the pension fund will decrease the available capital position of the institution, and should be taken into account in the capital adequacy assessment. There is thus an asymmetric relation between the pension fund and its sponsor, because the capital of the sponsor provides protection to the pension fund, but not vice versa.

To accommodate this asymmetry in the economic capital assessment of the sponsoring institution, economic capital for pension liability risk is best defined as the potential negative net asset value of the institution's pension plans. If the institution has a contractual or legal obligation to ensure that the net asset value of the pension fund has always some minimum positive value, and is required to provide funds directly if the net asset value falls below this minimum, then economic capital is best measured with respect to this minimum net asset value instead of a zero net asset value. This definition is an exception to the overall definition of economic capital that we have chosen, which is the potential downward deviation from the expected (net asset) value at the one-year horizon. The chosen definition of economic capital for pension liability risk ensures a fair comparison between economic capital and the institution's available capital in a capital adequacy assessment if a positive surplus of the pension fund is not included as part of available capital. For performance management, this definition is acceptable as well, because a positive surplus of an institution's pension fund will not increase the market value of the institution, due to the mentioned asymmetry.

The earnings approach for pension liability risk considers the impact on the institution's earnings of a decline in the net asset value of an institution's pension plans. The starting point for this approach is also the probability distribution of the net asset value of the pension plan at the economic capital horizon. An extra step is needed, however, to translate the change in net asset value into an impact on earnings for the institution. This translation may depend on accounting rules, as referred to earlier, but also on contractual and legal obligations that the institution has to provide funds to the pension fund in case the net asset value falls below a prespecified level. The earnings approach, however, considers only the potential impact on one-year earnings from such obligations. As we mentioned earlier, only the value approach is consistent with the choices we made for the general definition of economic capital.

A point of attention is the treatment of equity stakes that a pension fund may have in the sponsoring institution. In the extreme adverse scenario that corresponds to an unexpected decrease in net asset value corresponding to economic capital, these equity stakes are likely to have lost most of their value and, hence, should be valued close to zero for economic capital calculations. Debt instruments issued by, or other claims on, the sponsoring institution may receive a milder valuation treatment, but their value is obviously also highly correlated with the sponsoring institution's creditworthiness.

Allocation of Economic Capital

Allocating economic capital for pension risk to individual business lines can be done directly if these business lines have direct obligations to the pension fund. This may be the case if business lines are organized per country, because there

are usually different pension plans in different countries. If such a direct allocation is not possible, then economic capital has to be allocated indirectly. In such
a case, economic capital for pension risk often is allocated *pro rata* the "use" by
the business line of the services of the pension fund. Possible allocation keys are
the number of current (and former) employees that participate in the pension
plans, the expected contributions to the pension fund in the coming year, and
the technical reserves held by the pension fund against the claims of the employees in the business line. The most suitable allocation key will depend on the
actual circumstances and should be determined by management.

4.7.3 Fixed Asset Risk

Financial institutions own fixed assets for two main purposes: to use them as a
production factor and to act as a lessor and rent out the assets to clients. In
both instances the institution faces the risk that the value of the assets will
decrease below their expected value at the economic capital time horizon.

Assets that are used as a production factor are very diverse in nature. They
include real estate, office equipment, works of art, servers, and software. As
an alternative to owning the assets, institutions can rent the assets from a third
party. Thereby, they avoid the risk of unexpected value decreases. Depending
on the terms of the rental contract, the rental costs will appear as fixed or variable costs in the economic capital calculation for business risk.

As a lessor, institutions may rent out assets in the form of operational lease
contracts. For the lessee, this form of financing has the advantage that it is
off-balance, may reduce tax costs, and transfers the risk of an unexpected price
decrease to the lessor. The lessor carries the price risk with respect to the residual value of the asset at the end of the lease contract. The lessor can try to mitigate the residual value risk by increasing the tenor of the lease contract, as this
reduces the residual value of the asset at the end of the contract over which he
carries the price risk. Alternatively, the lessor can eliminate the residual value
risk by buying insurance from a third party, like the manufacturer of the asset
or a specialized insurer. With both risk mitigation strategies, the asset risk is
(partly) replaced by credit risk: the credit exposure on the lessee for the lease
payments, or the credit exposure on the guarantor/insurer for the residual
value insurance. These credit risk exposures can be included in the economic
capital calculations for credit risk. The unmitigated residual value exposure
will attract economic capital for fixed asset risk. Ideally, economic capital is
calculated in an integrated way, because the potential credit loss (loss given
default) and the fixed asset risk are highly correlated in case the lessee defaults.

Modeling Approaches

Economic capital for fixed asset risk measures the extent to which the fair value
of fixed assets may be lower than the expected value at the economic capital horizon, subject to the chosen confidence level. A first challenge is to determine the
fair value of fixed assets. For fixed assets that are used as a production factor, this

is difficult as they usually are not traded and often have unique features. For real estate, external appraisers may value the assets occasionally. For other fixed assets, the amortized value may be a reasonable estimate. For lease contracts, the fair value equals the sum of the present value of the remaining lease payments and the present value of the asset's residual value at the maturity of the lease contract, minus the present value of expected costs resulting from the lease contract.

To estimate potential changes in the fair value of fixed assets, historical price indices may be available from which it is possible to derive the historical price volatility and correlations with other asset prices. A liquidity discount may be considered if no buyers may be available immediately when the asset has to be sold. For some types of fixed assets, such as software developed specifically for the institution, the best assumption may be that it has no remaining value if it would have to be liquidated.

If we have information about the fair value and price volatility of fixed assets, then these assets can be included in the economic capital model for ALM risk. Diversification effects with the other assets of the institution can then be taken into account. If there is no relevant information available about the fair value or volatility of the fixed assets, rules of thumb may have to be used to estimate economic capital. One rule of thumb is to consider the advance rates applied by asset financing companies. The amount that is not advanced is then an indication of economic capital. There are many caveats to such a rule of thumb because the confidence level that the asset finance company uses may be unknown and the asset finance company may apply higher advance rates for more creditworthy borrowers.

For assets that the institution leases to clients, it bears the residual value risk. For the leasing of commoditized products such as cars, this residual value risk may be assessed based on historical data, using statistical analysis. For non-standard products, such as specialized manufacturing tools, the residual value risk is difficult to assess. This larger uncertainty (model risk) will typically be compensated by a higher margin in the required lease payments. An estimate of the uncertainty in the residual value needs to be included in the valuation of the lease contract at the economic capital time horizon if the lease contract has not ended by then. In some cases the lessee has the right to buy the asset at the end of the lease contract against a predetermined price. In these cases the lessor has *de facto* sold a call option on the asset to the lessee, and the expected residual value should reflect this feature. Economic capital is in all cases the difference at the time horizon between the expected residual value and residual value in the adverse scenario that economic capital represents. In these scenarios the call option is likely to expire worthless.

4.7.4 Tax Risk

Tax risk is the risk of loss due to an unexpected change in value of tax assets or liabilities. A change in value can occur because it becomes less likely that an institution can use existing tax assets in the future and has to write them down.

A loss can also result from compliance errors related to taxes to be paid, a contested interpretation of the tax law, or changes in the tax law. Tax risk is deemed relatively small for most institutions and, consequently, is seldom quantified for economic capital. This may not always be appropriate.

The risk of a compliance error is a type of operational risk. It is typically an administrative error that is usually small in size. An example is an error in the booking of a certain cost item as being tax deductible while in actual fact it is not. Later corrections will lead to (usually small) increases in the amount of tax to be paid.

An unexpected tax loss may also occur as a result of an interpretation of the tax law that is challenged by the tax authorities. When the tax law is not clear, companies take a position that later may not be approved by the tax authorities. A typical area of contention for international firms is intercompany transfer pricing. A transfer price is the price for a good or service that one entity within the institution charges to another entity. As a consequence, the taxable profit shifts from the paying entity to the receiving entity. If paying and receiving entities are in different tax jurisdictions or under different tax regimes, then the tax authorities of the paying entity are concerned that transfer prices are set too high.

Together with their auditors, firms assess the likelihood that their interpretation of the tax code will be accepted, and establish an allowance that reflects the expected loss. This allowance represents the tax claim in case the interpretation is not accepted, multiplied by the probability that it is not accepted. In some cases the firm's position will be vindicated. This was, for example, the case for the UK's National Westminster Bank versus the US Internal Revenue Service, when the US Court of Appeals affirmed in January 2008 that the interest costs on intercompany loans to the US branches were tax deductible.[89] In other cases, however, the outcome can be a significant tax claim. This was the case for the pharmaceutical company Glaxo SmithKline. The dispute was also about transfer pricing, but this ended with a settlement payment by Glaxo SmithKline of approximately USD 3.4 billion in 2006.[90]

Tax disputes can lead to reputation issues, in particular when it relates to structured products sold to clients. An example is the stock swap transactions that helped hedge funds avoid US dividend withholding tax by temporarily swapping the shares to a tax haven at the time that dividends were paid. Many reputable banks and hedge funds were involved in the execution of these transactions but were later criticized by the US Senate Permanent Subcommittee on Investigations in their report "Dividend Tax Abuse: How Offshore Entities Dodge Taxes on U.S. Stock Dividends."[91]

Changes to the tax code represent another source of tax risk. These changes typically apply only to future transactions and income. As such, they can alter the franchise value of the firm. Changes in the tax code can also change the value of deferred tax credits that are reported on the balance sheet. For example, the German insurer Allianz reduced in 2007 the value of its deferred tax credits with EUR 137 million because of a tax reform in Germany.

Value decreases of deferred tax credits can also occur because the firm's situation has changed, which makes it unlikely that the tax credit can be realized in practice. An example is the write down of deferred tax credits of USD 21.4 billion by Fannie Mae in the third quarter of 2008 as the company no longer believed it would be able to generate sufficient taxable profit soon enough to use the tax credits before they expired and would become worthless.[92]

The previous examples illustrate that tax risk can be material. In the case of the Dutch bank Van der Hoop Bankiers, tax risk even contributed directly to the demise of the bank in 2005. Van der Hoop Bankiers acted as intermediary between buyers and sellers of companies that had large cash reserves, but an outstanding tax liability at the same time (e.g., a holding company that has sold the shares in its operating company for cash and is still due the tax on the sale). Buyers of the companies could typically set off the tax liabilities against their own tax assets, thereby reducing the tax claim. As intermediary, Van der Hoop Bankiers gave warranties to the sellers of the companies with respect to the outstanding tax obligations. When the Dutch tax authorities found irregularities with the transactions, it imposed a tax claim on Van der Hoop Bankiers. The bank ultimately settled with a payment of EUR 5.5 million. Because the bank was small and not very profitable, this was a significant (unexpected) loss. When other banks declined to take over Van der Hoop Bankiers it went into bankruptcy in December 2005.[93]

The case of Van der Hoop Bankiers is a further illustration of the relevance of tax risk and the need for senior management to understand the nature of these risks. In some cases the losses can be very material and, consequently, the risk should not be disregarded for economic capital. How to estimate the amount of economic capital for tax risk is discussed next.

Modeling Approaches

The nature of tax risk is different for each of the potential sources of tax risk that we discussed. The modeling approach to quantify the aggregate tax risk therefore also may differ for each.

The risk of compliance errors can be modeled as a high-frequency/low-severity type of operational risk event, and be treated as an additional source for operational risk. We refer to the section on operational risk for modeling approaches.

Measuring the risk of tax disputes requires that we have an overview of potential contentious cases for which the probability and severity of future tax claims are assessed. In many firms this is common practice and done in consultation with the auditor to determine the allowance for tax claims. A loss distribution can be estimated on the basis of the estimated probability and severity of individual tax claims, by simulating many scenarios of potential future tax claims. In each simulated scenario, it is determined randomly which of the tax disputes results in a tax claim, using the estimated probabilities, after which their estimated severities are summed to give a total loss. This is similar to the way in which the credit loss distribution is estimated on the basis of probability-of-default and loss-given-default estimates of individual credit exposures. Most individual tax cases are probably unrelated to each other, but related tax cases have to be grouped together, or a positive correlation between them has to be taken into account in the simulation of the loss distribution.

The risk of changes in the tax law primarily has an impact on the franchise value of the firm. The more these changes apply to the distant future, the more uncertain and difficult to estimate they are. Measuring economic capital related to the franchise value of the firm was discussed earlier in the section on business risk.

The treatment of deferred tax credits was discussed already in Section 3.6.1, where we argued that deferred tax credits should be included at their full value in economic capital, or, alternatively, be deducted from available capital.

In conclusion, although tax risks may be relatively small for many institutions, we believe that this should not be taken for granted. In particular, the tax risks of structured, tax-efficient products such as the stock swap transactions discussed earlier, should be assessed as part of the product approval process. Also the associated potential reputation risk should be considered. Economic capital for tax risk should be estimated for these products in order to assess their risk-adjusted return properly.

4.7.5 Strategic Equity Investments

Many financial institutions have strategic equity investments in other firms, usually other financial institutions. These investments have a long-term nature, and sometimes are held to gradually acquire a controlling interest in the firms over time. When an institution owns more than 50% of the equity in another firm, it usually needs to be consolidated in the financial accounts. All of the firm's income, expenses, and losses are then included in the institution's income statement, and the assets, liabilities, and equity are included on its balance sheet. The share of the profit and equity that is attributable to other investors in the consolidated firms is represented as minority interests in the financial accounts. Consolidated entities are usually fully included in an institution's economic capital assessment, and the equity of the entities in the amount of available capital. This ignores the fact that the equity that is attributable to minority interests in consolidated subsidiaries can only cover losses related to the specific subsidiaries, and not for the institution as a whole. In the remainder of this section, we focus our discussion on strategic equity investments that are not consolidated in the institution's financial accounts, but are represented as an equity investment on its balance sheet.

Strategic equity investments that are not consolidated often are included at the historical acquisition price (historical cost) instead of the market value on the balance sheet of a financial institution, unless the (estimated) market value is below the historical cost. Hence, when assessing the potential impact of a decline in value of strategic equity investments on the institution's book value of equity, we need to consider the potential drop in value below the current book value instead of the market value. As we argued in Chapter 3, economic capital should reflect changes in market values of assets and liabilities instead of book values. This is therefore the point of view that we take when discussing modeling approaches.

Modeling Approaches

To estimate the potential decline in market value of a strategic equity investment, we can start from observed equity prices in the past if the firm in question has publicly traded equity. In that case, we can follow the modeling approaches that we described in the section on market risk to arrive at an estimate of the potential change in value at the economic capital confidence level over a one-year period. If no historical equity prices are available, the potential decline in market value needs to be estimated from the volatility of market values of comparable firms, or estimated using proprietary models. For example, structural credit risk portfolio models that we discussed in Section 4.2.2 could be used. When there are multiple strategic equity investments, a joint assessment on the potential decline in market value can be performed, taking correlations between the investments into account.

If there are only a few strategic investments, then economic capital is unlikely to be much lower than the current fair value. There are several reasons for this. First, for an undiversified equity portfolio the potential decline in value at the very high confidence level used for economic capital will be close to the current value. Second, if the strategic equity investment is in another financial institution, then the correlation with the institution itself is likely to be very high. This means that there is little diversification benefit with the other risk types of the investing institution. Third, the fact that it is a strategic investment implies that the investor is likely to be asked for additional capital in case the investment is in financial distress. Consequently, an estimate of the decline in value of strategic equity investments on the basis of historical equity prices may not fully capture the risk that the institution bears.

Regulatory Capital Treatment

The Basel II Accord requires that significant minority investments in banking, securities, and other financial entities, in which control does not exist, must be deducted from the banking group's capital or consolidated on a *pro-rata* basis.[94] National authorities can determine the threshold above which an equity investment is deemed significant. It usually lies around 10% of the equity of the entity in which the institution invests. The conservative treatment of such minority investments for regulatory capital purposes is motivated by the desire to maintain a sufficient level of capital within the financial industry as a whole. If such minority investments could be partly financed by debt, then this would reduce the overall level of capital in the system, thereby increasing systemic risk.

For other banking-book equity exposures, a bank can choose between various approaches under the internal-ratings-based (IRB) approach. These range from simple risk weights (between 300 and 400%, corresponding to capital requirements of 24 and 32% of book value) to the use of internal models for which the capital requirement is derived from the potential loss over a three-month period at a 99% confidence level (subject to certain floors). A special treatment applies if the total amount of equity investments of the bank exceeds a certain percentage of total Tier 1 plus Tier 2 capital (10% in general, and 5% if there are fewer than 10 individual holdings). In this way, the Basel II Accord addresses potential concentration risks in a bank's assets. In principle, such concentration effects can be included directly in an institution's economic capital methodologies.

4.8 Aggregation of Risks

In the previous sections we have reviewed economic capital modeling approaches for individual risk types. To obtain an estimate of overall economic capital, we need to aggregate the risk assessments across all risk types. How that can be done, and what issues may be encountered, is the topic of this section.

The modeling approaches that we described for the individual risk types each results in a distribution of potential value changes at the one-year economic capital horizon (loss distribution). For credit, market, ALM, insurance, pension, fixed asset, and strategic investment risks, the loss distribution represents potential changes in value of assets and liabilities, including earnings and losses on the assets and costs of the liabilities during the one-year horizon. The loss distribution can also represent potential changes in the value of revenues and costs related to future business (as for business risk), or direct financial expenses (as for tax and operational risk). When adding the expected value changes across all risk types, we obtain an estimate of the expected change in equity value of the financial institution as a whole. To obtain an estimate of overall economic capital, we need to combine the potential unexpected value changes across all risk types. Simply adding economic capital estimates for each of the individual risk types implies that large unexpected losses from all risk types would happen all at the same time. This is not realistic and would overestimate total economic capital. Instead, we want to incorporate the less than full correlation between unexpected losses from different risk types when aggregating risks and estimating overall economic capital. How to estimate correlations between unexpected losses from different risk types, and embed them in the calculation of total economic capital, constitutes the challenge of risk aggregation.

Table 4.9 Ranges of correlation parameter values between risk types used by banks for aggregating risks, with average correlation used in parentheses. (*Source*: IFRI/CRO Forum survey 2007[79])

	Market	Operational	Business
Credit	10–100% (66%)	10–100% (30%)	40–100% (67%)
Market		10–100% (30%)	0–100% (58%)
Operational			0–100% (60%)
Business			

A survey by the IFRI Foundation and the CRO Forum[79] reports the diversification effect that banks and insurance companies find as a result of including less than full correlation between unexpected losses across risk types. Among the banks that participated in the survey, the overall economic capital across risk types was between 10 and 30% lower than the sum of the economic capital amounts of all individual risk types. Among the insurance companies in the survey, the difference was around 40%. The inter-risk correlation parameters used by the participating financial institutions show significant variation. Among the banks, the ranges of correlation values used between credit, market, operational, and business risk are reported in Table 4.9, with the average value in parentheses. Among the insurers, the ranges of correlation values are included in Table 4.10. No average has been provided in the survey results for the insurance companies.

Comparing Tables 4.9 and 4.10 indicates that the ranges of correlations are generally wider for banks than for insurance companies. Furthermore, inter-risk correlations used by banks are generally higher than those used by insurance companies. For insurance companies, the correlations used for operational risk and the specific insurance risks (life, property and casualty (P&C)) with the other risk types are relatively low. These differences contribute to the higher inter-risk diversification effect reported by insurance companies compared to banks. The

Table 4.10 Ranges of correlation parameter values between risk types used by insurance companies for aggregating risks. (*Source*: IFRI/CRO Forum survey 2007[79])

	Market	Operational	Business	Life	P&C	Other
Credit	25–100%	0–15%	50–100%	0–0%	0–10%	0–50%
Market		0–10%	0–50%	0–25%	0–25%	0–50%
Operational			0–10%	0–35%	0–25%	0–50%
Business				0–100%	0–100%	0–20%
Life					0–0%	0–35%
P&C						0–35%
Other						

fact that within insurance companies more risk categories are distinguished in the survey also leads to a higher reported inter-risk diversification effect. For example, if the survey for banks would have contained ALM risk as a separate risk type from market risk, or the risk on private equity investments as a separate risk type from credit risk, then the inter-risk diversification effect for banks would have been higher than currently reported, although the overall risk profile obviously remains the same. Hence, the absolute size of the reported inter-risk diversification effect should be interpreted with some caution.

In a study that was commissioned by Dutch supervisory authorities, Oliver Wyman has analyzed the impact on economic capital of diversification benefits between banking and insurance activities within financial conglomerates.[95] The study estimates that the less than perfect correlation between aggregate banking and aggregate insurance losses results in overall economic capital for a financial conglomerate that is between 5 and 15% lower than the sum of the economic capital estimates for the banking and for the insurance activities on a stand-alone basis.

4.8.1   Fundamental Choices and Assumptions

Transferability of Capital

A central assumption underlying the inclusion of diversification effects between unexpected losses of different risk types is that there is a common pool of capital that can be used to absorb losses arising from any of the risks. In practice, this may not always be the case. This may be due to legal restrictions or economic reasons. Legal restrictions may limit the transfer of capital or investment returns in or out of a country. For economic reasons, some banks have used part of their capital to set up derivatives product companies (DPCs). These DPCs were capitalized to obtain a triple-A rating from rating agencies, which made them eligible to act as counterparty for derivatives transactions with other parties that required a triple-A counterparty (mostly institutional investors). The capital provided to such DPCs cannot be used to absorb unexpected losses in other parts of the institution. Restrictions on the transferability of capital typically apply to legal entities and specific geographies, and not to specific risk types.

If part of an institution's capital is set aside to support a specific subset of risks, and cannot be used to absorb unexpected losses arising from other risks within the institution, then this subset of risks should be looked at in isolation. That is, no diversification effects with other risks should be included when aggregating risks across the institution. This applies to the DPCs that we discussed in the previous paragraph, but also to minority interests in subsidiaries if they are included in available capital. This will increase the overall capital requirement, and consequently presents a cost for the institution.

In the discussion that follows we will ignore any restrictions on the transfer of capital between different parts of an institution, although it is important to take this into account in practical situations.

4.8.2 Modeling Approaches

The main approaches used to aggregate stand-alone economic capital estimates across risk types are the variance-covariance approach, and the copula approach. We will discuss the main features of both approaches next. Both approaches need estimates of correlations (or more general, the dependence structure) between risk types as input. Issues related to the estimation of dependencies will be discussed in the next section.

Variance-Covariance Approach

The variance-covariance approach is based on a formula that expresses the standard deviation of a sum of random variables in terms of the standard deviation of the individual random variables, together with the correlations between these random variables.[96] Although valid in general, this formula is particularly useful when summing random variables that all have a Gaussian distribution, because the sum of Gaussian random variables is fully characterized by its expected value and standard deviation. This calculation often is applied to calculate the distribution of possible returns on a portfolio of stocks, since the returns on individual stocks often are assumed to follow a Gaussian distribution.

For risk aggregation, the random variables that are summed are the potential value changes resulting from each risk type. If we know the standard deviation of potential value changes for each risk type, and the correlations between them, then we can apply the variance-covariance formula to calculate the standard deviation of potential value changes in total. However, as the probability distribution of potential value changes for many risk types is not Gaussian, and often strongly deviates from it because of the presence of fat tails as a result of a relatively high likelihood of large losses, we cannot reasonably assume that the distribution of total value changes is Gaussian. Consequently, knowing the standard deviation of potential value changes does not provide sufficient information on the full distribution, which is necessary to determine economic capital. We thus need to make some assumption how to translate the calculated standard deviation to a total economic capital estimate. This translation can be based on the ratio of economic capital to the standard deviation of value changes for each of the individual risk types (e.g., some weighted average of these ratios), or by assuming a specific functional form for the probability distribution of total value changes.

In the context of risk aggregation, the variance-covariance formula usually is not applied to the standard deviation of potential value changes of the individual risk types, but by inserting the risk-type specific economic capital estimates instead of the standard deviation in the variance-covariance formula. The outcome is then taken as a direct estimate of the overall economic capital. Assuming that correlations between risk types are available, this is a computationally simple approach to calculate overall economic capital. A question is how accurate the resulting economic capital estimate is. We will return to this question after discussing the copula approach.

Copula Approach

As we just saw, the variance-covariance approach does not use the full probability distribution of potential value changes for each of the risk types, but only one specific quantity derived from the distribution (i.e., the standard deviation or economic capital). In contrast, the copula approach uses the full probability distribution of each risk type. The copula "couples" these individual probability distributions through a dependence structure to get an overall probability distribution of value changes. There are various copulas, and the choice of copula determines the nature of the dependence structure. This provides more flexibility to model dependencies than the linear correlations that are embedded in the variance-covariance approach. For example:

- Copulas can incorporate tail dependence; that is, a positive correlation between arbitrarily large losses of two risks. Being able to incorporate tail dependence is important if we want to reflect stress correlations (see our discussion on stress correlations in Section 4.1.2).
- The use of copulas enables the use of more general measures of correlation, such as Spearman and Kendall rank correlations. They measure the correlation between the rank ordering of realizations from different random variables (in our situation, value changes or losses corresponding to different risk types) instead of considering the actual values. An important advantage of rank correlations is that they do not change under a (possibly nonlinear) scaling of the realizations as long as the rank ordering remains the same. Copulas make use of this feature.
- The copula approach can also take probability distributions for individual risk types as input that result from simulation methods, and for which no analytical expression is available.

The copula approach reduces to the variance-covariance approach if the individual probability distributions are all Gaussian, and if a Gaussian copula is used.[97] However, it can be shown that tail dependence is lost in this Gaussian setting.

The flexibility of the copula approach comes at the cost of being computationally more demanding than the variance-covariance approach. For any realistic set of probability distributions for individual risk types and less than full correlations, simulation methods are needed to determine the overall probability distribution of potential value changes.

Comparison of Approaches

The choice between the variance-covariance and the copula approach is primarily one between efficient computation and accuracy. In the IFRI/CRO Forum survey that we referred to earlier, 75% of all banks that participated use the variance-covariance approach, and the remaining 25% use a variety of other approaches. Although the copula approach is slightly more popular among insurance companies in the survey, twice as many insurance participants use the variance-covariance approach compared to the copula approach. That many financial institutions choose for the simplicity of the variance-covariance approach as opposed to the sophistication of the copula approach can be due to the fact that estimates of correlation between risk types typically are surrounded with significant uncertainty. The accuracy of the copula approach may therefore be compromised by the uncertainty surrounding the correlation estimates. We return to the estimation of correlations in Section 4.8.3.

Rosenberg and Schuermann[98] have performed numerical comparisons between the variance-covariance approach and the copula approach with a Gaussian copula. When the variance-covariance approach uses stand-alone economic capital amounts per risk type instead of standard deviations as inputs, this approach leads to somewhat higher aggregate economic capital estimates than the more accurate copula approach in all settings they consider. The difference ranges between 5 and 15 percent. Hence, the variance-covariance approach used in this manner results in somewhat conservative aggregate economic capital estimates compared to the more accurate copula approach. This result may be explained by the fact that the use of economic capital estimates directly in the variance-covariance formula imposes explicit correlations between large unexpected losses (represented by economic capital) for the individual risk types. When Rosenberg and Schuermann use copulas with more tail dependence (a Student-t copula) than the Gaussian copula, the results from the copula approach become closer, or even equal, to those of the variance-covariance approach. As a separate result, Rosenberg and Schuermann show that aggregate economic capital using the copula approach is more sensitive to changes in business mix (and thus the relative importance of various risk types) than to changes in correlations between risk types or the choice of copula.

The conclusion we can draw from the analysis of Rosenberg and Schuermann is that using the variance-covariance approach with stand-alone economic capital estimates per risk type as input instead of standard deviations, provides a reasonable and usually conservative approximation to the more accurate copula approach.

4.8.3 Special Topics

For risk aggregation approaches, important ingredients to calculate aggregate economic capital are correlation estimates between unexpected value changes (losses) stemming from individual risk types.

Estimating Correlations

A natural starting point to estimate correlations between unexpected value changes or losses from different risk types is to consider correlations between historical losses. For example, for credit risk we can consider historical loan impairments to calculate correlations (although this ignores fair value changes of credit-sensitive assets); for market risk, historical trading results; for operational risk, historical operational losses; for ALM risk in banks, the historical interest-rate result. However, for some risk types it is not easy to determine historical losses without overlap with other risk types. For business risk, we would need a time series of shortfalls of net operating earnings from expectations that are not due to losses resulting from other risk types. Such a time series is usually not directly available in institutions, and would require a careful filtering of profit-and-loss effects related to other risk types to construct it.

Moreover, in principle, we should consider for each risk type only the *unexpected* part of actual realizations. Actual realizations of losses or value changes thus should be corrected for expected losses or value changes. When no suitable historical loss data is available for a particular risk type, we can try to identify a market variable that has a strong correlation with gains and losses for the particular risk type, and for which historical observations are available. The historical realizations of this market variable can then be used to calculate correlations with other risk types. If that is not possible either, then we may have to resort to choose correlations with other risk types based on qualitative arguments.

When estimating correlations on the basis of historical loss data, the following issues may be considered:

- It is helpful to consider economic relationships when estimating correlations and validating outcomes. For example, in a downturn of the economy credit losses rise, and the interest rate curve tends to become steeper as a result of lower short-term interest rates following a looser monetary policy by central banks. Such an interest rate environment is attractive for banks from an ALM perspective. This can thus justify a negative (or, at most, a low positive) correlation between credit and ALM risk for banks. A positive correlation between equity prices and interest rates (equity prices and interest rates tend to rise and fall together in economic upturns and downturns, respectively) causes strong diversification effects between returns on investments in equities and in bonds for an insurance company or pension fund. For a life-insurer and pension fund, the positive correlation between equity prices and interest rates will result in a negative correlation between changes in the value of the equity investments and changes in the value of the liabilities. As a result, investing in equities is risky for a life-insurer or pension fund since the value of the equity investments is expected to decrease at the same time that the value of the liabilities increases. When they have large investments in equities, this can thus lead to a fast deterioration in the financial situation.
- There may be time lags between losses related to different risk types. For example, credit spreads may widen and equity prices may drop (impacting trading profit and loss) before loan impairments increase. Furthermore, in an economic downturn when credit losses will be high, revenues may recover after some time due to increasing margins (positively affecting income related to business risk). Taking these relationships over time into account can improve the reliability of correlation estimates.
- In some cases, historical losses may not be representative of potential future losses because business activities have changed significantly. Even if deemed

representative, the number of data points from which to estimate correlations is usually relatively small, giving rise to significant statistical uncertainty. Often, historical loss data per risk type is available only on a quarterly basis at best, in line with the frequency of external reporting. The small number of data points also does not allow for a statistical analysis to establish whether stress correlations are present (see also Section 4.1.2).

Unavoidably, there is significant uncertainty around the values of correlations between risk types. The fact that an individual risk type combines potentially very different exposures often makes it difficult to have a clear intuition on the sign and size of the correlation with other risk types. As a consequence, most institutions embed some level of conservatism in the correlation estimates that are used for risk aggregation purposes. In principle, the uncertainty about the values of the correlation parameters can be included explicitly in the economic capital calculation in the way described in Section 4.1.5 for parameter uncertainty in general.

4.8.4 Allocation of Economic Capital

We have described the overall economic capital calculation as consisting of two steps: first economic capital is estimated per risk type, and subsequently these estimates are aggregated across risk types. If we follow these steps, the calculation of the contribution of individual transactions and business units to aggregate economic capital also needs to be performed in steps. First, the contribution of a transaction or business unit to economic capital for each risk type is calculated, using the methods described in the sections for the individual risk types. Second, this risk-type contribution is lowered by the diversification effect for the risk type when it is combined with the other risk types. The risk-type contributions are thus scaled down. Subsequently, the scaled risk-type contributions are summed over all risk types to establish the contribution to aggregate economic capital.

To illustrate, suppose stand-alone economic capital for two risk types, A and B, is 100 each. We consider an institution that consists of two business units, X and Y. Suppose that business unit X contributes 40 to economic capital for risk type A and 70 to economic capital for risk type B. For business unit Y, the contributions are 60 and 30, respectively. Suppose that aggregate economic capital for the institution equals 180, to which risk type A and B each contributes 90. Hence, the diversification benefit by combining both risk types is 20, split equally between both risk types (as they have the same size on a stand-alone basis). To calculate the contribution of business unit X to aggregate economic capital, we first determine its contribution through risk type A as $40 \times (90/100) = 36$. Its contribution through risk type B can be calculated as $70 \times (90/100) = 63$. By adding the two numbers, we determine its contribution to aggregate economic capital as 99. For business unit Y it can be calculated in a similar manner, resulting in a contribution of 81 to aggregate economic capital.

In this example with two risk types of equal size, both contribute equally to total economic capital. However, there are more risk types in reality, and they will differ in size. When using the component economic capital contribution method to determine the contribution of individual risk types to aggregate economic capital, small risks generally are allocated a larger share of the diversification effect than large risks. For example, suppose that stand-alone economic capital for risk A equals 100, and 10 for risk B. Suppose that the correlation between unexpected losses on both risk types has been estimated at 50%. Using the variance-covariance approach for simplicity, this results in aggregate economic capital of 105.36. The contribution to the aggregate can be calculated as 99.66 for risk A and 5.69 for risk B. Hence, of the total diversification effect of 4.64 between risks A and B, the large risk A receives only 0.34 of the benefit and the small risk B receives the remaining 4.31. The reason that risk B gets attributed most of the diversification effect is that aggregate economic capital is nearly fully determined by unexpected losses from risk A. Potential losses resulting from risk B hardly matter for aggregate economic capital, and thus risk B is attributed a low economic capital contribution. In other words, if the institution experiences a very large loss, then it must be the case that a very large loss has materialized with respect to risk type A, and it is relatively immaterial what the loss in relation to risk type B is.

For business units that have a large exposure to risk types that are less important at the level of the institution as a whole (risk type B in the preceding example), this property means that they receive a relatively large diversification benefit compared to other business units. When the economic capital contributions are used in RAROC calculations, it can result in high RAROC numbers for these business units. They may therefore appear very attractive on a risk-adjusted return basis if the hurdle rate is not adjusted for the (implied) high leverage. It is, therefore, important for managers to understand what the impact is of aggregating risks, and how the resulting diversification benefits are allocated to the business units. We will discuss the setting of hurdle rates in Section 5.2.8.

4.8.5   Risk Aggregation in Regulatory Capital

Although the Basel II Accord allows for the inclusion of diversification effects within a given risk type, no diversification is applied between risk types. That is, regulatory capital requirements for individual risk types are added to determine the overall minimum required regulatory capital. This is thus more conservative than what usually is done in the aggregation of risk types for economic capital. However, Basel II minimum regulatory capital calculations consider only credit, market, and operational risk. In the internal capital adequacy assessment process (ICAAP) that is part of the Basel II Accord, banks are expected to include all material risk types, and in this assessment diversification effects between risk types can be included. In contrast to the Basel II Accord, the Solvency II proposal does allow for the inclusion of diversification effects between different risk types for the calculation of the solvency capital requirement.

4.9   Conclusion

In this chapter we have reviewed measurement approaches for economic capital for a large number of risk types. Most of these risk types will be relevant to a financial institution, although the materiality of each will differ between institutions. We also compared, where applicable, to what extent economic capital methodologies that are used by financial institutions differ from regulatory capital calculations.

We have emphasized the importance to ensure consistency between economic capital modeling approaches across the various risk types with respect to the following choices:

- Whether or not it is assumed that assets and liabilities that mature before the one-year economic capital horizon are replaced by similar assets and liabilities.
- Whether economic capital is intended to represent a through-the-cycle or point-in-time estimate of required capital.
- What method is used to calculate economic capital contributions for each risk as the basis for the allocation of economic capital. We have also discussed, however, that there may be practical reasons why different methods may be preferable for different risk types.

In addition, we have indicated how to take changes in fair value of assets and liabilities into account for each risk type, in line with the definition of economic capital that we arrived at in Chapter 3.

For each of the risk types, we discussed various modeling issues that relate to the specific nature of the risk in question and the particular modeling approaches employed. However, we also touched upon a number of recurring themes that are relevant to all or a majority of the individual modeling approaches:

- The estimation of the dependence structure between multiple events that can happen is the centerpiece of all economic capital models. For most risk types, large losses occur only when a number of bad things happen at the same time. The challenge in economic capital modeling is to estimate the likelihood that several bad things happen simultaneously. The only exceptions are operational risk and insurance risk, for which large losses may occur as a result of a single catastrophic event. In that case, the challenge is to estimate the likelihood and potential severity of such a catastrophic event.
- Although historical data is often a useful starting point for the estimation of parameters in economic capital models, large losses typically occur when patterns observed in the past change in a structural and persistent manner. Examples that we presented relate to the behavior of financial market variables, the dependence between industry sectors and geographic regions, the behavior of clients, the operating environment for institutions, and the frequency of occurrence of natural catastrophes. It is thus important to

complement the results of historical data analysis with a fundamental analysis of the economic environment, in order to assess whether the patterns observed in the past are representative for the future.

- Model risk arises in various ways in economic capital methodologies. It is present in the valuation of assets and liabilities at the current date and at the one-year economic capital horizon, in models describing the payment behavior of clients, and in the estimation of parameter values, for example. As we argued, it is desirable to include model risk explicitly in economic capital methodologies, if only in an approximate manner, since it can have a significant impact on economic capital estimates. We made several suggestions for how this can be done in a practical manner.

Estimating economic capital thus involves a number of significant modeling challenges. The implementation of economic capital within an organization entails a number of additional practical challenges. These challenges will be the topic of the next chapter.

Endnotes

[1]See, for example:

Chen JS, Ang A. Asymmetric correlations of equity portfolios. EFA 2001 Barcelona Meetings. 2001. Available at SSRN: http://papers.ssrn.com/sol3/papers.cfm?abstract_id=219495.

Koedijk KCG, Campbell RAJ, Kofman P. Increased correlation in bear markets. *Financial Analysts Journal.* 2002;58(1):87–94.

Alexander and Pézier report correlations between US Treasury yields and stock prices that are higher for large than for small changes in both, see:

Alexander C, Pézier J. Assessment and aggregation of banking risks. Working paper. ISMA Centre, University of Reading; 2003.

[2]Guha K, Tett G. Last year's model: Stricken US homeowners confound predictions. *Financial Times.* 2008;February:11.

[3]For a general overview and comparison of calculation approaches, see Hallerbach W. Decomposing portfolio value-at-risk: A general analysis. *Journal of Risk.* 2002;5(2):1–18.

[4]Epperlein E, Smillie A. Cracking VaR with kernels. *Risk.* 2006;August:70–74.

[5]The calculation of VaR contributions in portfolio credit risk models using the saddle-point method is described in:

Martin R, Thompson K, Browne C. Taking to the saddle. *Risk.* 2001;June:91–94.

Martin R, Thompson K, Browne C. VAR: Who contributes and how much? *Risk.* 2001; August:99–102.

Martin R, Ordovás R. An indirect view from the saddle. *Risk.* 2006;October:94–97.

[6]Glasserman P. Measuring marginal risk contributions in credit portfolios. *Journal of Computational Finance.* 2005;9:1–41.

[7]For the efficient calculation of expected shortfall contributions, see, for example:

Kalkbrenner M, Kennedy A, Popp M. Efficient calculation of expected shortfall contributions in large credit portfolios. *Journal of Computational Finance.* 2007;11(2):45–77.

[8]Basel Committee on Banking Supervision. Range of practices and issues in economic capital frameworks. 2008;March.

[9]Greenspan A. We will never have a perfect model of risk. *Financial Times.* 2008;March 17.

[10]Janes S, Tett G, Davies P. CPDOs expose rating flaw at Moody's. *Financial Times.* 2008;May 21.

[11]Moody's Finance & Securities. Credit default swaps: Market, systemic, and individual firm risks in practice. October 2008.

[12]Berkshire Hathaway, Inc. Chairman's letter to the shareholders 2001.

[13]For the classification of modeling approaches, we follow Crouhy M, Galai D, Mark R. *The essentials of risk management*. Forlag: McGraw-Hill;2006. The following books contain more extensive and technical descriptions of credit portfolio models:

Bluhm C, Overbeck L, Wagner C. *An introduction to credit risk modeling*. Boca Raton, FL: Chapman & Hall; 2002.

Crouhy M, Galai D, Mark R. *Risk management*. New York: McGraw-Hill; 2001.

Saunders A. *Credit risk measurement*. New York: John Wiley & Sons; 1999.

Servigny A, De Renault O. *Measuring and managing credit risk*. New York: McGraw-Hill; 2004.

[14]Merton R. On the pricing of corporate debt: The risk structure of interest rates. *Journal of Finance*. 1974;29(May):449–470. Also included as Chapter 12 of Robert Merton's book, *Continuous-time finance*, 1990, Cambridge, MA: Blackwell Publishers.

[15]Because KMV Portfolio Manager is a proprietary model, precise details of its implementation are not publicly available. The description in this section is based on a general understanding of the KMV Portfolio Manager implementation, and the description of the approach in other third-party sources. We have used in particular information contained in Crouhy M, Galai D, Mark R. *Risk management*. New York: McGraw-Hill; 2001.

[16]For a full description, see JP Morgan. *CreditMetrics—Technical document*. 1997.

[17]De Servigny A, Renault O. Correlations evidence. *Risk*. 2003;July:90–94. Also summarized in Chapter 5 of De Servigny A, Renault O. *Measuring and managing credit risk*. New York: Standard & Poor's. McGraw-Hill; 2004.

[18]Mashal R, Naldi M, Zeevi A. On the dependence of equity and asset returns. *Risk*. 2003;October:83–87.

[19]An extended version of CredtMetrics that includes credit spread volatility is described in Kiesel R, Perraudin W, Taylor AP. The structure of credit risk: Spread volatility and ratings transitions. *Journal of Risk*. 2003;6:1–36. Using both stylized and realistic portfolio compositions, they show that the inclusion of spread volatility per rating category significantly increases economic capital estimates. The increase is largest for high-quality loan portfolios.

[20]See Wilson T. Portfolio credit risk (I). *Risk*. 1997;September:111–117, and Portfolio credit risk (II). *Risk*. 1997;October:56–61.

[21]Another rating-migration model that relates the probability of rating migrations and defaults to macro-economic information is described in Bangia A, Diebold F, Kronimus A. Ratings migration and the business cycle, with application to credit portfolio stress testing. *Journal of Banking and Finance*. 2002;26:445–474. They construct two transition matrices, one based on observed rating migration and default rates that have occurred in periods of economic expansion, and one based on periods of economic contraction. They also estimate probabilities of switching from an economic expansion to an economic contraction, and vice versa. Using these estimates, Bangia et al. simulate whether an expansion or contraction takes place in each of a series of successive periods, and apply the corresponding rating transition matrix to a hypothetical bond portfolio. The assumption is made that rating migrations of different bonds are independent, conditional on the relevant transition matrix. Correlation between rating migration and default events of different bonds is embedded through the switch in transition matrix between expansions and contractions for all bonds. It is shown in Lucas A, Klaassen P. Discrete versus continuous state switching models for portfolio credit risk. *Journal of Banking and Finance*. 2006;30:23–35, that the embedded correlation in this model with only two possible states of the world is unrealistically low, however, resulting in underestimation of economic capital.

[22]Credit Suisse. *CreditRisk+: A credit risk management framework*. Credit Suisse Financial Products; 1997.

[23]Bürgisser *et al*. describe how to incorporate correlations between sectors by constructing the CreditRisk+ model with a single sector in which the standard deviation of this single sector is adjusted to reflect the standard deviations of, and correlations between, the multiple original

sectors (Bürgisser P, Kurth A, Wagner A, Wolf M. Integrating correlations. *Risk*. 1999;July:57–60). Giese generalizes CreditRisk+ to include a compound gamma distribution between sectors, which allows for non-zero correlations between sectors (Giese G. Enhancing CreditRisk+. *Risk*. 2003;April:73–77).

[24]Several modifications, generalizations, and applications of CreditRisk+ are contained in Grundlach M, Lehrbass F. (Eds.). *CreditRisk+ in the banking industry*. Berlin: Springer Finance.

[25]Alexandre Kurth and Dirk Tasche (Kurth A, Tasche D. Contributions to credit risk. *Risk*. 2003; March:84–88) also derive an expression for the contribution to expected shortfall, and illustrate the differences between the contribution to standard deviation, percentile, and expected shortfall numerically for a hypothetical loan portfolio.

[26]Various authors have tried to decompose observed credit spreads to assess what parts can be attributed to expected credit losses, other risks, and risk premiums. Elton *et al.* find that only between 30 and 70% of the credit spread can be attributed to expected credit losses (Elton E, Gruber M, Agarwal D. Explaining the rate spread on corporate bonds. *Journal of Finance*. 2001;56(1):247–277). The percentage is lowest for short maturities and good credit ratings. Similar findings, using a different approach, are reported in Huang J, Huang M. How much of corporate-treasury yield spread is due to credit risk? A new calibration approach. 14th Annual Conference on Financial Economics and Accounting (FEA); Texas Finance Festival; 2003. Available at SSRN: http://papers.ssrn.com/sol3/papers.cfm?abstract_id=307360. Driessen provides an empirical decomposition of expected corporate bond returns into risk premia, tax effects, and liquidity. He finds that all these factors are important drivers of the corporate bond return, with the most prominent role for default risk premia. In most cases, the risk premium on systematic variation in expected loss is larger than the risk premium on unexpected losses (Driessen J. Is default event risk priced in corporate bonds? *Review of Financial Studies*. 2005;18:165–195).

[27]Li D. On default correlation: A copula approach. *Journal of Fixed Income*. 2000;9:43–54.

[28]See, for example:
Duffie D, Singleton K. Simulating correlated defaults. Working paper. Graduate School of Business, Stanford University; 1999.
Duffie D, Gârleanu N. Risk and the valuation of collateralized debt obligations. *Financial Analysts Journal*. 2001;57(January):41–59.
Hull J, White A. Dynamic models of portfolio credit risk: A simplified approach. *Journal of Derivatives*. 2008;Summer:9–28.

[29]Koyluoglu and Hickman (Koyluoglu H, Hickman A. Reconcilable differences. *Risk*. 1998;October:56–62) show how structural credit risk portfolio models (such as KMV's PortfolioManager), CreditMetrics, CreditPortfolioView, and CreditRisk+ can be written in a similar mathematical form. For a simplified setting, in which only losses due to default are considered, all firms in the portfolio have the same probability of default, and correlations are driven by a single factor (which can be interpreted as assuming that all firms are active in the same region and industry), they also show how the parameters in each of the models can be chosen such that they imply the same expected default rate and standard deviation of the default rate for the portfolio. When the parameters are aligned in this manner, Koyluoglu and Hickman show that the shape of the tails is quite similar for the various models, using a general measure of tail correspondence. They do not look at potential losses corresponding to particular points (percentiles) of the loss distribution. Because each model uses different data to estimate the correlations between firms in the portfolio (equity or asset returns, macro-economic variables, or variation in historical default rates), and this data is available at different frequencies and precision, Koyluoglu and Hickman conclude that differences between the data and the methods used to estimate the parameters in each model are much more likely to result in substantial differences in economic capital estimates than differences between the mathematical formulation of the models. Bluhm *et al.* (Bluhm C, Overbeck L, Wagner C. Irreconcilable differences. *Risk*. 2001;October:S33–S37) look at specific percentiles in the tail of the loss distribution in the same setting that Koyluoglu and Hickman use. They show that at a high confidence level (99.98%) the structural models of KMV and CreditMetrics yields economic capital estimates that are between 25 and 40% higher than those resulting from

CreditRisk+ if all models imply the same expected default rate and volatility of the default rate. The differences are higher for higher confidence levels. They ascribe these significant differences to the difference in mathematical formulation and implied statistical behavior of the default rates between the models. They also show that the difference in economic capital estimate persists between the models when they consider more general portfolio compositions with variation in default rates and correlations.

Gordy (Gordy M. A comparative anatomy of credit risk models. *Journal of Banking and Finance.* 2000;24(January):119–149) shows that substantial differences between economic capital estimates from CreditRisk+ and a simplified version of CreditMetrics can arise, depending on how the factor model in CreditRisk+ is set up. In particular, a trade-off is possible between the weight that is assigned to a common factor (sector in the CreditRisk+ terminology) and the standard deviation of this factor. Although this leaves the standard deviation of the default rate unchanged, it significantly influences the shape of the tail of the credit loss distribution.

Lucas *et al.* (Lucas A, Klaassen P, Spreij P, Straetmans S. An analytic approach to credit risk of large corporate bond and loan portfolios. *Journal of Banking and Finance* 2001;25(9):1635–1664. Erratum in *Journal of Banking and Finance.* 2002;26(1):201-202) show that economic capital estimates from CreditMetrics depend significantly on the choice of copula used to model the dependence between the common factors in the correlation model. The choice of a t-copula instead of the standard Gaussian copula significantly increases the economic capital estimate, even if the implied volatility of default rates is the same in both cases.

[30]IACPM, ISDA. *Convergence of credit capital models.* 2006;February 21. Available from http://www.iacpm.org/

[31]Löffler G. The effect of estimation error on measures of portfolio credit risk. *Journal of Banking and Finance.* 2003;27:1427–1453.

[32]Several models to estimate probabilities of default are described in Caouette J, Altman E, Narayanan P. *Managing credit risk: The next great financial challenge.* New York: John Wiley & Sons; 1998.

[33]See, for example: Emery K, Gates D, Marshella T, Ou S. Migration of debt structures and revolver usage as firms approach default. Moody's Credit Policy, Special Comment, December 2008.

[34]For examples of credit risk portfolio models that include market risk variables to model variations in the exposure at default, see:
Jarrow R, Turnbull S. The intersection of market and credit risk. *Journal of Banking and Finance.* 2000;24:271–299.
Iscoe I, Kreinin A, Rosen D. An integrated market and credit risk portfolio model. *Algo Research Quarterly.* 1999;2(3):21–38.

[35]See, for example:
Araten M, Jabobs Jr M, Varshney P. Measuring LGD on commercial loans: An 18-year internal study. RMA 2004;
Moody's Investors Service. Back-testing Moody's LGD methodology. June 2007.

[36]See, for example, Schuermann T. What do we know about loss given default? Chapter 1 in Altman EI, Resti A, Sironi A (eds.) *Recovery Risk: The Next Challenge in Credit Risk Management.* London, UK: Risk Books; 2005.

[37]For example:
Acharya V, Bharath S, Srinivasan A. Understanding the recovery rates on defaulted securities. CEPR Discussion paper No. 4098, London Business School; 2003.
Altman EI, Brady B, Resti A. *The link between default and recovery rates: Theory, empirical evidence and implications.* Working paper. Stern School of Business, New York University; 2003.
Frye J. Depressing recoveries. *Risk.* 2000;November:108–111.
Frye J. A false sense of security. *Risk.* 2003;August:63–67.
Hu Y-T, Perraudin W. *The dependence of recovery rates and defaults.* Working paper. Birkbeck College; 2002.

Moody's Investors Service. Default and recovery rates of corporate bond issuers, 1920–2005. 2006;March.

[38]Empirical results show that estimated correlations tend to increase the longer the time interval is that is used; see, for example, results in Lucas A, Klaassen P, Spreij P. An analytic approach to credit risk of large corporate bond and loan portfolios. *Journal of Banking and Finance*. 2001;25(9):1635–1664.

[39]The variation of correlation over time has been documented in the literature for default correlation derived from historical default rate information (see Koopman SJ, Lucas A, Klaassen P. Empirical credit cycles and capital buffer formation. *Journal of Banking and Finance*. 2005;29:3159–3179), for equity return correlations (see, for example, Longin F, Solnik B. Is the correlation in international equity returns constant: 1960–1990? *Journal of International Money and Finance*. 2005;14:3–26), as well as for asset correlations (Düllmann K, Scheicher M, Schmieder C. Asset correlations and credit portfolio risk: An empirical analysis. *Journal of Credit Risk*. 2008;4(2), Summer). Correlations have both increased and decreased during different periods.

[40]For example, see:
Danthine J-P, Adjaouté K. Equity returns and integration: Is Europe changing? *Oxford Review of Economic Policy*. 2004;20(4):550–570.
Kearney C, Poti V. Correlation dynamics in European equity markets. *Research in International Business and Finance*. 2006;20(3):305–321.

[41]The dependence of asset correlations on firm size is found by Pitts A. Correlated defaults: Let's go back to the data. *Risk*. 2004;June:75–79.
Düllmann K, Scheicher M, Schmieder C. Asset correlations and credit portfolio risk: An empirical analysis. *Journal of Credit Risk*. 2008;4(2), Summer.

[42]Gordy M, Heitfield E. Estimating default correlations from short-panels of credit rating performance data. Working paper, US Federal Reserve Board; 2002.

[43]Heitfield E, Barger N. Treatment of double-default and double-recovery effect for hedged exposures under Pillar 1 of the proposed new Basel Capital Accord. White paper, US Federal Reserve; June 2003.

[44]Stuart Turnbull also mentions this point, as well as several other open issues in credit risk portfolio modeling, in his article Unresolved issues in modeling credit-risky assets. *Journal of Fixed Income*. 2005;June:68–86.

[45]Basel Committee on Banking Supervision. The application of Basel II to trading activities and the treatment of double default effects. July 2005.

[46]Canabarro E, Picoult E, Wilde T. Analysing counterparty risk. *Risk*. 2003;September:117–122.

[47]Reinhart CM, Rogoff KS. This time is different: A panoramic view of eight centuries of financial crisis. Manuscript. Harvard University, April 16, 2008.

[48]Gelpern A. Systemic bank and corporate distress from Asia to Argentina: What have we learned? *International Finance*. 2004;7(1).

[49]Indonesia in crisis, a macroeconomic update. *The World Bank*. July 16, 1998.

[50]Perry G, Servén L. The anatomy of a multiple crisis, why was Argentina special and what can we learn from it? *The World Bank*. June 2003.

[51]A structural model for private equity investments is described in Bongaerts D, Charlier E. Private equity and regulatory capital. Center Discussion paper No. 2008–52, Tilburg University; 2008. Forthcoming in *Journal of Banking and Finance*. 2009.

[52]For a detailed account of the origins of and events during the sub-prime crisis, see Crouhy M, Jarrow R, Turnbull S. The subprime credit crisis of 2007. *Journal of Derivatives*. 2008;16(4), Fall.

[53]UBS Investment Research. ABS CDO asset and liability downgrades. July 27, 2008.

[54]Our illustrations are in line with results reported in:
Coval J, Jurek J, Stafford E. The economics of structured finance. Working paper 09-060, Harvard Business School; 2008.

Heitfield E. Parameter uncertainty and the credit risk of collateralized debt obligations. Working paper, US Federal Reserve Board; July 15, 2008.

[55]Background on the capital requirement formula in the Basel II Accord can be found in:

Basel Committee on Banking Supervision. An explanatory note on the Basel II risk weight functions. July 2005. Available on www.bis.org.

Gordy M. A risk-factor model foundation for ratings-based bank capital rules. *Journal of Financial Intermediation*. 2004;12(July):199–232.

Wilde T. IRB approach explained. *Risk*. 2001;May:87–90.

Lucas A, Klaassen P, Spreij P, Straetmans S. An analytic approach to credit risk of large corporate bond and loan portfolios. *Journal of Banking and Finance* 2001;25(9):1635–1664. Erratum in *Journal of Banking and Finance*. 2002;26(1):201–202.

[56]Gordy M, Jones D. Random tranches. *Risk*. 2003:78–83.

[57]Case studies of a number of these trading losses can be found in: Lepus. Rogue trader: Executive summary. August 2002. Available on http://www.prmia.org/pdf/Rogue_Trader_Summary.doc.

[58]References for the VaR calculation in general are:

Dowd K. *Measuring market risk*. 2nd ed. New York: John Wiley & Sons; 2005.

Jorion Ph. *Value-at-risk: The new benchmark for managing financial risk*. 3rd ed. New York: McGraw-Hill; 2006.

[59]A full account of the fall of LTCM is described in Jorion P. Risk management lessons from Long-Term Capital Management. *European Financial Management*. 2000;6:277–300.

[60]Basel Committee on Banking Supervision. Guidelines for computing capital for incremental risk in the trading book. Consultative document, www.bis.org, January 2009.

Basel Committee on Banking Supervision. Revisions to the Basel II market risk framework. Consultative document, www.bis.org, January 2009.

[61]Basel Committee on Banking Supervision. Revisions to the Basel II market risk framework. January 2009.

[62]Sources:

J.P. Morgan to pay $ 2 billion in settlement. *Los Angeles Times*. March 17, 2005;

J.P. Morgan Chase to pay $2.2 bln in Enron settlement. CFO.com. June 16, 2005;

Citigroup agrees to pay $2 billion in Enron scandal. *New York Times*. June 11, 2005.

For more information on the way in which Citigroup assisted Enron with the establishment of off-balance sheet vehicles for Enron, see Appendix D to the Third interim report of Neal Batson, court-appointed examiner re: the Enron default, United States Bankruptcy Court of New York.

[63]Dangerous animals in the banking zoo. *Financial Times*. February 23, 2008.

[64]Analytic approximations exist for the loss distribution, which accommodate the "fat tail" behavior of empirical operational loss data that the subsequent paragraphs illustrate. Analytic approximations are described in:

Böcker K, Klüppelberg C. Operational VAR: A closed-form approximation. *Risk*. December 2005.

Koker R de. Operational risk modeling: Where do we go from here? In: *The advanced measurement approach to operational risk*. Risk Books; 2006.

Böcker K, Sprittulla J. Operational VAR: Meaningful means. *Risk*. December 2006.

[65]Consequences of combining data with different statistical properties for the estimation of economic capital for operational risk are described in Neslehová J, Embrechts P, Chavez-Demoulin V. Infinite mean-models and the LDA for operational risk. *Journal of Operational Risk*. 2006;1(1), Spring:3–25.

[66]ORX Operational Risk Report. May 2007. Graphs in the text included with permission from ORX, Balmer-Etienne AG, Dreikönigstrasse 34, CH-8002, Zürich, Switzerland +44 (0)1225 430394, www.orx.org.

[67]See, for example:

Frachot A, Moudoulaud O, Roncalli T. Loss distribution approach in practice. In: *The Basel handbook: A guide for financial practitioners*. 2nd ed. Risk Books; 2007.

Alderwereld T, Garcia J, Léonard L. A practical operational risk scenario analysis quantification. *Risk*. February 2006.

[68]The article by Pavel Shevchenko and Mario Wüthrich (Shevchenko P, Wüthrich M. The structural modeling of operational risk via Bayesian inference: Combining loss data with expert opinion. *Journal of Operational Risk*. 2006;1(3), Fall:3–26) describes how techniques from Bayesian statistics can be used to combine subjective assessments of the likelihood and severity of large losses with historical data, and how new data on operational losses can be used to update derived frequency and severity distributions over time.

[69]European Commission, Internal Market and Services DG. QIS 4 Technical Specifications (MARKT/2505/08) Annex to Call for Advice from CEIOPS on QIS 4 (MARKT/2504/08). March 31, 2008.

[70]This summary of the Savings & Loan crisis is based on:
Jameson R. US Savings & Loan crisis. E-Risk case study. www.prmia.org/pdf/Case_Studies/US_S&L.pdf; 2002.
Curry T, Shibut L. The cost of the savings and loan crisis: Truth and consequences. *FDIC Banking Review*. 2000;13(2):23–35.

[71]OECD. Pension markets in focus. December, Issue 5, www.oecd.org; 2008.

[72]Citadel joins rush to lock up funds. *Financial Times*. 14 December 2008.

[73]Basel Committee on Banking Supervision. Principles for the management and supervision of interest rate risk. July 2004.

[74]Towers Perrin. Economic capital for life-insurance companies. February 2008.

[75]Possible approaches to quantify the risk of increased funding costs as a consequence of changes in an institution's own credit rating are described in:
Allen B. Stemming the flow. *Risk*. 2006;August:47–49.
Allen B. The liquidity link. *Risk*. 2008;February:79–81.

[76]Paragraph 762 in Basel Committee on Banking Supervision. International convergence of capital measurement and capital standards: A revised framework. 2006.

[77]Is there a future? The loneliness of the independent Wall Street bank. *The Economist*. September 18, 2008.

[78]Annual Report 2007. Deutsche Bank.

[79]IFRI Foundation and CRO Forum. Insights from the joint IFRI/CRO forum survey on economic capital practice and applications. 2007.

[80]LGT Group results 2007. Business performance and strategic outlook; LGT Media Conference/Results 2007, March 4, 2008.

[81]In this section, we benefited greatly from the report of the International Actuarial Association. A global framework for insurer solvency assessment. 2004.

[82]Swiss Re. Natural catastrophes and man-made disasters in 2007: High losses in Europe. Sigma report 01/2008;
Swiss Re. Preliminary Swiss Re sigma estimates that over 238,000 people were killed by catastrophes in 2008, insured losses soar to USD 50 billion. December 18, 2008.

[83]Based on Filopovic D, and Rost D. "Benchmarking study of internal models." Carried out on behalf of the Chief Risk Officers Forum, April 2005.

[84]Influenza pandemics, a prominent example of a mortality shock event. CRO Forum Emerging Risk Initiative. Position Paper, September 2007.

[85]Swiss Re. Pandemic influenza: A 21st century model for mortality shocks. June 15, 2007.

[86]Swiss Re. Natural catastrophes and man-made disasters in 2007: High losses in Europe. Sigma report January 2008.

[87]Beursval kost AEX-fondsen jaarlijks 10% van de winst (in Dutch). Het Financieele Dagblad, March 22, 2008.

[88]International Accounting Standards (IAS) 19.

[89]Kirsten AP. IRS loses NatWest appeal. January 24, 2008. www.taxanalysts.com.

[90]IRS accepts settlement offer in largest transfer pricing dispute. IR-2006–142, September 11, 2006.

[91]United States Senate Permanent Subcommittee on Investigations, Committee on Homeland Security and Governmental Affairs. Dividend tax abuse: How offshore entities dodge taxes on US stock dividends. Staff report, September 11, 2008.

[92]Fannie posts loss of $29 billion, hit by write-down. *Wall Street Journal.* November 10, 2008.

[93]Onderzoek naar de oorzaken van het faillissement van Van der Hoop Bankiers N.V. te Amsterdam. Annex to the public report of the administrators (in Dutch), 10 November 2006.

[94]Paragraph 28, in Basel Committee on Banking Supervision (2006). International convergence of capital measurement and capital standards: A revised framework.

[95]Kuritzkes A, Schuermann T, Weiner S. *Study on the risk profile and capital adequacy of financial conglomerates.* London: Oliver, Wyman & Company; 2001.

[96]The *variance* of a random variable is the square of its standard deviation, and the *covariance* of two random variables is the product of the standard deviation of each random variable and the correlation coefficient between them.

[97]Technical details on the implementation of copulas in risk management applications can be found in:

Embrechts P, McNeill A, Straumann D. Pitfalls and alternatives. *Risk.* 1999;May:69–71.

Embrechts P, McNeill A, Straumann D. Correlation and dependence in risk management: Properties and pitfalls. In: Dempster M, ed. *Risk management: Value at risk and beyond.* Cambridge: Cambridge University Press; 2002:176–223.

Embrechts P, Lindskog F, McNeill A. Modelling dependence with copulas and applications to risk management. In: Rachev S, ed. *Handbook of heavy-tailed distributions in finance.* Elsevier; 2003:329–384 [Chapter 8].

[98]Rosenberg J, Schuermann T. A general approach to integrated risk management with skewed, fat-tailed risks. *Journal of Financial Economics.* 2006;79(3):569–614.

5 Facing Reality: Implementing Economic Capital

In the previous chapters we reviewed important choices and assumptions with respect to the definition and calculation of economic capital. In the actual implementation and use of economic capital in a financial institution, we encounter a number of dilemmas, requiring choices that impact the benefits that can be derived from the use of economic capital. In this chapter, we will discuss these dilemmas in relation to the primary purposes of economic capital: ensuring continuity (Section 5.1) and optimizing profitability (Section 5.2). Section 5.3 provides a summary of the discussion in this chapter.

5.1 Ensuring Continuity

To help ensure continuity and assess whether the institution has adequate capital available, the absolute amount of economic capital needs to be estimated correctly. First of all, this requires that consistent and comprehensive economic capital methodologies are employed, which we discussed in Chapter 4. In addition, we have to ensure that data and calculation results from different parts of an institution are combined in a consistent manner so as to properly capture diversification and concentration effects. We will review possible strategies for this in Section 5.1.1. Even if economic capital in aggregate is a good estimate of the capital that an institution needs, it is unrealistic to expect that it will encompass in full detail all features that determine the risk of each and every exposure. This is particularly true for complex products. In Section 5.1.2 we discuss how to deal with complex products in relation to economic capital. In Section 5.1.3 we review questions that may arise when performing a capital adequacy assessment at the level of the institution as a whole. Finally, in Section 5.1.4, we discuss capital adequacy assessments for subsidiaries and how they relate to the assessment for an institution as a whole.

5.1.1 Capturing Diversification and Concentration Effects

One of the main practical challenges in estimating economic capital is to combine the different risks of all different business lines in a single loss distribution for the institution. As individual exposures may reinforce or mitigate each other, it is important that they can be linked to each other to assess either concentration risks (reinforce risk) or diversification benefits (mitigate risk). The problem is that the data used for economic capital calculations is spread over many databases owned by different risk functions and business lines. To bring them together is a Herculean task that in practice often is done in steps. There are two main approaches that can be followed, each with specific consequences for economic capital calculations:

I.   First bring all data per risk type together across business lines, calculate economic capital per risk type, and then combine economic capital estimates across risk types to calculate economic capital at the level of the institution as a whole.

II. First bring the data together at the business line level, then calculate economic capital per business line comprising all material risks to which the business line is exposed, and then combine economic capital estimates across the business lines to calculate economic capital at the level of the institution as a whole.

In Graph 5.1, we depict the two approaches for two business lines A and B, where we have limited the scope to credit risk and ALM risk for illustrative purposes:

The process for calculating economic capital may depend in practice on the organization's infrastructure, processes, and culture. Approach I requires that groupwide the information per risk type is available in one place to perform the calculation. This data and system infrastructure may not always be in place. Furthermore, with a culture of independent business lines, the business lines may want to measure the risks and calculate economic capital as much as possible in the proximity of the business that uses these numbers, thus favoring approach II. Managers of the business line may also prefer that their economic capital numbers, and hence their RAROC, are not influenced by actions taken in other business lines, which they could fear would be the case for a combined calculation of economic capital following approach I.

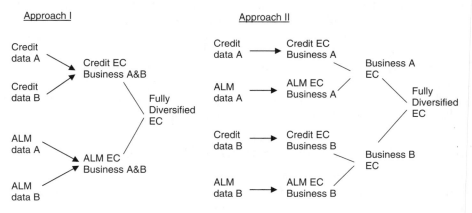

Graph 5.1 Calculation of economic capital (EC) for credit risk and ALM risk for the combination of business lines A and B.

Because economic capital models typically are developed per risk type, and can account for intra-risk correlations across the organization, approach I is more appealing from a computational perspective. In this approach, the diversification benefit between the credit risk resulting from, for example, a mortgage loan to a private individual and a commercial loan to an oil company will not depend on which business line has booked the exposures. Also, multiple exposures to the same oil company will be identified as a single obligor exposure regardless of whether they are booked in one or multiple business lines. Economic capital models for most risk types have no dependence on the organization structure, and hence treat exposures the same regardless of where they are booked within the institution.

This consistency is almost certainly not present with approach II. For example, in a credit portfolio the mortgage loans may be booked in the Retail Division and the loan to the oil company may be booked in the Wholesale Division. Although they will correlate and diversify within the credit portfolios of their respective business lines, it is not clear how to correctly include the correlation between these exposures across the business lines. If we add to the example an exposure to the same oil company, but booked in the Leasing Division of the bank, then we may miss the concentration effects of the combined exposure in the Wholesale and Leasing Division. Finally, the portfolio of the Leasing Division may differ substantially from that of the Wholesale Division, and, as a result, the respective exposures to the oil company may be subject to different diversification effects within the two portfolios. Thus, the economic capital attributed to the exposure to the oil company may differ between the two business lines even if the size of the exposure to the oil company is identical in both divisions. This is a drawback of approach II. It will almost certainly result in suboptimal decisions, because economic capital and related RAROC numbers will be distorted. Moreover, changes in the organization structure may cause the economic capital estimate to change even though actual exposures do not change. For example, if the Wholesale and Leasing Divisions are merged, then the economic capital attributed to the exposures to the oil company are most likely to change due to different diversification and concentration effects.

Because approach I is likely to result in a more accurate economic capital estimate, while being independent of the organizational structure, we prefer this approach. However, the trade-off between the advantages and disadvantages of each approach depends also on the actual organization structure and portfolios of the institution.

5.1.2 Dealing with Complex Products

When measuring an institution's risk and capital requirements, as well as risk-adjusted returns, a challenge is how to accommodate complex products of which the risk and return extend many years into the future. Examples are infrastructure capital transactions, long-term investments such as investments in structured finance products, as well as securitization transactions that a bank may enter into to eliminate part of its credit risk exposure. Within a one-year economic capital horizon, we have advocated to include potential market value changes at the one-year horizon in the determination of economic capital. However, a proper market value calculation at a future point in time is usually not straightforward for the products mentioned. To obtain a good picture of the risks inherent in such products over their full lifetime, financial institutions in practice often perform simulations over multiyear horizons to assess the risk profile and capital requirements, or the capital relief achieved.

For example, for a securitization of investment-grade loans, the economic capital relief obtained in the first year is most likely small because the probability of default of the loans in the first year is low. The default rate on investment-grade loans increases exponentially with time, however, as we have shown in Graph 3.3 in Section 3.5.1. Hence, the securitization is likely to realize its largest economic capital benefit in later years. To evaluate the attractiveness of such a transaction on a risk-adjusted return basis, we therefore must take the benefits in later years into account. Also for capital management and planning purposes, such a multiyear view on the capital consequences of major complex transactions is valuable.

The additional insights obtained from supplementary multiyear analyses for complex products emphasizes the more general point that the risk analysis using one-year economic capital should be complemented with other types of risk analyses.

5.1.3 Consolidated Capital Adequacy Assessments

A number of financial institutions publish consolidated group economic capital numbers. These provide analysts with information to assess the institution's risk profile and capital levels. When economic capital is higher than available capital, this signals that the institution is undercapitalized according to its own risk appetite. This raises obvious questions that the management of the institution should be prepared to answer. In general, however, published economic capital is lower than the available capital, implying that the financial institution has excess capital. In case economic capital is much lower than available capital, then at first sight this excess may look impressive from a financial soundness perspective. However, critical analysts will ask one or more of the following probing questions:

1. If economic capital is relatively low, are the published economic capital amounts comprehensive? That is, are all material risks reflected in economic capital?
2. If not, what risks are missing? Are they material? What would be a reasonable amount of capital to hold against them? Under Basel II, banks have to make these assessments and discuss them with their supervisor. Analysts will be curious to know the conclusions.
3. If the published economic capital amount is comprehensive and well below the amount of available capital, would it be possible for the institution to decrease its capital by the amount of the calculated excess and still maintain its credit ratings?

4. If the calculated excess can be reduced while maintaining the institution's credit ratings, then is there any specific action planned such as extra dividend payments or share buy-back programs? Alternatively, how does the institution intend to use its excess capital and make an attractive return on it?

In short, having excess capital may look desirable, but it can be too much of a good thing if these questions cannot be answered in a satisfactory manner. Nevertheless, in practice, excess capital is deemed a desirable feature by most managers and supervisors. This may be understandable if institutions do not measure economic capital comprehensively, or do not take model risk fully into account. The excess capital is then not a real excess, but a placeholder for the risks not included in economic capital. Even if economic capital is measured comprehensibly the question remains whether an institution should have a buffer on top of economic capital and if so, how large this buffer should be.

A first possible reason for an institution to have a capital buffer on top of the calculated economic capital is that an institution wants to avoid available capital falling below economic capital as soon as actual losses are only slightly higher than expected losses. In fact, actual losses may be quite frequently higher than expected losses. However, the unexpected loss is unlikely to lead to insolvency, which gives the institution's management the time to act and restore the capital ratios. Capital thus serves its intended purpose as buffer for unexpected losses, and consequently it may be temporarily above or below its target level.

The capital adequacy assessment may also show a shortage of available capital in case economic capital increases during an economic downturn. This will be the case, for example, if the credit risk portfolio model has a point-in-time character, which we discussed in Section 3.5.2. Note that this increase of economic capital will be reduced by the adjustment of the confidence level, which we argued should take place in case of point-in-time economic capital. Still, there may be a breach of the internal capital adequacy, and an institution may find it uncomfortable that the breach will occur precisely during an economic downturn. To avoid such a breach, economic capital should be calculated based on through-the-cycle model inputs. However, if it is unavoidable that some risk model inputs have point-in-time features, then for capital adequacy purposes we may want to introduce a cyclicality reserve, as part of economic capital, which compensates the impact of remaining point-in-time model inputs and parameters. This cyclicality reserve will be positive in favorable economic times and decrease to zero, or even become negative, during an economic downturn. In fact, this is not a buffer on top of economic capital but a practical way to estimate a truly through-the-cycle economic capital. Chapter 7 contains a discussion on the pro-cyclicality of economic capital, and suggestions how management of an institution can deal with this.

A specific concern that an institution may have when available capital ends up below economic capital, and why it wants to maintain a capital buffer, is that such a shortfall of available capital could affect the institution's credit rating.

This may impact funding costs and business revenues. The desire to prevent a rating downgrade can be viewed as a separate capital objective. In general, a downgrade of a through-the-cycle rating assigned to the institution by a rating agency will not occur for capital levels that are modestly below target and are likely to return to target within a reasonable period. Nonetheless, a rating downgrade may occur if the economic downturn is very severe or in case the institution suffers an unexpectedly large loss. To translate the concern about a rating downgrade into a capital objective, we first note that the chosen target debt rating implies a certain probability of a rating downgrade. For example, Standard & Poor's rating statistics over 1981 to 2007 show that 6.30% of A-rated companies have experienced a downgrade to a BBB rating within one year.[1] If the institution deems this probability of a downgrade too high, then it will need additional capital to reduce the risk of a downgrade. For example, if the institution's acceptable probability of a downgrade to BBB or below is less than 1%, then it should have capital as if it were an AA-rated institution, because on average only 0.76% of AA-rated institutions have been downgraded to a BBB rating or lower within one year, according to the Standard & Poor's statistics.

In addition to objectives related to insolvency and a rating downgrade, the institution may also have other objectives that imply a higher amount of required capital. If economic capital is used to indicate the amount of capital that the institution should have, its calculation should reflect the most demanding capital objective. No additional capital is needed on top of this most demanding capital objective.

A second possible reason for an institution to have excess capital is to allow the institution to grow or start new profitable businesses. To estimate the buffer needed to accommodate business growth, we need to know the institution's strategy and business plan, which normally is made operational in (multiyear) budgets. These budgets should also specify how much the risk exposures and, consequently, the economic capital will grow. Business growth is a valid reason to maintain a capital buffer, provided it is aligned with the institution's business strategy.

A third potential reason for excess capital is to satisfy regulatory capital requirements for subsidiaries. This is a form of capital inefficiency associated with the organizational structure. Ideally, an institution will try to avoid this inefficiency as much as possible. The issue is discussed more extensively in the next section.

5.1.4 Capital Adequacy for Subsidiaries

Assessing capital adequacy is done primarily at the consolidated group level. This assumes that capital can be transferred freely from one business line or legal entity to another. This is not always the case because local regulations can restrict the transfer of capital.

Local supervisors also may require an assessment of the capital adequacy for subsidiaries. For an institution that considers its subsidiaries as an indistinguishable part of the group, this may seem to be a less relevant exercise, but local supervisors and depositors have a valid interest that the subsidiary also is capitalized adequately. The default of the UK and Dutch subsidiaries and branches of Icelandic banks in 2008 and the resulting payments under deposit-guarantees by the UK and Dutch governments illustrate these valid interests. For these capital assessments at the subsidiary level, the question is whether we can apply economic capital models in the same way as we do at group level, or whether adjustments are necessary.

Capital assessments at the subsidiary level are a potentially sensitive issue because the subsidiary will not have the same diversification benefits as the group. In general, smaller entities will be less diverse and be exposed to higher concentration risks than larger entities. Consequently, if we calculate economic capital for a subsidiary as if it were a stand-alone entity, then economic capital for the subsidiary will be (significantly) higher than the amount of economic capital that it contributes to economic capital for the consolidated group. If we take the sum of the stand-alone economic capital estimates for all legal entities within a group, then typically this will be much higher than the economic capital of the entire group as a consolidated entity. This is due to the larger diversification benefits within the group as a whole. If banking supervisors would demand that available capital in the subsidiaries needs to be based on these stand-alone economic capital estimates, then the group as a whole would need to hold much more capital than the fully diversified economic capital for the entire group as consolidated entity. In this way the organization's legal structure can cause a higher capital requirement than otherwise would be required. These higher capital requirements are inefficient for an institution that aspires to optimize its return on capital.

There are a few options available to avoid this potential capital inefficiency as much as possible. The first option is that the holding company or parent guarantees all obligations of the subsidiary and thereby enables the subsidiary to be treated as part of the consolidated entity. This in principle avoids the need for stand-alone economic capital calculations and capital assessments for each subsidiary. To be able to accept a guarantee, the supervisor of the subsidiary should be comfortable that the guarantor is financially sound and well supervised, and that any claims on the guarantee would not de facto be subordinated to other claims on the group. Potential tax and legal impediments may also need to be considered for this option.

The second option is to calculate economic capital at the subsidiary level, but at a lower confidence level than is used at the group level. For smaller entities, it is not reasonable to expect that they can maintain the same level of continuity as larger and more diversified entities. What constitutes a reasonable confidence level for a subsidiary may require a constructive dialogue internally and with the supervisors of the subsidiary. The German insurer Allianz applies this approach to capital adequacy for subsidiaries as it uses a confidence level of 99.97% at the consolidated group level, but a lower 99.93% confidence level for local operating entities.[2]

A third option is that the exposures that contribute most to the subsidiary's economic capital are guaranteed by or booked at the parent. This is already common practice for large loans, which are extended by a subsidiary but booked at the parent because otherwise local legal lending limits would be breached. The economic capital framework can help to quantify the impact of these asset transfers or guarantees and optimize the choice of booking location.

5.2 Optimizing Profitability

When using economic capital to optimize profitability we have to deal with a host of practical issues. In Section 5.2.1 we start with a discussion of how to achieve confidence in and transparency about the complex methodologies that are used to estimate economic capital, so as to achieve support for its use across the organization. The use of economic capital for performance management also has clear implications for the budget process within institutions and the nature of information that business lines require to be able to improve their risk-adjusted performance. We discuss this in Section 5.2.2. A point of frequent debate within institutions is what risks to allocate to business lines, and whether and how to allocate diversification effects. This is the topic of Section 5.2.3. Section 5.2.4 discusses a number of practical choices when implementing the RAROC formula for performance measurement, and Section 5.2.5 considers how to use the RAROC formula for *ex-ante* and *ex-post* performance evaluation. A successful use of RAROC in an organization requires that it is embedded in a broader framework that ensures that managers and staff are provided with the right incentives to contribute to the optimization of the institution's profitability. We will review a number of important elements of such a framework in Section 5.2.6. In Section 5.2.7 we emphasize the importance of understanding the choices that are made in the definition and calculation of economic capital when comparing RAROC numbers between institutions and business lines. How to set a proper hurdle rate to which RAROC can be compared is the subject of Section 5.2.8. In Section 5.2.9 we discuss what role economic capital can play in strategic decisions, and when considering how to balance diversification and specialization.

5.2.1 Transparency and Governance

If economic capital and the related performance measures RAROC or economic profit are introduced for measuring performance, then these measures need to be trusted and accepted by management. This is not an easy hurdle since measuring risk and capital is complex and may be considered an esoteric activity by some. Managers of business lines often prefer simple and easy-to-understand performance measures to manage their business. However, these simple measures may provide the wrong incentives to optimize profitability.

To overcome this hurdle, there must be transparency about the risk models and the key assumptions underlying these models. This will involve discussions with business lines once they realize that their performance "depends" on these models. Model outcomes will be debated fiercely and proof will be requested where hard evidence may not always be available. However, these discussions also present an opportunity to improve the models with the practical knowledge contributed by the business.

As models will always have their limitations, it is important that decisions regarding the choice of models and key assumptions are made in a transparent way and within an appropriate governance framework. Not every manager can delve into the specifics of risk models, and hence he or she has to rely on the process to come to decisions that are relevant to how his or her performance will be measured. Given the importance of performance measurement for bonuses and strategic decisions by the institution, the key decisions about risk models should be taken at a senior level with appropriate involvement from risk management, finance, and business lines.[3]

5.2.2 Economic Capital and the Budget Cycle

When economic capital and RAROC are used to support management decision making and to allocate resources, these measures should be incorporated in the budgets of the organization. Capital as a scarce resource will be allocated to business lines depending on their growth and return projections. RAROC or economic profit targets will be agreed. The use of economic capital and RAROC in the budget process has consequences for the management of model changes and for reporting.

Over time, risk models will be refined and risk parameters need to be updated. As a consequence, economic capital estimates will change. Managers will, however, dislike these changes because their actual performance may appear less favorable as a result. Furthermore, some stability of methodology is required if managers are expected to manage their business on the basis of economic capital. This creates a tension between risk managers and supervisors on the one hand, who would like to see model improvements and updates of parameters to be implemented as soon as possible, and the finance department and business line managers on the other hand, who will demand that the models and parameters do not change during a budget period. To balance these interests, it is important that clear policies are in place regarding model and parameter changes, who is authorized to approve these changes, and when budgets will be adjusted. If a material model change is planned, then implementation may have to be delayed for budget process reasons. This is a price to be paid to have economic capital and RAROC used in the business processes of a financial institution.

If managers are to manage their business on the basis of economic capital and RAROC (among others), then they need to have the information to understand what drives changes in their economic capital and RAROC. This requires that not only revenues and costs are reported timely and accurately, but also that economic capital and the underlying risk drivers of economic capital are reported frequently. Such management information is desirable also without an economic capital framework; the additional challenge here is that changes in risk drivers should be related to changes in economic capital and that this should be reported in a transparent manner. This puts significant ongoing requirements on data, systems, risk analysis, and management reports.

5.2.3   Which Risks to Allocate to Business Lines?

When allocating economic capital to business lines, the overriding principle for performance management should be that risks are allocated to where revenues are earned that include a compensation for the risks. However, an individual manager will not be able to influence all risks to which his or her business is exposed. Should he or she still be accountable for a performance that is driven partly by (changes in) risks he or she cannot control? We will give a few examples of issues that may arise, and suggest ways to address them.

Risks that are inherent to the business may be deemed a "tax," in particular if they are relatively constant over time. The largest inherent risks are business and operational risk. For business risk, the market in which the business line operates determines to a large degree the revenue volatility. The primary risk mitigant for business risk is a flexible cost structure. It depends on the manager's level in the organization whether he or she can influence business risk by choosing different product/market combinations and optimizing the cost structure. Even if he or she can influence these choices, changing the business risk profile takes time. With respect to operational risk, all managers at all levels in the organization are responsible to manage this risk. The challenge is how to reflect management actions in the economic capital estimate for operational risk, as we discussed in Section 4.4.3. Since business and operational risks change only gradually over time, managers may perceive them as a "tax" but that does not change the fact that they are responsible to manage these risks. In any event, just like ordinary taxes, the inherent capital costs have to be paid and are part of the performance of a business line. Therefore, since the business line's overall return is a compensation for all the risks to which it is exposed, it is only consistent that all these risks should be allocated, not just the ones that a manager can directly influence.

Some risks are managed at a central level within a financial institution, and corresponding gains and losses would not be part of the revenues and costs of individual business lines. An example is foreign exchange translation risk, which we introduced as part of ALM risk in Section 3.3.1. It is the exchange rate risk involved in translating earnings and capital of a subsidiary in a foreign country to the reporting currency of the parent. The risk itself would not exist if the subsidiary were not owned by the current parent, but by a parent that reports in the same currency as the subsidiary. Although this risk clearly is related to the subsidiary, the subsidiary cannot influence this risk. The parent can choose to hedge the foreign exchange risk or not. In our view, a subsidiary's performance should not depend on the country of domicile and the reporting currency of the parent, and whether or not the parent hedges the foreign exchange risk. Consequently, we would choose not to allocate the risk and capital to the subsidiary, but keep it at the parent level where also the foreign exchange translation gain or loss is booked.

An issue that often stirs a lot of debate is whether to allocate diversification benefits back to the business lines. The diversification benefits arise as a result of combining the risk exposures of the different business lines. The diversification benefit is one of the benefits that a business line has from belonging to the group. On the one hand, business line managers will appreciate having the diversification benefits allocated back to the business lines because it will lower their economic capital. On the other hand, business line managers may prefer that their capital and related performance are not influenced by actions in other business lines. This dependence will exist, however, if diversification benefits that result from diversification of risks with other business lines are allocated back to each of the business lines. Actions by other business lines (e.g., new investments, large divestments) could result in changes in the overall diversification benefit and the resulting allocation back to the business lines. Changes in and volatility of these diversification benefits will depend on the size and volatility of the businesses and their risk exposures. For large diversified institutions the diversification benefits tend to be quite stable over time for major risk types like credit, business, and operational risk.

In Section 4.1.4 we discussed several methods according to which economic capital, and thereby diversification benefits, can be allocated to individual business lines. The choice of allocation method determines how stable diversification benefits are for a specific risk type. For example, the component economic capital contribution method may lead to volatile behavior when used to allocate ALM and traded market risk, because exposures with respect to these risk types can change quickly. For ALM and traded market risk, therefore, it may be preferable to allocate economic capital proportional to stand-alone economic capital estimates, despite the fact that this method has other drawbacks as we discussed in Section 4.1.4.

Other considerations that may play a role in deciding whether or not to allocate the diversification benefits relate to the organization's culture and business plan. Should a business line manager care about what happens in other business lines or not? In case a business line or subsidiary could be sold at short notice, then it may be appropriate not to allocate the diversification benefits back because this diversification benefit may disappear shortly.

In general, we will have to weigh the merits and drawbacks of allocating the diversification benefits to the business lines or not. In principle, to optimize group performance and provide the right incentives to business line managers to contribute to this objective, we should allocate the diversification benefits back to the business lines. The drawback may be some volatility of the diversification benefits and hence the economic capital numbers that are allocated to a business line over time. As illustrated for ALM and traded market risk, a solution may be found in alternative allocation methods that, although theoretically less optimal, reduce this volatility.

A specific attention point arises when RAROC is used to benchmark the performance of the business line with competitors. For example, a private bank that is part of a large institution may compete with other specialized independent private banks. The diversification benefit then gives it a capital advantage over its competitors. As will be discussed in Section 5.2.8, this should be compensated by a higher hurdle rate and therefore the comparison should focus on the difference between the realized RAROC and the respective hurdle rates. Alternatively, the comparison could be based on the return on the estimated economic capital as if the business line were a stand-alone unit. To perform such a stand-alone economic capital calculation, we must decide how to incorporate internal transactions of the business line with other parts of the organization to which it belongs. In a proper stand-alone view, these transactions should be considered as being conducted with another market participant. Assumptions need to be made on how to reflect the hypothetical counterparty risk on such transactions.

5.2.4 Calculating RAROC

We introduced the following formula for RAROC in Chapter 2:

$$RAROC = \frac{Revenues - Costs - ExpectedLoss - Tax}{EconomicCapital}$$

Although the formula is not complex, there are a few issues to consider when using it in practice. The first issue is how to deal with loss leaders—that is, products that are sold with a low profit margin in order to attract other more profitable business. Should part of the revenues of these other, more profitable, products be included in the RAROC calculation for the loss leaders? The business model of the institution will provide some guidance whether profitability per client, which allows that one product subsidizes another, or per product line, which typically does not recognize cross-product subsidies, is leading.

A second issue is the allocation of indirect costs. If indirect costs are significant, then the allocation of indirect costs can materially influence the returns for products and business lines. The allocation of indirect costs deserves as much attention as the allocation of capital when calculating and assessing RAROC. The allocation of revenues and indirect costs, however, is not unique to RAROC but applies to most performance measures; therefore, we will not discuss this further, but refer to other books on this topic.

A third issue relating to the use of RAROC is that the amount of economic capital that enters in the formula is a normative capital measure and not the actual capital employed. The actual capital employed by a business line (i.e., the available capital) may differ from this normative amount. This may have tax or regulatory reasons, for example. If the difference between economic and actual available capital is not accounted for in the RAROC calculation, then this will lead to an overstatement of RAROC for an institution or business line with a capital surplus (i.e., the amount of available capital is higher than economic capital). In this case, the business line will have lower funding costs than if the available capital would be equal to the normative economic capital amount, because the capital surplus does not have to be funded with interest-bearing debt. For the same reason, funding costs are higher, and RAROC will be underestimated, for an institution or business line with a capital deficit. Correcting the numerator for the debt costs of the capital surplus or deficit addresses the problem.

An alternative RAROC formula is sometimes used to avoid this correction for a difference between actual available capital and economic capital.[4] This formula is applied mainly for credit risk and is as follows:

$$RAROC = \frac{Revenues - Costs - ExpectedLoss - Tax + CapitalBenefit}{EconomicCapital}$$

The difference between the alternative RAROC formula and the original RAROC formula is the inclusion of a capital benefit and how revenues are calculated. To illustrate the impact of this difference, we consider a loan of USD 100,000 with an interest rate of 5%. If the matched funding rate is 4%, then the loan margin is 1%. The alternative RAROC formula assumes full debt funding and the net revenues are thus USD 1,000 (USD 100,000 × 1%). If we assume that economic capital of USD 10,000 needs to be held against the loan, then the formula assumes that this USD 10,000 is invested in risk-free bonds with an interest rate of, say, 3%. An investment in risk-free bonds is assumed because the alternative of a risky investment would give rise to additional credit risk, and the economic capital amount thus would increase as well, thereby distorting the calculation. In our example, the capital benefit is 300 (USD 10,000 × 3%). If we abstract from other costs, expected loss, and tax, then the RAROC is:

$$(1,000 + 300)/10,000 = 13\%.$$

The original RAROC formula does not invest the economic capital in risk-free bonds, but assumes that only the difference between the loan amount and the economic capital is funded with debt. The RAROC is thus:

$$(100,000 \times 5\% - 90,000 \times 4\%)/10,000 = (5,000 - 3,600)/10,000 = 14\%.$$

We observe that the same loan generates different RAROCs, depending on the formula we use. This raises the question, which of the two RAROC formulas is the correct one.

The alternative RAROC formula is easy to implement as it separates the loan revenues and costs from any capital structure considerations. It takes the loan margin over the full loan amount and deals with economic capital separately by reinvesting it in a risk-free bond. However, this assumes that the institution would attract more debt funding than strictly necessary, because USD 90,000 debt would be sufficient to fund the loan given available capital of USD 10,000, and will invest the remainder in a risk-free bond that has a lower return than the funding rate. This is irrational for a profit-maximizing institution and, not surprisingly, this investment strategy is not observed in practice.

We conclude that the alternative RAROC formula may be easy for calculation purposes, but that it underestimates RAROC. It is based on the artificial concept, that the amount of economic capital will be invested in risk-free bonds. This reduces the institution's profitability without lowering its risk and is thus irrational. The preferred RAROC calculation is, therefore, the original one.

5.2.5 Forward-looking Versus Backward-looking RAROC

Performance can be measured *ex-post*, looking back at the performance of business units, or *ex-ante*, when considering investment options. In both cases RAROC can be used.

When using RAROC to measure performance *ex-post*, it is standard practice to relate the operating result minus expected loss of the previous year(s) to the average economic capital allocated to that activity or investment over that period. This is comparable to how other return on capital measures are calculated, like return on equity (ROE), except that in RAROC expected loss is deducted instead of realized losses. We provided a motivation for this in Chapter 2, and will discuss in the next section the incentives to which it can give rise.

When RAROC is used to assess performance *ex-ante*, the use of a one-year time horizon of economic capital could lead to wrong decisions for new projects or investments with a longer time horizon because upfront fees and the like could boost the RAROC in the first year whereas RAROC in later years will look much less attractive. A correct *ex-ante* calculation of RAROC would avoid this problem by taking into account in the economic capital assessment the market value risk of the project or investment at the one-year horizon. However, instead of estimating a potential decline in the market value of the investment at the one-year horizon, it may be easier in practice to calculate an average RAROC over the entire tenor taking into account all the cash flows, the expected changes in the risk profile (e.g., rating migrations), and the resulting economic capital requirements. Such an analysis is comparable to the multiyear risk analysis that we suggested for complex products in Section 5.1.2. The economic capital assessment may also involve an estimate of the size of diversification effects that the new project or investment has with the institution's existing portfolio of risks.

5.2.6   Incentives and RAROC

RAROC and economic profit as performances measures create new incentives for managers. As we discussed in Section 2.3.1, the biggest difference with other performance measures is that they are risk sensitive by taking into account the expected loss and economic capital associated with the activity or investment.

The fact that we deduct expected loss instead of the realized loss in the numerator of the RAROC formula raises the question what incentives this creates. In theory, this could cause that managers are not interested anymore in the actual losses but only in the expected losses. First, when evaluating prospective investments, there are no realized losses and deducting expected losses ensures that these are taken into account in the investment decision. There are thus no incentive issues from deducting expected losses in RAROC when it is used to evaluate new projects or investments *ex-ante*. What incentives the deduction of expected losses causes when RAROC is used as an *ex-post* performance measure depends to what extent the losses can be controlled or managed by the manager. To the extent that actual losses are influenced directly by a manager, actual losses instead of expected losses should be subtracted in the numerator of RAROC to provide the correct incentives, i.e., to reward the manager for reducing actual losses. For example, operational losses classified as "execution, delivery & process management" could fall in this category.

With respect to credit risk, by deducting the expected credit loss the RAROC performance measure disregards whether a manager has been lucky that there have been few actual losses, or had the bad luck that the economy was in a downturn and credit losses were relatively high. However, credit losses may not be entirely outside the control of managers. Credit losses are not invariant to good monitoring of the risks and taking timely actions to mitigate the credit risk. This will have to be addressed by creating additional incentives to manage these risks, as markets do consider actual losses. It will not impress any shareholder, supervisor, or analyst if an institution reports a high RAROC while losing their shirts on credit losses.

Another incentive created by using RAROC is that commercial businesses may try to underestimate the risk as this will lower economic capital. This will allow them to do more business and increase the RAROC of their business with positive consequences for their bonuses and careers. If RAROC is measured on an annual basis while a transaction has a much longer tenor, then the real risks in the form of higher losses than expected may only materialize long after the bonuses have been paid. If products are very complex, then the likelihood that risks will be underestimated is relatively high. This incentive problem has been highlighted by many a commentator as being at the roots of the sub-prime crisis, because structured finance specialists had every incentive to structure the maximum volume of complex products with seemingly superior returns at inception of the transaction.[5]

In case risks are assessed by a strong independent risk management function and model risk is low, then we may trust that RAROC takes future risks appropriately into account and delayed incentive schemes may not be necessary. This would be the case for originators of commercial or consumer loans whose credits are screened and approved by experienced and independent risk officers. If an individual relationship manager would have the bad luck that his or her largest client would default, then this would not be held against him or her, nor would bonus payments have to be delayed. In case model risk would be high (e.g., new complex products or products with high operational risks), or in case there would not be a strong independent risk management function (e.g., business lines can approve loans themselves), then delayed bonus payments should be considered.

An incentive issue related to the RAROC for transactions that are subject to fair value accounting is that the income on such transactions will be realized at origination of a transaction. For example, when a transaction with a client is executed and hedged at the same time in the market, then the income, which is the difference between the fair values of the client and hedge transaction, immediately shows up in the income statement. Although the market risk is partly or fully hedged in this case, there is still counterparty credit risk on the client and the hedge counterparty for the remaining life of the transaction. To ensure that part of the initial income is reserved as compensation for the market and credit risk that remains, an income reserve can be established. This income reserve is released over time to spread out the income over the tenor of the transaction in line with the remaining risk exposure. Any intermediate corrections of the fair value are booked against the income reserve. This income reserve may not appear in the financial statements of the institution, but can be used solely for internal performance measurement.

In addition, a model reserve may be formed if there is considerable uncertainty about the determination of the fair value of transactions. This may be the case for transactions with long tenors, or of high complexity. The model reserve will decrease over time when the level of model risk around the determination of the fair value declines. The income that is included in the RAROC calculation should then be after additions to or releases from the model reserve.

Creating the right incentives is a challenge for any performance measure. To accomplish this, a performance measure may need to be supplemented by income and model reserves, as well as delayed bonus schemes. Still, RAROC and economic profit are a step forward compared to traditional performance measures as they take into account the cost of risk. Hence, they reduce the incentive for managers to take high risks on the books without adequate return.

5.2.7   Interpretation of RAROC

In Section 2.3.1, we discussed RAROC and its strength as a risk-adjusted profitability measure. In this section, we will discuss some issues that need to be taken into account when interpreting RAROC numbers. These issues relate directly to choices made for the definition and calculation of economic capital, which we discussed in Chapter 3.

The first issue relates to the potentially different definition of economic capital for the purpose of ensuring continuity and for the purpose of optimizing profitability, which we discussed in Section 3.6. We concluded that when the aim is to evaluate the creation of shareholder value we need to take account of the franchise value of the firm in the definition of economic capital. If the franchise value is not included in economic capital, then this will inflate RAROC in general, provided the franchise value is positive, and in particular for those business lines where the franchise value is relatively high.

In Section 3.6.2 we also noted that the franchise value is usually relatively high for private banking and asset management, and consequently we would expect superior RAROC for these business lines if economic capital does not include potential changes in the franchise value. Published RAROC figures for different business lines confirm this, as we show in Table 5.1.

In Table 5.1, the RAROC of business lines of Barclays Plc, ING Bank, and Credit Suisse are provided. These banks are among the few banks that disclose RAROC per business line and which have private banking operations (Barclays Wealth, ING Private Banking, Credit Suisse Wealth Management) and asset management units (Barclays Global Investors, Credit Suisse Asset Management, ING not specified). It is clear from the numbers that these business lines produce an

Table 5.1 Pre-tax RAROC of business lines of Barclays Plc, ING Bank N.V., and Credit Suisse Group (*Source*: 2007 Annual reports of Barclays and Credit Suisse, ING Group Statistical Supplement 2007)

Barclays	2006	2007
UK Retail	28%	28%
Commercial	37%	30%
Barclaycard	16%	19%
International	36%	16%
Barclays Capital	41%	33%
Global Investors	228%	241%
Barclays Wealth	40%	51%

ING Bank	2006	2007
Wholesale	19%	18%
Real Estate	59%	45%
ING Direct	19%	18%
Retail	44%	50%
Private Banking	57%	126%

Credit Suisse	2006	2007
Investment Banking	35%	20%
Asset Management	44%	50%
Corporate & Retail	39%	53%
Wealth Management	194%	245%

above-average RAROC, and sometimes significantly so. The exclusion of the franchise value in the economic capital estimates may be a (partial) explanation. We also observe large differences in RAROC between the asset management business lines of the three banks (Barclays 241% versus Credit Suisse 50%) and the private banking business lines (Credit Suisse 245%, ING 126%, and Barclays 51%). These differences may be caused by differences in performance and market circumstances, but can also result from differences between the definitions of economic capital employed, as well as from methodological differences. With respect to the latter, operational risk and business risk are the dominant risk types for these business lines, and these risk types are subject to high degrees of uncertainty and methodological differences to measure economic capital.

The second issue that needs to be kept in mind when interpreting RAROC numbers relates to whether economic capital is a through-the-cycle or a point-in-time measure. We discussed the difference in Section 3.5.2. Many banks calculate expected loss and economic capital based on through-the-cycle inputs. If this is the case, then we expect that RAROC will be low in favorable economic times and high in recessions. The reason is that economic capital and expected loss are relatively constant in a through-the-cycle system, but loan margins and revenues will vary with changes in market circumstances. Investors will require relatively low-risk premiums during favorable economic times, and loan margins will be low as a consequence. The opposite will be true during recessions. The result is high RAROC during a downturn, and low RAROC during good economic times. This may provide incentives to the business to expand lending during a recession and reduce lending during favorable times. Although countercyclical, increased asset growth at a time of increasing risks and below-average growth of available capital, or even a decline in available capital, may not be deemed desirable from the point of view of capital and balance sheet management of the institution. The issue can be addressed by using point-in-time parameters to estimate economic capital and RAROC for the purpose of originating transactions, or by adjusting the hurdle rates as a function of the economic situation, as we will discuss in Section 5.2.8.

In general, we should be suspicious of products that produce a consistently high RAROC. In an efficient market, that cannot last. As Abraham Lincoln was attributed to have said "you can fool some of the people all of the time, and all of the people some of the time, but you can't fool all people all of the time." In cases of lasting superior RAROC, we should analyze whether all risks are appropriately measured, in particular risks for which the measurement is subject to a significant amount of uncertainty.

5.2.8 Setting the Hurdle Rate

As we discussed in Chapter 3, economic capital can be viewed as an estimate of the amount of equity capital that a financial institution should possess to be able to sustain unexpected losses with a high probability. Investors are only willing to provide this equity capital if they expect to receive an adequate return. Hence, the management of a financial institution must ensure that the institution as a whole, and each individual business line within the institution, generates an adequate return for the providers of equity capital. This requires the determination of a hurdle rate of return for each of the businesses, and possibly even for individual transactions, that represents the minimum expected return required to adequately compensate the equity providers for the risk they take. If the RAROC exceeds the hurdle rate, the business line or transaction is said to create shareholder value. Because equity providers are interested in a return on the market value of equity, the amount of economic capital used in the calculation of RAROC should represent the market value of equity. As discussed, economic capital should then include the franchise value of an institution and its businesses.

The Capital Asset Pricing Model (CAPM)

The framework that commonly is used to establish the required return for risky investments, including therefore the equity investment in a financial institution, is the Capital Asset Pricing Model (CAPM). The question is whether the expected return that follows from the CAPM is a good choice for the hurdle rate on economic capital. And if so, do we need to determine different hurdle rates for different businesses within a financial institution?

In general, the risk of an investment can be split in two parts: idiosyncratic risk and systematic risk. Idiosyncratic risk is the risk that is specific to the investment, and that can be reduced or even eliminated by combining the investment with other investments. Systematic risk is the part of the risk that cannot be diversified by combining an investment with other investments. The central result of the CAPM is that a risky investment requires a return in excess of the risk-free interest rate only if it possesses systematic risk. For an investment without systematic risk, the required return would be equal to the risk-free interest rate. In the CAPM, systematic risk is reflected by a positive correlation with the market portfolio, which represents the universe of investment opportunities that is available to investors. The higher the correlation is between the return on an individual investment and the market portfolio, the higher the required return for the investment is in the CAPM. If a risky investment contains systematic risk, then its required return will in addition depend on the standard deviation of its returns. The higher the standard deviation of return is for an investment that contains systematic risk, the higher the required excess return above the risk-free interest rate will be. The precise relationship that the CAPM prescribes is:

$$R_I = R_f + Corr(R_I, R_M) \times \frac{Stdev(R_I)}{Stdev(R_M)} \times (R_M - R_f)$$

with R_I the expected return on the investment, R_f the risk-free interest rate, R_M the expected return on the market portfolio, $Corr(R_I, R_M)$ the correlation between the return on the investment and on the market portfolio, $Stdev(R_I)$ the standard deviation of the return on the investment, and $Stdev(R_M)$ the standard deviation of the return on the market portfolio. The correlation times the ratio of the standard deviations in the CAPM formula usually is referred to as the beta of the investment. It measures the sensitivity of the required return on the investment to the expected excess market return.

For equity investments, the volatility and correlation that are input into the CAPM usually are estimated from historical data. For the market portfolio, usually a broad equity index, such as the MSCI world index, is chosen. The difference between the expected return on the market portfolio and the risk-free interest rate often is called the market risk premium. This market risk premium may vary through time when the risk appetite of investors changes, for example, in different phases of an economic cycle. Also the risk-free interest rate may change. Such changes will therefore have an impact on the required return of a risky investment, even if its own risk characteristics remain the same.

CAPM and Economic Capital

Economic capital is not an input in the CAPM. As economic capital measures the potential decline in the equity value of a financial institution, it is most closely related to the standard deviation of the equity investment return in the CAPM. If there would be a fixed scaling factor between economic capital and the standard deviation of return on equity investments, and if this fixed scaling factor applies both to the equity value of individual institutions and to the market as a whole, then it does not matter whether we use the standard deviation of returns or economic capital in the CAPM formula. This requires that the probability distribution of changes in the equity value of an institution has a similar shape as the probability distribution of changes in value of the market portfolio—for example, if both would have a Gaussian (normal) distribution.

However, the probability distribution of changes in the equity value of a financial institution may well have much fatter tails than the probability distribution of changes in the market portfolio—for example, if the institution has significant exposure to credit or operational risk. The market portfolio, being the collection of all possible investment opportunities, has a probability distribution that is likely to resemble more closely a Gaussian (bell-shaped) distribution. Furthermore, the ratio of equity investment volatility to economic capital may vary between different firms. Hence, two institutions could have the same volatility of equity returns and correlation with the market portfolio, yielding the same hurdle rate of return according to the CAPM, while their economic capital estimates differ. The institution with the largest economic capital is obviously riskier, and it is reasonable to expect that equity investors require a higher expected return on an equity investment in that institution.

A Different Hurdle Rate per Business Line?

If we assume that the CAPM provides a reasonable approximation of what the minimum required return on economic capital of an institution is to create shareholder value, despite the caveats made earlier, the next question is whether the hurdle rate should vary between different businesses in the institution. The answer to this question is affirmative. If we use a single hurdle rate for an institution consisting of different businesses that would have a different hurdle rate when considered in isolation, then the institution risks foregoing investments that create shareholder value and accepting investments that destroy shareholder value.[6] We illustrate this with a numerical example.

We consider two different businesses, A and B. Each business has its own capital structure (composition of equity and debt funding), and we assume that the standard deviation of the equity return for each individual business equals 4%. We further assume that the correlation of the equity return of business A with the market is 0.75, and 0.25 for business B. Business A thus has a relatively high correlation with the market, and business B a relatively low correlation. If we further assume that the risk-free interest rate equals 4%, and that the market portfolio has an expected return of 8% (i.e., a market risk premium of 4%) with a standard deviation of 2%, then we can use the CAPM to calculate the expected return on the equity for both businesses A and B as stand-alone entities. The CAPM yields an expected return of 10% for business A and 6% for business B. The numbers are summarized in Table 5.2.

If we further assume that both businesses have the same amount of equity, and combine both businesses into one institution, then we can calculate that the standard deviation of returns on the combined equity value of the institution equals 3.08%. This is lower than the standard deviation of equity returns for each of the businesses individually, reflecting diversification effects between them when combined into one institution. We can further derive that the correlation of the equity return of the institution's equity with the market portfolio equals 0.65. It is higher than the average correlation of business A and B

Table 5.2 Using CAPM to derive expected returns for business A and B individually, and for the combination of both

Risk-free interest rate	4%		
Expected return on market portfolio	8%		
Standard deviation of return on market portfolio	2%		
	Business A	Business B	Business A+B
Standard deviation of equity return	4%	4%	3.08%
Correlation of equity return with market portfolio	0.75	0.25	0.65
Expected return from CAPM	10%	6%	8%
Weights	50%	50%	

because their combination in one institution reduces the amount of idiosyncratic risk. Using these values for the standard deviation of equity returns and correlation with the market, we obtain from the CAPM that the expected equity return for the institution equals 8% (which, as expected, is precisely equal to the average of the expected equity returns of businesses A and B).

If we would use a hurdle rate of 8% for the institution as a whole, then we run the risk of accepting projects in business A that in actual fact destroy shareholder value, and rejecting projects in business B that in fact create shareholder value. For example, if we have a project in business A that yields an expected return on equity of 9%, then we would accept this project if we compare it to the institutionwide hurdle rate of 8%. Given high correlation of projects in business A with the market, shareholders in fact require an expected return of at least 10% for such a project. Accepting the project with an expected return of 9% thus destroys shareholder value. Conversely, if we have a project in business B that yields an expected return on equity of 7%, then it would be rejected based on the hurdle rate of 8% for the institution as a whole. Given the low correlation of projects in business B with the market, however, shareholders require an expected return of only 6% to compensate for its risk. Hence, with an expected return of 7% the project would actually add value for the institution's shareholders.

This illustrates the need to differentiate hurdle rates for different businesses in an institution.[7] Moreover, for major investments it would be sensible to assess on an individual basis the volatility of return on the associated equity, as well as the correlation with market returns, to evaluate whether the investment creates shareholder value.

As noted earlier, the hurdle rate as implied by the CAPM also depends on the risk-free interest rate. This risk-free rate will depend on the currency, and this is therefore by itself a reason to differentiate hurdle rates between business lines that operate in markets with different currencies.

The Impact of Leverage on the Hurdle Rate

Using the earlier example, we can illustrate what happens if the institution decides to reduce the amount of equity after combining businesses A and B, and thus increase its leverage. We measure leverage as the ratio of the value of the assets to the value of the equity. A motivation for the increase in leverage could be that through the diversification between both businesses the default probability on the combined debt is lower than what is consistent with the target rating for the institution's debt. A reduction of the amount of equity, and thus increased leverage, will increase the volatility of returns on the remaining equity. As the correlation of the institution's equity returns with the market portfolio will not change, the required expected return for the institution according to the CAPM will increase. For example, if the institution would reduce its equity so that the standard deviation of the equity return would increase from 3.08 to 4%, then the required expected return on the equity would increase from 8 to 9.2% according to the CAPM. The hurdle rates for businesses A and B also would increase, as their leverage increases in line with the increased leverage for the institution as a whole, thereby increasing the standard deviation of return on the attributed equity.

When comparing RAROC to the CAPM hurdle rate for a business, a question is what amount of economic capital to use in the denominator of the RAROC formula: the stand-alone economic capital amount of a business line (at a chosen confidence level), or its contribution to economic capital for the institution as a whole? Since RAROC is a risk-adjusted return measure that considers risk at the level of an individual institution or even business line, whereas the CAPM is based on a marketwide view of risk, there is no natural choice. Fortunately, it does not matter that much as long as there is consistency between the amount of economic capital that is used in the RAROC calculation, and the amount of equity capital that is assumed for the calculation of the standard deviation of return on the equity in the hurdle rate.

Whatever the amount of economic capital that is used in the denominator of the RAROC formula, the hurdle rate should be calculated under the assumption that the equity investment in the business is equal to this amount of economic capital. If this consistency is ensured, then an increase in RAROC as a result of reducing the amount of economic capital in the denominator of RAROC (e.g., because of using economic capital contribution instead of stand-alone economic capital) leads to approximately the same proportional increase in the hurdle rate. It can be shown that the proportional changes are exactly equal if the average coupon rate on all debt equals the risk-free interest rate. For many financial institutions this is approximately satisfied in normal circumstances.

In practice, financial institutions use both stand-alone economic capital and economic capital contribution in the denominator of RAROC. When estimating the hurdle rate, however, many institutions estimate a beta directly from historical equity returns of institutions that are deemed comparable to a specific business line. This may be inconsistent with the amount of economic capital used in the RAROC formula, however, for two reasons. First of all, the amount of leverage of the comparable firms may differ from the leverage implied by the amount of economic capital that is used in the RAROC calculation for the business line. We then should adjust the estimated beta of the comparable firms for the difference in leverage with the business line under consideration. If the leverage (measured as the ratio of assets to equity) is lower for a comparable firm than for the business line in question, then the estimated beta should be increased proportionally for the business line. Second, if economic capital does not include the franchise value of the business line, then we must make a correction for the fact that the beta of the comparable firms is estimated from market values of equity that include the franchise value. This correction can be made by multiplying the estimated beta of a comparable firm with the ratio of the market to the book value of its equity. As illustrated in Section 3.6.2, the market-to-book value of equity may differ significantly between different business lines.

When Raising Equity Is Costly

In the CAPM as presented, we can determine the hurdle rate of a business independent of its interaction with other businesses in an institution. The only factors that are relevant are the standard deviation of its return on a stand-alone basis, and its correlation with the market at large. This is a consequence of the assumption underlying the CAPM that capital markets function frictionless. Specifically, it is assumed that there are no costs associated with attracting new equity capital when needed. In reality, however, there may be significant costs to attract new capital. Many banks and insurance companies experienced this when they had to attract new capital during the sub-prime crisis to shore up their capital reserves. New rights issues were offered at deep discounts to investors and very high interest rates were paid on preferred stock issues or mandatory convertible bonds.

Kenneth Froot and Jeremy Stein have shown that if it is costly for a financial institution to rebuild its capital base after incurring unexpected losses, then the hurdle rate that is required by investors for a business will not just depend on its stand-alone return volatility and correlation with the market, but also on the correlation of its return with the return on the rest of the institution's businesses.[8] The higher this latter correlation, the greater the likelihood that the business will contribute to the necessity for a required capital raise in the future. Because attracting new equity is costly for the firm, it reduces the value of the firm for the existing equity investors. The existing equity investors want to be compensated for this risk, and thus will require a higher expected return. Moreover, the closer the institution is to the point at which it needs to raise new capital, the more impact the correlation of the return of a business with the rest of the institution will have on the hurdle rate in the model of Froot and Stein. Since available capital will be close to economic capital if capital is deployed efficiently, we expect the contribution of a business line to the total risk of an institution to have an impact on the hurdle rate that investors require. The results of Froot and Stein further imply that business decisions that change the risk profile of an institution in a significant way (large investments, acquisitions, or divestitures) cannot be taken in an isolated manner (as would be the case in a pure CAPM world) but need to be considered in the context of the set of activities within the institution as a whole.

Froot and Stein present evidence that pricing decisions of financial institutions in reality are in line with the results of their model. In particular, it can explain why banks are more restrictive in lending when their capital levels have declined, since banks will be more critical on the returns they make on new business in such a situation, which can be viewed as an increase in the hurdle rate. Furthermore, the Froot and Stein model is consistent with the finding that the mark-up in insurance premiums for natural catastrophes such as earthquakes and hurricanes tends to increase across the board after the occurrence of a catastrophe that has reduced the amount of capital across the insurance industry. As the occurrence of natural catastrophes is not clearly related to the return on other investments, we would not expect a change in pricing according to the standard CAPM. However, the fact that pricing does change suggests that the level of available capital plays a role in the determination of hurdle rates.

Summary

In setting the appropriate hurdle rate for a business in an institution, both its stand-alone risk and its contribution to the risk of the institution as a whole are important. The available theory does not give a simple recipe, however, for how to set hurdle rates of return on economic capital in order to maximize shareholder value. Nonetheless, we can draw the following general conclusions:

- Despite a number of caveats, there is no clear alternative to using the CAPM as a starting point for determining the hurdle rate of return for an institution (as many financial institutions do). One caveat is that the CAPM does not reflect a compensation for tail risk. Equity investors are likely to care about tail risk, and because financial institutions typically are more exposed to tail risk than the market as a whole, the CAPM may understate the true required expected return. A second caveat is that the CAPM ignores the cost of raising equity when unexpected losses have reduced the amount of available capital. Accounting for this further increases the hurdle rate.

- The CAPM implies that hurdle rates for different businesses in an institution should be allowed to differ. If a uniform hurdle rate is imposed, projects that create shareholder value may be rejected, whereas projects that destroy shareholder value may be accepted. Given the cost of raising equity when needed, the more a specific business line contributes to the overall return volatility of the institution as a whole, the higher its hurdle rate should be compared to the one implied by the CAPM. In addition, the hurdle rate should depend on the main currency in which a business line operates, or in which a transaction takes place, since the risk-free rate varies between currencies.

- When RAROC is compared to the hurdle rate for a business line, it is important to ensure that there is consistency between the economic capital included in RAROC and the hurdle rate. The hurdle rate according to the CAPM specifies a required return on the market value of equity that is invested in the business line, and depends on the amount of leverage employed in the business line. If economic capital does not represent the market value of a business line, we must adjust the hurdle rate to reflect this. Furthermore, if the hurdle rate for a business line is estimated from observed equity returns of comparable firms, we should adjust the estimated hurdle rate if the amount of leverage of the comparable firms differs from the leverage of the business line in question.

The hurdle rate for an institution and its business lines may change as a function of the economic cycle, because the general risk premium in the market (incorporated as the difference between the expected return on the market portfolio and the risk-free interest rate in the CAPM) will change with the risk appetite of investors. It is thus advisable to recalibrate the hurdle rate calculation when economic circumstances change.

5.2.9   Strategic Decisions and the Balance Between Specialization and Diversification

Economic capital is an input to strategic decisions such as capital allocation and new investments. For new strategic projects or investments (e.g., acquisitions), the information available may not be sufficiently detailed to calculate the impact on economic capital in a precise manner. This will increase the uncertainty associated with such a decision, but limited information and the associated uncertainty are often inherent in these decisions. One method that can be applied to estimate economic capital on the basis of limited information is benchmarking the project or investment with another similar project, or investment, for which economic capital is known. For example, an acquisition target may not measure or disclose its economic capital, but internal economic capital ratios of similar business lines may be used to estimate economic capital, adjusting for scale and differences in risk indicators that are disclosed. Furthermore, we must assess to what extent the acquisition contributes to diversification or concentration of risks.

When taking strategic decisions, an important consideration for financial institutions is the balance between specialization and diversification. We already argued in Section 4.2 that a credit portfolio should be well diversified in order that no single event can cause an insurmountable loss. On the other hand, research indicates that institutions that specialize provide a significantly higher return to their owners than diversified institutions.[9] The benefits of specialization also were highlighted by Warren Buffett when he explained his risk management strategy to the shareholders of Berkshire Hathaway:[10] "We believe that a policy of portfolio concentration may well decrease risk if it raises, as it should, both the intensity with which an investor thinks about a business and the comfort-level he must feel with its economic characteristics before buying into it."

We conclude that for a financial institution it is of strategic importance to diversify the risks to which it is exposed, but balance this with specialized knowledge to understand the underlying risks and optimize the institution's profitability. How can economic capital help to balance diversification and specialization?

Risk models are designed to reward diversification, but how do they account for the benefits of specialization? For example, if a loan is granted to a Mexican company, then, *ceteris paribus*, the economic capital assigned to this loan will be less for an Italian bank with no business in Mexico than for a Mexican bank, because the diversification benefits will typically be higher for the Italian bank. Does this mean that the risk of the loan is smaller to the Italian bank? To answer this question we return to the issue of model risk. In general, model risks will be significantly lower for existing businesses that have a long track record than for new businesses and investments. The reason is that for existing businesses there will be better insight into what factors determine the risks and there will be more data available to estimate risk parameters reliably. In the example of a loan to a

Mexican company, an experienced lender in the Mexican market will be better placed to accurately estimate the default probability of the borrower. We discussed in Section 4.1.5 how model risk can be quantified and, consequently, how lower model risk can lead to a lower economic capital estimate for a seasoned lender than for a less experienced lender whose estimates are more uncertain.

Quantifying model risks for new projects is difficult and complex. However, as our illustration shows, model risks need to be considered because otherwise the institution will end up with projects and investments that appear to give large diversification benefits but that expose the institution to significant model risks. Because model risks are not uniform across the institution, they have to be assessed at a reasonably granular level, preferably at the level of individual models. Although a generic add-on for model risk may be acceptable to assess the institution's overall capital adequacy, for investment decisions it is necessary to specify the model risk at a more granular level. If such a specification is not feasible in a quantitative manner, then managers should at least take model risk into account in a qualitative manner in their decision making.

5.3   Conclusion

The implementation and use of economic capital bring a plethora of attention points, dilemmas, and choices. As attention points we classify the following issues that we discussed:

- Assessing capital adequacy at the level of the institution as whole. If available capital is well above economic capital, does this indicate inefficient use of capital? Does the economic capital calculation comprise all material risks?
- Assessing capital adequacy for subsidiaries. What confidence level do we use? Using the same confidence level as used at the group level may not be appropriate and may result in capital inefficiencies.
- Transparency and governance. Are all stakeholders represented and are decisions made at a sufficient senior level given the wider implications for performance management and strategic decision making?
- Calculate and interpret RAROC correctly. Is the franchise value included in economic capital? If not, is this acknowledged when the RAROCs of different business lines are compared?
- Take model risk into account when deciding how to balance specialization and diversification. When a new activity or transaction is contemplated that promises high diversification benefits with the existing portfolio of risks, is uncertainty about the risk assessment of the new activity or transaction fully accounted for? We concluded that it is of strategic importance for a financial institution to diversify its risks, but at the same time balance this with a specialized knowledge to understand the underlying risks and optimize the institution's profitablity.

In this chapter, we discussed the following dilemmas and choices to be made:

- How are diversification benefits calculated? From a risk management perspective we prefer to calculate economic capital in an integrated manner per risk type; that is, taking into account intra-risk diversification across business lines.
- Should the diversification benefits at consolidated level be allocated to business lines or not? To create the right incentives we argue that this should be the case. Choosing an appropriate capital allocation method may help to reduce the volatility of diversification effects.
- Do we need a buffer on top of economic capital, and if so, how much? We argued that this should not be the case except for growth of business and as a result of capital inefficiencies with respect to capital allocation to subsidiaries. However, this assumes that economic capital is calculated comprehensively and based on the most demanding of all capital objectives that the firm has.
- What incentives will the use of RAROC provide for managers and staff? What complementary measures are needed for sound performance measurement and compensation incentives? Although RAROC ensures that risk is taken into account at origination of the transaction, deferred performance payments may still be desirable if model risk is significant.
- How will hurdle rates be set? We argued that hurdle rates should be differentiated between business lines and that they may vary over time as a function of the business cycle. If hurdle rates are derived from equity returns of peer institutions, then adjustments may need to be made for differences in leverage, and for the possible absence of franchise value in the amount of economic capital that is used in the RAROC calculation.

Endnotes

[1]Standard & Poor's RatingsDirect. 2007 Annual global corporate default study and rating transitions. February 5, 2008.

[2]Allianz Group. Annual Report. 2007.

[3]Hall C. Economic capital: Towards an integrated risk framework. *Risk*. October, 2002; 33–38.

[4]See, for example: Jameson R. Between RAROC and a hard place. *ERisk*. 2001, February; and Belmont D. *Value-added risk management in financial institutions: Leveraging Basel II & risk adjusted performance measurement*. Singapore: John Wiley & Sons (Asia) Pte Ltd; 2004.

[5]Cohen W. Why Wall Street has to alter its financial incentives. *Financial Times*. February 25, 2008; and Reforms of bankers' pay in the spotlight. *Financial Times*. May 22, 2008.

[6]This point also is made in Crouhy M, Turnbull S, Wakeman L. Measuring risk-adjusted performance. *Journal of Risk*. 1999, Fall;2(1):5–35; and in Wilson T. Overcoming the hurdle. *Risk*. 2003; July: 79–83. Wilson also provides empirical evidence that US investment banks have significantly higher betas than insurance companies with the same credit rating. If the CAPM holds up in reality, this corroborates that equity investors require different expected returns for different financial businesses. Wilson also shows on the basis of empirical data that the beta of universal banks is larger if the credit rating is worse. Viewing the credit rating as a proxy for the leverage employed (as firms with the same rating have the same probability of default on their debt), the

CAPM thus implies a positive relationship between the amount of leverage and the required expected return on the equity of universal banks. In our formulation of the CAPM in the text, the increase in leverage will increase the volatility of the return on the equity investment ($Stdev$ (R_I)), and thereby the required expected return.

[7] Crouhy et al. (see endnote 6) suggest instead to use an adjusted RAROC measure in which one subtracts the risk-free interest rate from the traditional RAROC measure (see Section 2.3.1), and divides the remainder by the beta of the business or investment. This adjusted RAROC can then be compared to the excess return of the market portfolio above the risk-free interest rate.

[8] Froot K, Stein J. Risk management, capital budgeting, and capital structure policy for financial institutions: An integrated approach. *Journal of Financial Economics*. 1998;47:55–82. In fact, Froot and Stein show that it is optimal for an institution to hedge all risks to the extent it can do so at a fair price, and that the hurdle rate applies to the part of the risks that cannot be hedged at a fair price (or not at all).

[9] For property/liability insurers, see Liebenberg AP, Sommer DW. Effects of corporate diversification: Evidence from the property-liability insurance industry. *Journal of Risk and Insurance*. 2008, December:893–919. For banks, see Laeven L, Levine, R. Is there a diversification discount in financial conglomerates? NBER Paper, National Bureau of Economic Research; 2005.

[10] Chairman's Letter to the Shareholders of Berkshire Hathaway Inc. 1993.

6 Team Play: The Context of Economic Capital

In the previous chapters, we have discussed in detail how economic capital works. No single risk measure can capture all aspects of risk, however. In this chapter we consider how other risk management tools complement economic capital. Although economic capital can help to identify exposures that may give rise to large unexpected losses, it does not provide insight into the expected or potential loss if a specific event would occur. Stress testing can complement economic capital in this respect, as we will discuss in Section 6.1. Enterprise risk management (ERM) provides a wider risk management framework, in which economic capital has its place. We will discuss ERM in Section 6.2.

An institution cannot manage its available capital only on the basis of economic capital considerations; it must also comply with minimum regulatory capital requirements. We will discuss in Section 6.3 how regulatory capital constraints can be managed within an economic capital framework.

6.1 Stress Tests

Stress tests can serve several purposes:

- Assess the sensitivity of risk models to their assumptions.
- Understand the risk profile of the institution better.
- Prepare the institution for the eventuality of a crisis event and mitigate its impact.

The Basel Committee defines stress testing as follows:[1]

> Stress testing is a risk management technique used to evaluate the potential effects on an institution's financial condition of a specific event and/or movement in a set of financial variables.

This definition covers stress testing at to the level of individual institutions, but stress tests can be done also for entire industries, countries, or the world economy at large. For example, the IMF and World Bank perform stress tests covering multiple institutions in a country to identify vulnerabilities that could undermine the stability of a country's financial system.[2] In this section we will discuss how stress tests can be applied at the level of an individual institution so that they contribute to the main purposes of stress testing that we outlined above.

6.1.1   Types of Stress Tests

There are two main types of stress tests: sensitivity stress tests and scenario stress tests. A sensitivity stress test typically is related to a model and analyzes how much the model outcome changes if one of the variables of the model is changed. For example, how much does economic capital change if we double the correlations? A sensitivity stress test helps to understand if the model outcome is very sensitive to specific assumptions or parameter values. When combined with the degree of confidence that we have about these assumptions or values, this provides information on the reliability of model outcomes.

A scenario stress test analyzes the consequences of an event or sequence of events for an institution. Essential for a scenario stress test is the formulation of a realistic and relevant scenario. We distinguish two basic methods to formulate such a scenario.[3] First, event-driven scenarios can be formulated based on expert views of plausible events. These views may be based on historic or recent events, like changes in the oil price or political events, or on envisaged potential events like the outbreak of SARS. Second, portfolio-driven scenarios can be based on the identification of perceived vulnerabilities in the portfolio of an institution. The scenario then incorporates events that specifically affect the portfolio vulnerabilities, and cause losses as a result. In practice, portfolio-driven scenarios focus on large concentrated exposures in the portfolio. A particular example of a portfolio-driven scenario is a reverse stress test, for which first the size of the intended impact is specified, say a loss of USD 1 billion, and subsequently a scenario is developed that produces this loss.

An event-driven scenario is appealing because it relates to the actual environment in which the institution operates. However, it may not necessarily be relevant for the institution's portfolio. For example, a scenario could include a downturn in the UK housing market, but such a scenario may not be relevant for a Japanese bank with no UK mortgage exposures. A portfolio-driven scenario has the advantage that it is relevant for the institution's portfolio, but not necessarily for the actual situation. For example, the same Japanese bank may have significant exposures in Asia and a scenario that the Asia crisis of 1997 would repeat itself again may be relevant for this portfolio, but the likelihood of such a scenario may be deemed too small to be realistic because of the improved financial position of many Asian countries. Ideally, a scenario stress test combines both features so that it is relevant with respect to the actual environment as well as the institution's portfolio.

Institutions apply a large variety of stress tests for individual risk types. In market risk they are applied to complement the VaR models by reflecting events that are not covered in the VaR measurement. They consist of both sensitivity stress tests, in which specific market variables are stressed beyond what has been observed in recent history, and scenario stress tests, which represent extreme marketwide events that have occurred historically or are deemed plausible given the economic outlook. For example, a scenario stress test could consider what the expected impact on the value of a trading portfolio is if the 1987 equity crash would repeat itself. Stress tests also are used to manage liquidity risk, for example, to assess how well an institution is positioned to cope with the disappearance of an important source of funding. In the context of operational risk a stress test can be done to test the business continuity, for example, in the event that office buildings are not accessible anymore due to a natural disaster or fire. Notwithstanding the fact that a business continuity stress test is unlikely to use a quantitative model, it does test the impact of such an event and to what extent the institution is prepared for such an event.

Scenario stress tests can also address multiple risk types, and may even attempt to answer the question of how an institution will be impacted in its totality by an event. For example, how will a recession affect the institution's revenues, credit losses, profits, and capital position?

Although the use of models is not always necessary, the impact of a scenario commonly is assessed by calculating a loss distribution using an institution's economic capital models. Inputs and parameters are then changed to reflect the specific scenario under consideration. From this scenario-specific loss distribution, the expected loss can be estimated as well as losses at a specified confidence level. For example, the impact of a scenario in which a sovereign defaults, with contagion effects for neighboring countries and industries in these countries, can be assessed by estimating a loss distribution that is conditional on the sovereign default, taking into account the correlations between the defaulted sovereign and other sovereigns and industries in the region. The expected loss from this conditional loss distribution can be compared with the expected loss in the base case scenario to establish the expected impact of such a scenario.

6.1.2 The Use and Interpretation of Stress Test Results

Increasingly, regulators require that financial institutions perform stress tests. For example, regulators require that banks assess their capital adequacy in the light of the outcomes of a number of stress tests. The tests should include at least a so-called mild recession scenario. The results of the stress tests should assess the impact of a scenario on the bank's profitability, available capital, and required capital. Results of the stress tests need to be discussed with the bank's supervisors.[4] In reaction to the sub-prime crisis, the Basel Committee has formulated a number of principles for sound stress testing. They recommend that stress tests are geared toward events capable of generating the most damage to the institution. In particular, they recommend stress tests covering the effectiveness of hedging strategies (e.g., basis risk), complex products (e.g., securitizations), wrong-way risks, warehousing risks, and funding liquidity risk.[5] These risks caused significant losses to many institutions during the sub-prime crisis, and we discussed these risks in earlier chapters.

Danske Bank disclosed the results of two groupwide stress tests in its 2007 annual report. The two scenarios relate to a mild and a severe recession. They are characterized as follows:

Macro-economic variables	Severe recession	Mild recession
GDP change	−2.1%	1.4%
Unemployment	9.9%	6.4%
Change in property prices	−14.2%	0.7%

The values of the macro-economic variables represent the worst year of a 3-year scenario. The annual report states that default probabilities and loss severity have been estimated directly for each of the scenarios based on their historic relationship with the macro-economic variables.

Danske Bank has quantified the impact of the scenarios on expected credit losses, profitability, economic capital, and regulatory capital under Basel II. In the first year of the scenario, the profitability is expected to decrease by approximately 35 and 70% for the mild and severe recession, respectively. Under the severe scenario, the amount of economic capital is estimated to increase from approximately DKr 42 billion to DKr 48 billion. The expected increase of regulatory Basel II capital is a modest DKr 0.5 billion from a base case of approximately DKr 76 billion.

To be able to interpret the results of these stress tests it is important to know how sensitive the risk parameters are to changes in the economy. This relates to the question, to what extent the credit parameters represent through-the-cycle or point-in-time values. For regulatory capital, Danske Bank uses through-the-cycle values for its credit risk parameters. This explains why the impact on regulatory capital is small. However, through-the-cycle parameters are not suitable for estimating the impact of a scenario on next year's profitability of an institution because this is a point-in-time number. For the impact on profitability and economic capital, Danske Bank uses point-in-time values for its credit risk parameters. This point-in-time character explains that the amount of economic capital increases more than the amount of minimum required regulatory capital, in particular if the confidence level has not been adjusted for the phase of the economic cycle (see Section 3.5.2).

To assess the results of a stress test, we thus need to have insight into the methodological assumptions and choices that have been made. In practice, many banks use hybrid through-the-cycle/point-in-time parameters and, consequently, complex corrections may have to be made to account for the degree that the risk parameters are point-in-time or through-the-cycle. That is difficult, if not impossible, to convey in an annual report. In addition to knowing the character of the credit risk parameters, it is important to understand if and how risk types other than credit risk are incorporated in the scenarios. The risk types that may have a material impact will depend on the scenario. For example, in a recession scenario the impact of business risk, pension risk, and ALM risk can be significant.

Ideally, an analysis of stress test results is complemented by statements about whether the outcomes fall within the institution's risk appetite or tolerance.

Danske Bank adds the increases in regulatory and economic capital that result from the scenario to the amount of economic and regulatory capital in the base case. This raises a question on its capital adequacy objectives: Does it want to have a capital buffer on top of economic capital? It is desirable that an institution establishes a clear relation between the results of the stress test and the risk appetite and capital objectives of the institution.

Another example of a stress test is found in the 2007 annual report of Swiss Re. Swiss Re discloses the estimated pre-tax claims in case a specific event would occur, including an Atlantic hurricane, a European windstorm, a California earthquake, a Japanese earthquake, and a lethal pandemic. Risk limits are set to ensure that the losses will remain within the risk tolerance of the institution. However, no impact on economic or regulatory capital is disclosed. Swiss Re also describes a credit stress test on its portfolio. The credit stress test assumes that the portfolio is subject to the worst default rates by rating category that have been observed by Moody's between 1983 and 2004. Again, only the decrease in available capital (i.e., the loss in value) due to credit losses is shown and not the impact on regulatory required or economic capital. A question is whether it is reasonable to expect that economic capital will or should change as the result of a single event, which we will try to answer in the next section.

6.1.3 Stress Tests and Economic Capital

Typically, a single event does not change the originally estimated loss distribution and, hence, the associated economic capital. For example, if someone wins the lottery, that does not mean that the probability that he or she will win with the next draw has changed. In the same way, the occurrence of a single hurricane is not an indication that the probability of hurricanes has changed. Only when a number of hurricanes occur unexpectedly there may be a reason to review the model that estimates the probability that hurricanes occur. Consequently, economic capital for insurance risk may not change due to the occurrence of a single (large) hurricane.

For credit risk we have to ask ourselves the same question: why would an economic event such as a recession change the originally estimated loss distribution? This question is relevant in particular if the loss distribution has been estimated on the basis of through-the-cycle model parameters. In principle, the economic event produces a credit loss that is reflected already in the estimated loss distribution of the institution. The fact that the event occurs does not change the loss distribution. However, since credit risk is the result of economic processes influenced by (uncertain) human behavior, there may be second-order effects to consider. For example, during a recession there may be structural changes in the economy as companies and consumers adapt to the new recessionary situation. Furthermore, uncertainty may increase during a recession as the value of some assets may become more uncertain, established relationships may change, and the nature and duration of the adaptation process is uncertain. Model risk, therefore, may increase during an economic downturn. These second-order effects can change the loss distribution of the institution and thus its economic capital.

6.1.4 Limitations of Stress Tests

An event-driven scenario stress test starts with the specification of a realistic and relevant scenario. If the purpose is to timely identify risks in the portfolio, and possibly to take action to mitigate risks, then it is essential that a realistic scenario is applied. However, what constitutes a realistic scenario for the future is not easy to determine. Even an "ordinary" recession may be simple to define in terms of GDP growth, but in practice each recession differs with respect to underlying causes and industries that are affected by the recession. The problem is also one of timing, because doomsayers may ultimately be vindicated, but managers need to decide when to invest and when not to invest in order to optimize the profitability of the institution. We give three examples that illustrate the challenge to identify timely the relevant scenarios.

The first example is from the equity research group of Citigroup, which published a report in April 2006 with the telling title, "Where Are the Crocodiles?"[6] Analyzing the risks for European banks, the report observes that risk premiums were at all-time lows, and it argues that banks should be prepared for less benign circumstances. What are the risks that the report identified? As medium-term risks the report highlights the risk of lower trading income, worsening cost-to-income ratios, declining credit quality, and a downturn in emerging markets. It mentions HSBC and Commerzbank as banks most exposed to credit risks, whereas UBS is ranked among the least exposed banks. The sub-prime exposures were not mentioned, and judging by the fact that UBS lost much more on these positions than HSBC, that risk was not deemed a concern at the time of the report. To their credit, the analysts did identify Northern Rock as being heavily exposed to liquidity risks.

The second example concerns the Financial Services Authority (FSA) of the United Kingdom, which publishes at the start of each year a risk outlook to raise awareness about the key risks in the environment. In its Financial Risk Outlook 2007 it observed, like the equity analysts of Citigroup, that the global economic conditions were benign but also that there were considerable challenges ahead. Nevertheless, the FSA expected banks "to remain both profitable and highly capitalized in 2007, despite some deterioration in the business environment in 2007." A "possible weakening in the housing market" was envisaged, but evidently not with the devastating consequences that later became reality.

The final illustration is from the World Economic Forum in which Citigroup, Marsh & McLennan Companies, Swiss Re, and the Wharton School Risk Center participate.[7] On top of their list of concerns for 2007 was a collapse of asset prices. In their explanation, they refer to the house price increases in most mature markets, and they fear a correction that would impact consumption, economic growth, and other asset prices. In reality, many of these risks materialized: however, the impact that this would have on financial markets and the confidence in financial institutions was not foreseen. This illustrates that even when a scenario materializes, the impact may still be difficult to estimate.

6.1.5 Summary

To summarize, stress tests are a useful tool to identify and assess risks. They often make use of the same risk models that form the basis of economic capital calculations, and in this way they can be seen as an extension of and a complement to economic capital. However, to incorporate the impact of a stress scenario in economic capital is not straightforward because the former is a single (hypothetical) realization and the latter is a statistical quantity. Moreover, stress tests are as good as the scenarios that underlie them. Identifying relevant and realistic scenarios is a challenge, and even when a scenario materializes, it may manifest itself in unexpected ways and severity.

6.2 Enterprise Risk Management (ERM)

Economic capital and stress tests are useful techniques for the organization, but it is in the context of ERM that all these techniques are tied together into a comprehensive risk framework. There are many definitions of ERM, but the Committee of Sponsoring Organizations of the Treadway Commission (COSO) has provided the definition that is probably most commonly used:

> Enterprise risk management is a process, effected by an entity's board of directors, management and other personnel, applied in strategy setting and across the enterprise, designed to identify potential events that may affect the entity, and manage risk to be within its risk appetite, to provide reasonable assurance regarding the achievement of entity objectives.[8]

Organizations that have published on ERM, including COSO but also other organizations like the Casualty Actuarial Society (CAS),[9] describe ERM as a structured framework for risk management in which objectives are set, risks are identified and assessed, risk responses are formulated, and finally, risks are controlled and monitored. The structured approach helps management to ascertain that it is in control of the organization and its risks.

According to the COSO definition, ERM provides the link between the design of an organization (strategy, risk appetite) and the execution of its risk management activities (identify potential events, manage risk). The relationship of ERM with economic capital is apparent when considering our earlier discussion of economic capital in relation to these management activities in Section 2.4.

ERM came into vogue in part because of the increasing scale and complexity of financial institutions. Specialization occurred in many areas. Also in risk management silos of specialists started to appear in several areas such as credit, market, operational, and ALM risks. As a result, it became more difficult to have a comprehensive overview of all the risks to which an institution was exposed. However, as was apparent in our discussion in Section 2.2.1, the failure of an institution is often the result of a combination of factors. Consequently, it is necessary to have a comprehensive overview to prevent such a failure. The report on market best practices that the IIF published in 2008 in reaction to the sub-prime crisis observes: "the lack of a comprehensive approach to firmwide risk management often meant that key risks were not identified or effectively managed."[10] On top of that, there have been regulatory developments like SOXA that have contributed to the need to implement ERM-like approaches.[11]

A comprehensive overview starts with governance and consequently ERM has gone hand-in-hand with new governance practices at companies, including the emergence of an independent Chief Risk Officer (CRO). The aforementioned IIF report makes several recommendations in this regard:

- Senior management, in particular the CEO, is responsible for risk management and defining the firm's risk appetite.
- Risk management should be a key responsibility of the entire business-line management. All employees should have a clear understanding of their responsibilities in regard to the management of risks.
- An independent CRO should have sufficient seniority in the firm to affect decision making.

Economic capital has a natural fit with ERM because it takes a comprehensive firmwide view of risk. It is primarily a quantitative view. There is also a qualitative approach to ERM that focuses more on drivers or indicators of risks, which may not lend themselves to be quantified or aggregated readily. For example, a shortage of experienced staff may be an indicator that the institution is subject to increasing operational risks. However, there may not be a uniform method to measure experience, nor can the relation with operational risk losses be estimated reliably. Operational losses as a result of inexperienced staff will enter in an operational loss database, and as a consequence may feed into the economic capital calculation. However, this is after the loss occurred, whereas the intention of monitoring the qualitative indicators is to prevent losses from happening in the future. The qualitative approach does this by looking at a range of indicators out of which a holistic view of the institution's risk profile emerges, without necessarily quantifying these risks. Typically, the qualitative approach makes use of risk-based internal controls, balanced scorecards, and risk dashboards.

The choice between the quantitative and qualitative approach often depends on senior management's attitude toward, and comfort with, risk quantification.[12] In our view, the quantitative and qualitative views of ERM are complementary. The quantitative approach provides a link between the risk exposures, profitability, and capital targets of the institution and provides guidance how to balance the respective risks against each other. This is not obvious with the qualitative approach. However, qualitative indicators contribute to a holistic view of risk, and enable an institution to manage risk in those areas where risk drivers cannot easily be quantified, or where uncertainty is relatively high.

Rating agencies and supervisors have developed their own approaches to achieve a comprehensive risk overview of the institution. Rating agencies have started to assess ERM practices and disclose what elements they consider in their assessment.[13] Supervisors in the United States apply the CAMELS score, which consists of scores for Capital, Assets, Management, Earnings, Liquidity, and Sensitivity to market risk.[14] This score is used to determine the level of supervision to be applied. In the United Kingdom, the FSA uses the ARROW framework to assess business risk and control risk elements.[15] The business risk elements include, among others, external risks; types of clients of the institution and markets in which it operates; business processes (e.g., IT, key person risk); and credit, operational, liquidity, and insurance underwriting risk. The control risk elements include, among others, "Know Your Client" controls, financial controls, capital adequacy, IT security, corporate governance, compliance, and internal audit. In short, there are many different ways in which all relevant risk and control factors can be put together in an ERM framework. Each organization, supervisor, and rating agency will have its own preferences.

Comprehensive risk identification including quantifiable and non-quantifiable risks is needed for both the short term and for the medium to long term. The short-term view is used typically for the day-to-day management of the institution. It is concerned, for example, with increased volatility of financial markets or significant audit findings regarding IT security, which have to be addressed as soon as possible. The medium- to long-term risk outlook can be input to the institution's strategy and capital allocation. This includes, for example, expectations regarding the economic development of a country, the rise of new financial market players (like hedge funds in the past), or expected shortage of specialist staff. The medium- to long-term risk outlook can also serve to determine the relevant scenarios to be included in stress tests. In many institutions, scenarios are developed by economists but enterprisewide scenarios ideally should be comprehensive and combined with scenarios from a business and organization perspective. An ERM approach to define a scenario will help to formulate a comprehensive scenario and execute an enterprisewide stress test.

Besides a focus on risk identification, ERM also has operational aspects. First, there are aspects related to the organization. During a crisis it is good practice that a multidisciplinary crisis team is appointed to manage the crisis. The question is whether such a multidisciplinary approach is useful for risk prevention as well. If the answer is affirmative, then this may have consequences for the organization's structure and governance. Next, there are many risk-related processes that may be more efficient when they are integrated. For example, risk identification activities between compliance, operational risk, and internal audit may overlap or would improve if they could make use of each other's findings. Finally, breaking down the silos in the institution may also involve the establishment of cross-functional data definitions and repositories.[16] For example, finance and risk departments may both need information about actual credit risk exposures but may be using different definitions and data sources. Also, operational risk departments and internal audit departments may classify incidents in different ways and register them in separate databases. The result is potential confusion when each department issues its own report, and considerable effort is needed to reconcile the different information. Common definitions and data repositories may help to improve the quality and efficiency of management reporting overall.

To summarize, ERM provides the link between the design of the organization and the execution of its risk management activities. An objective of ERM is to provide a comprehensive, firmwide overview of the risks that are relevant to an institution. Economic capital is the quantitative view of such an overview and is thus integral to ERM. This needs to be complemented with a qualitative view on those risks and uncertainties that are difficult to quantify. An ERM framework provides a context within which economic capital is used. A comprehensive ERM framework will also address organization, processes, and data and systems.

6.3   Managing Economic and Regulatory Capital

Although maximizing the return on economic capital may be the primary objective of a financial institution, it also has to comply with regulatory capital requirements. To avoid the complication of having to deal with two measures of required capital, some institutions have chosen to maximize the return on regulatory capital instead of economic capital. Maximizing the return on regulatory capital may conflict with the creation of shareholder value through the optimization of RAROC or economic profit, however.

6.3.1   Economic Capital Versus Regulatory Capital

The difference between return on regulatory capital and RAROC is illustrated by numbers of Danske Bank,[17] as displayed in Table 6.1. The numbers in Table 6.1 show that the return on capital allocated on the basis of regulatory capital can be materially different from the return on capital allocated on the basis of economic capital. For some business areas the return on economic capital is higher, and for others lower, than the return on regulatory capital. Also, the rank ordering of returns is different. Danske Markets was the most profitable business line when measured by return on regulatory capital but not when

Table 6.1 Risk-adjusted returns, Danske Bank, 2007

Business area	Return on capital allocated on the basis of Basel I regulatory capital	Return on capital allocated on the basis of economic capital
Banking in Denmark	31%	36%
Banking outside Denmark	17%	15%
Danske Markets	44%	29%

measured by return on economic capital. Because Basel I regulatory capital requirements are only to a very limited extent risk-based, the return on Basel I capital does not incorporate an adequate representation of risk. Its use can therefore lead to different conclusions when compared to the return on economic capital, as the numbers of Danske Bank illustrate.

In many countries, the Basel I capital regulations have been replaced by Basel II, which make the regulatory capital calculations more risk sensitive. In particular, the advanced approaches of Basel II are more aligned with economic capital than the Basel I capital calculations were. One important improvement of Basel II is that the regulatory capital formula for credit risk is based upon the same type of economic risk framework as economic capital. Furthermore, institutions are allowed to use their own estimates of risk parameters, such as default probabilities, as input in the capital formula. Moreover, institutions can use internally developed value-at-risk models for operational risk, as was already the case for market risk. However, there are also significant differences between the advanced approaches in Basel II and economic capital. In Table 6.2 we list the most material differences. More detail on differences between the models used for economic and regulatory capital calculations for credit, market, and operational risk has been provided in the corresponding sections in Chapter 4.

Because correlations are fixed and concentrations are not reflected, Basel II regulatory capital is less suitable for credit risk portfolio management. Although regulatory capital under Basel II is more risk sensitive than under Basel I, it is still some distance from being an accurate risk measure that can be used to optimize risk-adjusted returns and maximize shareholder value. For this purpose, economic capital and RAROC are the superior measures. Nonetheless, regulatory capital constraints are applicable. The question is how an institution can best manage these. This is the topic of the next section.

6.3.2 Optimizing Economic Profit under Capital Constraints

Many institutions establish budgets for both regulatory and economic capital. The amount of available capital may differ between economic and regulatory capital, as different capital definitions may be used. Subject to the budgets

Table 6.2 Key differences between Basel II advanced approaches and economic capital

Characteristic	Basel II advanced approaches	Economic capital
Risks in scope	Credit, market, and operational risk	All risk types
Confidence level	99.9%	Chosen by the institution, often 99.95% or higher
Credit correlations	Fixed: same for all institutions and static	Best estimate, specific to institution. Can change over time.
Credit concentration risks	Not included	Included
Securitizations	Capital based on fixed rules and percentages	Internal model
Diversification between risk types	None	Best estimate by the institution
Expected income	Not accounted for	Expected income is assumed to cover expected losses. Expected income in excess of expected loss may be added to available capital or deducted from economic capital.

for economic capital and regulatory capital, the overall objective of a financial institution is to maximize economic profit (or, equivalently, the return on economic capital).

We illustrate how this can be done by means of an example. We consider an institution that consists of three business lines: A, B, and C. Relevant data for each of the business lines, as well as for the institution as a whole, are presented in Table 6.3. As is clear from the table, the different business lines consume economic capital and regulatory capital in different proportions. Business A is expected to generate the highest return on economic capital,

Table 6.3 Data for a financial institution consisting of three business lines, A, B, and C

Business line	A	B	C	Institution (A + B + C)	Expansion B
Expected income net of EL (I)	12	10	8	30	3
Economic capital (EC)	100	100	100	300	25
Regulatory capital (RC)	150	100	72	322	25
RAROC ($=I/EC$)	12%	10%	8%	10%	12%
Hurdle rate on EC (h)	11.5%	10%	7.6%	9.7%	10%
Economic profit ($=I - h \cdot EC$)	0.5	0	0.4	0.9	0.5

and business C the highest return on regulatory capital. RAROC for business lines A and C is higher than the required hurdle rate for each, and thus they expect to generate an economic profit.

Suppose business B expects that it can generate additional income of 3 units by expanding its business by 25% and exploiting economies of scale. We have included this proposed expansion in the last column of Table 6.3. Economic capital and regulatory capital scale linearly with the figures for business line B, and the hurdle rate equals the one of business B because the risk characteristics remain unchanged (in Section 5.2.8 we have discussed the factors that influence the hurdle rate). Pursuing this expansion will create shareholder value because the economic profit of the expansion is positive.

Without restriction on the use of additional economic and regulatory capital, the institution can just allocate the associated economic and regulatory capital for the expansion of business B and realize the economic profit of the expansion. If the institution has reached its limit for economic capital or regulatory capital, and is not able or willing to raise additional capital, then the question is how it can still try to realize (part of) the economic profit that the expansion of business B promises.

Suppose first that the institution is constrained in its regulatory capital. The question is whether it is attractive from an economic profit perspective to scale back one of the existing businesses A or C to allow business B to expand and realize the associated economic profit. Scaling back business A to allow for the expansion of business B without increasing regulatory capital usage for the institution as a whole requires that business A shrinks by one-sixth (25 out of the current regulatory capital usage of 150). This will cost business A one-sixth of its economic profit, or 0.083, assuming all quantities scale linearly with the size of the business. The additional economic profit from the expansion of business B is 0.5, however, so the net increase of economic profit for the institution as a whole would be 0.417. It is thus attractive to scale back business A to allow for the proposed expansion of business B.

Scaling back business C to enable the expansion of business B without increasing regulatory capital usage for the institution as a whole requires that business C shrinks by approximately 35% (25 out of the current regulatory capital usage of 72). This will cost business C an equivalent percentage of its economic profit, or 0.139, assuming again that all quantities scale linearly with size. The net increase of economic profit for the institution as a whole would thus be 0.361. Although it is attractive as well to scale back business C to allow for the proposed expansion of business B, the analysis indicates that scaling back business A instead of C will result in a larger economic profit for the institution as a whole. Table 6.4 shows the result if business A is scaled back to enable expansion of business B without increasing regulatory capital. Note that the hurdle rate for the institution as a whole changes because of the shift from business A to business B. Also the amount of economic capital for the institution as a whole has increased from 300 to 308.

Table 6.4 Data for the financial institution of Table 6.3 when business A is scaled back to allow for expansion of business B without increasing regulatory capital

Business line	A	B	C	Institution (A + B + C)
Expected income net of EL (I)	10	13	8	31
Economic capital (EC)	83	125	100	308
Regulatory capital (RC)	125	125	72	322
RAROC ($=I/EC$)	12%	10.4%	8%	10.1%
Hurdle rate on EC (h)	11.5%	10%	7.6%	9.6%
Economic profit ($= I - h \cdot EC$)	0.417	0.5	0.4	1.317

We can summarize this analysis by looking at the economic profit per unit of regulatory capital for each of the businesses if regulatory capital acts as a constraint for the institution. The expansion of business B promises an increase in economic profit of 0.02 per unit of regulatory capital (0.5 divided by 25). Business A expects to generate 0.003 in economic profit per unit of regulatory capital (0.5 divided by 150) and business C, 0.006 (0.4 divided by 72). Comparing these numbers shows immediately that it is attractive to let business B expand, and that it is most attractive to do so by letting business A shrink.

The economic profit per additional unit of regulatory capital for each of the businesses is the *marginal price* of regulatory capital—that is, the maximum price a business would be willing to pay if it could use one additional unit of regulatory capital (or the minimum price it wants to receive to give up the use of one unit of regulatory capital). The *shadow price* of regulatory capital is the increase in economic profit that the institution as a whole could generate if it could use one more unit of regulatory capital. In our example, it would equal 0.02, the maximum of the marginal prices of the different business lines. The shadow price on regulatory capital is zero if regulatory capital is not a constraint for the institution, because in that case being able to use one additional unit of regulatory capital does not provide any benefit to the institution.

If economic capital instead of regulatory capital is the constraint for the institution, we can perform an analogous evaluation. Expansion of business B promises an increase in economic profit of 0.02 per unit of economic capital (0.5 divided by 25). Business A expects to generate 0.005 in economic profit per unit of economic capital (0.5 divided by 100) and business C, 0.004 (0.4 divided by 100). Hence, it is most attractive to expand business B by shrinking business C. Table 6.5 shows the resulting composition of the institution, for which economic profit has increased from 0.9 to 1.3. Due to the shift from business C to business B, the hurdle rate for the institution as a whole has increased. Also regulatory capital usage has increased because business B uses relatively more regulatory capital than business C.

Table 6.5 Data for the financial institution of Table 6.3 when business C is scaled back to allow for expansion of business B without increasing economic capital

Business line	A	B	C	Institution (A + B + C)
Expected income net of EL (I)	12	13	6	31
Economic capital (EC)	100	125	75	300
Regulatory capital (RC)	150	125	54	329
RAROC (= I/EC)	12%	10.4%	8%	10.3%
Hurdle rate on EC (h)	11.5%	10%	7.6%	9.9%
Economic profit (= $I - h \cdot EC$)	0.5	0.5	0.3	1.3

In the illustrative example of Table 6.5, we have assumed that all quantities scale linearly with the size of a business unit. In reality, this will likely not be the case. To perform the preceding analysis, we then need to look at the marginal costs and benefits of increasing or decreasing a business. In addition, specific costs may be incurred when reducing the size of a business (e.g., redundancy compensations), which should also factor into the analysis.

The analysis as described earlier in principle can be carried out at a central level in the organization, although it will be more complex with many business lines and investment opportunities than in the previous example. If the number of business lines and investment opportunities is very large, mathematical optimization techniques can help to find a reallocation of capital that optimizes economic profit while satisfying constraints on regulatory and economic capital.

Instead of allocating capital budgets centrally, it is possible to establish an internal market for capital that enables business lines to sell and buy capital budgets for a price. Capital is then a scarce resource needed to produce a good, which is priced as any other production factor. In such a market, different business lines can provide bid and offer prices for the scarce capital resource, for example, regulatory capital. These bid and offer prices are related directly to the marginal prices that we discussed. In the previous example, when regulatory capital is a constraint for the organization, business B should be willing to bid up to 0.02 for a unit of regulatory capital to expand its business (its marginal price for regulatory capital), and business lines A and C should be willing to offer at any price above 0.003 and 0.006, respectively (their marginal prices for regulatory capital). A market price in between the bid and offer prices can result in an economic profit increase for both the buyer and the seller of regulatory capital.

We note that the technique of using marginal prices can be applied irrespective of the nature of the regulatory capital calculation rules—that is, whether an institution is subject to a simple leverage ratio or to the Basel II advanced approaches. However, the more regulatory capital is aligned with economic capital, the less likely it is to become a constraint if an institution already manages its available capital on the basis of economic capital. In this case, the shadow price of regulatory capital will be relatively low. The introduction of the Basel II advanced approaches has thus added value to regulated institutions by lowering the shadow price of regulatory capital for institutions.

6.4 Conclusion

In this chapter, we provided the broader context in which economic capital is used.

Economic capital is a measure for the risks to which an institution is exposed, and the losses it may experience as a result, but it does not provide insight into the causes and consequences of specific events. Stress tests help to understand what the impact of an event or sequence of events could be for the financial position of an institution and whether risk-mitigating action is necessary. The risk models that are used for economic capital often are used to perform stress tests as well. The Achilles heel of stress tests is, however, the formulation of a relevant and realistic scenario. An open issue is further how to use the results of stress tests in relation to economic capital.

Enterprise Risk Management provides a general framework in which strategy, economic capital, stress tests, the management of non-quantifiable risks, risk governance, and risk infrastructure are integrated into a coherent whole. A comprehensive approach to identify risks for the medium and long term may provide the relevant scenarios that stress testing needs as input.

Finally, we have discussed the practical issue of how to manage regulatory capital constraints within an economic capital framework. Under the objective to maximize an institution's economic profit, we described how to deal with constraints on regulatory capital and economic capital usage by calculating marginal and shadow prices for these constrained resources. Using these marginal and shadow prices, optimal use of both economic and regulatory capital can be achieved through central (re)allocation of capital, or by establishing an internal market.

Endnotes

[1]Committee on the Global Financial System. Stress testing at major financial institutions: Survey results and practice. Bank for International Settlements. January 2005.
[2]Marina M, Stolz S, Swinburne M. Stress testing at the IMF. IMF Working Paper 08/206 September, 2008.
[3]Committee on the Global Financial System. Stress testing at major financial institutions: Survey results and practice. Bank for International Settlements. January 2005.
[4]Committee of European Banking Supervisors. Consultation paper 12 on stress testing under the supervisory review process. June, 2006.
[5]Basel Committee on Banking Supervision. Principles for sound stress testing practices and supervision. Consultative Document, Bank for International Settlements. January 2009.

[6]Citigroup Global Markets. Where are the crocodiles? Mapping risk for European banks. April 10, 2006.

[7]World Economic Forum. Global risks 2007. A World Economic Forum report in collaboration with Citigroup, Marsh & McLennan Companies, Swiss Re, and Wharton School Risk Center. January 2007.

[8]The Committee of Sponsoring Organizations of the Treadway Commission. Enterprise risk management—Integrated framework. September 2004.

[9]Casualty Actuarial Society—Enterprise Risk Management Committee. Overview of enterprise risk management. May, 2003.

[10]Institute of International Finance. Final report of the IIF Committee on market best practices: Principles of conduct and best practice recommendations, financial services industry response to the market turmoil of 2007–2008. July 2008.

[11]The Conference Board. Emerging governance practices in enterprise risk management. 2007.

[12]Mikes A. Enterprise risk management in action. Discussion Paper No. 35, ESCR Centre for Analysis of Risk and Regulation, London School of Economics. August 2005.

[13]Standard & Poor's. Assessing enterprise risk management practices of financial institutions. September 22, 2006.

[14]Federal Financial Institutions Council. Uniform Financial Institutions Rating System. *Federal Register*. 1996;61:245.

[15]Financial Services Authority. The FSA's risk assessment framework. August 2006.

[16]Calandro J, Fuessler W, Sansone R. Enterprise risk management—An insurance perspective and overview. *Journal of Financial Transformation*. March 2008.

[17]Danske Bank. Risk management report 2007. 2007.

7 What Is Next? The Future of Economic Capital

In the previous chapters, we reviewed many choices and assumptions with respect to the definition, calculation, and use of economic capital. For a successful application of economic capital within a financial institution, it is important that these choices and assumptions are made in a conscious and consistent way. They should be consistent with the purpose for which management of a financial institution aims to use economic capital, because the choices and assumptions not only define the applicability of economic capital but also its limitations. For example, we have seen in Chapter 3 that the definition of economic capital itself may depend on whether it is used in the context of ensuring continuity or of optimizing profitability. In this chapter we have gathered a number of unresolved issues regarding the calculation and application of economic capital that are worthwhile areas for future thought and analysis. But the question we turn to first is: Do economic capital models have a future?

As mentioned in the Introduction, doubts were raised during the sub-prime crisis about the value of quantitative models for managing a financial institution. Quantitative models even have been blamed for the crisis itself. However, decisions to take on risks are made by people, not models. To the extent that such decisions are based on models, it is important for decision makers to understand the assumptions underlying the models, since models are only as good as the assumptions upon which they are based. We cannot develop a reliable model without first having a solid understanding of the risks that the model should capture. An important cause for the sub-prime crisis has been that financial institutions that exposed themselves to complex new credit products had an insufficient understanding of the risks involved. Consequently, the credit and market risk models in use were not amended to properly reflect the underlying risks of these products. Moreover, many market participants heavily relied on models developed by other parties (*in casu*, the rating agencies) instead of trying to quantify the risks themselves. Few serious questions were raised about the economic rationale of the persistent, seemingly attractive returns on these instruments. As the sub-prime crisis has shown again, there is no substitute for a thorough, independent risk analysis. Models can add value in this respect by forcing an institution to make explicit how various factors influence the risk profile of particular transactions, or the institution as a whole. Inherent to the use of models is model risk—that is, the risk that a model does not reflect the real world correctly. The presence of model risk does not invalidate their use, however, but means that the outcomes and implications of the models should be tested by comparing them to the real world. In case there is a large discrepancy, we have to go back to the assumptions underlying the model to investigate in which way they do not reflect reality correctly, or lack an important ingredient. When used in this way, models can aid in risk management by enforcing additional discipline in the analysis of risks.

As a matter of fact, financial institutions have become too large to manage without the use of models that enable a consistent and comprehensive view of the risk profile. In addition, financial products have become too complex to value and risk manage them without the use of models. The lesson of the sub-prime crisis is, therefore, not that risk modeling is an esoteric activity best disregarded, or even to abandon models completely, but that managers have to be aware of the purpose and limitations of models. As the Basel Committee writes in early 2009, "with respect to new or complex products and activities, senior management should understand the underlying assumptions regarding business models, valuation and risk management practices."[1]

We see a number of directions for the further development of economic capital. Some of these developments are of a technical nature, relating to a more accurate or complete measurement of risk. Other developments are of a practical nature, concerning a more effective application of economic capital to help an institution achieve its objectives. We provide some first thoughts on each of them, recognizing that more work is needed on all of them. This overview also consolidates a number of open issues that we have encountered throughout this book.

We will discuss in Section 7.1 how an economic capital framework may be extended to incorporate multiple capital objectives of a financial institution. In Section 7.2, we present a number of ideas how pro-cyclicality concerns of regulators may be addressed. Subsequently, we emphasize the need for continuous improvements in risk measurement methodologies in Section 7.3, and the explicit consideration of model risk in Section 7.4. As risks are not managed by models but by people, it is important that incentives schemes are properly designed. On this subject, we provide in Section 7.5 our view why economic capital and RAROC are important ingredients for the incentive schemes of institutions. In Section 7.6, we discuss the relevance of economic capital within the context of a number of ideas that have been put forward regarding the future regulatory framework for financial institutions. We end in Section 7.7 with some observations of supervisors and researchers on the added value of ERM and economic capital.

7.1   Consider All the Institution's Capital Objectives

We discussed in Chapter 3 that the institution's solvency objective is reflected in the confidence level that is chosen for the calculation of economic capital. The confidence level equals the probability with which the institution wants to remain solvent within the chosen time horizon, and typically is related to the target rating of the institution's debt. Although the chosen confidence level determines the probability of insolvency, in practice a financial institution may face a situation of discontinuity well before it is technically insolvent. This is in particular the case if an institution is confronted with funding liquidity risk. In Section 3.3.4, we argued that funding liquidity risk should not attract economic capital but that being sufficiently capitalized will help to avoid funding liquidity problems to materialize.

An open question is at what level of capital a financial institution would start to experience funding liquidity problems. Further research is needed to determine this. For insurers, the Minimum Capital Requirement as included in the Solvency II proposal could be such a capital level. For banks, the minimum capital requirement according to the Basel II Accord could be used, or the minimum level of capital that is consistent with an investment-grade credit rating. If a minimum level of capital has been established that is required to avoid funding liquidity problems, then the probability needs to be specified that is accepted for the actual capital level to fall below this minimum capital level. This is thus the probability that the institution will experience funding liquidity problems during the time horizon used for economic capital. This probability of discontinuity will obviously be higher than the probability of insolvency because a situation of discontinuity will manifest itself (long) before available capital is depleted.

To illustrate the idea, suppose that the accepted probability of insolvency is 0.05% and the accepted probability of funding liquidity problems 0.5%. Furthermore, suppose that the minimum level of capital to avoid funding liquidity problems is estimated to be USD 8 billion. If it has been calculated that there is a probability of 0.5% that the institution's available capital would decrease by USD 4 billion or more in the coming year, then the minimum required capital to avoid funding liquidity problems with the specified probability of 99.5% equals USD 12 billion. If economic capital at the confidence level of 99.95% is calculated to be USD 11 billion, then the capital objective related to funding liquidity is more restrictive than the solvency objective.

In Chapter 1 and in Section 5.1.3, we discussed the possibility that an institution may have more than one capital objective, and that the most restrictive capital objective would determine the required amount of capital. Besides a maximum probability of becoming insolvent or experiencing funding liquidity problems, additional earnings objectives may also be formulated that influence the risk profile of the institution. They could, for example, relate to a maximum probability of missing dividend payments, or a maximum expected loss once every 10 or 20 years. Such earnings objectives may have an impact on the acceptable distribution of potential losses, and thereby on economic capital and required capital.

To calculate the contribution of individual businesses and transactions to the minimum amount of capital that satisfies all of the institution's capital and earnings objectives, we could determine at what confidence level the economic capital calculation yields this amount of capital. In our example, we would calculate what confidence level corresponds to a total economic capital amount of USD 12 billion. This confidence level will be higher than the 99.95% that was chosen for the solvency objective, as economic capital at a confidence level of 99.95% equaled USD 11 billion. Using the chosen methods to calculate economic contributions, the economic capital amount of USD 12 billion can then be attributed to business lines and transactions.

In conclusion, the reality of capital management is that most institutions want to achieve a variety of capital and earnings objectives, and not just a maximum probability of insolvency associated with a target debt rating. It is important that all these objectives are identified when evaluating an institution's risk profile, and its interplay with economic capital, regulatory capital, and available capital. This will ensure that the amount of required capital is not underestimated in relation to any of the institution's capital objectives, and the risk profile is in line with its risk appetite.

7.2   Address the Pro-cyclicality of Capital Requirements

Another issue for further exploration is the potential pro-cyclical behavior of economic capital—that is, the feature that economic capital increases when the economic situation deteriorates. Such an increase may be caused by a deterioration of the creditworthiness of borrowers, which is reflected by lower credit ratings in the credit risk economic capital model. When economic capital is pro-cyclical, institutions will have to shrink their credit portfolios in an economic downturn in response to the increased capital requirements. As a consequence, consumers and companies cannot consume and invest as much as they otherwise would, which will contribute to a deepening of the economic downturn. This is undesirable from society's point of view because it could exacerbate the volatility of the economic cycle. From the institution's point of view, pro-cyclicality generally is considered an undesirable feature for assessing capital adequacy as well, because it creates uncertainty regarding how much economic capital will increase during a downturn of the cycle, and thus how much available capital is needed in those circumstances. A board of directors will prefer stability of the amount of economic capital throughout a cycle because it will make management of available capital significantly easier and less costly.

In a perfect through-the-cycle system, economic capital will remain constant during an economic cycle and pro-cyclicality will not be an issue. However, in practice, model inputs for economic capital often have point-in-time characteristics. For example, the price volatilities that are used in market and ALM risk may be estimated over relatively short historic periods and not include periods with high volatility. If the economic capital calculations have point-in-time characteristics, then we should adjust the confidence level for economic capital over the cycle, as we discussed in Section 3.5.2. This will have some dampening effect on the variability of economic capital. However, accurately adjusting the confidence level over time can be difficult because subportfolios may be in different phases of the economic cycle, for example, because they are exposed to different economies or industries. Furthermore, inputs and parameters of economic capital models may not all have the same point-in-time or through-the-cycle character. For example, retail credit models may use point-in-time inputs but corporate credit models may use through-the-cycle inputs.

To address the pro-cyclicality of economic capital while keeping the confidence level constant over time, we could assess for each risk type and portfolio how much the point-in-time inputs vary over an economic cycle and how this would cause economic capital to change. The calculated amount of economic capital can then be corrected for the impact of using point-in-time instead of long-term average values. Such corrections can be both positive and negative, depending on whether the inputs are above or below the long-term average values. If the correction is based on comparing the point-in-time inputs with their value at the bottom of the cycle, then these additions can only be positive. The total economic capital can then be characterized as a "bottom-of-the-cycle" estimate. In both cases, the adjustment to economic capital to correct for cyclicality varies over the economic cycle, but the net result will be a relatively constant amount of total economic capital.

Although this approach ensures that economic capital will be fairly stable over time, available capital will fluctuate because actual losses vary with the economic cycle. As a consequence, the ratio of economic capital to available capital may change through the economic cycle. This can be accommodated within the risk appetite of an institution if it is prepared to allow the ratio of economic capital to available capital to fluctuate within predetermined bands that do not jeopardize its continuity. In favorable economic times the solvency ratio would be higher than average, and during an economic downturn it would be lower than average. The CRO Forum also suggests specifying bounds for potential variation of solvency targets in relation to Solvency II.[2]

To avoid pro-cyclicality completely, not only economic capital but also the amount of available capital should not change materially during a cycle. To smooth the variability of net profit and, as a result, available capital over the cycle, a through-the-cycle system of credit allowances can be used. A variant of such a system already is applied by Spanish banks at the instigation of their regulator. The idea is that the profit and loss account is not charged for the actual credit losses, but for the average through-the-cycle credit losses. The result is that in favorable economic times, credit allowances are higher than actual losses. These excess allowances are kept in a credit reserve, which can be drawn upon during an economic downturn when credit losses are higher than the through-the-cycle credit allowances. With a through-the-cycle system of credit allowances, the credit reserve that appears on the balance sheet has all the characteristics of equity capital and, consequently, available capital still increases with the credit reserve in favorable times and decreases during a downturn.

Thus, available capital continues to behave in a pro-cyclical manner. However, by ear-marking this part of capital as a credit reserve, managers (and regulators) signal that it is not available to cover other risks nor is it available for distribution to the shareholders. For an internal capital adequacy assessment, through-the-cycle economic capital should be compared with available capital excluding the credit reserve. This latter amount will be much more stable.

Another way to address the risk that available capital decreases during an economic downturn is by ensuring that the institution has access to new capital when it needs it. One method to do so is the introduction of a capital insurance product as suggested by Kashyap, Rajan, and Stein.[3] At inception of the insurance, the insurer(s) would put the insured amount in the form of government bonds into a custodial account (i.e., a "lock box"), thus avoiding counterparty risk for the insured institution. The insurance pays out in case a predefined condition is met—for example, if a large number of institutions suffer large unexpected losses. If there is no event over the life of the policy, then the government bonds are returned to the insurer(s). The insurance provides relief in situations of systemic risk—that is, when a large number of institutions suffer large losses. An instrument that can be a source of additional capital in case of institution-specific losses is debt that is convertible in equity at the option of the institution. The institution must then be able to exercise the option in case it would suffer large unexpected losses, or in case its market value would decrease below a certain threshold amount.[4] These kinds of financial instruments may address situations of high unexpected losses that decrease the institution's amount of available capital.

In conclusion, the pro-cyclicality of economic capital can best be addressed through the use of through-the-cycle model inputs and parameters. To account for any model inputs and parameters that are point-in-time, an amount of capital for cyclical risk can be maintained to balance fluctuations in economic capital. As a result, we have a truly through-the-cycle economic capital number. Still, available capital may decrease during an economic downturn because actual losses are cyclical. This can be accommodated within the risk appetite of the institution if it is prepared to allow the ratio of economic capital to available capital to fluctuate within predetermined bands that do not jeopardize its continuity. To dampen the variability of available capital during an economic cycle, a system of through-the-cycle credit allowances can be used. In addition, financial instruments can be issued or bought that provide the flexibility to increase the amount of capital when the institution needs it.

7.3 Continuously Improve Risk Measurement

The dynamic nature of financial markets and products requires that risk models are updated and refined on an ongoing basis. It is no coincidence that the largest losses have occurred in those areas where risk modeling has been less developed. This can be viewed as a failure of the models but, equally well, it could be attributed to the result of arbitrage behavior. To add value to the organization, bankers and traders are trained to identify and make use of market inefficiencies. However, they can, consciously or unconsciously, also exploit internal risk measurement inefficiencies and generate superior results by taking on risks that are underestimated. As a general observation, good arbitrageurs identify areas of imperfection and try to make maximum use of it. For managers, the challenge is to ensure that these are external and not internal imperfections. Although it is unavoidable in today's financial markets to use complex models, it is important to understand the risks that are embedded in new products and markets and to what extent these risks are not fully captured in the models used by the institution. If certain risks are not captured, then other measures need to be taken to protect the institution against large unexpected losses.

A specific area of further work is the integrated measurement of risks, as referred to earlier in Section 4.1.7. Estimating risks separately and then estimating their overall correlation may result in incorrect estimates of the impact of common risk drivers. It is natural that a complex calculation as is necessary for economic capital is performed initially using a building block approach, in particular if each building block is already quite complex to produce. The next step in the evolution is that economic capital is estimated with a single integrated model. An incremental approach may be most efficient to achieve this objective. For example, we could start with the integration of credit and ALM risk in one model. A common risk driver such as changes in interest rates could then explicitly be modeled to influence credit default rates, asset and liability values, as well as pension liabilities. The correlations between the respective risk types would be embedded in these modeled relationships, rather than resulting from a separate estimation. Such an integrated approach to risk measurement will increase the accuracy of the results (provided the modeled relationships are correct, of course). In addition, it provides more insight into how the overall risk profile can be managed by considering the integrated exposure to a number of common risk drivers.

7.4   Explicitly Account for Model Risks

In Chapter 3, we introduced model risk and discussed its relevance for a financial institution. Model risk arises in the estimation of the fair value of assets and liabilities, both at the current date if no market prices are available, and at the economic capital horizon. Hence, model risk is present in the reported profit-and-loss statement, the balance sheet, as well as in the economic capital calculation of the institution. Economic capital methodologies are also subject to model risk with respect to the way in which they include (or do not include) the factors that drive potential losses. On several occasions in Chapter 5, we have discussed that it is important to include model risk explicitly in economic capital for capital adequacy assessments, performance management, and investment decisions.

Model risk is especially relevant if human behavior has to be modeled, as is the case when measuring ALM risk, for example. In Chapter 4, we have explained how model risk can be reflected in economic capital. Ideally, model risk is quantified and integrated along the way with each relevant aspect of the model. However, there is always some inherent model uncertainty as relationships between risk factors may change due to unknown future events. For example, correlations may change due to technological change and this may only become apparent when model outcomes deviate from reality. Furthermore, model risk may also be the result of faulty implementation (i.e., human error). These types of model risks may be difficult to attribute to individual models. A possibility is to include them with operational risk as a type of event risk. The relevant risk mitigation measures, such as good model governance, may also fit well in the operational risk management framework of an institution.

Quantifying model risks is relatively new and not very common yet. Given the importance of model risk, institutions should consider to explicitly take model risk into account in their economic capital models. They also need to be aware of model risk when interpreting and using economic capital outcomes. In the Basel II Accord, regulators require that institutions apply a sufficient degree of conservatism to their estimates of the risk parameters to account for model risk, without specifying how this should be done. Our concern with this approach is that conservatism becomes a purpose in itself: after a crisis more conservatism typically is deemed better than less conservatism. However, models that are overly conservative quickly lose their credibility and purpose. It is like the weatherman who forecasts rain every day in order to prevent his audience from getting wet by surprise. Although the objective is laudable, he would probably soon lose his audience and his job.

We are of the opinion that an attempt should be made to quantify model risk in a risk-sensitive manner in order that the amount of capital that is attributed to each risk is accurate, and that it provides proper incentives for reducing model risk.

7.5 Create Risk-sensitive Incentives

In Chapters 2 and 5 we have argued that RAROC and economic profit can be valuable performance metrics when the aim is to maximize risk-adjusted profitability and create shareholder value. In order to add value, the performance metrics need to balance the interests of the various stakeholders.

This became apparent during the sub-prime crisis when short-term profit incentives were blamed for the reckless behavior of bank managers and traders. In response, regulators and banking industry associations emphasized the importance of longer time horizons to evaluate profitability and deferred bonus payments to align the incentives of managers and traders with those of the institution and its stakeholders. In our view, this should be complemented by a performance measure that takes the costs of risk into account as well. For example, consider a trader who writes many put options that are far out-of-the-money. If the options expire out-of-the-money then the institution makes a profit equal to the received premiums, and the trader may be rewarded with a large bonus. However, the strategy can also lead to significant losses for the institution if the options end up in-the-money and the institution has to pay significant amounts to the option holders. In such an event, the trader would likely not receive a bonus. From the perspective of the trader, this incentive scheme presents him or her with an option-like payoff because if the put options expire out-of-the-money, then he or she will receive a bonus; however, if they do not, then the losses are for the institution's account. Even worse for the institution, even if the premiums received were below market, the trader typically still receives a bonus if the options expire out-of-the money. The fact that the bonus is paid only at maturity of the transactions does not change these features. We note that traditional bank lending is also a form of writing put options that are far out-of-the-money and that the same incentives may apply here. If we assign economic capital to the risk exposures and use RAROC as a performance measure, then the trader will be eligible for a bonus only if the return was sufficient for the risks taken. Consequently, the trader will receive a bonus only if he or she was able to write put options that generated sufficiently high premiums to meet the hurdle rate. The risk that the trader adds to the institution is measured by the total amount of economic capital allocated to his or her transactions and should fall within the institution's risk appetite. In conclusion, in our view, a good incentive program not only avoids undue focus on short-term gains but also applies a risk-adjusted performance measure such as RAROC. As argued in Section 5.2.6, deferred payments should be applied in particular when model risk is high.

7.6   Align Regulatory Capital Further to Economic Capital

The concept of economic capital has been adopted to a significant degree in the Basel II Accord and the Solvency II proposal. It forms the basis for the calculation of the minimum required regulatory capital, and plays a central role in how the institution's capital adequacy needs to be assessed by management and supervisors. As a result of the sub-prime crisis, there have been a number of proposals to reform or revise the capital requirement regulations. In this section, we will discuss whether economic capital is compatible with the suggested regulatory reforms.

A number of prominent commentators have argued that the focus of regulation should shift from the prudential practices of individual institutions to the health of the financial system as a whole.[5] The external consequences of the institution's behavior should be of concern to regulators. In particular, these commentators highlight the undesirability of the pro-cyclical effects of capital regulations. Earlier in this chapter, we have discussed how the pro-cyclicality of economic capital can be addressed by individual institutions. We concluded that economic capital can be held relatively constant though the cycle without losing its risk sensitivity. We are, therefore, of the opinion that the use of economic capital is compatible with the desire to dampen, or at least not increase, the contribution of the financial sector to the volatility of the economic cycle.

Another criticism that has been levied at the regulatory capital calculations in the Basel II Accord is that they are subject to model risk. This model risk arises from the internal models that banks are allowed to use for (the inputs in) regulatory capital calculations, as discussed in Chapter 4. We already discussed the relevance of model risk and how it should be included in a risk-sensitive manner in an economic capital framework.

The Basel II Accord also has been blamed for not preventing excessive leverage of bank balance sheets, despite its reliance on internal risk models. To limit this leverage, a simple leverage ratio that does not rely on model outcomes and, hence, is deemed more difficult to circumvent, is advocated by some commentators and regulators. In some countries, for example, Switzerland, a leverage ratio already has been introduced.

The benefits of a risk-sensitive method over a simple leverage ratio can be illustrated by the concept of shadow prices as introduced in Section 6.3. In that section, we calculated the shadow price of regulatory capital, which can be interpreted as the cost of regulation to the institution that will be borne by its clients and shareholders. The shadow price increases the more regulatory capital is a constraint to optimize the institution's economic profit. Provided that economic capital is measured comprehensively and at a confidence level that gives sufficient comfort to all stakeholders, institutions and regulators have an interest to minimize these regulatory costs. As such, a regulatory capital regime that gradually becomes more risk-sensitive and moves toward an economic capital framework will lower the shadow price of regulatory capital and, thereby, creates value for individual institutions and for society at large. The speed of this transition is for regulators to determine. However, simple risk-insensitive regulations always have led to market inefficiencies that smart arbitrageurs have been able to turn to their advantage. At best, simple measures such as the leverage ratio should be temporary until the underlying issues are addressed.

7.7 The Promise of Economic Capital

We stated in the Introduction that economic capital is an important risk measure for managers of financial institutions. In Chapter 2, we elaborated on the purpose of economic capital, responding to the challenge: "Show me the money." In reaction to the sub-prime crisis, regulators and associations of the financial industry have analyzed risk management practices at financial institutions. For example, the Senior Supervisors Group reported that relatively successful institutions distinguish themselves by a comprehensive view of their exposures, critical judgment and discipline in the valuation of holdings of complex or potentially illiquid securities, treasury functions that are closely aligned with risk management processes, internal pricing mechanisms that provide incentives for individual business lines to control their activities, reliance on a wide range of measures of risk, and balancing the use of quantitative rigor with qualitative assessments.[6] Similar best practices were identified by the International Institute of Finance.[7] All these practices are closely related to a sound economic capital framework and have been discussed in earlier chapters.

A quantitative test of the added value of a comprehensive approach to risk management was performed by Robert Hoyt.[8] He researched the added value of ERM for the US insurance industry for a sample of 125 firms that started to implement an ERM program during an 11-year period. The conclusion was that insurers who engaged in ERM were valued 16.7% higher than other insurers. This difference was statistically significant. Although ERM is broader than economic capital, as we explained in Section 6.2, and although economic capital was not a necessary condition for an ERM program in the research, the findings do indicate the potential value to measure and manage risk in a comprehensive manner. Economic capital is an important ingredient to such an approach. By using a comprehensive and internally consistent economic capital framework of which the purpose and limitations are well understood, we strongly believe that financial institutions are in a better position to ensure their continuity and optimize their profitability.

Endnotes

[1]Basel Committee on Banking Supervision. Proposed enhancements to the Basel II framework. Consultative Document. January 2009.

[2]CRO Forum. Addressing the pro-cyclical nature of Solvency II. November 2008.

[3]Kashyap AK, Rajan RG, Stein JC. Rethinking capital regulation. Paper prepared for Federal Reserve Bank of Kansas City symposium on "Maintaining Stability in a Changing Financial System." August 21–23, 2008.

[4]See, for example, Flannery MJ. No pain, no gain? Effecting market discipline via reverse convertible debentures. In: Scott HS, ed. *Capital adequacy beyond Basel: Banking securities and insurance*, Chapter 5. Oxford: Oxford University Press; 2005.

[5]See, for example, Summers L. Six principles for a new regulatory order. *Financial Times*. June 2, 2008; and Wolf M. Why financial regulation is both difficult and essential. *Financial Times*. April 16, 2008.

[6]Senior Supervisory Group. Observations on risk management practises during the recent market turbulence. March 6, 2008.

[7]International Institute of Finance. Final report of the IIF Committee on market best practises: Principles of conduct and best practice recommendations, financial industry response to the market turmoil of 2007–2008. July 2008.

[8]Hoyt RE, Liebenberg AP. The value of enterprise risk management: Evidence from the U.S. insurance industry. www.ermsymposium.org/2008/pdf/papers/hoyt.pdf; January 2008.

Index